Heart-Centered
Metaphysics

Heart-Centered
Metaphysics

Paul Hasselbeck

unity®
HOUSE
Unity Village, MO 64065-0001

Heart-Centered Metaphysics

First edition 2010

Unity House books are available at special discounts for bulk purchases for study groups, book clubs, sales promotions, book signings or fundraising. To place an order, call the Unity Customer Care Department at 800-251-3571 or e-mail *sales@unityonline.org*.

The publisher wishes to acknowledge the editorial work of Dan Rebant; the copy services of Lila Herrmann and Peter Harakas; and the project management efforts of Julie Boles.

Cover design by: Doug Brown
Interior design by: The Covington Group

Library of Congress Control Number: 2008910995
ISBN: 978-0-87159-334-4
Canada BN 13252 0933 RT

ACKNOWLEDGEMENTS

I want to recognize and acknowledge the work of the ministers who created the first two versions of *Metaphysics I* and *II*. The original version, with a brown or tan cover, was the work of Rev. Marvin Anderson and Rev. Ed Rabel. The second, or blue, version was the work of Rev. Leona Evans and Rev. Susan Scott Downs. These versions were the basis for updating and amplifying the concepts that resulted in the 2005 and 2006 versions. I also want to thank and acknowledge Rev. Toni Boehm for her vision, support and encouragement for the updating of this material. The following people also helped with these versions: Rev. Bob Barth, Rev. Daisy Guevara and ministerial candidate Dagmar Mikkila, as well as the ministerial classes of 2004, 2005 and 2006. Useful suggestions and input were also received from those who attended classes at Unity Village and Unity Church of Overland Park, Overland Park, Kansas.

For this new text, I want to acknowledge Revs. Tom Thorpe, Norma Iris Rosado, Sandra Kale and Eileen Goor for their encouragement and assistance. I also want to thank the hundreds of students who worked with the drafts of the chapters for this updated version. Their feedback surely helped to make this material clearer.

INTRODUCTION

Heart-centered metaphysics is a large and comprehensive subject consisting of powerful Divine Ideas, Principles and Laws that can be used to improve everyday life. Studying this material is the first step in learning how to use it.

Metaphysics explores beliefs and concepts that are above and beyond the physical plane. However, with the advent of quantum physics, metaphysics and physical science have been found to be intricately interrelated. In this text, metaphysics focuses on beliefs about the nature of Ultimate Reality, or Oneness, from a Unity perspective. In Unity, *metaphysics* is considered synonymous with *theology*; thus the study of Unity metaphysics is the study of Unity theology. This can be a rather heady intellectual exercise even though classic Unity literature emphasizes the importance of both our thinking and feeling natures.

Heart-centered metaphysics explores Ultimate Reality through the "lens of the heart," insuring that these beliefs represent more than cold, hard facts. The compassionate application and practice of heart-centered metaphysics is central to realizing a loving and peace-filled life and world.

ULTIMATE GOAL

The ultimate goal of this exploration is for each person to become a heart-centered metaphysician by embodying and expressing these spiritual concepts. We could even say a Christian heart-centered metaphysician since Unity is a Christian-based community. A heart-centered metaphysician:

1) Deeply realizes the underlying unity and Oneness of all.

2) Knows and understands the Principles and Laws of Ultimate Reality, or God.

3) Compassionately and lovingly applies and practices these Principles and Laws in his or her own life.

4) Compassionately and lovingly sees each and every person in the highest light, Christ.

5) When invited, quietly and humbly assists other people in understanding and applying these Principles and Laws in their own lives.

THE LANGUAGE OF ONENESS

In reading this text, you may notice some departures from the way language is conventionally used. A conscious decision was made to write this new text in what I am calling "The Language of Oneness."

The Power of the Word is foundational to classic Unity literature. Language and the use of words are very important. Our goal in this text is to use language that embraces the classic teachings while expressing them in current-day vernacular. Here are a few examples:

> *Know that the word of God is in your mouth and in your heart. Rejoice that this is true, and speak the words of Truth with joy, and power, and love. Expect your words spoken and sung to bring results. Weed out all the destructive and negative thoughts and words and tones.* (Healing Letters, *Myrtle Fillmore, p. 120*)

> *Because the word is the mind seed from which springs every condition, great stress is laid on the power of the word, both in the Scriptures and in metaphysical interpretations of the Scriptures ... All metaphysicians recognize that certain words, used persistently, mold and transform conditions in mind, body and affairs.* (Christian Healing, *Charles Fillmore, p. 137*)

> *Words charged with power and intelligence increase with use, while material things decrease.* (Atom-Smashing Power of Mind, *Charles Fillmore, p. 50*)

Our language has already shifted to reflect changing times. Most people would agree that the use of "male language" that was common well into the 20th century is now regarded as politically incorrect. In fact, it sometimes seems odd to read classic Unity books that use male-centric language so freely. We have been given permission in this text to update the early Unity writings with gender-neutral language as long as the meaning is not changed.

Further, the language in the classic Unity texts was rooted in the late 19th century and early 20th century and was "traditional Christian" in nature. While a keen reader discerns that these terms were redefined and used in unconventional ways, some fail to notice and continue to interpret them in traditional ways, which leads to misconceptions about Unity metaphysics.

Terms such as *Christ*, *Holy Spirit* and *forgiveness* (to name a few) are so habitually used that it can be difficult to discern the assumptions and meanings embedded in them. Many of our underlying, even subconscious, assumptions stem from the spiritual traditions in which we were raised. As a result, our language is imprecise and vulnerable to misinterpretation.

As we move deeper into the 21st century, re-examining the use of language to express Unity beliefs and theology is essential. This text attempts to develop a new language that more accurately and precisely conveys these beliefs. This language has been created to avoid 1) being misunderstood; 2) reinforcing the embedded theology of the listener/reader; and 3) reinforcing the embedded theology of the speaker/writer. Updated language will inevitably shift consciousness to new heights of understanding, due to the Power of the Word. Here are some examples.

Unity believes what Jesus taught: The kingdom of heaven is within and the Christ is within. That is why we routinely say, "I behold the Christ in you!" The language creates the mistaken impression that the kingdom of heaven and the Christ are within us like a wiener in a bun, i.e., that while the kingdom and Christ are within, the real me is the vessel, the bun, containing them. This perception may be so subtle that we are not even aware of it until someone points it out. But the teaching is really that the kingdom of heaven is a state of *consciousness*. The kingdom of heaven is within consciousness and the Christ within is within consciousness. Neither can be separate from us.

Another Unity belief is that God is not a person or Divine Entity. God is Spirit; God is Principle; God is Law; God is Love; God is Divine Mind. Therefore it is really not accurate to refer to God with any of the usual pronouns like He and the increasingly popular She. When we refer to God as He, She or even Father-Mother God, we continue the personification and anthropomorphizing of Divine Mind. These pronouns are so loaded that they easily take us back to the beliefs of our childhood, when we imagined a separate God with a long gray beard living in a far-off place called heaven. When we use this language, we are keeping one foot rooted in the old theology while trying to gain traction in the new.

Traditional language that is even more Bible-based is particularly troublesome. Even though classic Unity literature refers to God as Father, Charles Fillmore defined the Father within as the Christ-Nature within consciousness. If one does not know this, it is nearly impossible to hear or read these words without reinforcing one's embedded theology. Similarly, when we refer to ourselves as a son of God, daughter of God, or child of God, we continue to reinforce the misconception of an anthropomorphic God.

The key point is that these references reinforce the traditional notion that we as humans are "less than." It may be a step up from the belief that we are broken and depraved, but the implication is still that we are less than God, or Divine Mind. Other common phrases also support this "less than" theology. For example: "We are like a drop of water in the ocean that is God." This metaphor implies that even though we have all the qualities of God, we are not the totality of God. And it implies that a piece of God, or Divine Mind, can be separated from the whole, just as a drop can be separated from the ocean. This is impossible since Oneness is the Truth. Eric Butterworth said, "God is in us, not like a raisin in a bun but like the ocean in a wave." The wave is just as much ocean as any other aspect of the ocean. Here is what Charles Fillmore wrote in *Christian Healing*: "Individual consciousness is like an eddy in the ocean—all the elements that are found in the ocean are also found in the eddy, and every eddy may, in due course, receive and give forth **all** that is in the ocean." (Emphasis mine.)

We say that there is only Oneness and then say, "We are one *with* God." This is an oxymoron. Although we say there is no separation between God, or Divine Mind, and us, the use of the word "with" implies "two or more" not One. There is only one Divine Mind.

Finally, I advocate that the use of the term *God* be kept to a minimum and that it be explicitly defined when it is used. God is the most traditional and common word for Spirit, Oneness, Beingness and Divine Mind. However, the term God is loaded with baggage from the spiritual traditions in which we were raised—some of it conscious and some subconscious. We also must acknowledge that the meaning of the word *god* is a supernatural male being while *goddess* is a supernatural female being. Perhaps by not using the term God we can free ourselves from all the meanings that have been heaped on the word.

Vigilance in our use of language will help us better understand Unity theology and raise our consciousness. As we claim Unity theology with language that does not activate our embedded beliefs, we will more quickly grow into the awareness of Oneness, or Divine Mind. Our parents were correct: We really do need to "watch our language."

CONTENTS

Section 3: The Basic Tool Kit for Living

Section 4: Proving the Truth We Know

Foundational Principles and the Highest Form of Mind Action

Heart-centered metaphysics focuses on the building of consciousness, growing spiritual awareness that integrates head and heart, intellect and compassion. The practices of the Silence, meditation and prayer form the foundation of becoming a heart-centered metaphysician.

CHAPTER ONE

METAPHYSICS AND TRUTH

INTRODUCTION

Metaphysics is the branch of philosophy that is concerned with the fundamental nature of Reality and Being. In its broadest sense, the study of metaphysics explores areas that are considered to be above and beyond the physical sciences.

In this chapter, we will define our understanding of metaphysics from a Unity perspective and discuss our beliefs about the nature of Ultimate Reality.

1A METAPHYSICS DEFINED

The systematic study of the science of Being; that which transcends the physical. By pure metaphysics is meant a clear understanding of the realm of ideas and their legitimate expression. (Charles Fillmore, *The Revealing Word: A Dictionary of Metaphysical Terms,* 2nd ed., Unity House, Unity Village, Mo., 2006, p. 132)

Metaphysics is the branch of philosophy that studies the Ultimate Reality beyond the physical realm and is generally concerned with asking these questions: What is the nature of Being? What is the nature of the Spiritual Universe and the physical universe? How do we know what we

know? When we study Unity metaphysics, we are studying one perspective within this branch of philosophy. What we, in Unity, discern in the study of metaphysics are those Realities that are True concerning the inner life of every human being, regardless of time, place and circumstance.

Unity heart-centered metaphysicians ask such questions as "What is the nature of God?" "What is the nature of humankind?" and "What is the relationship between God and humankind?" They believe that God is Spirit, the invisible Life and Intelligence underlying all physical things. As the Consciousness underlying all things, God is Divine Mind, Oneness, or Beingness, which are explored in detail in Chapter 10.

Unity heart-centered metaphysics asserts and recognizes that Divine Ideas are the fundamental, eternal Truth that underlie and transcend all physical manifestation. Divine Ideas are Spiritual Patterns that pertain to all of us. They are all the components known to our mind that constitute what we call Good. The most essential and basic of all Divine Ideas are what we now experience as our Twelve Spiritual Powers (Faculties or Abilities): Faith, Strength, Love, Power (Dominion, Mastery), Imagination, Understanding, Order, Zeal, Will, Judgment (Wisdom, Discernment), Elimination (Renunciation) and Life. (For more on the Twelve Spiritual Powers, read Chapters 24 and 25.)

Heart-centered metaphysics deals with this Ultimate Reality through the "lens of the heart" insuring that these beliefs are more than mere cold, hard facts. It is the compassionate application and practice of heart-centered metaphysics that is vitally important to the realization of a loving and peace-filled life and world.

1B WHAT IS TRUTH?

What we mean by Truth is concerned with the great fundamental questions that have always perplexed and at the same time engaged the profoundest attention of humankind:

- *What is the character of God?*
- *How does God create?*
- *What is the real character of humankind?*
- *What relation does humankind bear to its Source?*
- *What is the ultimate destiny of humankind and the universe?* (Charles Fillmore, *Atom-Smashing Power of Mind*, 2nd ed., Unity House, Unity Village, Mo., 2006, p. 84)

The Absolute; that which accords with God as divine principle; that which is, has been, and ever will be; that which eternally is. (The Revealing Word, p. 200)

God is Truth: the eternal verity of the universe and humankind. (Charles Fillmore, *Jesus Christ Heals*, 2nd ed., Unity House, Unity Village, Mo., 1940, p. 30)

All truth has its origin in Divine Mind. (Charles Fillmore, *Talks on Truth*, Unity House, Unity Village, Mo., 1926, p. 116)

There is a special meaning for the word *Truth* as used in Unity. We do not mean "all the truth there is." Nor do we mean "all the facts that are known." The Unity usage of the word Truth is in connection with Divine Ideas as they relate to God. Anything that acknowledges, verifies, supports or expresses Divine Ideas is called "Truth" in Unity terminology. Anything that contradicts or attempts to negate Divine Ideas is called " error" in Unity terminology.

Unity acknowledges that the term Truth represents these perfect Divine Ideas. Truth is absolute, unlimited, unchanging and complete. We understand that Truth is universal and that every human being has the capacity to know the Truth by engaging in the activity of metaphysical thinking as well as investing time in the Silence. We do this by looking beyond the physical realm to the Realm of Pure Thought.

1C ABSOLUTE TRUTH/ RELATIVE TRUTH

It is only from the plane of mind that one can know Truth in an absolute sense. That which we pronounce truth from the plane of appearances is relative only. The relative truth is constantly changing, but the absolute Truth endures; and what is true today always was and always will be true. (Atom-Smashing Power of Mind, p. 88)

Absolute Truth consists of the sum total of all Divine Ideas in their origi-

nal purity and power. Absolute Truth describes the pure, ideal Good that encompasses Divine Mind. The Absolute is changeless. Relative truth is that aspect or dimension that we experience in the physical realm. The relative is constantly changing.

The human mind has the unique ability to identify with the Absolute and at the same time to participate in the changing processes of the relative. Learning the difference between Absolute Truth and relative truth helps us apply metaphysics in a practical way in our own lives. In the Absolute, we can never be sick, poor or anything less than the perfect Divine Ideas that exist in Divine Mind. Relative truth deals in the world of human thoughts and feelings, where we can experience sickness, poverty and death.

The Realm of God-Mind is Divine Ideas. All things rest on changeless Divine Ideas. Thus, a Divine Idea behind the flower is Beauty and a Divine Idea behind music is Harmony. Relative truth comes from our human experience of the appearance of things in the physical world. It is anything we can say or observe about the physical world that is subject to change, qualification or limitation. Although the flower will appear to eventually fade, wither and die (relative truth), the Divine Idea of Beauty is changeless and timeless (Absolute Truth).

By shifting our awareness from the relative to the Absolute, we change our thinking and use the power of thought to manifest greater good in our lives.

1D RELATIVE EXISTENCE

When we say that our mind is our world, we do not mean to deny the existence of a material world or a material body in which we function, but only its independent existence. (Richard Lynch, *Know Thyself*, Unity House, Unity Village, Mo., 1935, p. 46)

The Ideas of God are potential forces waiting to be set in motion through proper formative vehicles. The thinking faculty of [humankind] is such a vehicle, and it is through this that the visible universe has existence. (Atom-Smashing Power of Mind, p. 93)

It is most important to gain a clear understanding of the relationship between the Absolute and relative. The relative world, or world of the senses, certainly seems to exist, but it does not exist independently from the Absolute Realm. It comes into manifestation solely through the formative power of thought. Since the relative world is a product of thought and feeling, it is not ultimate or eternal in nature, even though it may seem so from our human perspective.

Divine Ideas are in the Absolute. They do not change. Thoughts that are related to a Divine Idea or about Divine Ideas are in the relative since they can and do change. Since that which is relative is impermanent and changeable, any condition existing on the relative plane (the realm of the senses) has the potential to be healed and restored to wholeness in our awareness. Moving our awareness from the relative to the Absolute helps to accomplish this and requires a great deal of practice.

Think of it in this way:

First Cause is the Absolute Realm. It is God, or Spirit; it is Good. It is also known as Primal Cause.

Beauty, a Divine Idea, is First Cause. It is in the Absolute; therefore, this Divine Idea does not change.

Effect: Thoughts and feelings about Beauty or thoughts and feelings about creating a beautiful garden are effects of the Divine Idea of Beauty. These are in the relative realm since thoughts and feelings about Beauty or creating a beautiful garden can and do change.

Second cause is in the relative realm. Second cause is an effect of First Cause, or Primal Cause. So, if the First Cause is God, or Divine Ideas, then the second cause would be thoughts and ideas that are generated from these Divine Ideas.

Thoughts and feelings about creating a beautiful garden are second, or secondary, to the First Cause. These are in the relative realm because thoughts and feelings about what makes up a beautiful garden change.

Effect: A beautiful garden is made in the physical realm, the realm of the senses. It is made up of things like flowers and trees and does change.

SUMMARY STATEMENTS

▼ *Metaphysics is the study of the Ultimate Reality that underlies and transcends the physical realm. In Unity, we refer to this reality as Divine Ideas.*

▼ *Heart-centered metaphysics deals with Ultimate Reality through the "lens of the heart" insuring that these beliefs are more than mere cold, hard facts.*

▼ *Absolute Truth is the Realm of Divine Ideas. Truth is absolute, universal, unlimited, unconditional, unchanging and complete.*

▼ *Relative truth refers to the world of the senses. Time, space, form, changeability, experience and perspective are components inherent in the concept of relative truth. It is our experience as humans living on the physical earth plane.*

▼ *The relative world, or the world of appearances, does not have independent existence from the Absolute Realm. It exists solely through the formative power of thought and feelings and is based on humankind's present understanding of Divine Ideas.*

▼ *Even though relative experiences are not considered to be eternal Truth and therefore are not in the same Realm as the Absolute, we tend to experience them as if they were real. They feel very real. This is why it is important to cultivate balance in our lives as we learn to acknowledge our humanity and affirm our Divinity.*

▼ *By shifting our awareness from the relative to the Absolute, we change our thinking and use the power of thought to make and manifest greater good in our lives.*

TOPICS FOR DISCUSSION

1. Discuss your understanding of the Absolute and relative.

2. Is it appropriate to speak of the relative world as "unreal"?

3. What steps can we take to cultivate a balanced state of mind when conditions in the relative appear to be overwhelming?

4. Share a time in your life when you were able to know the Absolute Truth despite appearances to the contrary. How did you relate your understanding to others? What was the outcome?

THOUGHTS FOR REFLECTION AND MEDITATION

"Those who have honestly studied metaphysics and applied its rules in their daily work will tell you that it has made them over physically, mentally and morally. They will tell you that they are better men and women; that life has new zest for them, and that they can now do good and help others where before they were helpless."

(Charles Fillmore, *Dynamics for Living: A Topical Compilation of Essential Fillmore Teachings*, Unity House, Unity Village, Mo., 1995, p. 24)

SUPPLEMENTARY READING

Know Thyself by Richard Lynch, Unity House, Unity Village, Mo., 1935, Chapter 1, "Knowledge of Truth."

Lessons in Truth by H. Emilie Cady, Centennial Edition, Unity House, Unity Village, Mo., 2003, Chapter 1, "Bondage or Liberty, Which?"

What Are You? By Imelda Shanklin, 2nd ed., Unity House, Unity Village, Mo., 2004, Chapter 4, "The Real and the Fictitious."

CHAPTER TWO

LIFE IS CONSCIOUSNESS

INTRODUCTION

Although metaphysical Principles and Truths may be used to manipulate and change our outer lives and circumstances to a certain degree, they are used most effectively to change our own consciousness. As we expand our own awareness, we change our experience of the world and may change our outer lives and circumstances. This process must be entered into with a healthy dose of compassion. Jesus said to seek the kingdom of God first, and seeking the Kingdom ultimately leads to changing consciousness. This is an ongoing process through learning about and applying our commonly held Principles and Truths.

2A PLANES OF LIFE

There are many planes of life, one above or below another, yet not conflicting. All creation is based on life activity, or as it is called in physical science, rates of vibration. A certain activity in the life current forms worlds on a plane, which we may call the physical; a little increase in the vibratory rate makes another system, which we may designate as the psychical; a still higher rate makes a universe where spiritual ideas prevail. These are all interlaced and interblended in the presence around and within us, hence, the *"kingdom of God is within you"* (*Lk. 17:21*), or *"among you,"* as one translator gives it. (Charles Fillmore, *Revealing Word*, Unity House, Unity Village, Mo., 1994, p. 150)

"The kingdom of God is within you" (*Lk. 17:21*). *The pivotal point around which Spirit creates is within the structure of consciousness.* (Charles Fillmore, *Jesus Christ Heals*, 2nd ed., Unity House, Unity Village, Mo., 1940, pp. 76-77)

God ideated two universal planes of consciousness, "the heavens and the earth." One is the realm of pure Ideas, the other of thought forms. God does not create the visible universe directly, as a person makes a concrete pavement, but God creates the Ideas that are used by the intelligent "image and likeness" to make the universe. Thus God's creations are always spiritual. Humankind's creations are both material and spiritual, according to humankind's understanding. (Charles Fillmore, *Mysteries of Genesis,* 2nd ed., Unity House, Unity Village, Mo., 2007. pp. 27-28)

The above paragraphs help in eliminating the confusion which sometimes occurs when people believe that because omnipresent Divine Mind is the one Presence and Power, everything in existence is *one* in all respects. This is not metaphysically correct. True, there is the essence of Oneness that binds, blends, harmonizes and is back of all things; but there are also differences in scale, planes of existence and vibratory rates. These differences are what require recognition of polarity and scale of being. To overlook this is to call everything the same in all respects, which is not practical Christianity. Consciousness is the only thing that is able to cope with the paradox of Oneness and all of Beingness with the polarity and diversity of planes of existence. In our existential universe, consciousness is the key that unlocks all the mysteries of this paradox.

2B INTELLECT

"The power or faculty of knowing" (Webster). *Intellect is not wise. Wisdom is not its office. Intellect is the executive officer of wisdom and can do right only when faithfully carrying out the instruction of its principal. Intellect follows the letter of the law.*

It is hard for the intellect to realize the spiritual "I AM THAT I AM" (Ex. 3:14). The intellect always argues back and forth, endeavoring to prove that it is the highest authority. Jesus condemned the sins of the intellect, of which self-righteousness is the greatest, as worse than moral sins. People who live wholly in the intellect deny that humankind can know anything about God, because they do not have quickened faith. (Revealing Word, p. 108)

Innately we are in harmony; but complete dependence on the intellect and its findings and recordings is dampening our spiritual response. (Unity Correspondence School Records, Box 16, Folder 205, Thinking Lesson Material [Lessons in Truth #3])

Too great a dependence on books and teachers dampens our individual response to the call of Spirit. We are leaning on books and teachers instead of developing our own spiritual ability, approach and response. ... We must use a faculty or lose it. Or lose a great deal of its adaptability and elasticity of response. (Unity Correspondence School Records, Box 16, Folder 205, Thinking Lesson Material [Lessons in Truth #3])

When we speak of consciousness building, we are not talking about an intellectual process. However, our consciousness can use the intellect. The intellect is the ability to know, and it tends to follow the letter of the law. The intellect is not wise but has dominion over Wisdom. We can know what our inner Wisdom is saying and yet use our intellect to override or ignore this Wisdom. Dependence on the intellect alone leads to less and less reliance on Spirit, or Divine Mind. Depending entirely on the intellect weakens our ability to respond to the inner promptings of Spirit and is not heart-centered.

2C **Mind**

mind—The starting point of every act and thought and feeling; the common meeting ground of God and humankind. ...

The mind is the seat of perception of the things we see, hear and feel. It is through the mind that we see the beauties of the earth and sky, of music, of art, in fact, of everything. That silent shuttle of thought working in and out through cell and nerve weaves into one harmonious whole the myriad moods of mind, and we call it life. (Revealing Word, p. 133)

Thinking is essentially control, organization [and] direction of mind. If the mind is set upon the external as the criterion of all activity, we will have one kind of life and that not a very satisfactory one even to [oneself] or on earth. If the mind is set on righteousness or on the rightness of things or truth and we yearn to know really, to discern, the shadow from the substance, we will have quite a different sort of life. We cannot find God and peace when we stand on sense experiences alone. We do not sow the physical thought and attitude and reap the fruit of the spirit. What we think about God is going to make the difference between a haunting fear that weighs us down and keeps us back, or an exhilarating strength and inspiration that [stimulate] us to our highest achievement. (Unity Correspondence School Records, Box 16, Folder 205, Thinking Lesson Material [Lessons in Truth #3])

Conscious mind—The mind that makes one know of one's mental operations and states of consciousness; that phase of mind in which one is actively aware of one's thoughts. The mind through which one establishes one's identity. (Revealing Word, p. 41)

Mind—By the term Mind, *we mean God—the universal Principle, which includes all principles.*

Humankind in the consciousness of the one Mind has no sense of apartness. Through affirmation one can attune oneself to Being, transmute one's thought into ideas, and accomplish the seemingly impossible. (Revealing Word, p. 133)

It is useful to distinguish between mind, conscious mind and Mind. The mind is the beginning point of every thought, feeling and act. It is what perceives everything we see, hear and feel. Conscious mind is the mechanism that allows us to know our mental operations and states of consciousness. It is aware of thoughts, feelings, actions and what the body senses. "Mind" is another term for God; It is the Universal Principle. When we are in the consciousness of the one Divine Mind, Oneness is experienced. We must not let our human mind depend entirely on sense consciousness (See section 2E). We must use and direct our minds to have "Divine Mind thoughts" (thoughts based on Divine Ideas) in order to experience the fruits of Spirit.

2D CONSCIOUSNESS

The sense of awareness, of knowing. The knowledge or realization of any idea, object or condition. The sum total of all ideas accumulated in and affecting a person's present being. The composite of ideas, thoughts, emotions,

sensation and knowledge that makes up the conscious, subconscious and superconscious phases of mind. It includes all that humankind is aware of—spirit, soul and body.

It is very important to understand the importance of our consciousness in spiritual growth. Divine ideas must be incorporated into our consciousness before they can mean anything to us. An intellectual concept does not suffice. To be satisfied with an intellectual understanding leaves us subject to sin, sickness, poverty and death. To assure continuity of spirit, soul and body as a whole, we must ever seek to incorporate divine ideas into our mind. A consciousness of eternal life places one in the stream of life that never fails. (Revealing Word, p. 41)

The mind of humankind is like a clear stream that flows from some lofty mountain. It has nothing at its point of origin to corrupt or to distort it, but as it flows out into the plain of experience, it meets the obstruction of doubt and fear. It is here that dams are built and its course is turned in many ways. (Charles Fillmore, The Essential Charles Fillmore: Collected Writings of a Missouri Mystic, Unity House, Unity Village, Mo., 1999, p. 398)

Your consciousness is like a stream of water. If the stream is in any way dammed up, the water settles in all the low places and becomes stagnant. The quickest way to purify and reclaim the low, "swampy" places in your consciousness is to let in the flood from above by opening the dam. (The Essential Charles Fillmore, p. 279)

Remember that you cannot perform a single act without putting your consciousness into it. All things are sustained by your conscious thought projection. Every time you indulge in any of the sensations of the flesh, you are binding the I AM to the fleshly consciousness.

Spiritual thinking is the pioneer that opens the way into the new birth, but it must be followed by spiritual acting on the part of every faculty. (The Essential Charles Fillmore, p. 300)

The development of consciousness is key to demonstrating our good and overcoming the "stuff" that happens in this relative realm. Kindhearted development of consciousness requires self-awareness, self-knowledge and awareness of the processes of the evolution of the awareness of Spirit, or Divine Mind. It also requires substantial time invested in meditating in the Silence and prayer.

2E TYPES OF CONSCIOUSNESS

Christ [Spiritual] Consciousness—Consciousness built in accordance with the Christ ideal, or in absolute relationship to God. The perfect mind that

was in Christ Jesus. (Revealing Word, p. 42)

Illumined Consciousness—A mind purified by the light of Truth. (Revealing Word, p. 42)

Child of God Consciousness—A state of mind that is conscious of God's ideal human. (Revealing Word, p. 42)

Inner Consciousness—The realm of the supermind as contrasted with the outer or conscious mind. (Revealing Word, p. 42)

Centers of Consciousness—The subconscious realm in humankind has 12 great centers of action. Each of these 12 centers has control of a certain function in mind and body. (Revealing Word , p. 42)

Positive Consciousness—A mind filled with God thoughts such as power, strength, generosity, purity and optimism. (Revealing Word, p. 42)

Body Consciousness—The subconscious mind in its work in the body—repairing, renewing and conducting the functions of the body in harmony and health if right ideas are given to it, or disintegrating the organism and producing inharmonious action of the functions if untrue thoughts are sown in the mind. (Revealing Word, p. 42)

Material Consciousness—A state of mind based on belief in the reality of materiality, or things as they appear. It is carnal mind expressing its unbelief in the omnipresence of God. (*Revealing Word*, p. 42)

Sense Consciousness—A mental state that believes in and acts through the senses. To rise out of sense consciousness, we determine to return to conscious oneness with God. "I will arise and go to my Father" (Lk. 15:18 RSV). (*Revealing Word*, p. 42)

Negative Consciousness—A mind filled with un-Godlike thoughts, such as fear, hate, greed, lust, resentments, discouragement, sickness and poverty. (*Revealing Word*, p. 42)

It is useful to subdivide consciousness into various categories. But more than simply identifying various forms of consciousness, our goal is to understand the ways in which we *use* our consciousness. For example, one could be operating one moment in sense consciousness, then realize that life works better when lived from a Christ Consciousness.

2F LEVELS OF CONSCIOUSNESS

Victim consciousness—occurs when I believe and feel that everything is happening TO ME. I am a victim of the world I see and experience. I have little or no control about what is happening to me.

Victor consciousness—occurs when I believe that I do have some ability to control the world and events around me and especially my experience of them. A certain amount of the world, events and my experiences are controlled BY ME. I have discovered the innate power of my mind. This state of consciousness still contains some victim consciousness; in order for there to be a victor, there must be a victim.

Vessel consciousness—occurs when I have realized there is something greater or bigger than I think, feel or believe I am. This something greater is God, Spirit, Christ or Divine Mind, to identify a few of the names by which It is known. I believe I am an instrument, conduit or vessel of God, Spirit, Christ or Divine Essence. This consciousness is when I believe It is IN ME. An even higher state of vessel consciousness is when I believe I am an *expression* of God, Spirit, Christ or Divine Essence; but this is still not quite Oneness. To illustrate, the expression of a piano is sound. The sound is an effect of playing the piano; it is not the piano. Vessel consciousness is also when I believe God is showing up AS ME. However, a person can go to a Halloween party as a ghost but is never truly the ghost. This state of consciousness still contains some victim consciousness. Notice that victim consciousness is about everything happening to me and this is usually in a negative sense. In vessel consciousness there is still that sense that something is happening to me; the only difference is that now I believe and feel that God is happening to me.

Verity Consciousness—occurs when I finally come to realize Oneness. This is when I realize there is no such thing as God, or Divine Mind, *and* me. This is when I realize Christ Consciousness. This is when I realize that my most profound understanding is that It IS ME.

At any given time we seem to live in and from one of these levels of consciousness. The level of consciousness that we are in the greatest amount of time is the *stage* we are living in and from. While we are living in this particular level of consciousness (stage), we can also temporarily experience another level of consciousness (state). While living in and from a particular stage, a person might temporarily jump to another level and operate in that other state for a brief time. For example, Jesus on the night before his death had been clearly living in Verity Consciousness (stage) and slipped into a victim consciousness state when he said " Take this cup from me." A person who is learning to be a heart-centered metaphysician learns to not be hard on herself/himself when slipping temporarily into lower levels of consciousness, especially victim consciousness.

2G INVOLUTION AND EVOLUTION OF CONSCIOUSNESS

Involution (infolding) always precedes evolution (unfolding). That which is involved in mind evolves through matter. (Revealing Word, p. 109)

God makes all things [perfect ideas, divine ideas] in God Mind first, which is involution; then they are made into form and shape, and this is evolution. … The image-and-likeness man [Christ], pours into "mankind" a perpetual stream of ideas that the individual man arranges as thoughts and forms as substance and life. While this evolutionary process is going on there seem to be two entities, one ideal and spiritual and the other intellectual and material, which are united at the consummation, the ideal man, Christ. (Mysteries of Genesis, p. 26)

Evolution—The development achieved by humankind working under spiritual law. It is the result of the development of ideas in mind. What we are is the result of the evolution of our consciousness, and this consciousness is the result of seed ideas sown in the mind. In the beginning, God implanted God's perfect word—involved this seed word into each person. Evolution is the unfolding in consciousness of that which God involved in humankind in the beginning. (Revealing Word, p. 65)

Evolution, spiritual—The unfolding of the Spirit of God into expression. The

Christ ... evolution in humankind is plainly taught in the New Testament as the supreme attainment of every person. (Revealing Word, p. 65)

I AM—Spiritual identity; the real or Christ Mind, of each individual. The I AM Being. God is I AM, and humankind ... is also I AM. I AM is the indwelling Lord of life, love, wisdom and all the ideas eternally in Divine Mind.

The I AM is the metaphysical name of the spiritual self, as distinguished from the human self. One is governed by Spirit, the other by personal will. Christ and Jehovah are the scriptural names for spiritual I AM. Jesus called it the Father. I AM is eternal, without beginning or ending: the true spiritual human who God made in God's image and likeness. (Revealing Word, pp. 100-101)

Involution precedes evolution. First we go inward (involution) to the Silence to realize Truth. We realize that in the midst of our "being," in the midst of consciousness, is a seed. It is the perfect Word; it is of God and it is God, or Divine Mind. We know this seed as Divine Ideas. We then evolve our consciousness (evolution) from this perfect Word and the development of ideas in mind. This "perfect Word" is the I AM; it is the metaphysical name of our Spiritual Self. It is the real or Christ Mind.

2H PURPOSE OF THE EVOLUTION OF CONSCIOUSNESS

What is the chief object of humankind? To glorify God in the body; this is the true answer. Have the courage to make the heroic attempt to give personal expression to God. And how shall we do this? By mentally agreeing that we are potentially the Christ and capable of making a divine presentation of ourselves to God. We must rise to the conscious realization that every thought of mind, every atom of body, every molecule of being, every function of nature, and every force is divine, and that all of these do and shall vibrate to the harmonies of Spirit. This is the resurrection of humankind; there is none other. By so doing we establish our ego, our I AM identity, with Divine Mind, and enter with Jesus into joint heirship to the heavenly inheritance of power, peace, prosperity and perfection. (Charles Fillmore, *Atom-Smashing Power of Mind*, 2nd ed., Unity House, Unity Village, Mo., 2006, p. 123)

It is set forth in the New Testament and whoever adopts the life of purity and love and power there exemplified in the experiences of Jesus of Nazareth will in due course attain the place that He attained.

The way to do this is the way Jesus did it. He acknowledged Himself to be the Child of God. The attainment of the Christ consciousness calls for nothing less on our part than a definite recognition of ourselves as children of God right here and now, regardless of appearances to the contrary. (Charles Fillmore, *Talks on Truth,* Unity House, Unity Village, Mo., 1926, p. 170)

Our grand purpose is to express our Christ Potential. This purpose is not one given by some external God. God, or Divine-Mind, only "knows" of Oneness. As each person wakes up to the Reality of Oneness and the Christ Potential, he or she begins to choose the grand purpose of realizing and expressing It. Until a person wakes up to this Reality, he or she may have life purposes based on the outer world and sense consciousness. We must establish our I AM identity with the Divine Mind and stop empowering as well as arguing for our personalities (egos), which are expressions of separation and limitation, masks hiding our True Identity.

SUMMARY STATEMENTS

▼ *Consciousness is the only thing that is able to cope with the paradox of the Oneness of God's creation and all of Beingness with the polarity and diversity of planes of existence.*

▼ *The intellect is the ability to know, and it tends to follow the letter of the law. It has dominion over Wisdom.*

▼ *The mind is the beginning point of every thought, feeling and act.*

▼ *Conscious mind is the mechanism that allows us to know our mental operations and states of consciousness. It is aware of thoughts, feelings and actions. It gathers a great deal of information from the senses.*

▼ *"Mind" is another term for God. It is the Universal Principle.*

▼ *The development of consciousness is key to demonstrating our good and overcoming the stuff that happens in this relative realm.*

▼ *It is useful to subdivide consciousness into various categories that, while they are not literal, do help create an understanding of the ways we use consciousness.*

▼ *It can also be useful to speak of <u>four levels of consciousness</u>; <u>victim</u> (to me), <u>victor</u> (by me), <u>vessel</u> (in me, as me) and <u>Verity</u> (Is Me).*

▼ *<u>Involution</u> precedes <u>evolution</u>. First we go inward (involution) to the Silence to realize God's perfect Word. This seed Word is then the basis of the evolution of our consciousness.*

▼ *<u>The grand purpose</u> we can choose for ourselves is our spiritual wakening and evolution to realize and express the Christ potential.*

TOPICS FOR DISCUSSION

1. *How does your understanding of* involution *and* evolution *assist you in your spiritual evolution?*

2. *Compare and contrast a time when you decided something strictly from your intellect with a time when you utilized your Spiritual Consciousness.*

3. *What are some of the tools you might use to build your consciousness?*

THOUGHTS FOR REFLECTION AND MEDITATION

"We have the key to life; and that key is the knowledge that life is a state of consciousness. The explanation of all your problems, the explanation of your difficulties, and the explanation of your triumphs in life boil down to this: Life is a state of consciousness. That is the beginning and the end. That is the final step in metaphysics. All the other steps but lead up to that."

(Emmet Fox, *Life Is Consciousness*, a pamphlet from Unity School of Christianity, Unity Village, Mo., 1949)

SUPPLEMENTARY READING

Dynamics for Living: A Topical Compilation of Essential Fillmore Teachings by Charles Fillmore, selected and arranged by Warren Meyer, Unity House, Unity Village, Mo., 1967, Chapter 5, "Consciousness."

Jesus Christ Heals by Charles Fillmore, 2nd ed., Unity House, Unity Village, Mo., 1940, Chapter 3, "Realization Precedes Manifestation."

Talks on Truth by Charles Fillmore, Unity House, Unity Village, Mo., 1926, Chapter 1, "Reform Your God Thought," and Chapter 7, "Ye Must Be Born Again."

CHAPTER THREE

SELF-KNOWLEDGE

INTRODUCTION

Our quest for Truth must begin with self-knowledge. Our first step toward building consciousness and spiritual enlightenment is the awareness that we have an inherent knowledge of the Truth.

In this chapter, we will consider the concept of self-knowledge in relation to our spiritual unfoldment. We will also discuss self-observation as a technique for gaining greater self-awareness.

3A **KNOW THYSELF**

Our most important study is our own mind, not only the intellectual mind but the spiritual mind. "Know thyself" was inscribed on the temple of Apollo at Delphi; and it must be inscribed on our own temple, over the door of our mind." (Charles Fillmore, *Keep a True Lent,* 2nd ed., Unity House, Unity Village, Mo., 2005, p. 38)

"Know thyself" ; know who and what you are, where you came from, what you are doing here, and where you are going. If you want to know all this, meditate on the I AM. (Charles Fillmore, *Talks on Truth,* Unity House, Unity Village, Mo., 1926, p. 76)

There is ordinary self-knowledge that is about the personality (ego), or who we think we are. And there is genuine Self-knowledge that is about the Christ, or What we are. However, Self-knowledge is the true prelude to Christ Consciousness, What we are. Without genuine Self-knowledge, other knowledge often becomes a kind of clutter in the mind. With genuine Self-knowledge, however, other knowledge has meaning and ripens into wisdom. We begin our quest for Self-knowledge by realizing that the Source of all wisdom is within the spectrum of our own consciousness. One of the most effective ways to gain greater Self-knowledge is to realize that we have a dimension of our minds that is even greater than our "think-ing self," or who we think and feel we are. It can evaluate what it observes. It can make decisions about what it observes. If it chooses, it can control, change and adjust what the thinking self is doing. It is from this higher level that true Self-knowledge is attained.

3B KNOWLEDGE IS WITHIN

Heretofore we have sought knowledge and help from outside sources, not knowing that the source of all knowl-edge, the very Spirit of truth, is lying latent within each one of us, waiting to be called on to teach us the truth about all things. (H. Emilie Cady, *Lessons In Truth*, Centennial Edition, Unity House, Unity Village, Mo., 2003, p. 19)

In education the emphasis is normally placed on the acquisition of knowledge. ... However, progressive educators are beginning to realize, as the ancient Greeks did, that true education is the process of waking up to life and releas-ing the effusion of light. (Eric Butterworth, *In the Flow of Life*, revised paperback edition, Unity House, Unity Village, Mo., 1994, p. 69)

The key to self-knowledge and Self-knowledge is the awareness that True Knowledge comes from within. We must keep in mind that the gaining of wisdom is not merely the result of pouring a sufficient number of facts

into our heads; rather, it is "remem-bering" or calling forth the Spiritual Truths that are inherent within our consciousness.

3C MORE THAN OUR MIND

A key to God Mind is with everyone—it is the action of the individual mind. Humankind is created in the "image" and "likeness" of God; humankind is therefore a phase of God Mind, and the individual mind must act like the orig-inal Mind. Study your own mind, and through it you will find God Mind. In no other way can you get a complete understanding of yourself, of the uni-verse, and of the law under which it is being brought forth. (Charles Fillmore, *Christian Healing*, 2nd ed., Unity House, Unity Village, Mo., 2005, p. 19)

We do not actually find God, or Divine Mind, since Omnipresence is never absent. What we must find is the point of awareness of Divine Mind/Oneness, and that can only be within our own consciousness. We are actually more than our seeming "own mind," which we can study from an observer self. If we were only our own mind, we could not rise to a dimension above it in order to observe or study it.

3D OUR MANY SELVES

We have no independent mind—there is only universal Mind—but we have consciousness in that Mind, and we have control over our own thoughts, and our thoughts fill our consciousness. By analyzing ourselves we find that we unconsciously separate our self into different personalities. (Charles and Cora Fillmore, *Teach Us to Pray*, 2nd ed., Unity House, Unity Village, Mo., 2007, p. 138)

We do not have an independent mind, in the sense that we have created it and it belongs to us exclusively. We each partake of the One Mind to the degree of our current capacity. However, we do have something called a "sense of I AM." We have the freedom of choice concerning what to do with our sense of I AM. We can use this sense to choose and make so many different "selves," or aspects of personality. In most of us, our sense of I AM is not really unified or totally coherent. It is usually fragmented and a bit chaotic. Thus, most of us are functioning as many selves.

3E PIVOTAL CONSCIOUSNESS

The conscious can look in two directions—to the outer world where the thoughts that rise within it give sensation and feeling, which ultimate in a moving panorama of visibility; or to the world within, whence all its life, power and intelligence are derived. (*Talks on Truth*, p. 10)

Ideas are hinged; they swing in and they swing out. Not everyone has observed this. But everyone must observe it, and note also the swing of his particular ideas. An idea that swings in has a mission. It is of Spirit, and has power to do far beyond an idea that swings out and dissipates its forces in the whirl of the periphery. On the inner side, ideas behold the great wisdom and attach themselves to it; then they lose their identity as limited things and take on the unlimited. (*Talks on Truth*, p. 29)

Our pivotal consciousness gives a wonderful advantage in life: We are able both to view realities and to evaluate them correctly. We utilize our pivotal consciousness to choose whether to swing our ideas to the outer and have them based primarily on sense consciousness or to swing our ideas to and from the inner and have them based primarily on Christ Consciousness.

The inner life should have priority, for it is the Realm of Causes and of spiritual resources. In the symbolism of the story of Jesus with Martha and Mary, the lesson of the relative value of our two worlds is brought out. Martha stands for our concerned feelings for the outer life, Mary for our serene contemplation of our inner life. Jesus respected both women, meaning that both aspects of our life have value. But Jesus indicates that "Mary has chosen the better part, which will not be taken away from her" (Lk. 10:42).

3F THE GREAT WORK

All things are in the consciousness and you have to learn to separate the erroneous from the true, darkness from the light. The I AM must separate the sheep from the goats. This sifting begins right now and goes on until the perfect child of God is manifest and you are fully rounded out in all your Godlike attributes. (Charles Fillmore, *Atom-Smashing Power of Mind,* Unity House, Unity Village, Mo., 1949, p. 49)

The great work that each individual may choose is the perfection of consciousness through individual evolution. This is the "seed" planted in the collective consciousness by Divine Mind. This is the purpose of metaphysical Christianity. We utilize our higher awareness in self-observation to separate goats from sheep—error from Truth—so that Christ Consciousness, the "perfect child of God," is manifest.

3G SELF-OBSERVATION

We must learn to watch our consciousness, its impulses and desires, as the chemist watches his or her solutions. We form our own consciousness from the elements of God, and we alone are responsible for the results. (Charles and Cora Fillmore, *The Twelve Powers,* Unity House, Unity Village, Mo., 1999, pp. 163-164)

One of the most effective ways to gain greater self-knowledge is through the process of compassionate self-observation. The primary purpose for self-observation is to discern the movements of beliefs, thoughts, feelings, attitudes and opinions in our own consciousness. Only in this way can we distinguish between what is desirable and what is undesirable at any given moment. Some persons never take time for sincere and calm self-observation and consequently find it difficult, even impossible, to change their consciousness. Error is a choice and it originates in consciousness. Self-observation is a method to detect error. It is important to point out, however, that self-observation must not become self-condemnation. Self-observation is a tool that must be used with all Twelve Powers (inherent yet often undeveloped Spiritual Faculties) and particularly the Powers of Love, Understanding and Judgment (Wisdom). (See Chapters 24 and 25 to learn more about the Twelve Powers.) Our goal is not to reproach ourselves or enter into self-loathing for our thoughts, feelings and actions; rather, we are seeking to carefully observe our thought patterns and how we choose and construct them moment to moment. Then the ones we realize are in error may be released or transformed. We want to remember that an important part of self-knowledge is *self-acceptance.*

3H **OUR GOAL**

The most profound knowledge that you can attain is that your whole existence flows forth inexorably from a universal process, which is always from within-out. (Eric Butterworth, *In the Flow of Life,* revised paperback edition, Unity House, Unity Village, Mo., 2004, pp. 4-5)

There are not thousands of things to learn in life. There is only one thing to learn: to know the Knower within and to sincerely and regularly "acknowledge God in all our ways." (*In the Flow of Life*, p. 80)

The ultimate aim of each individual is to gain a consciousness of Truth. In this knowledge each person finds himself or herself and the particular work he or she is intended to do. Each person brings a gift into the world, a donation to its progress. Each is restless and unsatisfied until he or she has delivered a contribution. Each becomes free from the ignorance that binds and hampers him or her only in proportion to his or her knowledge of Truth. False thinking makes one's way hard, but Truth is always liberating. (Richard

Lynch, *Know Thyself,* Unity House, Unity Village, Mo., 1935, pp. 6-7)

Once we become aware of the "Knower within," we are able to seek True Knowledge through prayer and meditation. We come to realize that we each have unique and special talents to share. We begin to understand that true success in life is not dependent solely on formal education but on the knowledge of Christ, or Self-knowledge. We are then able to *use* our education and the knowledge we acquire in life to kindheartedly serve others.

3I **SECURITY AND SELF-CONFIDENCE**

Security comes from knowing the truth of who and what we are. (Sue Sikking, *Only Believe,* Unity House, Unity Village, Mo., 1976, p.133)

Self-confidence is a great asset, and we cannot succeed in life without it; but self-confidence must have its base in the knowledge of who and what we are. (Martha Smock, *Halfway Up the Mountain,* Unity House, Unity Village, Mo., p. 209)

The *who* of us is the personality (ego), the mask worn over the *What* of us, Christ. A true sense of security and self-confidence does not come from reliance on the personality. Rather, it comes from a deep inner conviction and realization of the *What* we are. All that we ever need to know is available at any time and under all circumstances because *What* we are is Christ and "It is the true teacher and guide" to the *who* of us, the personality or ego.

In remembering and bringing the Christ—*What* we are—to the forefront of awareness, we are acknowledging and celebrating Oneness, or omnipresent Divine Mind.

SUMMARY STATEMENTS

▼ *The most important knowledge humankind can attain is <u>Self-knowledge</u>. Through knowledge of our own mind, we will find the key to Divine Mind.*

▼ *The key to Self-knowledge is the understanding that True Knowledge is a process of calling forth the Spiritual Truths <u>inherent within us</u>.*

▼ *One of the most effective ways to cultivate self-knowledge and Self-knowledge is through the process of <u>self-observation</u>. Only by watching our thought patterns can we distinguish between what is desirable and undesirable in our consciousness.*

▼ *While we must <u>use all Twelve Powers, or Spiritual Faculties,</u> in the process of distinguishing between the desirable and undesirable, we must especially utilize the Powers of Understanding, Love and Wisdom.*

▼ *We must be careful not to turn self-observation into self-condemnation. The key to successful self-observation is <u>self-acceptance</u>.*

▼ *When we seek Self-knowledge through <u>prayer</u> and <u>meditation</u>, we have the opportunity to uncover our gifts and talents that are based on our Christ Nature.*

▼ *True <u>success</u> and <u>self-confidence</u> come from the knowledge and realization that Christ is the* What *of us.*

TOPICS FOR DISCUSSION

1. *Explain your understanding of self-knowledge. Why is it emphasized in the Unity teachings?*

2. *What is the importance of self-observation to our spiritual unfoldment?*

3. *What part does Judgment play and how does that square with the admonition to "judge not"?*

4. *What role does formal education play in the process of self-knowledge?*

THOUGHTS FOR REFLECTION AND MEDITATION

"The old Greeks recognized this and wrote over the door of one of their temples: 'Man, know thyself.' The [S]elf of humankind is spiritual, and when it is in direct conscious unity with the [Divine] Mind it has permanent formative power."

(Charles Fillmore, *Christian Healing, 2nd ed.*, Unity House, Unity Village, Mo., 2005, pp. 62-63)

SUPPLEMENTARY READING

In the Flow of Life by Eric Butterworth, revised paperback edition, Unity House, Unity Village, Mo., 2004, Chapter 4, "The Effusion of Light."

CHAPTER FOUR

EVOLVING SPIRITUAL AWARENESS, BUILDING CHRIST CONSCIOUSNESS

4A OUR PROCESS AND GOAL

If you would bring forth the very best that is in you, study the methods of Jesus. Study them in all their details, get at the spirit of everything that is written about this wonderful man, and you will find the key to the true development of your soul [conscious mind and subconscious mind] and your body. If you will carry out His system, there will be revealed to you a new person, a person of whom you never dreamed, existing in the hidden realms of your own subconsciousness. (Charles and Cora Fillmore, *The Twelve Powers*, Unity House, Unity Village, Mo., 1999, p. 40)

Unspeakable joy, glory and eternal life are promised to those who with unselfish devotion strive to develop Christ consciousness. (*The Twelve Powers*, p. 6)

The desire to become new is universal in the hearts of humankind and contains within it the promise of fulfillment. No matter how good a person is, how many advantages are enjoyed, how much satisfaction there is, the desire for newness is always present. The potential for being new exists in everyone; however, spiritual mastery is usually not accomplished in one realization or one affirmation. We reach spiritual mastery through active, committed participation in a process of practicing Truth Principles in every area of our lives. Our wholehearted investment in this process of awakening to our True Spiritual Nature—Christ—will result in our experiencing rich and wondrous blessings.

4B EVOLUTION OF SPIRITUAL AWARENESS

Step by step, thought added to thought, spiritual emotion added to spiritual emotion—eventually the transformation is complete. It does not come in a day, but every high impulse, every pure thought, every upward desire adds to the exaltation and gradual personification of the divine in humankind and to the transformation of the human. The "old person" is constantly brought into subjection, and his or her deeds forever put off, as the "new person" appears arrayed in the vestments of divine consciousness. (Charles Fillmore, *Atom-Smashing Power of Mind,* Unity House, Unity Village, Mo., 1949, p. 124)

In every person the Christ, or Word of God, is infolded; it is an idea that contains ideas. Evolution is the result of the development of ideas in mind. What we are is the result of the evolution of our consciousness, and our consciousness is the result of the seed ideas sown in our mind. Therefore spiritual evolution is the unfolding of the spirit of God into expression. It is the development achieved by humankind working under spiritual law. ... The Christ, or Word (Son) of God evolution of humankind is plainly taught in the New Testament as the supreme attainment of every person. (Charles Fillmore, *Keep a True Lent,* 2nd ed., Unity House, Unity Village, Mo., 2005, p. 165)

In the second quote, Charles Fillmore is very explicit that Christ is the Word of God and is not an entity. Christ, the Word, is an Idea that contains Ideas. We could say it is a composite Divine Idea. In Unity we would say that this Idea, Christ, contains the twelve Divine Ideas that make up the Twelve Powers (see Chapters 24 and 25).

Often there is a misconception that the Christ is already in "full bloom" in us. Sometimes the mistake is made by thinking that what is true in potential is the same as whatever is manifesting at any given moment. However, awakening spiritual awareness supports our evolution from simply believing in who we are to realizing What we are, the composite Divine Idea called Christ. We progress in our development by first becoming aware of What we are (Christ, Divine Mind, Spirit, Oneness) and then by choosing and allowing this Divine Mind to be expressed from Christ Consciousness. We grow in consciousness by using head and heart to let go of erroneous thought patterns, holding in mind Truth ideas and applying them to our everyday lives. The attainment of Christ Consciousness is the result of this process; it is not an instant achievement. We succeed because of the Christ or Word of God "infolded" in us.

4C EVOLUTION OF CONSCIOUSNESS

Jesus was Himself a parable. His life was an allegory of the experiences that humankind passes through in developing from natural to spiritual consciousness. (Charles Fillmore, *Christian Healing,* 2nd ed., Unity House, Unity Village, Mo., 2005, p. 74)

… the Christ in Jesus existed before the personality. This is true for all of us. Christ is the spiritual mind in every individual, and the spiritual mind is the offspring of the universal or Jehovah-Mind. (*Atom-Smashing Power of Mind*, p. 100)

All the divine perfection that exists in the universal Jehovah-Mind can be brought into direct contact with its image and likeness, the Christ, imprinted in the beginning in each individual. As each individual develops spiritually, he or she releases, rounds out, and fully expresses that divine perfection which is potentially in his or her soul." (*Atom-Smashing Power of Mind*, pp. 100-101)

The method by which Jesus evolved from sense consciousness to God consciousness was, first, the recognition of the spiritual selfhood and a constant affirmation of its supremacy and power. Jesus loved to make the highest statements: " I and the Father are one." … Secondly, by the power of His word He penetrated deeper into omnipresence and tapped the deepest resources of His mind, whereby He released the light, life, and substance of Spirit, which enabled Him to get the realization that wholly united His consciousness with the God Mind. (*Atom-Smashing Power of Mind*, pp.37-38)

It is important to recognize that Christ, the Word, the composite Divine Idea, preexisted Jesus' personality and body as well as ours. This Christ (Word or Logos) was there in the beginning. John 1:1 tells us that this Logos is in fact God, or Divine Mind. This is because Divine Mind is not separate from Its Divine Ideas. We have hidden Christ behind the mask of the personality that we assume and believe. Just as Christ is the Word, the Idea that contains Ideas, so, too, is our personality nothing more than a conglomeration of ideas and thoughts about ourselves. Jesus went through a process of awakening to, developing and fully expressing the potential of this composite Divine Idea (Christ); and so shall we. We are to use him as our model and way-shower in our quest to be heart-centered metaphysicians. Jesus constantly affirmed his spiritual nature. He recognized its supremacy and power. He used the power of the spoken word to penetrate deeper and deeper into the awareness of Omnipresence, Divine Mind, thereby removing the mask of personality while realizing Oneness. He then lived from that Oneness.

4D THE FIRST AND SECOND BIRTH

"Ye must be born anew" was the proclamation of Jesus. *The first birth is the*

human—the self-consciousness of a person as an intellectual and physical being; the second birth, the being "born anew," is the transformation and translation of the human to a higher plane of consciousness as the Child of God. The second birth is that in which we "put on Christ." It is a process of mental adjustment and body transmutation that takes place right here on earth. "Have this mind in you, which was also in Christ Jesus," is an epitome of a mental and physical change that may require years to work out. But all people must go through this change before they can enter into eternal life and be as Jesus Christ is. (Christian Healing, pp. 25-26)

The "first birth" refers to our physical birth as a human being that is self-conscious, intellectual and physical. The "second birth," being "born again," accurately describes the significant change we undergo when we commit ourselves to living spiritually oriented lives, or living from Oneness, Christ. This new birth occurs when we make a commitment to awaken to Spirit as our Christ Nature, to make the effort to change the level of our thinking. When we do, we can let go of inadequate concepts of God, or Divine Mind, resulting in feeling brand-new as we express ourselves in productive and fulfilling ways. We are born again each time we consciously dedicate ourselves to living a life centered in and from Divine Mind. In other words, the sec-

ond birth is not an event, but an ongoing process of spiritual unfoldment.

The concept of a second birth lends itself to the concept that we are sons, daughters or children of God. It is important to realize that these are simply metaphors to somehow enhance our understanding. In Truth, in the Absolute Realm of Oneness, there cannot be a separate Christ, the composite Divine Idea, that is somehow different and separate from Divine Mind. Further, we must always be aware that such phrases as sons, daughters or children of God can subtly reinforce the beliefs we have carried from the spiritual understanding of our childhood. These phrases directly support the personification or the humanizing of God. God is not a person or entity; God is Mind.

4E CHEMICALIZATION

Chemicalization—A condition in the mind that is brought about by the conflict that takes place when a high spiritual realization contacts an old error state of consciousness. ... Whenever a new spiritual idea is introduced into the mind, some negative belief is disturbed. It resists. With this resistance comes more or less commotion in the consciousness. This is called chemicalization. This can be greatly modified or eliminated by putting the mind in divine order through denial. (Charles

Fillmore, *The Revealing Word: A Dictionary of Metaphysical Terms,* 2nd ed., Unity House, Unity Village, Mo., 2006, pp. 32-33)

Chemicalization is the experience of inner conflict and upheaval that often occurs when aspects of our consciousness resist the transformation process. This happens when a high spiritual realization conflicts with a belief that is contrary to the new realization. Chemicalization may show up as nervousness, the appearance of symptoms in the body, sleeplessness, or the return of old desires and habits that had previously been overcome. We must remember that these elements of our life are coming into our awareness and attention in such undeniable ways so that we can choose to release, heal or transform them. When chemicalization takes place, we have a wonderful opportunity to let our Christ Mind strengthen and restore us. If we meet our challenges with a nonresistant attitude, a kind heart and accept them as *part* of our growth process, we will feel more comfortable with the aspect of spiritual evolution that involves letting go of old thought patterns. Frequently, a person will view this upheaval as evidence they are doing something wrong, when, in fact, this chemicalization is proof they are doing something right!

4F NONRESISTANCE

"Agree with thine adversary quickly," remembering that the adversary is not the person or situation that stands before you but your reaction to or feeling about it. It has been said, "Things may happen around you, and things may happen to you, but the only things that really count are the things that happen in you." We can't always control what happens to us. But we can control what we think about what happens—and what we are thinking is our life at any particular moment.* (Eric Butterworth, *Discover the Power Within You*, 40th Anniversary Edition, HarperOne, New York, 2008, p. 87)

To have a good and rich life does not mean being set free from worldly experiences. It means having dominion and authority over them. (Sue Sikking, *A Letter to Adam,* Unity School of Christianity, Unity Village, Mo., 1965, p. 157)

The only "adversary" to our spiritual awakening and seeming evolution is found within our own consciousness. The adversary is not the situation or person before us; it is what we think and feel about the person or situation before us that gives rise to our reaction. This happens entirely within our own consciousness. Resisting, resenting and fighting the adversary only increases it. We want to find a way to harmonize and blend our desire and our adversary. If we are compassionate with ourselves and accept instead of fight these processes, we can use them for our growth. We will be able to proceed with poise and inner peace. Nonresistance eliminates an oppositional attitude. Our attitude of nonresistance enables us to meet all challenges victoriously.

4G CRUCIFIXION

The crossing out in consciousness of errors that have become fixed states of mind … . (Revealing Word, p. 46)

Having once seen Truth, having once had the illumination, you find that the next step is to demonstrate it and not be cast down or discouraged by the opposite. When the crucifixion comes and you are suffering the pangs of dying error, you may cry out, "My God, my God, why hast thou forsaken me?" forgetting for the time the promises in the mount of Transfiguration. This is when you need to realize that you are passing through a transforming process that will be followed by a resurrection of all that is worth saving. (Atom-Smashing Power of Mind, p. 155)

Feeling like we are being crucified can be a form of chemicalization. As we let go of old error beliefs and thinking, we can use the crucifixion experience to remember to let go of error thinking.

We can also use the experience to let go of some cherished aspect of our personality or of our personal life in order to unfold more of our Spiritual Potential, Christ (the composite Idea). It usually feels very painful to us even if we recognize how necessary it is to go through. The amount of pain involved in the act of letting go relates directly to the level of attachment we had to the cherished aspect of our personality along with whether we have engaged our heart in the process or not. Crucifixion is the crossing out of error thinking; it is "dying" to our old ways of error thinking in order to be reborn in the resurrection.

4H RESURRECTION

The "resurrection" of the body has nothing whatever to do with death, except that we may resurrect ourselves from every dead condition into which sense ignorance has plunged us. To be resurrected means to get out of the place that you are in and to get into another place. Resurrection is a rising into new vigor, new prosperity; a restoration to some higher state. It is absurd to suppose that it applies only to the resuscitation of a dead body. (Atom-Smashing Power of Mind, pp. 119-120)

The restoring of mind and body to their original, undying state. This is accomplished by the realization that God is

Spirit and that God created humankind with power like that which God Itself possesses. When a person realizes this, his or her mind and body automatically become immortal. ... The resurrection takes place in us every time we rise to Jesus' realization of the perpetual indwelling life that is connecting us with God. A new flood of life comes to all who open their minds and their bodies to the living word of God. (Revealing Word, p. 169)

Ordinarily the word *resurrection* means to regain that which one has lost. In these quotes we can see resurrection as something more. It is not only regaining a state from which one may have fallen, but it is actually rising to a higher state of new vigor, prosperity and restoration than ever before. There is an element of "ascension" in this definition of resurrection.

The resurrection experience can be a daily one for any person who is seriously committed to realizing more Divine Mind. Paul said in 1 Corinthians 15:31, "I die daily"; he dies to the old self and resurrects himself into a newer Self continually. Resurrection follows crucifixion and is an ongoing experience in our spiritual unfoldment. It is evidence of overcoming the belief in lack and limitation through spiritual mastery. We do this by taking on Divine Ideas, new thought forms and habit patterns that are from and in alignment with Christ

Mind. Each effort is directed from the awareness of Oneness, or Divine Mind, producing a new resurrection experience, new energies, truer thoughts, purer emotions and happier attitudes. These are all evidence of the resurrection of Christ Nature in our consciousness. It is not that Christ Nature, or Christ Consciousness, is ever dead or gone. It is simply that our awareness of It is dead and we must resurrect this awareness.

41 REGENERATION

When people begin to follow Jesus in the regeneration they find that they must cooperate with the work of their disciples or faculties. Heretofore they have been under the natural law; they have been fishers in the natural world. Through their recognition of their relation as the Son of God, people cooperate in the original creative law. The person calls his or her faculties out of their materiality into their spirituality. This process is symbolized by Jesus' calling His apostles. (Charles and Cora Fillmore, *The Twelve Powers*, Unity House, Unity Village, Mo., 1999, p. 50

A change in which abundant spiritual life, even eternal life, is incorporated into the body. The transformation that takes place through bringing all the forces of mind and body to the support of the Christ ideal. The unification of

Spirit, soul and body in spiritual oneness. (Revealing Word, p. 165)

Regeneration follows generation in the development of humankind. Generation sustains and perpetuates the human; regeneration unfolds and glorifies the divine. (The Twelve Powers, p. 3)

As the mind changes from error to Truth, corresponding changes take place in the body, and the ultimate of these changes is perfection and wholeness in every part. (Keep a True Lent, p. 96)

As a serious commitment to follow the teachings of Spiritual Truth is made, a person immediately becomes aware of Laws that are higher and finer than before. Up to this point, most people are almost entirely dominated by the laws of nature as well as the most mechanical level of cause and effect. As we recognize our True Nature, Christ, this changes. Life seems to become more simplified. One's life starts to be lived from the awareness of Oneness. One knows and feels guidance and protection coming from their Christ Nature. This guidance is from the Higher Self (Individuality) to the lower self (the personality). Up to this point the Twelve Powers (Spiritual Faculties or Abilities) had been used from the awareness of separation and from sense consciousness. As a person becomes aware of Christ Nature, these Powers, the Divine Ideas that make up

the composite Divine Idea, are expressed from It.

Regeneration is the process that reveals and unfolds our Divinity (Christ). Regeneration of the Twelve Powers is how we unfold our Divinity. It begins and ends in consciousness. Regeneration results in the transformation of our souls (conscious mind and subconscious mind), as well as corresponding changes in the physical body that express perfection and wholeness. Thus, the transformation process enables the realization of wholeness on all levels of our being. (See Chapters 24 and 25 for more on the Twelve Powers.)

4J ETERNAL LIFE

God is life. Life is a principle that is made manifest in the living. Life cannot be analyzed by the senses. It is beyond their grasp; hence it must be cognized by Spirit. (Charles Fillmore, Jesus Christ Heals, 2nd ed., Unity House, Unity Village, Mo., 1940, p. 30)

God is life, and humankind [humankind's Divine Nature] is life. But life in its essence and life as seen in the living are not identical. The sense man [the personal person] looks on living, moving things and says, "This is life." It is not life, but only the evidence of life. Each person may know the life that is back of the living. When a person feels the thrill of that life within him/her, he/she has touched the divine energy that changes not. (Keep a True Lent, pp. 61-62)

Thus humankind must understand the nature of God and awaken in itself that divine nature through which to effect its conscious union with Him. God is Spirit. We are the offspring of this Spirit. God is Mind: a person is the thinker. God is Life: a person is the living.(Charles Fillmore, Dynamics for Living: A Topical Compilation of Essential Fillmore Teachings, compiled by Warren Meyer, 1967, pp. 90-91)

We all have life, and it is God's eternal life, but it does not become ours in reality until we consciously realize it. The one who enters into eternal life, as did Jesus, must lay hold on that omnipresent life and make it one with his body. This is the secret of inheriting eternal life. (Keep a True Lent, p. 22.)

Life is divine, spiritual, and its source is God, Spirit. The river of life is within all people in their spiritual consciousness. They come into consciousness of the river of life through the quickening of Spirit. They can be truly quickened with new life and vitalized in mind and body only by consciously contacting Spirit. This contact is made through prayer, meditation and good works." (Revealing Word, p. 22)

God is Spirit; God is Life; God is Divine Mind. Life is an eternal Divine Idea. Since God is not a person or entity, to say we are offspring of God is a metaphorical way of indicating that our True Nature is Divine; It is Spirit; It is Mind; It is Life. However, there is a difference between the eternal Divine Idea of Life and what we call *living*. Eternal Life is an aspect of our True Nature; the experience we call *living* is how the seeming personal self utilizes this Life Principle. The consciousness that Life is eternal is arrived at (quickened) by becoming aware of Divine Mind through prayer, meditation and good works.

4K REINCARNATION

When a soul leaves the body, it rests for a season. Then innate desire for material expression asserts itself, and the ego seeks the primal cell and builds another body. This is reincarnation. Reincarnation will continue until the ego awakens to the Christ Mind and through it builds an imperishable body …. But reincarnation is not a part of the divine plan and does not lift humankind out of mortal limitations. It is not an aid to spiritual growth, but merely a makeshift until full Truth is discerned. (Revealing Word, p. 166)

A new soul is not created with every physical birth. A physical birth simply means that a soul is taking on another body. Every person inhabiting this earth and the psychic realms immediately surrounding it has gone through this process of dying and being reincarnated many times. (The Twelve Powers, p. 138)

Although belief in reincarnation is not necessary for Unity students, it is found in Charles Fillmore's writings. Reincarnation is the process by which we express the desire for physical expression and is another way in which the sense of separation expresses the eternal Divine Idea of Life. The way Fillmore is using the term *soul* here is not equivalent to the word *Spirit*. Spirit is already whole and perfect and has no desire or need for physical expression. Soul is the sum of conscious mind and subconscious mind. It may seem that we need successive bodies for our souls to inhabit in order to achieve " salvation." However, this method keeps us mired on the wheel of karma: it does not help our spiritual growth. As Fillmore said, it is " merely makeshift until full Truth is discerned." We must individually and collectively awaken to Oneness, Christ Nature.

SUMMARY STATEMENTS

▼ *Our <u>desire</u> to unfold our spiritual potential contains within it the <u>promise of fulfillment</u>.*

▼ *<u>Evolving spiritual awareness</u> is the unfoldment of Divine Nature from our consciousness.*

In Unity, being "<u>born again</u>" refers to a continual process of commitment and rededication to our spiritual awakening and unfoldment.

▼ *<u>Nonresistance</u> is not about the outer; it is not resisting thoughts, feelings and attitudes about the outer.*

▼ *<u>Nonresistance</u> and the exercise of the Power of Dominion over life's experiences allow the awareness of poise and inner peace to be achieved.*

▼ *<u>Chemicalization</u> is when the awareness of new Spiritual Truths meets old beliefs and error thoughts in consciousness, resulting in conflict and upheaval. It sometimes shows up as physical, emotional or mental symptoms.*

▼ *Crucifixion* is how we sometimes feel when chemicalization occurs. It is the experience of crossing out (letting go of) error thinking or some cherished aspect of our personality or personal life. This results in heightened awareness of Oneness.

▼ *Resurrection* is the experience of having overcome our error thinking or our attachment to some cherished aspect of our personality or personal life. This can be the overcoming, through spiritual mastery, of the belief in lack and limitation.. The crucifixion/resurrection experience is an ongoing process.

▼ *Regeneration* is the process that reveals and unfolds our Divinity (Christ). Regeneration occurs when we consciously choose to begin to use the Twelve Powers from the awareness of Oneness rather than from sense consciousness.

▼ *Eternal Life* is a Divine Idea. It is utilized by the seeming personal self to manifest the experience called living as well as reincarnation.

▼ *Reincarnation* is the makeshift process by which humankind experiences successive embodiments on the earth plane for the purpose of soul unfoldment until we individually and collectively awaken to the Reality of Oneness, Christ Nature.

TOPICS FOR DISCUSSION

1. *Describe your understanding of evolving spiritual awareness.*

2. *What does it mean to you to be "born again"?*

3. *Share a time in your life when you had a "crucifixion and resurrection" experience. What did you learn from this experience?*

THOUGHTS FOR REFLECTION AND MEDITATION

"We must meet the experiences of life
with the knowledge and understanding of their part in life.
To do this is to have power over the events of life.
We cannot stay in any place and say:
'Here is where I want to be.
I don't want anything else to happen to me.
I want to be away from the fret and worry of common life.
I want to stay on this high mountain or in this ivory tower.'
This isn't the way life is.
This isn't the way to happiness or contentment.
Strange as it may seem,
happiness, joy, contentment, and victory
belong to the overcomer."

(Sue Sikking, *A Letter to Adam*, Unity School of Christianity, Unity Village, Mo., 1965, p. 160)

SUPPLEMENTARY READING

Discover the Power Within You by Eric Butterworth, 40th Anniversary Edition, HarperOne, New York, 2008, Chapter 8, "The Law of Nonresistance."

What Are You? by Imelda Shanklin, 2nd ed., Unity House, Unity Village, Mo,, 2004, Chapter 6, "Your Objective," and Chapter 9, "Nonresistance."

CHAPTER FIVE

OUR PURPOSE, DIVINE WILL, DIVINE PLAN, AND DIVINE GUIDANCE

INTRODUCTION

Normally people speak about God's will, God's plan and God's guidance. These terms lend themselves to consciously or subconsciously humanizing God, a tendency that reinforces the idea that there is literally a God outside of us giving guidance and that God has a very specific will and plan for each individual. It might be better to think in terms of Divine Will, Divine Plan and Divine Guidance. In Unity, however, these concepts are very different from the way they are more traditionally understood.

God, or Divine Mind, is ever-present Spirit. In Truth, we are Spirit; we are Christ (the Idea that is made up of Ideas). We come to the awareness of Spirit, or Divine Mind, in the Silence as we seek the Kingdom. It is from the Silence and therefore from our Christ Nature that Divine Will, Divine Plan, and Divine Guidance arise.

While Divine Will, the Divine Plan, and Divine Guidance are frequently used interchangeably, we are not doing that here.

◆ Divine Will is that each person ultimately reveals and expresses Christ (the composite Divine Idea). This Divine Will is generic, amorphous, nonspecific and is for everyone.

◆ Divine Plan is how each person decides to go about bringing forth, developing and expressing Divine Will. Each person's consciousness determines the direction he or she takes in expressing the Christ, the Divine Idea that is made up of Ideas.

◆ Divine Guidance is the supportive flow of Divine Mind. It uses the amorphous Divine Idea of Wisdom emerging from one's Divine Mind to discern the road ahead and to formulate and implement the Plan.

In summary, from the awareness of Oneness, or Divine Mind, it is through and from the Divine Guidance of the Higher Self that we, as heart-centered metaphysicians, give shape and form to a Divine Plan out of the awareness of Divine Will.

5A **OUR PURPOSE**

Purpose gives joy and zest to living. When our eye is on the goal we are not so easily perturbed. Purpose awakens new trains of thought into new fields of achievement. Really to succeed we must have some great purpose in mind, some goal toward which we are to work. (Charles Fillmore, *Talks on Truth,* Unity House, Unity Village, Mo., 1926, p. 45)

Our purpose is to realize, be and express our Divine Potential, which is Christ. The Christ Nature is always maximal and is seemingly only potential until we first realize Its presence. This purpose is not imposed upon us from some separate, external, micro-managing God. Rather, it is the purpose we create at the point of ourselves as we experience the dissonance between who we think we are (personalities) and What we are, Christ (the composite Divine Idea), or

Individuality. We might also consider motivation along with purpose. Both are generated in the consciousness through the Power of Zeal, one of the Twelve Spiritual Powers covered in Chapters 24 and 25. We use quickened Zeal to increase awareness of our true potential, Christ.

5B **DIVINE WILL**

God Mind expresses its thoughts so perfectly that there is no occasion for change, hence all prayers and supplications for the change of God's will to conform to human desires are futile. God Mind does not change, or trim thought, to meet the conflicting opinions of humankind. Understanding the perfection of God thoughts, people must conform to them; so conforming, they will discover that there is never necessity for any change of the will of God in regard to human affairs.

(Charles Fillmore, *Christian Healing,* 2nd ed., Unity House, Unity Village, Mo., 2005, p. 18)

Will of God—God's will is always perfection and good for all God's children. ... *God does not will suffering or imperfection in any form.* (Charles Fillmore, *The Revealing Word: A Dictionary of Metaphysical Terms,* 2nd ed., Unity House, Unity Village, Mo., 2006, p. 87)

God, or Divine Mind, is only Absolute Good (Good without opposite) in the form of Divine Ideas that consist of both thinking and feeling natures. Since Good is the ultimate Truth about Divine Mind and Its Divine Ideas, wanting It to change does not make sense. Divine Will is that each person ultimately reveals and expresses Christ (the composite Divine Idea), or Good. This Divine Will is generic, amorphous, nonspecific, and is for everyone. We are all partaking of and participating in the generic Divine Will; there is no separation from It. This Divine Will is not the Spiritual Power of Will. The Power of Will is the ability to choose. There is no choosing in Divine Mind since all "choices" already are. We "create" the experience of this Will because of the gap we sense between who we think we are (egos/personalities) and What we already are, Christ. It may also be experienced simply as an urge to express more and more of our Christ Potential.

5C DIVINE PLAN

In order to get at the very heart of Being, it is necessary to realize that it is manifesting in the least as well as in the greatest, and that, in the bringing forth of a universe, not one idea could be taken away without unbalancing the whole. This brings us to fuller realization of our importance in the universe and to the necessity of finding our right place. (*Christian Healing,* pp. 10-11)

In some such way then we can think of humankind represented by an x *in God's plan or calculations. God is carrying humankind along in God Mind as an ideal quantity, the image-and-likeness human [the Christ] of God's creation, and God's divine plan is dependent for its success on the manifestation by humankind of this idea. The divine plan is furthered by the constant idealism that keeps humankind moving forward to higher and higher achievements. The image-and-likeness human [the Christ] pours into humankind a perpetual stream of ideas that the individual person arranges as thoughts and forms as substance and life.* (Charles Fillmore, *Mysteries of Genesis,* 2nd ed., Unity House, Unity Village, Mo., 2007, p. 26)

The only predestiny in life is the ulti-mate unfoldment of the divine creature you are. But the direction you take in realizing this outforming of the Christ indwelling will always be determined by your consciousness. However, there is a creative intention working in you. It is a force that transcends mistakes and wrong choices and makes all things work for good. It is like an organist who may touch a wrong note and create a dissonance, and who skill-fully uses that wrong note as a leading tone by which to modulate into a new key. He or she makes it appear as if the whole progression was intended that way, as if it were the only way it could have been.

You cannot really make a wrong choice, a bad decision. Any step you take will lead eventually to your good, because a negative experience encountered will produce the challenge in which to out-grow the kind of consciousness from which the choice was made, leading to a higher consciousness from which more constructive steps will be taken. So a wrong choice is a right choice at that particular time. Know this: you are free from the fear of bad decisions. You can stand still and believe that there is no decision to be made, only a direction to discover. (Eric Butterworth, *In the Flow of Life,* revised paperback edition, Unity House, Unity Village, Mo., 1994, p. 77)

The Divine Plan is how each person decides to bring forth, develop and express Divine Will. It is not the same thing as predestination because there is not a predetermined way for each person. While the Divine Plan is about revealing and expressing our Divinity, we still have free will, the freedom of choice. At any given moment, each person decides whether and/or how much Christ Nature he or she will reveal and express. The beauty of this is that, in the big picture, the Divine Will is fixed and does not change, while the Divine Plan is designed and crafted by each individual. Each per-son's consciousness determines the direction he or she takes in expressing the Christ indwelling consciousness. It is with joy and gratitude that we must dedicate and consecrate our lives to unfold Christ Nature and fully partici-pate in this joyous process of fulfill-ment.

As we consciously recognize that this powerful creative intention is within us and *is* us, we can transcend the level of mistakes. If we make a mis-take, it is made right by tuning in to the creative flow of consciousness that we are; we can choose to make every-thing work for good. While in the awareness of the creative flow of con-sciousness, we, like the organist, may in any given moment transform a mis-take into a moment of genius.

5D **DIVINE GUIDANCE**

What is called "divine guidance" is a flow of Infinite Mind. It is universal in that it is a principle of mind action and not dependent upon a special appeal. It is personal in that it is a process of the presence of this Mind that "knows what you need before you ask him" (Mt. 6:8). It makes no choice for you, but it is the urge and energy through which you can make the choice that is best in terms of your own consciousness. It is not a special act of God but a specialization of the omniscience and omni-action of the presence of God.

Divine guidance is not prejudiced. It does not come with one fixed and unalterable step to be taken. It is, rather, a wisdom, a light, a supportive flow that enables you to see the road ahead with amazing clarity and to use your own wisdom at its highest level of development. Divine guidance can never lead you to take a step that is beyond your ability to understand or rightly use.

Some persons puzzle over the question "How can one distinguish between divine guidance and human will?" The very question implies a duality—a sense of God "out there" who would or could desire for you something contrary to your personal desires. Divine guidance is not an exterior force acting upon you. It is the seed of your divinity (the Christ of you) seeking to fulfill its pattern in the outforming process of

your life. God could never do for you that which you do not inherently want for yourself." (In the Flow of Life, pp. 70-71)

Light is where you are, and it is the complete answer to what you need, now and always. ... The light you seek is not somewhere else, but where you are. Don't ask God to guide you or beg God to make the choice for you. Instead, affirm that you are in the flow of light, and God is the light. You are in it. It is in you. It is the reality of you. It is not something to reach for but a truth to accept. Know that there is that in you that knows the right and perfect direction for your life and affirm that you are now acting under that guiding light.

You are forever in the flow of guidance. Don't wait to be guided. We are told to "wait on the Lord," but the word wait *comes from the root word that means "to bind together." This kind of "waiting" implies plugging in to the divine circuits. It is not a question of time but a depth of consciousness. Expect to be guided; then get in motion. (In the Flow of Life, p. 75)*

At first, it might seem shocking to learn that God, or Divine Mind, makes no choice for us. Divine Mind simply ideates. And yet it is freeing to learn that we do not have to invest hours and hours trying to get God to reveal what to do. There is no exterior force acting upon us. Divine Guidance is a magnificent flow of Divine Mind. It is an "urge and energy through which *you* can make the choice that is best in terms of your own consciousness." It is the amorphous Divine Idea of Wisdom emerging from Divine Mind as a supportive flow to discern the road ahead and to formulate the Divine Plan. Step by step, Divine Guidance also helps us implement the Divine Plan.

SUMMARY STATEMENTS

▼ *Our purpose is to express our Divine Potential that is inherent in Divine Ideas. When we are aware of our purpose in life, we find a joy and zeal for living.*

▼ *Divine Will is simply that we experience and manifest as much of the Absolute Good (Christ, the Idea that is made up of Ideas) as we can at our current level of consciousness.*

▼ *Divine Will is not something that is imposed upon us.*

▼ *The Divine Plan is what we ultimately create using Divine Guidance to discover, unfold, reveal and express the composite Divine Idea (Christ).*

▼ *Divine Guidance is a magnificent flow of Infinite Mind that discerns the road ahead and helps formulate and implement the Divine Plan. It is an "urge and energy through which you can make the choice that is best in terms of your own consciousness."*

TOPICS FOR DISCUSSION

1. *If God is not guiding us step by step, how might you understand the personal experience people have when they say they have received guidance?*

2. *How does one go about utilizing the divine urge and energy to make decisions?*

CHAPTER SIX

THE SILENCE

INTRODUCTION

The Silence is often thought to be the most important subject Unity teaches. It is the most fundamental starting point for becoming a heart-centered metaphysician. It is simple and yet, at the same time, the most advanced of all Unity teachings. There is sometimes confusion because there is both the practice of the Silence and the state of consciousness called the Silence. The purpose of the meditation practice of the Silence is to enter into the Silence. While sometimes referred to as prayer, the Silence is more accurately a state of non-awareness that arises during some forms of meditation. It is the medium in which and from which our True Nature, Christ, expresses. It is the Source of creativity. It is both the means and the goal of the path to all spiritual attainment.

In Unity, we do not claim to possess all Truth, nor do we actually reveal the inner mysteries; we merely point the way to discovering them. Do not depend on what you read or hear. Trust, rather, in the Silence and Christ Nature (composite Divine Idea), the teaching of the Spirit of Truth. Depend only on what is revealed to you in the Silence and therefore the Christ.

This chapter ends with excerpts from the book *Myrtle Fillmore's Healing Letters*. These excerpts describe a process of going into the Silence. We include them for historical reasons, yet they also provide an appropriate conclusion to this chapter and a transition to the next chapter on meditation.

6A THE SILENCE

A state of consciousness entered into for the purpose of putting each person in touch with Divine Mind so that the soul may listen to the " still small voice" (1 Kings 19:12 KJV). (Charles Fillmore, *The Revealing Word: A Dictionary of Metaphysical Terms,* 2nd ed., Unity House, Unity Village, Mo., 2006, p. 179)

There is a vast difference between mere intellectual silence and that constructive Silence which always gives the victory within the soul. The intellectual silence, which is limited in its power, is the silence where one's whole attention is fixed on the intellect. (Charles and Cora Fillmore, *Teach Us to Pray,* 2nd ed., Unity House, Unity Village, Mo., 2007, p. 22)

Realization—The deep inner conviction and assurance of the fulfillment of an ideal. It means at-one-ment, completion, perfection, wholeness, repose, resting in God. It is the dawning of Truth in the consciousness. When realization takes place, one abides in the light of God-Mind. (The Revealing Word, p. 164)

The Silence is a state of consciousness and nonawareness to which we may retreat from the relative realm of sense consciousness. It is always there like the sun. It is a place of inner stillness and quiet that is the source of Divine Revelation and from which we make discoveries of the eternal Truths and therefore, ultimately, ourselves.

Experiencing the Silence is more than merely rearranging our thoughts, and it is not a process of demonstration. We do not seek things or form there at any time. It is a state of consciousness, a state of nonawareness, from which realization arises. After investing time in the Silence, we see with the inner eye That which is eternal and realize and know That which has always been.

In the Silence, we look away from and release the errors of sense consciousness and enter into the Truth. We enter into the consciousness of True Beingness. It is a state of consciousness in which there is only Oneness. However, since it is actually a state of NO AWARENESS (no time, space, experience or awareness from the senses), we actually discern Oneness, or Beingness, after having been in the Silence and we realize " I Am" as an effect, a result of being in the Silence.

The actual practice of the Silence is a state of gentle mental alertness that may be the simplest operation of which the mind is capable as well as the simplest practice of human experience. It is more than merely keeping still and being quiet or silent; and yet, the first step of practicing the Silence is becoming physically still. It is the gateway of the mind to the state of nonawareness, from which we make spiritual discoveries and come into an understanding of spiritual things. One discovery is that Christ is the Truth of What we are. When we discover this fact, we find true freedom. When we practice the Silence, our entire consciousness is affected and there is subsequent overflowing into every department and aspect of our being and life.

From the Silence we discern our True Intuitional Nature and can distinguish between who we think we are and What we are. We see with our inner eye, not with our two outer, physical eyes. We see inwardly to our Beingness. We begin to realize What we want to *be* and not what we want to possess or do. Ultimately, we want to be as radiant, as wise and as Christlike as Jesus demonstrated. This Christ Nature is the heart of consciousness. This Truth is discovered by investing time in the Silence.

6B THE FOUNDATION

The first step is to discipline the mind in the knowledge that there is God alone. This is the path of illumination. It is also the path of elimination, as it causes a dropping away of all ungodliness. (E.V. Ingraham, "The Silence," unpublished Unity class notes of L.E. Meyer, 1933)

The starting point for all success is always One Truth or simply Oneness.

It is complete; nothing needs to be added. Oneness is not discernible to the human senses. Our experience of It is that It *seems* to be indwelling; consequently, all Truth must be individually discerned. It is the One Power and One Presence. Paradoxically, Oneness is understood from the awareness of Divine Nature in consciousness. It becomes apparent to those who have the eyes to see and ears to hear. As we focus on the awareness of Divine Nature, we become more and more conscious of Oneness. In the process, error is eliminated. We are renewed, and our awareness is filled with Truth.

6C THE OUTER

The intellect is always busy, jumping from one thing to another, much of the time dwelling on the daily routine of the workaday world or on conditions in the world at large. The first step in scientific Silence is simply to still these outer intellectual thoughts so that the consciousness may become subservient to the Spirit within. (*Teach Us to Pray*, p. 24)

Things are not to be sought first, or at any time. Our first, last and entire attention must be to God. (Unpublished Unity Training School course work of L.E. Meyer, transcript of a class entitled "The Silence," taught by E.V. Ingraham, Lesson Two, 1933)

It is easy to get wrapped up in sense consciousness and to get lost in the maze of the outer world. The intellect easily jumps from one thought to another, from one experience to another. The outer must be released so that one can enter into the Silence. Ironically, the meditation practice presented in the next chapter utilizes and works with the way thoughts naturally arise in mind.

6D **WHY**

A period of quiet and rest each day is your opportunity to establish yourself at the center of your being, the one place where the supply of life and substance is inexhaustible. (Myrtle Fillmore, *Myrtle Fillmore's Healing Letters,* revised paperback edition, Unity House, Unity Village, Mo., 2006, p. 28)

The sabbath is a very certain, definite thing. It is a state of mind that a person enters or acquires when he/she goes into the silence, into the realm of Spirit. There he/she finds true rest and peace. … Humankind had become so lost in the darkness of sense consciousness that it could not save itself, so the Saviour came. When each person lays hold of the indwelling Christ, the Saviour, he/she is raised out of the

Adam consciousness into the Christ consciousness. The person then enters the seventh stage of … unfoldment, where he/she finds sweet rest and peace. (Charles Fillmore, *Keep a True Lent,* 2nd ed., Unity House, Unity Village, Mo., 2005, p. 171)

While living from sense consciousness, one can become aware of a longing for something higher. This longing is a kind of unrest that is fueled from the dissonance between who we think we are (Adam consciousness, a personality, ego) and What we are, Christ. We are not satisfied with life that manifests from sense consciousness. We are not satisfied with the search for things and projects to do. The psalmist once said, "I shall be satisfied, when I awake, with thy likeness" (Ps. 17:15 KJV). Until we begin to go within consciousness, this Oneness, Christ

Nature, is only potential.

This desire to know Christ Nature is frequently experienced as trying to get pleasure from things. This pleasure is fleeting and does not last, though we may try for years. Eventually we begin to feel empty and unsatisfied, perhaps even enslaved by the process. We learn that things which fill our outer senses never truly satisfy us; and yet, like the moon reflects the light of the sun, this outer fulfilling of our desire is a reflection of our true desire to know Oneness, to know our Divine Nature.

6E **PURPOSE**

The Silence is designed primarily to enable us to come into an understanding of spiritual things. As we drop away all habits of thought, speech and action which are now known to us, we shall quickly come into an understanding of newer, lovelier and greater things. Practice of the Silence expands the consciousness to include the things of the Spirit. (Unpublished Unity Training School course work of L.E. Meyer, transcript of a class entitled "The Silence," taught by E.V. Ingraham, Lesson Two, 1933)

The Silence is not a process of demonstration. The purpose of the Silence and prayer is a matter of revelation. It opens up new avenues of mind and paths in consciousness to illumination. ("The Silence" class, Lesson Two, 1933)

The Silence is for the purpose of seeking out the inner faculties. Hidden within the ethers about us, and within us, are the powers of the universe. God is Spirit. We discern spiritual things through the activities of our inner being. ("The Silence" class, Lesson Two, 1933)

The purpose of the Silence is to still the activity of the individual thought so that the still small voice of God may be heard. For in the Silence, Spirit speaks Truth to us and just that Truth of which we stand in need. (Teach Us to Pray, p. 17)

The practice of the Silence is not a process *of* or *for* demonstration. The purpose of the Silence is to turn the mind away from the outer world of things perceived by the senses to that which is in consciousness and eternal—essentially turning away from the world of form to the realm of Spirit. It is to seek our inner treasures as if we are "spiritual prospectors" working in an infinite mine of possibilities. The raw ore of Mind/mind contains rich treasures yet to be discerned.

The purpose of the Silence is interior discovery through revelation. The Silence awakens understanding and feeds our beingness as Life, Spirit, energy and action. The Silence opens up the mind to new avenues and paths of consciousness leading to illumination. Ultimately, this inner discovery reveals the fundamental Divine Nature.

Practicing the Silence (meditation) and resting in the Silence do result in the stilling of individual thought (Adam consciousness) and the five senses. Ironically, this does not happen by actively trying to still, quiet or silence the mind. It happens by working with the way mind works.

With respect to the last excerpt above, it is more accurate to say that the Still

Small Voice is not actually "heard" while one is in the Silence. The Silence is actually a state of spiritual non-awareness. We become more aware of Spiritual Truth *after* having been in the Silence. The impetus for the Still Small Voice and Spiritual Truth arises *from* the Silence.

6F HOW MUCH TIME TO INVEST IN THE SILENCE?

In the beginning, many students try to stay too long in the Silence. Forget about the question of time. <u>*Cultivate the habit of turning the attention to God. Do it a thousand times a day by*</u> *realizing, "I am in the presence of God."* (Unpublished Unity Training School course work of L. E. Meyer, transcript of a class entitled "The Silence," taught by E. V. Ingraham, Lesson Three, 1933)

Students should not try so hard to "go into the Silence." When your growth brings you to the place where your consciousness may be so completely merged with Christ ideas in God Mind that you lose all sense of things about you, it is time to seek to go into the Silence. But one should not try to hurry this experience. (*Myrtle Fillmore's Healing Letters*, p. 27)

Trying to get into the Silence simply does not work because trying or striving is the antithesis of Oneness. Any sense of urgency to go into the Silence is counterproductive.

Many ask, "How much time should I invest in the Silence?" It is important not to focus too much on time because awareness and consciousness are turned toward the outer when the focus is on time. A starting place is to simply cultivate the habit of turning awareness to Divine Nature as often as can be remembered and affirming, *I am the Presence of Divine Mind* or, more boldly, *I am Divine Mind.*

In order to train the mind, work up to establishing regular periods of meditation of 20 minutes once or twice a day. Choose a time that is convenient and not rushed. At times you will feel a kind of pull or nudge from your Higher Nature to simply sit, be still and to go into the Silence. Eventually, as the awareness of Oneness intensifies, all disturbing and distracting influences will drop away with ease and grace during these times of meditation. As these ways are practiced, there will always be time to accomplish what needs to be done if you desire it enough.

6G PREPARATION

Relaxation is not inertia, but a light, spontaneous, buoyant spirit. Tension comes through suppression. The first step in relaxation is to "cast thy burden upon the Lord" (Ps. 55:22 KJV). This is not accomplished through effort, but through ease. It is well not to take ourselves too seriously. God created by letting the true come forth, and not in making them. The Spirit is within us and comes forth as we let it. (Unpublished Unity Training School course work of L. E. Meyer, transcript of a class entitled "The Silence," taught by E. V. Ingraham, Lesson Four, 1933)

Relaxation—A letting go of tenseness in mind and body. Abatement of strain. Loosening the tight mental grip we have on ourselves in order that the healing Christ life may flow freely through our being. "Come unto me … and I will give you rest" (Mt. 11:28). (*The Revealing Word*, p.166)

We shall guard well the inner processes of our nature. We shall let go of limitation that the inner limitless One will come forth. ("The Silence" class, Lesson Four, 1933.)

Relaxation is essential to the process since the tense habits of our minds and bodies inhibit our progress in realizing our Spiritual Nature. Relaxing the body can occur in many ways: stretching, yawning, sighing or wiggling in our seats as well as laughing. It is also important not to take oneself too seriously. Let go of the personality and the body while letting Divine Nature come to the forefront of awareness.

Avoid those things that cause unpleasant mental or emotional reactions. If you notice that there are unpleasant mental and/or emotional reactions, do not resist them. Simply do not give them power or set them up in residence in your consciousness. Release anything that feels oppressive or stifling. Embrace anything that strengthens the power of the awareness of Oneness, or Spirit. Ultimately, this is letting go of anything that limits or restricts so that the experience of limitless Oneness fills your awareness.

6H HOW-TO BASICS

The first step in life's process is to discipline the mind in the knowledge that there is God alone. This is the path of illumination. It is also the path of elimination, as it causes a dropping away of all ungodliness. (Unpublished Unity Training School course work of L. E. Meyer, transcript of a class entitled "The Silence," taught by E. V. Ingraham, Lesson Two, 1933)

Do not seek vibrations. Do not seek experiences; do not expect any outer results from prayer. ("The Silence" class, Lesson Three, 1933.)

We do not experience illumination until we become conscious of Oneness, which is why realizing Oneness comes first. We arrive at this point by stilling the human mind; however, it cannot be accomplished by willing it. Ironically, we actually use how our mind works as the way the mind is stilled. By remaining poised in a state of relaxed mental alertness or receptivity, the realization and awareness of the Spirit of Truth, or Oneness, is enlivened or " quickened."

Stilling the mind is more than rearranging thoughts; it is actually working with the thinking process. In this process, we move from the limitations of our own thinking into the Realm of Divine Mind. The process requires that we let go of the outer and contemplate the Divine. As we drop away all habits of thought, speech and action by working with the way we think, we allow the awareness of Spirit to quicken in consciousness. As we dwell in the Silence, Divine Nature is not directly experienced in any way. One is simply aware of this Divine Nature after leaving the Silence. We discover that Oneness, or Divine Mind, *is* and that *I Am Oneness, Divine Mind.*

Do not seek for experiences, demonstrations or answers in the Silence since these do not actually occur while one is resting in the Silence. Remember that the Silence is a state of consciousness that is timeless, spaceless and sensationless; it is a state of no awareness. If we do have experiences, answers or demonstrations, they occur "just this side" of the

Silence because these involve awareness. It is wise to call them good and relate them to Divine Mind, as they most likely arose from the Silence.

It is worth repeating that the Silence is not accomplished through straining, striving or effort. It happens with ease and grace, and without taking ourselves too seriously.

The only way we can be finished with our troubles is to forget them and release the personal self by turning to the awareness of Divine Nature, or Spirit. All we have to do is accept the inner revelation as the Truth. We become still and know; we let go of the outer sense consciousness. We enter into the stillness to cultivate a spiritual sense of Oneness.

Ordinary thoughts, error thoughts and evil (a consciousness of error) are not overcome by trying to eliminate them. The mind can be silenced through the law of substitution that works with the thinking process by interesting the mind in something else. Error thoughts are overcome by substituting a single word or phrase for them. We can take a word or phrase for the meditation and use it as our path from outer separation and chaos to inner joy and unity. In the process, we become more aware of our own Divine Nature. A few examples of useful phrases are:

1. *I am satisfied with the Christ life.*
2. *Peace, be still.*

3. *I am Christ.*
4. *One.*
5. *Om.*

6| **RESULTS**

The Silence is like the sun: it is always shining. It brings forth the best that is within us, the image and likeness of God that is waiting to be brought into activity, that will show itself after the fashion that God intended it should. (Myrtle Fillmore, *How to Let God Help You*, 3rd ed., Unity House, Unity Village, Mo., 2000, p. 89)

When you get very still and go into the Silence where you commune with your indwelling guide, you will be shown the easy, pleasant, harmonious, orderly way out of every situation. (Neal Vahle, *Torch-Bearer to Light the Way: The Life of Myrtle Fillmore*, Open View Press, Mill Valley, Calif., 1996, p. 70)

As you still all the outer thoughts and meditate upon the indwelling Christ, you will be spiritually quickened, uplifted, strengthened. You will be inspired with new and rich ideas and will demonstrate good things for you as you use them. (Torch-Bearer to Light the Way, p. 71)

The result of dwelling in the Silence is that there may or may not be outer change; our eyes are simply opened to what has been eternally True. We learn to be free of the limitations of personality and focus on Truth, Divine Mind or Oneness through practicing the Silence. This Truth is pondered in our hearts. Wisdom is there for every need. Joy is present—a wonderful inward joy that no one can take away.

The Silence is the answer and solution to everything; the Truth is finally understood. We come into an understanding of newer, lovelier and greater things. Our expanding consciousness becomes aware of the omnipresence of Divine Mind, which is always the Truth of What we are, even when we are living from our limited sense consciousness. It is from and after resting in the Silence that we may become aware of the highest seeing, hearing and knowing of the things of Spirit. We know that Spiritual Consciousness, Divine Mind, or Oneness is, in Truth, our own Higher Consciousness. Our seemingly limited consciousness is the result of error thinking. Oneness is merely waiting to burst forth into awareness and then activity. The "voice of Spirit" is actually our "True Voice," informing What we are and can do. We are not what we seem to be, hard and solid, flesh and blood. We are not who we think we are, personalities. We are really Spirit, Divine Mind. The more quickly we find this out, the more quickly we can apply It. Then our experience of the world changes, we engage life with both head and heart and the outer circumstances may also change.

6J MYRTLE FILLMORE ON GOING INTO THE SILENCE

This compilation of quotes from *Myrtle Fillmore's Healing Letters* gives a window of understanding into how Myrtle Fillmore viewed and entered into the Silence. They are as written. These quotes, like others in this book, are rooted in the language of the late 1800s and early 1900s. Much of it is better viewed and understood as metaphorical rather than literal. At the same time, many spiritual seekers find comfort in Myrtle's wording.

Purpose/Union—*When we seek God, our temporal as well as spiritual needs are supplied. The providing law will always work for us when we work with it.*

"By wisdom a house is built, and by understanding it is established; by knowledge the rooms are filled with all precious and pleasant riches." (Prov. 24:3-4)

It is through the development of our minds that we find the way to success. God is mind. We have the mind of Christ, and it is for us to make conscious union in the Silence with the all-providing Mind, lifting our thoughts to its standard of truth and holding them in this truth as we go about our duties

of living. (*Myrtle Fillmore's Healing Letters*, pp. 33-34)

God gives freely; it is for us to keep the receiving channels open, to keep attuned to the realities so that our intellect does not take us out among the limited ideas of the world. The manifest human must have the sustenance that can come only from within. (p. 29)

Regularity—*A period of quiet and rest each day is your opportunity to establish yourself at the center of your being, the one place where the supply of life and substance is inexhaustible. God is this eternal life that we make into living. Each day you should have a period of stillness when the soul may gather sustaining power and restoring life.* (pp. 28-29)

Relaxation—*When you start to go into the Silence, you should breathe evenly in the happy feeling that you are taking in great drafts of God's pure life-sustaining air ….* (p. 28)

Anything that is an effort and that disturbs the natural functioning of the body is not going to bring your mind into conscious at-one-ment with the source of your light and every good. (p. 27)

Letting Go—*You cannot listen to God while your ear is given to your affairs. You can gain nothing by incessantly milling around in negative thought. You can gain all by quietly letting go of* these outer appearances and laying hold of God. (p. 31)

Attention—*You owe God attention. You owe God the full measure of your faith, of your thought, of your service.* God abides in your mind as the wisdom that will reveal the way to you if you will quiet your thoughts from their ceaseless outer searching for ways and means. (pp. 30-31)

Concentration—*So when you turn to the secret place for Silence, be sure that you get away from yourself, your old ideas and desires, and bring your mind into perfect harmony with Christ ideas.... The more you think about the Christ within, the stronger will grow your consciousness of the Divine Presence and your oneness with Him, until you can " be still and know that I am God" (Ps. 46:10); until you can still all the outer thoughts and meditate upon " Christ in you, the hope of glory" (Col. 1:27). Many have been helped ... in finding the Silence, by repeating "Jesus Christ" time after time, with short intervals between.* (p. 30)

Jesus Christ—*You love Jesus Christ and He is now with you, guiding you and teaching you, bringing you consciously into oneness with God. His prayer was: "That they may be one, as we are one" (Jn. 17:11). His mission is to bring us into unity with God, and His promise is "I am with you always" (Mt. 28:20). He taught us to pray in this way: "Whenever you pray, go into*

your room and shut the door and pray to God who is in secret" (Mt. 6:6).* (p. 31)

The Silence—*The inner chamber is that quiet place within the heart. We are taught to center our thoughts within, and then to shut the door; that is, to close our minds to all other thinking and think about God and God's goodness and love.* (p. 31)

Speak to God in the quiet of your heart, just as you would speak to me; tell God how much you desire to know and feel God's loving presence and how glad you are to receive God's blessings and to do God's will. Then be very still and feel God's love enfold you. (p. 32)

Be Still. Be Still. Be Still. God in the midst of you is substance. God in the midst of you is love. God in the midst of you is wisdom ... Let wisdom fill [your thoughts] with thesubstance and faith of God. (p. 32)

Be still and know that at this moment [your heart] is the altar of God, of love; love so sure and unfailing, love so irresistible and magnetic that it draws your supply to you from the great storehouse of the universe. Trust God, use God's wisdom, prove and express God's love. (p. 32)

Thanksgiving—*As you come out of the Silence, count your blessings and give thanks for them. Realize that only good exists in you and in your world, that the power you contacted in the Silence may have opportunity to multiply and increase your blessings. Give thanks that you have already received the good for which you looked to God in the Silence, feeling the assurance, "Before they call I will answer" (Isa. 65:24). (p. 32)*

Application—*On the "mountaintop" we receive new illumination, inspiration and insight into the providing law. Then we have a work to do away from the mountaintop, lifting our thoughts to the Truth standard. We should carry the light, joy, peace and strength we receive on the spiritual heights of consciousness into our everyday life for the purpose of redeeming the human part of us. (p. 33)*

The thing to bear in mind is to take with you and hold onto all that you gain on the mountaintop of prayer, and not let go of it when you meet the thoughts and states of mind on the material plane that need to be spiritualized. In other words, maintain your spiritual poise and control when you meet adverse thoughts. (p. 33)

Instead of spending too much time in the Silence, make practical use of what you have already gotten from study and from the Silence. It is possible to waste strength and energy and substance in dwelling in that passive mental state sometimes called the Silence, or in the personal effort to make certain thoughts go out and accomplish results that are not based on the divine order and plan of life.... Work definitely to bring those [Christ] ideas to bear upon your thought centers, and then come forth to practice what you have seen with spiritual vision and declared for yourself. (pp. 29-30)

SUMMARY STATEMENTS

▼ *The Silence is a state of Spiritual Consciousness to which we may retreat from the relative realm of sense consciousness.*

▼ *The Silence is a state in which there is no experience of time, space or sensation. One only knows that he/she has been in the Silence after returning from It.*

▼ *Any experience of a voice, guidance or answers is an effect of having been in the Silence and does not actually occur in the Silence.*

▼ *The foundation for all success is always that there is One. The origin of Truth is the Spirit of Truth, Divine Mind, our True Nature.*

▼ *We are trying to find our* <u>Wholeness, or Christ Nature</u>*. The outer fulfilling of our desire is a reflection of our true desire to know Divine Mind.*

▼ *We begin to learn that things which fill* <u>our outer senses</u> *never truly satisfy. And yet, as the moon reflects the light of the sun, this outer fulfilling of our desire is a reflection of our true desire to know Divine Mind.*

▼ *One of the* <u>purposes</u> *of the Silence is to open up the mind to new avenues and paths of consciousness leading to illumination.*

▼ *To start, keep free of the outer focus on* <u>time</u>*.*

▼ <u>*Preparation*</u> *for being in the Silence includes relaxation and avoidance. While relaxation is not inertia or standing still, it is a joyous and buoyant attitude. Avoid those things that cause unpleasant mental or emotional reactions.*

▼ *The* <u>basics</u> *of dwelling in the Silence are: (1) Realize that there is only Oneness, or Divine Mind. (2) Never seek for experiences or demonstrations in the Silence. (3) Stilling the mind is not accomplished through straining, striving or effort, and it is more than rearranging our thoughts. (4) Let go of your own thoughts, words and feelings and contemplate the Divine. (5) Become still, be and know. (6) Let go of the outer and looking for things. (7) Enter into the quiet where there is only Oneness, or Divine Mind. (8) Interest the mind in something else by using a word or phrase.*

▼ *The* <u>result</u> *of dwelling in the Silence is that in reality* there may or may not be outer change. *Our eyes are simply opened to what has been eternally True. We are not who we seem to be, hard and solid, flesh and blood. We are really Spirit, Divine Mind, Christ.*

TOPICS FOR DISCUSSION

1. *What is the Silence?*

2. *What do you see as your biggest obstacles to experiencing the Silence, and how might you overcome them?*

3. *How are the Silence and the Kingdom of Heaven related?*

THOUGHTS FOR REFLECTION AND MEDITATION

"When entering the Silence, close the eyes and ears to the without. Go to [Divine Mind] within [consciousness] and hold the mind steadily on the word until that word illumines the whole inner consciousness."

(Charles Fillmore, *Dynamics for Living: A Topical Compilation of Essential Fillmore Teachings*, compiled by Warren Meyer, Unity House, Unity Village, Mo., 1967, p. 98)

SUPPLEMENTARY READING

Effectual Prayer by Frances W. Foulks, 3rd ed., Unity House, Unity Village, Mo.,, 2000, Chapter 6, " The Silence."

How to Let God Help You by Myrtle Fillmore, 3rd ed., Unity House, Unity Village, Mo., 2000, Chapter 15, "The Secret Place of Spirit."

Lessons in Truth by H. Emilie Cady, Centennial Edition, Unity House, Unity Village, Mo., 2003, Chapter 9, " The Secret Place of the Most High."

Myrtle Fillmore's Healing Letters by Myrtle Fillmore, revised paperback edition, Unity House, Unity Village, MO, 2006, Chapter 5, "Going Into the Silence," and Chapter 27, "Going Into the Silence."

CHAPTER SEVEN

MEDITATION

INTRODUCTION

In Unity, meditation and prayer are intertwined, and frequently the terms are used interchangeably. In the Unity five-step prayer process, the first three steps are the same as for meditation. While some forms of meditation might be considered a type of prayer, for simplicity, clarity and precision, the subjects of meditation and prayer have been separated into two chapters. Strictly speaking, meditation as "resting in the Silence" is not prayer.

In this chapter, we will explore a specific form of meditation. While there are many ways to meditate, the meditation technique recommended here has been traditionally called *centering prayer*. (Note how the name for this type of meditation underscores how meditation and prayer are sometimes intertwined and even confused.)

7A THE FOUNDATION

In our silent meditations and prayers we must infuse into the inner mind realms the same energy that, used without, would make us notable in some worldly achievement. But unless we do this inner work and lay the foundation of strength and power in the subjective mind, we shall find ourselves in failing health when called upon for extra exertion in some great effort. (Charles and Cora Fillmore, *The Twelve Powers,* Unity House, Unity Village, Mo., 1999, p. 123)

Energy can be utilized in two ways: (1) investing it in some outer aim to accomplish a result, good or bad, and (2) investing it as a "reserve pool" in the inner realms of consciousness. Both are necessary; however, we must be vigilant to do this "inner investing" so that an inner reserve is available in times of challenge and even crisis. Involution precedes evolution.

7B MEODITATION

Continuous and contemplative thought; to dwell mentally on anything; realizing the reality of the Absolute; a steady effort of the mind to know God; humankind's spiritual approach to God. The purpose of meditation is to expand the consciousness Christward; to bring into realization divine Truth; to be transformed in spirit, soul and body by the renewing of the mind. (Charles Fillmore, *The Revealing Word: A Dictionary of Metaphysical Terms,* 2nd ed., Unity House, Unity Village, Mo., 2006, p. 131)

In one of his unpublished talks ("The Historical Jesus and the Living Christ," December 21, 1913), Charles Fillmore states that "going into the Silence" is what Unity calls meditation. Recall that there is the practice of the Silence, more the subject of this chapter and the state of consciousness (total nonawareness) that is the Silence. It is certain that meditation is the process by which we enter the Silence. One form of meditation is the gentle process of concentration on a word or phrase of Spiritual Truth; it is a gentle focusing of one's thoughts in such a way as to create the opportunity to enter the Silence. One meditative process that allows the Silence to arise is *centering prayer.* Even though this particular technique has been called

prayer for many years, it is actually a meditation technique.

7C THE SILENCE

By quieting the mental, by passing through the discipline of intellectual silence, we arrive at the very threshold of God's workshop, the threshold of Being. As we pass into the inner chamber we find we are entering the holy of holies, where noiselessly, silently a mighty work is always going on. (Charles and Cora Fillmore, *Teach Us to Pray,* 2nd ed., Unity House, Unity Village, Mo., 2007, p.24)

The silence is not something mysterious. It is that inner place of stillness where you feel and know your oneness with God. (May Rowland, *The Magic of the Word,* Unity House, Unity Village, Mo., 1972, p. 144)

The purpose of the silence is to still the activity of the individual thought so that the still small voice of God may be heard. For in the silence Spirit speaks Truth to us and just that Truth of which we stand in need. (*Teach Us to Pray,* p.17)

God is mind. "We have the mind of Christ," and it is for us to make conscious union in the silence with the all-providing Mind, lifting our thoughts to its standard of Truth and holding them in this Truth as we go about our duties of living. (Myrtle Fillmore,

Myrtle Fillmore's Healing Letters, revised paperback edition, Unity House, Unity Village, Mo., 2006, p. 34)

The reader is directed to Chapter 6 on the Silence for a more thorough discourse on the topic. While the excerpts above indicate that we may hear, feel or experience the Divine, it is more accurate to say that the Silence is the "still point" or "void." It is a state of no time, no space, no thought, no sensation and no awareness. The Silence, then, is the matrix *out of which* come guidance, inspiration and realization from our Higher Self. Guidance ("the Voice,") inspiration, and realization are the effects of having been in the Silence. These experiences occur "just this side" of the Silence. Since Divine Ideas have their origin in the Silence, we must persist in our practice of daily meditation to be able to recognize Truth and act upon it and from it.

7D **MEDITATION TIPS**

1. Use a room where you will not be disturbed. Ask to not be disturbed while you are meditating unless there is an emergency. Turn off phones and pagers!

2. Have the room at a comfortable temperature. The room should not be so warm as to promote sleep or so cool as to be uncomfortable.

3. Keep the room softly lighted.

4. Wear comfortable clothing.

5. Be well rested. If you are tired, you will tend to fall asleep rather than meditate.

6. Since we are creatures of habit, it is helpful to work with this tendency. Keep the same routine until your meditation practice is firmly established. Once a meditation practice is established, you will be able to meditate anywhere. Here are some habits to establish:

a. Meditate at approximately the same time every day.

b. Meditate in the same room and in the same chair.

c. If you like to have music, use the same music at a background level. Use music that does not contain lyrics and that you can utilize to promote a peaceful, restful state.

d. If you like to use candles, light one or more before you begin.

e. If you like to use incense, burn the same incense, using an aroma that promotes a restful yet alert state.

f. Consider setting up an altar in your meditation room.

7. Start gently. If you have not meditated before, begin with an amount of time that is a stretch but not so much so as to keep you from achieving your goal. Twenty minutes once or twice a day is a great goal to work toward. Begin with five minutes a day for the first week, and then increase your time by five minutes each week until you reach 20 minutes a day.

7E HOW TO MEDITATE

Please remember that this is a meditation *experience*. Practice it for a period of time. Test it for yourself and notice if love, joy, peace and kindness seem to be more evident in your experience.

1. RELAX: Sit comfortably. For some that might mean sitting with the legs crossed; for others it might mean sitting with feet on the floor, hands resting in the lap and eyes closed. For some it might mean lying down; however, if you are tired, lying down may promote sleep rather than meditation. Do not rush or hurry this step. (Some teach that crossing the legs blocks the energy flow. Since energy blockage from this practice has not been proven true, we leave it to the comfort of the individual.)

2. TURN YOUR AWARENESS TO "WITHIN CONSCIOUSNESS": Turn your attention from the outer world of the senses to the inner world of Oneness. We know by faith and experience that this Presence, or Oneness, is *within* consciousness. In fact, "we" are it. In love, turn yourself over to your Beingness, Christ. This time is a pure gift, a gift to yourself of resting in the awareness of Oneness, Christ.

3. CONCENTRATE: To abide in the Oneness quietly and attentively, use a simple word (or short phrase) that expresses your heart's desire to be aware of the Presence that you are. Simply allow that word to be there in your mind, and silently repeat it. It may be *Jesus, Father, love, peace, one* or *om*. Use whatever is personally meaningful. Other examples of sacred words that can be used for centering prayer are *Adonai, Elohim, Yahweh, El Shaddai, Rabboni, Abba, Emmanuel, Maranatha*. If you elect to use a phrase, keep it short (not to exceed seven words is recommended). This is also a perfect opportunity to use an affirmation such as *I am love* or *I am Christ*.

• Remember, this is *not* a process of actively trying to clear your mind of thoughts, which is counterproductive. This process *works with* the mind's desire to think. Thinking is what the mind does. When you become aware of thoughts other than your word or phrase, gently return your mind to it. Do this by simply allowing the word or phrase to easily bubble up into your awareness. Allow your "mantra" to come naturally and easily to mind like any other thought would arise in your mind. You simply and gently repeat it. As soon as you become aware that you are again thinking about something else, return to it again. This process of moving back and forth from your mantra to extraneous thoughts ("monkey-mind" thoughts) allows the Silence to arise. During this time, you do not seek anything for yourself or others; this is a time of simply *being*. All your attention is gently aware of repeating your mantra or being aware of other thoughts and then gently moving back to your word or phrase. This *process* will allow the Silence (a state of total nonawareness) to begin. Ironically, the process of working with your thoughts, a kind of thinking, is what stills the mind. It is outside this time of meditation (centering prayer) that you will discern the difference in your life—the love, peace, joy and kindness that will begin to flourish.

• It is during the concentration process that entering the Silence will occur. The process creates the container in which the Silence may begin, just like the parts of a box create the space in which something may be placed. In a sense, it is the process of concentration that creates the opportunity to slip into the Silence. There is no forcing one's way into the Silence; one merely slips into it while concen-

trating. It is almost as if one slips and dwells in the gap between the words as well as the gap between thoughts.

4. PRAY: If the meditation time is intended to be preparation for prayer, this is when we begin to pray. It is when we come out of the Silence and before giving thanks that we can claim the Truth for any situation or condition.

5. GIVE THANKS: At the end of your time in the Silence, feel gratitude for being able to dwell in the awareness of Oneness. Please remember that we are not being grateful for God or to God; we are simply grateful. Whatever we praise and are grateful for increases. "The purpose of praise is to awaken in ourselves a higher realization of the omnipresence and power of God." (*The Revealing Word*, p. 152)

6. GENTLY CONCLUDE: Do not jump right back into activity when you finish your meditation. You will want to end your meditation time gently. You have gone very deeply, even if it may not feel that way. One suggestion is to silently and slowly say words of affirmation or repeat a favorite Bible passage. As you do this, be aware of the meaning you give to each word and phrase. If you find that you feel any irritability after your meditation, you have probably come out too quickly. Simply sit back down, begin the meditation again for a few minutes, and come out more slowly. If you feel sleepy and want to sleep (assuming you have time), feel free to do so.

7F BENEFITS OF MEDITATION

Maybe meditation isn't so mysterious after all. Neuroscientists have found that meditators shift their brain activity to different areas of the cortex. Brain waves in the stress-prone right frontal cortex move to the calmer left frontal cortex. This mental shift decreases the negative effects of stress, mild depression and anxiety. There is also less activity in the amygdalae, where the brain processes fear. (Colin Allen, *www.psychologytoday.com/articles/pto-20030424-000003.html*)

One of the most important health benefits of meditation is how it releases stress from our bodies. Meditation practiced regularly will lead you to a deeper level of relaxation and contemplation. If you want to be free of constant worry, pressure and stress, meditation can give you a life that is calm, peaceful, happy and relaxed. Even 10 minutes of meditation a day will help alleviate stress. Some of the health benefits of meditation are:

- Reduces anxiety attacks as it lowers the levels of blood lactate.
- Builds self-confidence.
- Increases serotonin which influences moods and behavior. Low levels of serotonin are associated with depression, headaches and insomnia.
- Enhances energy, strength and vigor.
- Helps keep blood pressure normal.
- Reduces stress and tension.
- Creates a state of deep relaxation and general feeling of well-being.
- Helps with P.M.T. [Pre-Menstrual Tension].
- Increases concentration and strengthens the mind.
- Helps reduce heart disease.
- Helps with weight loss.

If you regularly practice meditation, you will begin to feel so much calmer and in control. Ability to concentrate will be far greater. You won't become stressed about things and you'll feel more peaceful and relaxed about everything. You'll simply go with the flow and things that used to irritate you before will become insignificant. (Hilary Reese, *www.project-meditation.org/bom/health_benefits_of_meditation.html*)

Our primary purpose for meditating is to strengthen the awareness of Oneness. However, over many years, research has proven that there are many additional benefits to meditating every day.

SUMMARY STATEMENTS

▼ *Since the material world is merely a shadow of the* <u>*Spiritual Universe,*</u> *the inner world of consciousness (Cause) is even more important to us than the outer world of effect.*

▼ *We must do our inner work in order to lay the* <u>*foundation*</u> *of strength and power to do our outer work.*

▼ <u>*Meditation*</u> *is the process by which we enter the* <u>*Silence.*</u>

▼ <u>*Daily meditation*</u> *is the time when we take the opportunity to rest from all activity and simply be. Sometimes as we come out of meditation, we "hear with the inner ear" guidance or words of inspiration "from" our Christ Nature. (See the chapter text for meditation tips and a step-by-step guide to learn how to meditate.)*

▼ <u>*The Silence*</u> *is the name for that "inner place" in consciousness where there is no time, space, awareness or experience of any kind. It is after the Silence that we feel, know, and realize that we were in the Oneness.*

▼ <u>*The benefits of meditation*</u> *include the alleviation of constant worry, pressure and stress; meditation can also give you a life that is calm, peaceful, happy and relaxed. (See section 7F, "Benefits of Meditation.")*

TOPICS FOR DISCUSSION

1. *What is the importance of meditation in one's spiritual practice?*

2. *What are some obstacles to establishing a regular meditation practice, and how can they be overcome?*

3. *Describe your understanding of the Silence.*

THOUGHTS FOR REFLECTION AND MEDITATION

"A daily half hour of meditation will open up the mind to a consciousness of the inner One and will reveal many things that are hidden from the natural human."

(Charles Fillmore, *Christian Healing, 2nd ed.*, Unity House, Unity Village, Mo., 2005, p. 15)

SUPPLEMENTARY READING

Beyond the Relaxation Response: How to Harness the Healing Power of Your Personal Beliefs by Herbert Benson, M.D., with William Proctor, Times House, New York, 1984.

Lessons in Truth by H. Emilie Cady, Centennial Edition, Unity House, Unity Village, Mo., 2003, Chapter 9, "The Secret Place of the Most High," and Chapter 10, "Finding the Secret Place."

Myrtle Fillmore's Healing Letters by Myrtle Fillmore, revised paperback edition, Unity House, Unity Village, Mo., 2006, Chapter 5, "Going Into the Silence."

The Relaxation Response by Herbert Benson, M.D., William Morrow and Company, Inc., New York, 1975.

Teach Us to Pray by Charles and Cora Fillmore, 2nd ed., Unity House, Unity Village, Mo., 2007, Chapter 3, "Intellectual Silence and Spiritual Silence."

CHAPTER EIGHT

PRAYER

INTRODUCTION

Along with meditation, prayer is one of the most important spiritual activities in which we can participate. The more we understand about the activity of prayer, the more we come to realize that the time we devote to it is an investment in our process of attaining spiritual mastery and enlightenment. Consistently setting aside portions of our day for prayer provides the opportunity to experience healing at the deepest, most satisfying levels of our lives.

In this chapter, we will explore Unity's concept of affirmative prayer and how to pray in this manner utilizing a five-step prayer process. Affirmative prayer is the act of claiming and declaring what is already True in the Absolute Realm. As we said in the previous chapter, this form of prayer is so rooted in the awareness of our Oneness, or Christ Nature, that it is inextricably linked to meditation. This is because one must first become still, if only for a few moments, and center through meditation into the awareness of Oneness. In heart-centered metaphysics, prayer is both a head and heart, thinking nature and feeling nature process.

8A MIND

Mind is the common meeting ground between God and humankind, and it is only through the most highly accelerated mind action, as in prayer, that we can consciously make union with God, *the one and only Creator. Prayer is the language of spirituality and improves the quality of humankind's being. Prayer makes humankind master in the realm of creative ideas. The inner silence of prayer is a great source of spiritual power. (Charles Fillmore,*

Keep a True Lent, 2nd ed., Unity House, Unity Village, Mo., 2005, p. 10)

God is a great mind reservoir that has to be tapped by the human mind and poured into visibility through human thought or word. (Charles Fillmore, *Jesus Christ Heals,* 2nd ed., Unity Books, Unity Village, Mo., 1940, p. 68)

The point of prayer is not so much about the goodies we get but the Goodness we realize we are. (Paul Hasselbeck, *Point of Power,* Prosperity Publishing House, Raleigh-Durham, N.C., 2007, p. 56)

Words like *meeting ground* and *union* imply that we can actually be separate from Oneness, or Divine Mind, when there can never be separation in Oneness. From our relative experience it only seems that we are making union with Divine Mind when what is really occurring is the awakening of awareness.

The process of affirmative prayer utilizes the power of the mind. True prayer requires much more than the repetition of memorized words. Prayer is an attitude of the heart that is more about being than doing. It is through our minds we can remember and become aware of Oneness, or God. Affirmative prayer is not about asking an external deity for things or to fix situations in our lives. The primary benefit is more the realization of Oneness and Divine Ideas.

8B AFFIRMATIVE PRAYER

"The kingdom of God is within you." The pivotal point around which Spirit creates is within the structure of consciousness. This is true of the primal cell as well as of the most complex organ. The throne on which the divine will sits is within one's consciousness, and it is to this inner center that one should direct attention when praying or meditating. (*Jesus Christ Heals*, p. 76)

Prayer is the most highly accelerated mind action known. It steps up mental action until a person's consciousness synchronizes with the Christ Mind. It is the language of spirituality; when developed it makes a person master in the realm of creative ideas. (Charles Fillmore, *The Revealing Word: A Dictionary of Metaphysical Terms,* 2nd ed., Unity House, Unity Village, Mo., 2006, p.152)

Instead of a supplication, prayer should be a jubilant thanksgiving. This method of prayer quickens the mind miraculously, and, like a mighty magnet, draws out the spiritual qualities that transform the whole person when he or she is given expression in mind, body and affairs. (Charles Fillmore, *Christian Healing,* 2nd ed., Unity House, Unity Village, Mo., 2005, p. 76)

Prayer is more than supplication. It is an affirmation of Truth that eternally exists, but which has not yet come into consciousness. It comes into consciousness not by supplication but by affirmation. (The Revealing Word, p. 152)

Affirmative prayer is the spiritual activity in which we enter into conscious remembrance of Oneness, or Divine Nature. In an attitude of gratitude and love, affirmative prayer celebrates this Oneness. It is not praying to God nor being grateful to God, nor is it asking God *for* something or to *do* anything. Affirmative prayer is praying *from* the Consciousness of Divine Mind (Oneness) knowing, realizing, claiming and declaring what is already True. While the thinking nature is certainly involved, it is vital that we feel what is True.

8C DIVINE IDEAS

True prayer is not asking for things, not even the best things. Prayer is the lifting of the consciousness to the place where these things are. (Sue Sikking, *A Letter to Adam,* Unity School of Christianity, Unity Village, Mo., 1965, p.13)

We often hear the remark that God "gives" us answers to our prayers, but we need to realize that these answers come to us in the form of ideas. These ideas may flash into our minds in answer to prayer, or they may be conveyed to us through the words of other people, or through books, magazines, or newspapers. (Vera Dawson Tait, *Take Command!*, Unity Books, Unity Village, Mo., 1981, p. 55)

Divine ideas are our inheritance; they are pregnant with all possibility, because ideas are the foundation and cause of all that humanity desires. ... Get behind a thing into the mental realm where it exists as an inexhaustible idea, and you can draw upon it perpetually and never deplete the source. (Christian Healing, p. 13.)

Divine Ideas are the Primary Cause for everything and most especially all that is good in life. To say that God "gives" us Divine Ideas is another way of humanizing (anthropomorphizing) God and should be understood metaphorically. It is more like becoming aware of Divine Ideas; they are always fully available and cannot be depleted or annihilated. Nor are they cause in the same sense that a person causes the movement of the hand. In relation to Divine Ideas, Cause is more like the primary basis or starting point. The human mind lays hold of Divine Ideas (our Supply) and then has thoughts and ideas about those Divine Ideas according to a person's level of consciousness. Then these thoughts and ideas are made manifest.

Prayer is the most effective way we can fulfill our creative potential. It is most important to keep in mind that when we pray, we pray for the awareness of Divine Ideas and not things; we become aware of Divine Ideas as the "answer to prayer." It is through our awareness and realization of these Ideas that we realize our good.

8D FIVE-STEP PRAYER PROCESS

Prayer is both invocation and affirmation. Meditation, concentration, denial and affirmation in the silence are all forms of what is loosely termed prayer. (Jesus Christ Heals, p. 70)

We start with an intention to gratefully and lovingly enter into a time of prayer. This attitude of the heart should include the entire prayer process. When Jesus "thanked God" in advance of prayer, we now assume that Jesus was not thanking some outside Deity or Being.

There are many ways to pray, each having its own process and/or step-by-step procedure. One of these procedures commonly used in Unity is called the Five-Step Prayer Process. The steps are as follows: Relaxation, Concentration, Meditation, Realization, and Thanksgiving. Notice that the first three steps are actually the steps of meditation, and they lead us into the Silence.

We may wish to approach our time of affirmative prayer by acknowledging the presence and power of Oneness, or Divine Mind, then relaxing physically

and mentally. We may use denials (Chapter 22) to gently release error beliefs as we begin to affirm the activity of Oneness, or Divine Mind, in our lives. If denials are used, always follow them with affirmations of Truth (Chapter 22). As we continue to focus on Truth Ideas, we find our former cares and concerns transformed into feelings of peace and well-being. Then, with a sense of joy and gratitude, we simply know that all is truly well.

8E RELAXATION

The Mind of Spirit is harmonious and peaceful, and it must have a like manner of expression in one's consciousness. When a body of water is choppy with fitful currents of air it cannot reflect objects clearly. Neither can one reflect the steady strong glow of Omnipotence when the mind is disturbed by anxious thoughts, fearful thoughts or angry thoughts. (Jesus Christ Heals, pp.176-177)

A letting go of tenseness in mind and body. Abatement of strain. Loosening the tight mental grip we have on ourselves in order that the healing Christ life may flow freely through our being. (The Revealing Word, p. 166)

In order for us to physically and mentally prepare for the experience of resting in the Silence, we need to consciously relax ourselves and release all tension—physical and mental. The most conducive environment in which to attain relaxation and receptivity is one which is comfortable, peaceful and free from distractions. If the body feels really tense it can be helpful to tense all the muscles at the same time, hold that tension for about a minute, then release the tensing of the muscles. Mental tensions and distractions are released by utilizing denials and affirmations. Some may find journaling another helpful way to process and release distracting thoughts.

8F CONCENTRATION/INTENTION AND ATTENTION

In prayer attention is the concentration of the mind upon a statement of Truth. Attention is focalizing the I AM or inner entity upon a word of prayer, until the inner meaning is realized and the soul is aware of a definite spiritual uplift. As a lens focalizes the sun's rays at a given point—and we know how intense that point of light may become—so concentration focalizes the mind on a single idea until it becomes manifest and objective. (Charles and Cora Fillmore, *Teach Us to Pray*, 2nd ed., Unity House, Unity Village, Mo., 2007, p. 31)

Concentration, one-pointed attention, forms a mental magnet in the mind to which thought substance rushes like iron filings to a loadstone. Then follows confidence or faith in one's ability to accomplish the desired end. (*Jesus Christ Heals,* p. 44)

The centering of the attention on a particular idea. (*The Revealing Word,* p. 39)

Concentrated attention of the mind on an idea of any kind is equal to prayer and will make available the spiritual principle that is its source in proportion to the intensity and continuity of the mental effort. (*Jesus Christ Heals,* p. 48)

Similar to contemplative prayer, concentrated attention is the gentle focusing of the mind on a particular statement or thought of Truth. The intention is to access the Superconscious Mind (see Chapter 17, "The Three Phases of Mind") and therefore gain a deeper understanding and realization, an inner meaning. This uplifts the soul (conscious and subconscious minds) leading to a higher level of consciousness. In prayer, we concentrate on an Idea of Truth related to the prayer. For instance, in praying about prosperity, the Truth Idea concentrated upon might be Abundance. In praying for healing, the Truth Idea might be Life that expresses as wholeness and health. In a way, holding these thoughts serves as a kind of mantra during meditation.

8G MEDITATION

To open yourself to the inspiration of your indwelling Lord and then to listen for Its inspiration, this is meditation. (May Rowland, *The Magic of the Word*, Unity Books, Unity Village, Mo., 1972, p. 143)

Through the practice of meditation we can establish a center of peace and quietness within. We can turn to this center and gain great strength to help us meet all of life's experiences. (*The Magic of the Word*, p. 149)

Meditation is the process of our conscious intention to gain awareness of Oneness. Meditation is the process that invites the Silence. It is from the Silence that we are inspired with Divine Ideas. Remember, as we rest in the Silence, there is nothing—no time, space, sensation or awareness; It is a state of *total nonawareness*. We are "just this side of the Silence" when we become aware of Divine Ideas and Divine Inspiration. To build a solid foundation for our prayer practice, it is most important to invest time each day to rest from all activity and focus our complete attention on the Oneness we are in Truth.

8H REALIZATION

To a metaphysician, realization is the conviction that a person gets when he or she has persistently concentrated attention on an ideal until assurance of the fulfillment of that idea is felt. (*Jesus Christ Heals*, p. 45)

The deep inner conviction and assurance of the fulfillment of an ideal. It means at-one-ment, completion, perfection, wholeness, repose, resting in God. It is the dawning of Truth in the consciousness. When realization takes place, one abides in the light of God Mind. It is the inner conviction that prayer has been answered, although there is as yet no outer manifestation. (*The Revealing Word*, p. 164)

The scientific metaphysician fixes attention powerfully on the consummation of a certain idea until he or she has a realization, which means that the idea has nucleated a certain amount of thought substance. When this realization is had, the metaphysician rests 'from all work.' Through faith and work the person has fulfilled the law of mind and rests in the conviction that the ideal of health will appear in manifestation in due season. (*Jesus Christ Heals*, p. 45)

Somewhere in all effectual prayer, and in every quiet miracle of answered prayer, a point of release can be discovered, a point in time where the one who is praying experiences a sense of assurance. (Ernest C. Wilson, *Soul Power*, Unity School of Christianity, Unity Village, Mo., 1963, p. 77)

It is from the awareness of Oneness during meditation that we can enter into the state of realization. It is from the awareness of Oneness, or Divine Mind, that we pray. It is from dwelling in the Silence that specific aspects of universal Truth become real to us. Realization does not occur in the Silence since it is a state of no awareness. Realization is an effect of having been in the Silence; it may be experienced as a deep, inner "click" of knowing Truth despite outer appearances. One knows and feels the Truth. Realization makes Truth a permanent possession of our minds. It is a process in which metaphysical thinking causes the Power of Faith (our Ability to believe and have conviction; see Chapter 24, section C) to "clothe" the Divine Idea with Spiritual Substance. At a certain point, the degree of attention is sufficient to cause a breakthrough from the invisible to the manifest. Realization is followed with rest from external effort or even thinking about why we turned to prayer. For example, if the prayer focus is on healing, then from the meditative state we enter into the realization of Wholeness and with our mind's eye and heart we see unfolding Wholeness from Oneness, or God Mind. Persist in prayer until realization is achieved. Persist in prayer until there is a deep inner knowing, a deep conviction of Truth, and then stop thinking about or even looking for manifestation. This realization, or deep conviction of Truth, is answered prayer. Realization naturally results in an attitude of love and gratitude partly because the feeling nature is fully engaged.

8| THANKSGIVING

As you come out of the silence, count your blessings and give thanks for them. Realize that only good exists in you and in your world, that the power you contacted in the silence may have opportunity to multiply and increase your blessings. Give thanks that you have already received the good for which you looked to God in the silence, feeling the assurance, "Before they call I will answer, while they are yet speaking, I will hear." (Myrtle Fillmore, *Myrtle Fillmore's Healing Letters,* revised paperback edition, Unity House, Unity Village, Mo., 2006, p. 32)

Praise and thanksgiving impart the quickening spiritual power that produces growth and increase in all things. (Charles Fillmore, *Prosperity,* Unity Books, Unity Village, Mo., 1936, p. 105)

As we have seen, thanksgiving is an attitude of the heart for the entire prayer process. What we are grateful for increases. It is also an important last step in response to the blessings and Divine Ideas realized during the prayer experience. We are not actually grateful *to* Oneness, or Divine Mind, as that implies separation; we are grateful *from* Divine Mind, from the awareness of Oneness.

Also recall that we are grateful *before* our answer appears, before the realization of Divine Ideas. Then manifestation in the relative realm is a potent expression of the Power of Faith which is defined as "the perceiving power of mind linked with the ability to shape substance." (Charles Fillmore, *Dynamics for Living: A Topical Compilation of Essential Fillmore Teachings,* Unity Books, Unity Village, Mo., p. 52)

8J PRAYER WITHOUT CEASING

We pray without ceasing when we habitually meet whatever comes to us with faith and with love, with a mind to draw from the event all that it has to give, with a willingness to do whatever has to be done to make the most and the best of it. (James Dillet Freeman, *Prayer: The Master Key,* Unity Books, Unity Village, Mo., 1975, p. 41)

To pray without ceasing is to put God in charge of your life. It is to look for direction. It is to expect inspiration. (*Prayer: The Master Key,* p. 42)

Prayer is not a duty or a habit, but a pouring forth of the heart in gratitude for every breath, every moment of life, every experience. (*A Letter to Adam*, p. 13)

At some level all thoughts are prayers. So we are always praying without ceasing even though we may not be intentional about it. We are always laying hold of Divine Ideas and manifesting them according to our level of consciousness. "Putting God in charge of our lives" means putting Divine Mind in charge of our lives; it is investing ourselves in the awareness of Divine Mind, or Oneness, so that we are living *from* It. As we learn to source every thought, word and deed from the awareness of Oneness, we become more intentional about our prayer. If prayer is to be truly effective in our lives, it must be an intentional, perpetual activity. This is what it truly means to pray without ceasing.

SUMMARY STATEMENTS

▼ *Prayer is a spiritual activity where we become aware of <u>conscious Oneness</u>.*

▼ *Our prayer method in Unity is called "<u>affirmative prayer</u>." The affirmative prayer process engages mind and heart.*

▼ *Pray for the awareness of Divine Ideas* and not things; awareness of Divine Ideas is the "answer to prayer."

▼ *The Unity Five-Step Prayer Process is relaxation, concentration, meditation, realization and thanksgiving.*

▼ *The relaxation step is the release of all physical and mental tension.*

▼ *Denials and affirmations cleanse our consciousness of error beliefs as well as help to release mental tensions and distractions so we are able to claim the Truth we know.*

▼ *Attentive concentration is similar to contemplative prayer in that the mind is concentrated upon a word or statement of Truth until an inner meaning is realized, uplifting the soul (conscious and subconscious minds).*

▼ *Meditation is the process of our conscious intention to gain awareness of Oneness, or Divine Mind; it invites the Silence.*

▼ *It is from the Silence that we are inspired with Divine Ideas. It is important to recall that while resting in the Silence there is nothing—no time, space, sensation or awareness; it is a state of nonawareness.*

▼ *Realization is our sense of assurance and deep inner knowing of Divine Ideas. It includes both thinking and feeling natures.*

▼ *Praying without ceasing is putting the awareness of Oneness, or Divine Mind, first in every area of our lives.*

▼ *We are always praying without ceasing because at some level all thoughts are prayers, even though we may not be intentional about it.*

TOPICS FOR DISCUSSION

1. *What is our Divine Inheritance?*

2. *What does "affirmative prayer" mean? How does it differ from beseeching prayers or prayers of supplication?*

3. *Share a time in your prayer activity when you experienced a "realization." Tell how you felt when it happened and what transpired in your life as a result.*

THOUGHTS FOR REFLECTION AND MEDITATION

The fruit of silence is prayer.
The fruit of prayer is faith.
The fruit of faith is love.
The fruit of love is service.
The fruit of service is peace.

—Mother Teresa

SUPPLEMENTARY READING

Effectual Prayer by Frances W. Foulks, 3rd ed., Unity House, Unity Village, Mo., 2000, Chapter 1, "Effectual Prayer."

Lessons in Truth by H. Emilie Cady, Centennial Edition, Unity House, Unity Village, Mo., 2003, Chapter 9, "The Secret Place of the Most High" and Chapter 10, "Finding the Secret Place."

Myrtle Fillmore's Healing Letters by Myrtle Fillmore, revised paperback edition, Unity House, Unity Village, Mo., 2006, Chapter 5, "Going Into the Silence."

Teach Us to Pray by Charles and Cora Fillmore, 2nd ed., Unity House, Unity Village, Mo., 2007, Chapter 1, "The God to Whom We Pray," Chapter 2, "True Prayer," and Chapter 3, "Intellectual Silence and Spiritual Silence."

CHAPTER NINE

PRAYING WITH OTHERS

INTRODUCTION

In this chapter, praying with others is explored in the context of a request for healing. To be clear, our use of the term *healing* does not mean "cure." For the purposes of this text, cure is when a person moves from illness to health without a change of consciousness. Healing is always about a change in consciousness first; it is a change from error thinking to Truth. The concepts discussed here may then be generalized to any context with only the Divine Ideas, or Spiritual Truths, changing based upon the particular prayer request. As heart-centered metaphysicians we pray from our compassionate hearts with an attitude of loving kindness.

9A **PRAYING FROM, NOT TO**

Many good people think that God is a person located in a place in the skies called heaven. They pray to Him for what they want and are satisfied. This is the prayer of the primitive, personal man, and it meets his needs; but this is not direct communion of the Father and the Son, the communion with reference to which Jesus said, "I and the Father are one." We must have this more intimate acquaintanceship or communion with creative Mind if we are in all ways to do His will. (Charles and Cora Fillmore, *Teach Us to Pray,*

2nd ed., Unity House, Unity Village, Mo., 2007, p. 13)

So prayer is not something we do to God, or a ceremony we perform for God. It is an experience of our own God-potential. ... We do not really pray to God, rather we pray from a consciousness of God. Prayer is not conditioning God with our needs, but conditioning our lives with the activity of God. Prayer is self-realization, self-expansion. It is getting centered within, and reestablishing ourselves in the flow of the infinite creative process. (Eric Butterworth, *The Universe Is Calling: Opening to the Divine*

Through Prayer, HarperSanFrancisco, 1993, p. 23)

A man was distraught over his young son who was into drugs and alcohol ... realizing that as long as his thoughts about the son were focused on worry and parental concern, he was giving support to the weakness. ... This father worked diligently to alter his anxious concern, and then he prayed, not to God about his son, but from the consciousness of God, projecting this consciousness to the son, saluting the divinity in him, seeing him strong and whole. (The Universe Is Calling, p. 121)

The first step in praying with others is the recognition that Divine Mind is not only active at the point of you and those with whom you pray, but Divine Mind is also the Truth of you and those you bless with prayer. We do not pray *to* God, or Divine Mind, because there is not a separate Divine Mind to which to pray. Rather, we center ourselves in the awareness of Oneness and experience our own Divine Potential (Christ Nature) and pray *from* the awareness of Oneness. In the case of a health challenge, we pray from the awareness of Oneness, knowing and realizing that Divine Mind is Life and Life expresses as wholeness and health.

When we read anything that refers to God as "Father" and us as the "Son," we must understand this as metaphor.

In *Talks on Truth* (p. 35), Charles Fillmore said, "But this Kingdom within [consciousness] is not material—it is spiritual. ... This inner country is the domain of that superior wisdom which we term the Christ. Jesus called this place of wisdom the Father within Him, and to it he ascribed all His power and wisdom."

9B THE OBJECT

Remember that the object of all treatment is to raise the mind to the Christ consciousness, through which all true healing is accomplished. (Teach Us to Pray, p. 178)

What we need to know above all is that there is a place within our soul where we can consciously meet God and receive a flood of new life into not only our mind but also our body. (Teach Us to Pray, p. 7)

Greater awareness and realization of Christ Consciousness should be the primary aim of any spiritual endeavor. The cause of any worthwhile activity for us is our forward ("Christward") direction of consciousness, our evolving spiritual awareness. We can realize Christ Consciousness through becoming still and meditating in a way that leads us into the Silence. It is from this Christ Consciousness that all true healing is accomplished; wholeness is realized.

9C **MIRACLES**

The underlying meaning is that when a person unifies with God, a spiritual power works for him or her in ways that are incomprehensible to human reason and superior to human might. (Elizabeth Sand Turner, *Be Ye Transformed: Acts Through Revelation Metaphysically Interpreted,* 3rd ed., Unity House, Unity Village, Mo., 1984, p. 30)

When the free flow of unobstructed life takes place, we, often in awe, term it a "miracle." (Vera Dawson Tait, *Take Command!* Unity House, Unity Village, Mo., 1981, p. 102)

The forces invisible are much closer than we think, and when we turn our attention in their direction the response is usually so pronounced and so swift that we cannot but feel that a miracle has been performed. A more intimate acquaintance with the divine law convinces us that under it all, things are possible if we only believe, and if we at the same time conform our thoughts to its principle. (Charles Fillmore, *Christian Healing*, 2nd ed., Unity House, Unity Village, Mo., 2005, p. 92)

By the power of his thought Elijah penetrated the atoms and precipitated an abundance of rain. By the same law he increased the widow's oil and meal. This was not a miracle—that is, it was not a divine intervention supplanting natural law—but the exploitation of a law not ordinarily understood. Jesus used the same dynamic power of thought to break the bonds of the atoms composing the few loaves and fishes of a little lad's lunch—and five thousand people were fed. (Charles Fillmore, *Atom-Smashing Power of Mind*, 2nd ed., Unity House, Unity Village, Mo., 2006, p. 10)

Miracles do not exist, if by miracles we mean there is some Divine Intervention supplanting natural law. Seeming miracles are the result of Divine Ideas, Principles and Laws of which we are not yet aware.

Not all realizations of Life take place in the same amount of time. Some occur so quickly that we feel a miracle has occurred. This does not mean there is no process involved in the healing demonstrations (the outpicturing of Wholeness) that occur instantly. All realizations of wholeness begin with the claiming of Divine Life here and now; all healing is the expression of a definite realization of Life expressing as wholeness and health.

9D **RELEASING**

If you would help someone else in need of healing, you first must be free in your own mind from anxious thoughts concerning him or her before you can give a real blessing. Anxious thoughts will leave as you consciously know that the healing power of God is active in the person now, that the healing work is being done perfectly. (Martha Smock, *Halfway Up the Mountain,* Unity House, Unity Village, Mo., 1971, p. 202)

To begin your prayer process, sometimes called a "treatment," release any thoughts of fear concerning the one with whom you are praying. Denials can be used to release those thoughts and affirmations to realize Truth (see Chapter 22). Then, as you consciously know and feel that Oneness, Divine Mind, is active at the point of you *and* the consciousness of the person you're blessing with prayer, the healing work is achieved. It is achieved when you acknowledge that Divine Ideas are the Truth of you both.

9E RESISTANCE AND PERSISTENCE

By experimentation, modern metaphysical healers have discovered a large number of laws that rule in the realm of mind, and they agree that no two cases are exactly alike. Therefore, one who prays for the health of another should understand that it is not the fault of the healing principle that the patient is not instantly restored. The fault may be in the healer's own lack of persistency or understanding; or it may be due to the patient's dogged clinging to discordant thoughts. In any

case, the one who prays must persist in this prayer until the walls of resistance are broken down and the healing currents are tuned in. Metaphysicians often pray over a critical case all night. (Charles Fillmore, *Jesus Christ Heals,* 2nd ed., Unity House, Unity Village, Mo., 1940, p. 85)

Each health challenge we encounter is unique; however, the Principle of Life expressing as wholeness and health remains the same. Even though the symptoms may appear to be identical to those of another, the case itself is not exactly like any other because the cause in consciousness may differ. We cannot judge by appearances.

If the person you are praying with is not "instantly restored," it could involve the challenge of subconscious (or unconscious) resistance. Human resistance to the realization of Truth is a great mystery that can necessitate much persistence in prayer. In a case where an individual simply will not give up inner resistance, the person praying need not feel guilty about it. Each individual has freedom of choice. It could also be due to the lack of persistence and understanding on the part of the one praying. Whatever the case, the solution is always the same: persist in prayer until confident that realization has been fully achieved and then let go.

9F REALIZATION

The starting point in spiritual realization is a right understanding of that One designated as the Almighty. It is strictly logical and scientific to assume that humankind comes forth from this One, who is named variously, but who, all agree, is the origin of everything. Since people are the offspring of the Almighty, they must have the character of their Parent. ... God must be in God's universe as everywhere—intelligent power; otherwise it would fall to pieces. God is in the universe as its constant "breath" or inspiration; hence it is only necessary to find the point of contact in order to understand the One in whom we all "live, and move, and have our being." (Christian Healing, p. 8)

Mind is the common meeting ground of God and humankind, and only through its study and the observation of all the conditions and factors that enter into its operation can we come into the realization of God as abiding health and sustenance. (Jesus Christ Heals, pp. 31-32)

A spiritual realization is a realization of Truth. A spiritual realization of health is the result of holding in consciousness a statement of health until the logic of the mind is satisfied and a person receives the assurance that the fulfillment in the physical must follow. In other words, by realizing a healing prayer a person lays hold of the princi-ple of health itself and the whole consciousness is illumined; he or she perceives principle working out the health problems. (Jesus Christ Heals, p. 39)

However when a person lays hold of the principle of wholeness, that person finds that he or she is automatically working with God and that much new power is added. (Jesus Christ Heals, p. 39)

Realization is a deep inner conviction of Truth; it occurs when you know and feel something is True regardless of outer circumstances. In a healing need, this realization is NOT the realization of healing. This is so because healing is the process of moving from error thinking to Truth in consciousness, and from disease or illness to health in physicality. Realization in a seeming healing need is a deep inner conviction in consciousness; it is the knowing that *you* know, knowing and feeling, that Life expresses as wholeness and health.

Prayer for healing is about realizing Life, Wholeness and Health; it begins with going to that still point of the awareness of Divine Mind, or Oneness. From this awareness, one can achieve the realization of the Truth of Life at every level of being. It is in and from this conscious realization that we then see ourselves and others as whole and perfect. When realization occurs, there is often the awareness of what has been described as an "inner click."

9G NO EFFORT WASTED

The law of spiritual healing involves full receptivity on the part of the one under treatment. God does not do things in us against our will, as will acts in both the conscious and subconscious realms of mind. However much it may appear that the word is thwarted in its original intent, this is never true; it goes on, and it enters where reception is given it. In this way people are quickened, and whether we see the result with our physical vision or not, the process is as sure as God. (Jesus Christ Heals, p. 112)

As our awareness of Oneness increases, we develop a heartfelt desire to bless anyone overcoming a health challenge. We must remember to persist and not become discouraged by appearances. As we persist in our faith-filled prayers to achieve the realization of Life, we cannot insist on any particular result in those with whom we pray. Forcing a result is the antithesis of the state of Oneness; therefore, we must remain receptive. We can be confident that all our prayers will have the appropriate results according to the consciousness of the person with whom we pray. God does not do things in us because God is not a Being, Deity or Entity that acts upon us. Therefore, however defined—as Oneness, Divine Mind, Divine Truth, Law or Principle—God cannot act against a person's will because God simply is.

9H SEEING PERFECTION

The important need is not to try to effect some change in other people, but to make some changes in your thoughts about them. Don't try to set them right, but rather to see them rightly. And to see them rightly you must get rid of some narrow frames of reference, and get out of the feeling of concern. ... There is a divine milieu in which you live and move and have being ... and the same is true for the one about whom you are concerned. (The Universe Is Calling, p. 119)

Some of the most miraculous cures ever made have been where the healer simply saw perfection in the patient. The healer saw with the eye of Spirit that which really exists, and the shadow conformed to that seeing just to the extent of his or her realization of that spiritual reality. (Charles Fillmore, Talks on Truth, Unity House, Unity Village, Mo., 1926, p. 93)

Misunderstandings often arise about Unity teachings on "seeing perfection," or "seeing the good," in others. Unity uses the word "see" in a very special sense in these instances. We do not mean "to pretend," we do not mean "to see" in the literal sense. We are speaking, rather, of an inner acknowledgment and realization regardless of whether or not the appearance matches the acknowledgment at the moment. This is also sometimes called "holding the thought" or "laying hold of the Truth." As Eric Butterworth said, "Don't try to set them right, but rather to see them rightly." When we focus on people's illnesses we are not seeing them rightly; we are not seeing their Reality. As heart-centered metaphysicians we are kind hearted; true compassion is when we can perceive their Divine Perfection, or Christ Nature, then we are seeing them rightly.

9| A SUGGESTED PROCESS

While this overall process is applicable to any circumstance that motivates prayer, we will continue to use a health challenge as the example. (In other circumstances, the focus would be on different Principles, Truths and/or Divine Ideas.) Again, it is important to remember that we are not actually praying for healing, as healing is the process of moving from error thought to Truth in consciousness and it is moving from the appearance of illness and disease (or dis-ease) to wholeness and health in physicality. In a seeming healing need, we must remember that the focus is on a change in consciousness through the realization of the principle of Life. The process is as follows:

1. Refuse to see and acknowledge any appearance of illness. This may require the use of denials and affirmations (see Chapter 22).

2. Focus your attention and awareness on Oneness, or Divine Mind. Meditate for a while until you are dwelling in the Silence.

3. Once you have become still and at peace, feel and "think after" the principle of Life.

4. Focus your attention on Life, Spiritual Life—the vital, energizing Divine Life that produces wholeness and health. Hold on to the Principle of Spiritual Life until you have as full a realization of it as possible, until you have that sensation of the internal click that comes with knowing that you know. Know and feel the Truth of Divine Life.

5. Once centered in as full a realization as you can have of Life, bring into consciousness the person with the health challenge. See Spiritual Life coursing from that person's Divine Nature through every level of his or her being, radiating wholeness and health. Fully engage your thinking and feeling natures using the power of the spoken word to claim these Truths through your Spiritual Faculty of Dominion/Power (Chapter 24, section G).

6. Give praise for these Truths and be in gratitude for this vitalizing Life expressing wholeness and health.

7. Continue to refuse to see and acknowledge any appearance of illness. Whenever you think of or see this person, see only Perfection. See that he or she is whole and perfect, vitalized by Spiritual Life from Divine Mind. Behold only wholeness and health.

SUMMARY STATEMENTS

▼ *We do not pray to God, or Divine Mind. We <u>pray from</u> a consciousness of Oneness.*

▼ *Our goal in any challenging circumstance is to raise our consciousness to <u>Christ Consciousness.</u>*

▼ *The power of praying with others is a reality because of the one <u>Christ Mind</u> that indwells the consciousness of all humankind.*

▼ *When we are in complete alignment with Spiritual Truths, we often experience an immediate manifestation that <u>seems miraculous</u>.*

▼ *<u>Miracles do not exist,</u> if by miracles we mean that there is some Divine Intervention supplanting natural law. Seeming miracles are the result of Divine Ideas, Principles and Laws of which we are not yet aware.*

▼ *We must <u>become still</u> and recognize that "indwelling Oneness, Divine Mind," is in charge, and <u>release</u> all anxious thoughts about the one with whom we are praying so we can know the Truth for that individual.*

▼ *Even if they appear the same, <u>each health challenge is unique</u> because the cause in consciousness differs. While no two cases are the same, the Principle of Life expressing wholeness and health remains the same.*

▼ *We must not <u>be insistent</u> upon particular results for an individual. Each person chooses a unique path to spiritual unfoldment, and therefore, human <u>resistance</u> to Divine Truth may be present.*

▼ *<u>Persistence</u> on the part of metaphysicians calls for prayers continuing until the walls of resistance are penetrated and realization occurs.*

▼ *No effort is ever wasted because prayers quicken the expression of Life, whether we see results in the physical or not.*

▼ *We choose to see only perfection (Life) regardless of outer appearances.*

TOPICS FOR DISCUSSION

1. *How can we know the Truth for another in spite of appearances to the contrary?*

2. *What is meant by a miracle healing?*

3. *Why do we pray from and not to God?*

THOUGHTS FOR REFLECTION AND MEDITATION

"One who prays for the health of another should understand that it is not the fault of the healing principle that his patient is not instantly restored. The fault may be in his own lack of persistency or understanding; or it may be due to the patient's dogged clinging to discordant thoughts. In any case the one who prays must persist in this prayer until the walls of resistance are broken down and the healing currents are tuned in. In treating others see patients as perfect."

(Charles Fillmore, *Dynamics for Living: A Topical Compilation of Essential Fillmore Teachings*, Unity House, Unity Village, Mo., p. 64)

SUPPLEMENTARY READING

Myrtle Fillmore's Healing Letters by Myrtle Fillmore, revised paperback edition, Unity House, Unity Village, Mo., 2006, Chapter 17, "Helping Others."

Prayer: The Master Key by James Dillet Freeman, Unity House, Unity Village, Mo., 1975, Chapter 12, "Praying for Others."

Section 2:

God—Jesus Christ— Humankind

Heart-centered metaphysics explores the basic Unity teachings around God, Jesus Christ and humankind. These topics are important to the understanding of our True Nature and the application of Divine Laws and Principles in our everyday lives so that we can be heart-centered metaphysicians.

CHAPTER TEN

BEINGNESS, ONENESS, DIVINE MIND

INTRODUCTION

The excerpts used in this chapter and the entire book frequently use the word *God* for the Divine because they were mainly written during the first half of the 20th century. *God* is one of the most traditional words we have for what we also call Spirit, Oneness, Beingness or Divine Mind. The term God is loaded with understandings from the spiritual traditions in which people were raised. To further complicate its meaning, the word god refers to a supernatural male being (deity) while *goddess* refers to a supernatural female being (deity). For these reasons, the term God is used sparingly in the commentaries of this book, and only where it is deemed appropriate. This text uses synonyms for God that include but are not limited to those mentioned above—Spirit, Oneness, Beingness and Divine Mind—as well as Principle, the Sacred, Mind, Super Conscious Mind, Christ and I Am.

The purpose of this chapter is to explore the ways Beingness, Oneness or Divine Mind is perceived. We will explain our understanding that Beingness is Principle, All-Good, Divine Mind, Spirit, Substance, Source, Law, Love, Life and Power and so much more. In explaining what we perceive about Oneness or Divine Mind, it is important to realize that we cannot truly and fully define It since an *experience* of It is what is most important. From our relative perspective it may seem difficult, and some would say impossible, to know all there is to know about Beingness, Oneness or Divine Mind, which is always greater and beyond our current relative perception. And, what we know or perceive about Beingness, Oneness or Divine Mind is exceeded by our experience of It that is difficult to put into words. And yet, even though some people say that the finite cannot know the infinite, in Truth we are not finite. Our mind functions like Divine Mind because it is Divine Mind. We are infinite, in Truth, because Divine Mind is infinite. However, for us to communicate with one another in meaningful ways about Oneness, Beingness or Divine Mind, we need to clearly identify and use terms that reflect our common understanding of them.

10A ONENESS, BEINGNESS IS NOT A BEING, PERSON OR ENTITY

God is not a being or person having life, intelligence, love, power. God is that invisible, intangible, but very real, something we call life. God is perfect love and infinite power. God is the total of these, the total of all good, whether manifested or unexpressed. (H. Emilie Cady, *Lessons in Truth,* Centennial Edition, Unity House, Unity Village, Mo., 2003, p. 18)

We must relieve our minds of a personal God ruling over us in an arbitrary, manlike manner. God is not person but Principle. By Principle is meant definite, exact, unchangeable. It best describes the unchangeableness that is an inherent law of Being. The fundamental basis of practical Christianity is that God is Principle. (Charles Fillmore, *Atom-Smashing*

Power of Mind, 2nd ed., Unity House, Unity Village, Mo., 2006, p. 30)

We are studying spiritual science to get a broader conception of God, rather than holding to the view that He is a personal being with parts like a man, a being subject to change and capable of varying moods. Though personal to each one of us, God is IT, neither male nor female, but Principle, *God is not a cold, senseless principle like that of mathematics, but the Principle of life, love, and intelligence.* (Myrtle Fillmore, *How to Let God Help You,* 3rd ed., Unity House, Unity Village, Mo., 2000, p. 25)

But this Kingdom within [consciousness] is not material—it is spiritual. ... This inner country is the domain of that superior wisdom which we term the Christ. Jesus called this place of wisdom the Father within Him, and to it he ascribed all His power and wisdom. (Charles Fillmore, *Talks on*

Truth, Unity House, Unity Village, Mo., 1926, p. *35)*

It is understandable that it can be very difficult to let go of the notion of a God that is a person, being or entity. Almost all the words we are accustomed to hearing about God are words we use when we are talking about people. Even Jesus personified his realization of God by using the term "Father." But Charles Fillmore suggested that Jesus was not "defining" God when he spoke of the Father, he was naming his feeling of *relationship* with God. Jesus was referring to that inner Wisdom we call Christ. God is Divine Mind; God is Principle, Life, Love, Power, Wisdom and so much more.

10B **ALL GOOD**

God as principle is the absolute good expressed in all creation. (Charles Fillmore, *Keep a True Lent,* 2nd ed., Unity House, Unity Village, Mo., 2005, p. 9)

The central proposition in the inspiration of Spirit is that God, or primal Cause, is good. (Charles Fillmore, *Christian Healing,* 2nd ed., Unity House, Unity Village, Mo., 2005, p. 10)

God is not a being having qualities, but God is the good itself. Everything you can think of that is good, when in its absolute perfection, goes to make up

that invisible Being we call God. (Lessons in Truth, pp. *19-20)*

Jesus used the simple word *Good* in describing God. Therefore, Unity's first premise concerning Divine Nature is that Divine Mind, the Absolute Omnipresence, is Good. It is Good without an opposite. Divine Mind, Oneness or Beingness is not a person. Good is not a person; Good is Principle beyond precise definition.

That Divine Mind is Good can be difficult to understand from a relative, dualistic perception. In reference to Divine Mind, the term *Good* refers to the totality of Divine Ideas like Order, Harmony, Wholeness and Perfection that comprise the fundamental Divine Nature of the Spiritual Universe. They also underlie or "lie back of" all physicality (the manifest universe). They make up the Absolute Realm and provide the basis of the relative realm. They underlie every person, thing and situation, even though they do not always seem apparent in the "relative" because of what humankind's consciousness does with them.

When we say that Divine Mind, or Oneness, is All-Good everywhere present, it does not mean that everything we see or experience in the relative world is good. It simply means that the Good (Order, Harmony, Perfection, etc.) underlies everything as Divine Ideas and is ever available regardless of the situation. We do well, however, to remember that the Source is Truth and decide to see only Good and express only Truth. In every situation, these personal questions can be asked: What do I make of it? How do I use this for Good? Do I choose to see and affirm the Divine Essence and Potential, or do I see and affirm that which is less than Perfection?

10C BEING/BEINGNESS

God; the Mind of the universe composed of archetype ideas: life, love, wisdom, substance, Truth, power, peace, and so forth. Being is omnipresent, omnipotent, omniscient; it is the fullness of God, the All-Good. (Charles Fillmore, *The Revealing Word: A Dictionary of Metaphysical Terms,* 2nd ed., Unity House, Unity Village, Mo., 2006, p. 22)

God, the source of our existence every moment, is not simply omnipotent (all-powerful); God is omnipotence (all power). God is not alone omniscient (all-knowing); God is omniscience (all knowledge). God is not only omnipresent, but more—omnipresence. God is not a being having qualities, but God is the good itself. Everything you can think of that is good, when in its absolute perfection, goes to make up that invisible Being we call God. (Lessons in Truth, p. 19)

The word *Being* is frequently used as a synonym for God. This is not intended to mean a being or entity in the way we use it in the term *human being.*"The meaning of God as Being is used here more like a verb denoting action or energy than as a static noun. However, this sense of action or energy is better conveyed by the word *Beingness,* which is preferred in this text. Likewise, Divine Ideas such as Love and Wisdom are used as synonyms for Divine Mind, Oneness, Beingness (God is Love; God is Wisdom, etc.). Beingness does not possess or have these Divine Ideas; Beingness *is* these Divine Ideas. We must also keep in mind that in the Absolute Realm, Divine Mind is all there is. Divine Mind consists of Divine Ideas such as the Twelve Powers: Love, Wisdom (Judgment/Discernment), Power (Dominion/Mastery), Life, Imagination, Faith, Order, Understanding, Zeal, Elimination (renunciation), Will, and Strength. Since the Essence or Omnipresence of Divine Mind can be experienced, it is appropriate to use these terms as synonyms for Oneness.

10D TWO ASPECTS OF BEINGNESS

Being has two aspects: the invisible and the visible, the abstract and the concrete. The visible comes forth from the invisible, and this coming forth is always according to a universal method of growth from minute generative centers. All forms are built according to this law. From center to circumference is the method of growth throughout the universe." (*Atom-Smashing Power of Mind*, p. 134)

Jesus emphasized the supremacy of the invisible aspect of Beingness. Unity founders Charles and Myrtle Fillmore did the same throughout their writings. This is not to imply that the visible aspect of life should be ignored; such an attitude is not healthy for abundant living. The visible is simply an effect of the invisible and is secondary in priority under the Creative Law of Spirit.

Since metaphysics deals mainly with what is True about the inner life of every person, it is easy to understand that the invisible aspect of Beingness is considered of primary importance. The invisible realm of consciousness (both Mind and mind) is the matrix from which everything becomes visible, just as ordinary silence is the matrix from which all sounds become audible. The invisible realm of consciousness (mind) has its existence in the invisible Source (Divine Mind or Superconscious Mind); our focus and attention should always be in and from this invisible Source. The visible is "legitimate" in that it derives from the invisible Source (Divine Ideas).

The visible arises through an orderly process of manifestation—mind>idea>expression (Divine Order)—first in consciousness and then in outward manifestation. First, we appropriate Divine Ideas from the awareness of Source, or Divine-Mind. Next, through our own thought processes and from our own level of consciousness, we form these Divine Ideas in mind and then into outward manifestation.

10E SOURCE

Mind is the great storehouse of good from which man draws all his supplies. If you manifest life, you are confident that it had a source. If you show forth intelligence you know that somewhere in the economy of Being there is a fount of intelligence. So you may go over the elements that go to make up your being and you will find that they draw their sustenance from an invisible and, to your limited understanding, incomprehensible source.

This source we term Mind, because it is as such that our comprehension is best related to it. Names are arbitrary, and we should not stop to note differences that are merely technical. We want to get at the substance which they represent.

So if we call this invisible source Mind, it is because it is of like character with the thing within our consciousness that we call our mind. (Atom-Smashing Power of Mind, pp. 90-91)

"There is but one Source of Being. This Source is the living fountain of all good, be it life, love, wisdom, power— the Giver of all good gifts. ... You have power to draw on this Source for all of [the] good you are, or ever will be, capable of desiring." (Lessons in Truth, p. 24)

Divine Mind (Beingness) is the unchanging, unlimited Source of all existence; the underlying Cause of all that is. All the Good we could ever be and/or want is Divine Mind or is derived from Divine Mind based on Divine Ideas. Oneness or Beingness, is our limitless supply, which is unfailingly available in abundant ways. We bring "our" supply from the awareness of Oneness into mind and then into the manifest realm.

10F PRINCIPLE

The fundamental basis and starting point of practical Christianity is that God is principle. By principle is meant definite, exact and unchangeable rules of action. That the word principle *is used by materialistic schools of thought to describe what they term the "blind forces of nature" is no reason why it should convey to our minds the idea of an unloving and unfeeling God. It is used because it best describes the*

unchangeableness that is an inherent law of Being. (Charles Fillmore, Jesus Christ Heals, 2nd ed., Unity House, Unity Village, Mo., 1940, p. 34)

The unchangeable life, love, substance and intelligence of Being. Principle does not occupy space; neither has it any limitations of time or matter, but it eternally exists as the one underlying cause out of which come forth all true ideas. (The Revealing Word, p. 84)

God is the name we give to that unchangeable, inexorable principle at the source of all existence. (Lessons in Truth, p. 22)

The word *principle*, as commonly used, denotes an unfeeling set of rigid rules or formulas. This is not at all the meaning we have in mind when the word is used here as a synonym for God. Principle is not an unfeeling force; It consists of both thinking and feeling natures. When we say Divine Mind is Principle, we are referring to It as eternal, unchanging and unlimited. It is the Principle of Absolute Good, which differs from the principles of mathematics, chemistry or pathology. Consider music and art: When a musician creates music and an artist creates art, they use principles to which they usually add a feeling component. In music, for example, a song can be played very mechanically by strictly playing the music as written. This results in a very unsatisfactory, mechanical experience for the listener.

When the feeling nature is added, the musician adds his or her personal expression to the music, resulting in a very satisfying experience for the listener. God as Principle is much like this.

"God is Absolute Good" is the most accurate statement because Absolute Good cannot be precisely defined, even though we can know that this Good has no opposite. It is always beyond formal definition.

10G LAW—DIVINE PRINCIPLE IN ACTION

... a clear understanding of ourselves and of the unchangeableness of Divine Mind makes us realize that everything has its foundation in a rule of action, a law that must be observed by both creator and created. (Charles and Cora Fillmore, *The Twelve Powers*, Unity House, Unity Village, Mo., 1999, p. 38)

Law—God as law is Principle in action. Everything has its foundation in a rule of action, a law. Divine law is the orderly working out of the principles of Being. Divine law cannot be broken. It places first things first. Divine order is the first law of the universe. Indeed, there could be no universe unless its various parts were kept in perfect order. (Charles Fillmore, *Dynamics for Living: A Topical Compilation of Essential Fillmore*

Teachings, compiled by Warren Meyer, Unity House, Unity Village, Mo., 1967, p. 31)

"Law" is yet another name for God as perfect Order and Harmony in action. God as Law provides for the consistent and orderly outworking of Divine Ideas into manifestation. A fundamental law of the universe is the Law of Cause and Effect—that is, every effect we experience in Mind, our Higher Consciousness, and see in our outer world is the result of a thought held in mind. One example of Cause and Effect is Divine Order: Mind-Idea-Expression.

10H SPIRIT

Spirit is not matter. Spirit is not person. In order to perceive the essence of Being we must drop from our mind all thought that God is in any way circumscribed or has any of the limitations that we associate with things or persons having form or shape. (Charles Fillmore, *Prosperity*, Unity House, Unity Village, Mo., 1936, p. 14)

God as Spirit—God is Spirit, and Spirit is located and appears wherever it is recognized by an intelligent entity. It thus follows that whoever gives his attention to Spirit and seals his identification with it by His word, starts a flow of Spirit life and all the attributes of Spirit in and through his consciousness. To the extent that man practices identifying himself with the one and only source of existence, he becomes Spirit, until finally the union attains a perfection in which he can say with Jesus, "I and the Father are one" (Jn. 10:30). (The Revealing Word, p. 84)

Divine Mind, or Oneness, is Spirit, the infinite invisible Essence of all life. Spirit is the activity of Divine Mind that underlies everything. Spirit is everywhere equally and totally present; we refer to Spirit, or Divine Mind, as *Omnipresence* rather than *Omnipresent.* Spirit that is "us" is the Divine Pattern, our eternal, unchanging, indestructible perfection. We express Spirit by what we are being; not in what we are doing. Through the practice of identifying oneself with Source, one realizes Spirit.

101 DIVINE MIND

God Mind; ever-present, all-knowing Mind; the Absolute, the unlimited. Omnipresent, all-wise, all-loving, all-powerful Spirit.

There is but one Mind, and that Mind cannot be separated or divided, because, like the principle of mathematics, it is indivisible. All that we can say of the one Mind is that it is absolute and that all its manifesta-

tions are in essence like itself. (The Revealing Word, p. 56)

... The connecting link between God and humankind. God Mind embraces all knowledge, wisdom and understanding and is the source of every manifestation of true knowledge and intelligence. God as principle cannot be comprehended by any of the senses. But the mind of humankind is limitless, and through it one may come into touch with Divine Mind. The one Mind is a unit and cannot be divided. The individual mind is a state of consciousness in the one Mind. (The Revealing Word, p. 84)

One might ask, How can the Absolute that is unchanged, unchanging and unchangeable and is ever One have manifestations and therefore "more?" In the first excerpt, it might be better for us to use the word *emanations* rather than *manifestations.* The emanations are "in essence like" Divine Mind, but are not, in and of themselves, Divine Mind. This is true because Divine Mind does not *exist*, or "stand forth out of" anything, but simply *is.* The emanations of Divine Mind, first in the form of Divine Ideas, are always perfect. Although the expressions formed by humans are in *essence* like Divine Mind, they may not be in *expression* like Divine Mind.

There is only one Mind and that is Divine Mind. Divine Mind is the realm of all Divine Ideas. Divine Mind encompasses the Truth that It is the Source from which all intelligence and everything else is derived. Since Divine Mind is the capacity or ability to know, we refer to God as *Omniscience* rather than Omniscient. Our seeming "individual mind" is a state of consciousness in the One Mind. It is a state of consciousness that erroneously believes it is separate from Oneness.

10J SUBSTANCE

The divine idea of the underlying reality of all things. Substance is everywhere present, pervades all things, and inspires to action. It underlies all manifestation and is the spiritual essence, the living energy out of which everything is made. (The Revealing Word, pp. 186-187)

God is not a dispenser of divine substance, God is the allness of ever-present substance in which we live, move and have being. (Eric Butterworth, *Spiritual Economics: The Principles and Process of True Prosperity,* 2nd revised paperback ed., Unity House, Unity Village, Mo, 1998, p. 2)

This does not mean matter, because matter is formed while God is the formless. The substance that God is lies back of all matter and all forms. It is that which is the basis of all form yet enters not into any form as finality. It cannot be seen, tasted, or touched. Yet it is the only enduring substance in the universe. (The Revealing Word, p. 85)

Divine Mind is Substance, the Realm of Pure Potential. We often think of things such as homes, cars and money as substance, but these things will sooner or later disappear. True Substance is Divine Mind. Divine Mind is not a thing we possess, It is What we are in Reality. It is the invisible Realm of Pure Potential that is the basis for, lies back of, and is utilized to manifest all thoughts, matter and form. It is important to keep in mind that Substance does not enter into form as finality. This means that Substance is never "trapped" or "contained" within any object or entity, or limited in any way by time and/or space. You cannot find Divine Substance in any matter as, for example, you cannot find the idea or thought of *table* in the table.

Our Supply is Divine Substance, or Divine Ideas. Out of Divine Substance, we form whatever we choose according to our faith, understanding and consciousness. We become conscious of Divine Substance from the awareness of Oneness that is quickened by investing time in the Silence. Spiritual realization enriches our awareness of the omnipresence of invisible Substance. It is ever ready to take form like spiritual clay, but always in accordance with our mental pattern that is based on our present consciousness and understanding of the Divine Idea. This may be made active by affirming: *The rich Substance of the Realm of Pure Potential is ever available at and from the point of my mind. I am in all ways prospered* (adapted from *The Revealing Word*, p. 187, on "Substance," and p. 194, on "Thought-stuff").

(NOTE: The following three sections on Love, Life and Power are a sampling of the Twelve Powers. Please see Chapters 24 and 25 for a more complete exploration of all 12 of these Powers.)

10K LIFE

That expression of Being which manifests as animation, activity, vigor. Life and substance are ideas in Divine Mind. Life is the acting principle; substance is the thing acted upon. ... Life is divine, spiritual, and its source is God. (*The Revealing Word*, p. 121)

Oneness, or Divine Mind, is Life, the Source and sustainer of all energy, vitality and activity. Life is the Principle that expresses as wholeness and health. Divine Mind is the Life Essence that permeates and underlies every level of our being—Spirit (Superconscious Mind), soul (conscious and subconscious mind), and body.

This Life is perfect and eternal and is our True Beingness.

10L LOVE

The pure essence of Being that binds together the whole human family. Of all the attributes of God, love is undoubtedly the most beautiful. In Divine Mind, love is the power that joins and binds in divine harmony the universe and everything in it; the great harmonizing principle known to humankind.

Divine love is impersonal; it loves for the sake of loving. It is not concerned with what or whom it loves, nor with a return of love. Like the sun, its joy is in the shining forth of its nature. ...

Love is that mighty power, that divine quality of God that is expressing through all humankind, and cannot be suppressed by any outside force. (*Keep a True Lent*, p. 152)

Divine Love is the harmonizing, unifying and attracting Principle. Divine Love is unconditional and continues to give of Itself wholly and completely throughout any and all circumstances. Love is the unifying Principle, and we can use it to draw ourselves away from sense or belief in separation into an awareness of Oneness.

Love is the inner quality through which we desire. Used from a higher state of consciousness, we continually do our best to see good everywhere and in everyone. From lower states of consciousness we desire based on sense consciousness; therefore, we can desire erroneously. Love also harmonizes and unifies everything to match our desire, whether we are desiring from higher or lower consciousness.

10M **POWER**

God is power; humankind is powerful. God is that indescribable reservoir of stored-up energy that manifests no potency whatever until set in motion through the consciousness of humankind yet possesses an inexhaustible capacity that is beyond words to express. When that power is manifested by man it becomes conditioned. It is described as powerful, more powerful, most powerful, and it has its various degrees of expansion, pressure, velocity, force and the like. (Jesus Christ Heals, p. 25)

God is power. Not simply God has power, but God is power. In other words, all the power there is to do anything is God. (Lessons in Truth, p. 19)

Divine Mind is Power/Dominion. Divine Mind, or Oneness, is the unfailing, limitless, invincible capacity to accomplish good. Oneness is the Source of all power, all authority, mastery and all dominion. Divine Mind is

Power, the ability or capacity to master, dominate and control. All the power there is in the universe is based on Divine Mind being *Omnipotence*, not *omnipotent.*

10N **AWARENESS OF ONENESS, BEINGNESS, DIVINE MIND**

God is already in every part of your being, so it is just a matter of being conscious of oneness with God. (Myrtle Fillmore, *Myrtle Fillmore's Healing Letters,* revised paperback edition, Unity House, Unity Village, Mo., 2006, p. 96)

God is all, and to live and dwell in this realization makes every moment so full of meaning that we cannot put into words the sheer joy of living we feel. (Martha Smock, *Listen, Beloved,* Unity House, Unity Village, Mo., 1980, p. 16)

In studying the terms and concepts pertaining to Divine Mind, we are not seeking so much to learn *about* Divine Mind, or Beingness, as we are to deepen our experience and realization of It. As we do so, we become aware that Divine Mind is the Truth of us (What we are, not who we think we are) and therefore is always available for use in every facet of our lives.

SUMMARY STATEMENTS

▼ *The term* <u>*Principle*</u> *refers to the unlimited, unchanging, eternal Divine Mind.*

▼ *Unity's first premise concerning Divine Mind is that It is* <u>*Absolute Good*</u>*.*

▼ *Oneness, or Beingness, is* <u>*Mind*</u>*, Divine Mind, the Source of all knowledge. Divine Mind is* <u>*Omniscience*</u>*.*

▼ *Oneness, Beingness, is* <u>*Spirit*</u>*, the infinite invisible Essence of all life. Spirit is the activity of Divine Mind and can be experienced in all creation.*

▼ *Divine Mind, Oneness, Beingness is* <u>*Omnipotence*</u>*. Divine Mind does not have power; Divine Mind is the one and only* <u>*Power*</u>*.*

▼ *Divine Mind, or Oneness, is* <u>*Substance*</u>*; Substance is not matter. Substance lies back of and underlies all matter and forms. It is the basis of all form yet does not enter into any form as finality. It cannot be seen, tasted or touched.*

▼ *Divine Mind is the unfailing* <u>*Source*</u> *of our supply. Our supply is Divine Ideas.*

▼ *Oneness, or Beingness, is* <u>*Law*</u>*, Principle in action. A fundamental law is the Law of Cause and Effect; Divine Order (Mind>Idea>Expression) is one example of it.*

▼ *Divine Mind is* <u>*Life*</u>*, the eternal activity and vitality.*

▼ *Oneness, or Beingness, is* <u>*Love,*</u> *the unifying, harmonizing and attracting Principle. Divine Mind is Love and It is ever-present and unconditional.*

TOPICS FOR DISCUSSION

1. *Describe your understanding of Divine Mind as Principle.*

2. *Name an attribute of Divine Mind and tell how it has worked in your life.*

3. *Share a time in your life when you have experienced Divine Mind as Love.*

4. *What does it mean to you to know that Divine Mind is Absolute Good?*

THOUGHTS FOR REFLECTION AND MEDITATION

"Eden is a pleasant, harmonious, productive state of consciousness in which are all possibilities of growth. When man is expressing in harmony with Divine Mind, bringing forth the qualities of Being in divine order, he dwells in Eden, or in a state of bliss in a harmonious body."

(Charles Fillmore, *Dynamics for Living: A Topical Compilation of Essential Fillmore Teachings*, compiled by Warren Meyer, Unity House, Unity Village, Mo., 1967, p.57)

SUPPLEMENTARY READING

Christian Healing by Charles Fillmore, 2nd ed., Unity House, Unity Village, Mo., 2005, Lesson 1, "The True Character of Being."

How to Let God Help You by Myrtle Fillmore, 3rd ed., Unity House, Unity Village, Mo., 2000, Chapter 6, "Fundamental Propositions."

Lessons in Truth by H. Emilie Cady, Centennial Edition, Unity House, Unity Village, Mo., 2003, Chapter 2, "Statement of Being."

CHAPTER ELEVEN

THE SPIRITUAL UNIVERSE AND THE PHYSICAL UNIVERSE

INTRODUCTION

One of the most commonly held beliefs is that God, a supernatural Being, created the physical universe, including our bodies. This belief is so strongly held that many do not even "see" or discern where Unity founders Charles and Myrtle Fillmore and other Unity teachers clearly state in their writings that Divine Mind did not create the physical universe.

11A DIVINE IDEAS

God is mind, and all God's works are created in mind as perfect ideas. (Charles Fillmore, *Mysteries of Genesis,* Unity Classic Library edition, Unity House, Unity Village, Mo., 1998, p. 25)

God creates through the action of God Mind, and all things rest on ideas. (*Mysteries of Genesis,* p. 14)

The idea is the directing and controlling power. Every idea has a specific function to perform. (*Mysteries of Genesis,* p. 21)

Mental activity in Divine Mind represents two phases: first, conception of the idea; and secondly, expression of the idea. In every idea conceived in mind there is first the quickening spirit of life, followed by the increase of the idea in substance. Wisdom is the "masculine nature" or expressive side of Being, while love is the "feminine" or receptive side of Being. Wisdom is the father quality of God and love is the mother quality. In every idea there exist these two qualities of mind, which unite in order to increase and bring forth under divine law. (*Mysteries of Genesis,* p. 27)

Every idea is a seed that, sown in the substance of mind, becomes the real food on which humankind is nourished. Humankind has access to the seed ideas of Divine Mind, and through prayer and meditation, one quickens and appropriates the substance of those ideas, which were originally planted in his or her I AM by the parent mind. (Mysteries of Genesis, p. 27)

Divine Mind creates/ideates through the action of Mind. Everything in the Spiritual and material universes is based on Divine Ideas in Divine Mind. These operate under the Laws of Divine Mind, or Divine Order: Mind, Idea in mind, and Expression (Manifestation). At the level of Divine Mind, this expression might be more accurately worded as Consciousness (Mind-Idea-Consciousness). Humankind manifests through the same sequence, the same law of thought (mind-idea-expression). Mind-idea-expression first results in feelings, thoughts and images. Then humankind utilizes these thoughts, feelings and images to manifest form.

There are two phases of activity in Divine Mind. First, the idea quickens the Spirit of Life followed by the expression of the Idea in Substance. In order to increase and bring forth according to Divine Law, two qualities must be present: Wisdom and Love; like thinking and feeling in the relative realm. Wisdom is the expressive side of Being, while Love is the receptive side of Being. Humankind has "access" or becomes aware of Divine

Ideas (seed ideas) in the I AM, Christ. Through prayer and meditation, a seed idea sown in Substance is quickened and appropriated for manifestation.

11B CREATION (IDEATION) OF THE SPIRITUAL UNIVERSE

The creation described in these six days or six "steps" or stages of God Mind is wholly spiritual and should not be confounded with the manifestation that is described in the succeeding chapters. God is mind, and all God's works are created in mind as perfect ideas. (Mysteries of Genesis, p. 25)

In the six mental steps or "mind movements," called days, Elohim God creates the spiritual universe and spiritual humankind. God then rests. God has created the ideas or patterns of the formed universe that is to follow. (Mysteries of Genesis, p. 9)

... we see that God did not create the worlds directly; God created that which produced or evolved them. (Mysteries of Genesis, p. 21)

Ideas are productive and bring forth after their kind. They express themselves under the law of divine imagery. The seed is within the thought and is reproduced through thought activity until thought habits are formed. Thoughts become fixed in the earth or

formed consciousness. In Divine Mind all is good.

Again a definite degree of mind unfoldment has been attained. Humankind, in forming its world, goes through the same mental process, working under divine law. (Mysteries of Genesis, p. 19)

"Created" means "ideated." The "heavens" is the realm of ideas, and the "earth" represents ideas in expression. Heaven is the idea and earth the mental picture. A comparison is found in the activity of our own mind: we have an idea and then think out a plan before we bring it forth. (Mysteries of Genesis, p. 15)

God ideated two universal planes of consciousness, "the heavens and the earth." One is the realm of pure ideas, the other of thought forms. God does not create the visible universe directly, as a person makes a concrete pavement, but God creates the ideas that are used by God's intelligent "image and likeness" to make the universe. Thus God's creations are always spiritual. Humankind's creations are both material and spiritual, according to its understanding. (Mysteries of Genesis, pp. 26-27)

The creation as depicted in the first chapter of Genesis is entirely Spiritual and should not be confused with manifestation. At this level a better word for creation is *ideation*. It is "Elohim God" that creates (ideates) the Spiritual Universe and the "Spiritual Human." God does not create (ideate) the visible universe directly. Divine Mind ideates the Divine Ideas that are the basis of and are used to manifest the visible universe. Divine Mind simply ideates Divine Ideas, and these are always Spiritual.

The physical universe is made from Divine Ideas, including Substance, and manifests according to the consciousness that is imaging it. This is why "humankind's creations" are both "Spiritual and material." They are Spiritual in that they are based on Divine Ideas that are of the Absolute. Humankind's creations are material in that they are in space and time, are changing and therefore of the relative realm.

11C "SPIRITUAL HUMANKIND"— CHRIST

The human that God created in God's own image and likeness and pronounced good and very good is spiritual human. This human is the direct offspring of Divine Mind, God's idea of [the] perfect human. This is the only-begotten Offspring, the Christ, the Lord God, the Jehovah, the I AM. In the second chapter [of Genesis] this Jehovah or divine idea of [the] perfect human forms the manifest human and calls his name Adam. (Mysteries of Genesis, p. 12)

In the beginning was the Word, and the Word was with God, and the Word was God. He was in the beginning with God. All things came into being through him, and without him not one thing came into being (Jn. 1:1-3).

Numbers are used throughout the Bible in connection with faculties or ideas in Divine Mind. There are twelve divine faculties. ... All of these have a threefold character: first, as absolute ideas in Divine Mind; secondly, as thoughts, which are ideas in expression but not manifest; and thirdly, as manifestations of thoughts, which we call things. In humankind this threefold character is known as spirit, soul, and body. Therefore in studying humankind as the offspring of God, it is necessary to distinguish between the faculties as they exist in the body. We find heaven to be the orderly arrangement of divine ideas within humankind's true being. Earth is the outer manifestation of those ideas, this manifestation being humankind's body. (Mysteries of Genesis, pp. 11-12)

God is carrying humankind along in God Mind as an ideal quantity, the image-and-likeness human of God's creation, and God's divine plan is dependent for its success on the manifestation by humankind of this idea. The divine plan is furthered by the constant idealism that keeps humankind moving forward to higher and higher achievements. The image-and-likeness human pours into "humankind" a perpetual stream of ideas that the individual person arranges as thoughts and forms as substance and life. While this evolutionary process is going on there seem to be two people, one ideal and spiritual and the other intellectual and material, which are united at the consummation, the ideal human, Christ. (Mysteries of Genesis, p. 26)

The "image-and-likeness Human" is the Spiritual Human also referred to as Christ, the Lord God, Jehovah, the I AM and in John 1: 1-3 as the Word. All the language around the image-and-likeness Human is that It is an Idea in Divine Mind ideated by Divine Mind. And yet, John 1:1- 3 says the Word, the Christ, is God.

In *Keep a True Lent*, Charles Fillmore defined Christ as the Idea that is made up of ideas. Charles Fillmore subdivided the Spiritual Human, Christ, into Twelve Faculties, Powers or Ideas based on the metaphysical interpretation of Jesus calling his 12 disciples. It may be more useful to think of these as Twelve Abilities. These Ideas are threefold in nature: they are Absolute Divine Ideas in Divine Mind, thoughts (ideas in expression), and the manifestation of thoughts. The threefold nature of humankind (Spirit, soul, body) reflects this threefold nature of the "Spiritual Human." Heaven is the orderly arrangement of these Divine Ideas in humankind's True Spiritual

"Beingness." The earth and the entire physical universe are the outer manifestation or "body" of the collective consciousness, while our individual bodies are a manifestation of both collective and individual consciousness.

The common perception of there being a Divine Plan results from the dissonance experienced between who we think we are as separate personalities and What we are, Christ. The actual Divine Plan arises from this dissonance as an urge to express more and more of Divine Nature, or Christ Nature, at the current level of consciousness. This urge is amorphous, not specific. Each person individualizes it according to his or her own consciousness. The success of this "plan" depends on humankind manifesting Divine Ideas more and more clearly. The image-and-likeness Human, the Spiritual Human, "pours forth" Divine Ideas from the Absolute into the relative. Each individual then arranges the Divine Ideas into thoughts (soul), forms (physical reality that can be touched and felt) and life. This is not a purely intellectual process; it includes the thinking and feeling natures. This is a single evolutionary process where there seem to be "two," one ideal and spiritual and the other intellectual and material. These two aspects of the one process are united at the consummation, the Ideal Human: Christ.

11D THE SPIRITUAL BODY

... the words "body of Christ" refer to man's spiritual body. "Until Christ be formed in you." When we appropriate words of Truth, "eat them," so to speak, we partake of the substance and life of Spirit and build the Christ body. This is partaking of the body and blood of Jesus Christ, the true sacrament that vitalizes the body by renewing the mind. Every student of Truth builds the Christ body as he constantly abides in the Christ Mind through daily meditation upon words of Truth. (Charles Fillmore, *Atom-Smashing Power of Mind*, 2nd ed., Unity House, Unity Village, Mo., 2006, p. 78)

The limited concept of matter and of a material body must be transformed so that the true spiritual body may appear. (Atom-Smashing Power of Mind, p. 154)

All thoughts and ideas embody themselves according to their character. (Charles Fillmore, *Dynamics for Living: A Topical Compilation of Essential Fillmore Teachings,* compiled by Warren Meyer, Unity House, Unity Village, Mo., 1967, p. 47)

Spiritual thoughts make a spiritual body. (Dynamics for Living, p. 48)

The spiritual body of man is the conception of Divine Mind, the creation of Spirit for us. Our work is to make this spiritual body manifest. (Dynamics for Living, p. 141)

From these excerpts, we clearly see that Fillmore believed in something he referred to as the Spiritual Body. It is made up of Truth, or Spiritual Thoughts, appropriated from the awareness of Oneness. It is revealed by transforming the limited concepts of matter and of a material body so that the true Spiritual Body may appear. Daily meditation on words of Truth and abiding more *in* and *from* the Christ Mind builds up the Spiritual Body.

11E THE PHYSICAL BODY

Body—The outer expression of consciousness; the precipitation of the thinking part of a person. God created the idea of the body as a self-perpetuating, self-renewing organism, which a person reconstructs into his or her personal body. God creates the body idea, or divine idea, and that person, by his thinking, makes it manifest. As God created us in His [Its] image and likeness by the power of His [Its] word, so we, as God's image and likeness, project our bodies by the same power. (Charles Fillmore, *The Revealing Word: A Dictionary of Metaphysical Terms,* 2nd ed., Unity House, Unity Village, Mo., 2006, p. 26)

Material thoughts make a material body. (Dynamics for Living, p. 48)

This section presents another startling concept for those who believe that God, a supernatural Being, made our physical bodies. In the first excerpt above, Charles Fillmore in *The Revealing Word* emphatically states that the thinking aspect of humankind makes the personal body. These quotes point the way to the understanding that the material body, the physical body, is not directly manifested by Divine Mind. Fillmore postulated that there was a Body Idea or Divine Idea that humankind (collective and individual) uses to manifest a physical body through thought, the thinking and feeling nature. If Fillmore believed that humankind manifests their individual physical bodies, then it is not logical to think that Fillmore believed that God or even Divine Mind is manifesting the rest of the physical universe. For him, the entire physical universe is manifested by collective consciousness

11F CREATION OF THE MATERIAL UNIVERSE

We are by birth a spiritual race, and we should never have known matter or material conditions if we had followed the leadings of our higher consciousness. (Charles Fillmore, *Talks on*

Truth, Unity House, Unity Village, Mo., 1926, p. 164)

God is not matter nor confined in any way to the idea of substance termed matter. God is that intangible essence which man has "formed" and called matter. Thus matter is a limitation of the divine substance whose vital and inherent character is above all else limitless. (Charles Fillmore, *Jesus Christ Heals,* 2nd ed., Unity House, Unity Village, Mo., 1940, p. 27)

The Christ man has dominion over every idea emanating from Divine Mind. (*Mysteries of Genesis,* p. 25)

When wisdom and love are unified in the individual consciousness, a person is a master of ideas and brings forth under the original creative law. (*Mysteries of Genesis,* p. 27)

... That mind has ideas and that ideas have expression; that all manifestation in our world is the result of the ideas that we are holding in mind and are expressing. (Charles Fillmore, *Christian Healing,* 2nd ed., Unity House, Unity Village, Mo., 2005, p. 16)

Ages of thought upon the reality and solidarity of things have evolved a mental atmosphere that has produced the present material universe. These and millions of other concepts are the work of humankind and not God, as is popularly supposed. However they all rest on the original God Mind and can be restored to the perfect law and order of that Mind by those who free themselves from the mental entanglements with materiality and identify their thinking with that of the Mind that is Spirit. "Ye shall know the truth, and the truth shall make you free." (*Jesus Christ Heals,* foreword)

But God does not form things. God calls from the depths of Its own being the ideas that are already there, and they move forth and clothe themselves with the habiliments [clothes] of time and circumstance in humankind's consciousness. (*Jesus Christ Heals,* pp. 35-36)

The ideas of Divine Mind are whole and complete in their capacity to unfold perpetually greater and more beautiful forms according to the thinking capacity in humankind. A person catches mental sight of an idea in Divine Mind and proceeds to put it in terms comprehensible to that person on his or her plane of consciousness. All ideas have their origin in Divine Mind, but their character as unfolded by people depends entirely upon their acquaintance with God. The idea of a house as formulated by people varies all the way from a wigwam to the most magnificent castle. The original idea of a house, as it exists in God's mind, cannot be anything less than the perfected consciousness of humankind, of which the body is a symbol. This is the temple "not made with hands," and it is the only temple acceptable to God. (Atom-Smashing Power of Mind, p. 94)

But we should not assume that all manifestation is good because the originating idea came from Divine Mind. All ideas have their foundation in Divine Mind, but humankind has put the limitation of negative thought upon them, and sees them "in a mirror, darkly." (Christian Healing, p. 45)

Charles Fillmore believed that we would have never known physicality if Oneness had remained the focus. These quotes indicate that Fillmore was clear that Divine Mind created (ideated) the Spiritual Universe and the Divine Ideas that make the material (physical) universe possible. The Christ has dominion and mastery over all Divine Ideas. As Fillmore wrote, "When wisdom and love are unified in the individual consciousness, a person is a master of ideas and brings forth under the original creative law." Ideas in individual consciousness manifest according to Divine Law. It is the Christ, I AM, or Jehovah God that uses these Ideas to manifest the physical universe. It is this Spiritual Human that clothes the Divine Ideas in time and circumstance.

Further, humankind has been entangled with materiality, and therefore some of that manifestation is not necessarily good. This is because the manifestation of Divine Ideas is related to the level of consciousness of the collec-

tive mind as well as the individual mind. Thus, Charles Fillmore makes statements that indicate that our mental sight of Divine Ideas is dependent on our plane of consciousness and that the character of their unfoldment is dependent on our realization of Oneness. He indicates that we put the limitation of our own negative thinking on Divine Ideas and see them "'in a mirror dimly" (1 Cor. 13:12).

11G **WHAT HAPPENED?**

When it [consciousness] looks wholly without, upon sensation and feeling, it loses its bearings in the maze of its own thought creations. Then it builds up a belief of separateness from, and independence of, a causing power. Humankind sees only form, and makes God a personal being located in a city of dimensions. This belief of separateness leads to ignorance, because all intelligence is derived from the one Divine Mind, and when the soul thinks itself something alone, it cuts itself off in consciousness from the fount of inspiration. Believing ourselves separate from our source, we lose sight of the divine harmony. We are like a musical note standing alone, looking upon other notes but having no definite place upon the great staff of nature, the grand symphony of life. (Talks on Truth, p. 10)

We can readily see how a whole race might be caught in the meshes of its own thought emanations and, through this drowsy ignorance of the human ego, remain there throughout eternity, unless a break were made in the structure and the light of a higher way let in. This is exactly what has happened to our [human] race. In our journey back to the Father's house we became lost in our own thought emanations. (*Talks on Truth,* p. 165)

... humankind must learn that we have within ourselves all the potentialities of Being. When this tremendous truth is revealed to us we sometimes forget that our potentialities are to be expressed according to plans inherent in Being and we proceed to make our worlds after our own design. (Charles Fillmore, *Keep a True Lent,* 2nd ed., Unity House, Unity Village, Mo., 2005, p. 54)

This is the first step in the fall of humankind—the belief that we can act wisely without first knowing the plan of God. This fall takes place in our own consciousness. We follow the dictates of the animal nature rather than those of the higher wisdom, and indulging them we eat the fruit of "the tree of the knowledge of good and evil," which is a consciousness of nakedness and separation from God. (*Keep a True Lent,* p. 54)

The Garden of Eden or Paradise of God is in the ether, and we see that the "fall of man" antedated the formation of this planet as we behold it geologically. (*Talks on Truth,* p. 54)

We who have studied these creative processes through thought action know how states of consciousness are formed and how persistent a certain mental state is after it has once crystallized. The human ego seems to lose its identity in its own formations, and forgets for the time all its past experiences and powers. (*Talks on Truth,* p. 165)

Instead of [the I AM] recognizing the power to think as simply a faculty of mind, it assumes it to be the whole mind and all of itself. This identification of the free I AM with its creations brings about a world of illusion. (*Talks on Truth,* p. 89)

And Jehovah God (a limited concept of Elohim, the Almighty) caused a deep sleep (mesmeric state) to fall upon the man (Adam). Nowhere in Scripture is there any record to show that Adam was ever awakened; and he (humankind) is still in this dreamy state of consciousness. In this dream he creates a world of his own and peoples it with ideas, dimly alive, corresponding to his own sleep-benumbed consciousness. (*Mysteries of Genesis,* p. 40)

These excerpts present quite a cross section of views concerning what happened to humankind in its "fall" from Oneness. The conclusion is that somehow our focus and attention got all wrapped up in the outer, what was being made or manifested from Divine Ideas. This focus was at first entirely in consciousness and preceded geology; it preceded physicality. Such a focus builds up a belief in separation and independence from First Cause. Charles Fillmore postulates that we became entangled and maybe even enthralled in sense consciousness and forgot Source. This identification with manifestations brought about a world of illusion, a mental state that became persistent and crystallized. It is as if we lost our Identity in our own formations.

In any event, these reasons do not ultimately satisfy, as they raise as many questions as they attempt to answer. However, the basic premise is that Divine Mind (Oneness) is perfect, unchanged, unchanging and unchangeable. "Something" must have happened since each of us seems to experience and witness separation and error. But rather than dwell on what happened, it is more useful and productive to focus on what we can do about it now.

11H THE REMEDY

Every act of man has its origin in thought, which is expressed into the phenomenal world from a mental center that is but a point of radiation for an energy that lies back of it. That point of radiation is the conscious I, which in its correct relation is one with Cause, and has at its command all the powers potential in Cause. The conscious I can look in two directions—to the outer world where the thoughts that rise within it give sensation and feeling, which ultimate in a moving panorama of visibility; or to the world within, whence all its life, power, and intelligence are derived. When the I looks wholly within, it loses all sense of the external. (Talks on Truth, p. 9)

Life is a problem solvable by a principle whose essence is intelligence, which the wise person always consults. (Talks on Truth, p. 10)

It is the recognition of this higher consciousness and the reorganization of our place in Being that we are seeking. We are emerging from the darkness of Egyptian bondage—we see the Promised Land, and we want to know the shortest way to it. That way is the Jesus Christ way. The demonstration of Jesus relates Him to us in a metaphysical sense, because it is only by a study of states of consciousness formed by thought that it can be understood. (Talks on Truth, p. 164)

When you have renounced the fleshly consciousness and have resolved to live in the Spirit, you have made a covenant with the Most High to leave the domain of the flesh forever. You have entered into an agreement with your invisible self that is far more binding than any man-made contract could possibly be. (Talks on Truth, p. 84)

So each of us is a son of God. We shall come into conscious recognition of the Christ mind, affecting the junction between our mind and God's mind just as soon as we let go of the limitations of mortal sense. God has but one Son, the Christ, the one ideal man. This divine conjunction was accomplished by Jesus, and the Christ shone out through His mortal self and illumined it, until it lost its personality and disappeared into divine individuality. (Talks on Truth, p. 167)

To comprehend the atonement requires a deeper insight into creative processes than the average man and the average woman have attained; not because they lack the ability to understand, but because they have submerged their thinking power in a grosser thought stratum. So only those who study Being from the standpoint of pure mind can ever understand the atonement and the part that Jesus played in opening the way for humanity into the glory that was potentially theirs before the world was formed. (Talks on Truth, p. 164)

The way out of the entanglement in sense consciousness is the path that Jesus demonstrated. Jesus played an important role in renting the veil that prevented the awareness of the perception of separation and therefore the awareness of our True Divine Nature. The remedy is to claim our True Divine Nature, as Jesus did. We must study "Beingness" from the standpoint of pure Mind. On an individual basis, this means becoming so aware of our "own" Christ Nature that it shines right through the personality; in this way, the personality disappears into the Divine Individuality. This also requires making a commitment to live in and from Spirit, Divine Mind. It means ceasing to look to the outer and

---

SUMMARY STATEMENTS

▼ *Divine Mind creates/ideates through the action of Mind.*

▼ *The Spiritual Universe is composed of Divine Ideas.*

▼ *Everything in the material universe is based on Divine Ideas in the Spiritual Universe, Divine Mind.*

▼ *The body is the precipitation of the thinking part of humankind, collective consciousness and individual consciousness.*

▼ *Material thoughts* make a material body. *Spiritual thoughts* make a Spiritual Body.

▼ *Humankind has "access" to Divine Ideas*, seed ideas, in the I AM. Through prayer and meditation, Substance is quickened and appropriated for those Divine Ideas.

▼ The *creation* as depicted in the first chapter of Genesis *is entirely spiritual* and should not be confused with manifestation. It is Elohim God that creates (ideates) the Spiritual Universe and the Spiritual Human, Christ.

▼ The *"Image-and-Likeness Human" is the Spiritual Human,* also referred to as the Christ, the Lord God, the Jehovah, the I AM. The Spiritual Human is made up of Twelve Faculties, Powers, Abilities or Divine Ideas.

▼ The *Image-and-Likeness Human, the Spiritual Human*, "pours forth" Divine Ideas from the Absolute into the relative. Each individual then arranges those Divine Ideas into thoughts (soul), forms (physical reality that can be touched and felt) and life.

▼ *God created/ideated the Spiritual Universe* and the Divine Ideas that make the material (physical) universe possible. It is the *Christ*, I AM, Jehovah, God that *uses these Ideas to manifest the physical universe.*

▼ Humankind is *entangled with materiality* and therefore some manifestation is not necessarily good; the manifestation of Divine Ideas is related to the level of consciousness of the individual as well as collective consciousness.

▼ The *physical universe* is the result of entanglement with our sense consciousness.

▼ *The way out is the way in*. The way out of the entanglement in sense consciousness is the path that Jesus demonstrated for us. It is about claiming our True Divine Nature.

TOPICS FOR DISCUSSION

1. In what ways do you experience error and separation?

2. Think of a time when you were aware of responding to life's challenges from Christ Nature?

3. How can you make this experience happen more often?

THOUGHTS FOR REFLECTION AND MEDITATION

"God creates through the action of His mind,
and all things rest on ideas. ...
Evolution is the working out in manifestation
of what mind has involved.
Whatever mind commands to be brought forth
will be brought forth
by and through
the law of evolution inherent in being.
This applies to the great and the small.
In mind there is but one."

(Charles Fillmore, *Mysteries of Genesis*, p. 14)

SUPPLEMENTARY READING

Mysteries of Genesis by Charles Fillmore, Unity House, Unity Village, Mo., 1998, Chapter 1, "Spiritual Man."

Prosperity by Charles Fillmore, Unity House, Unity Village, Mo., 1936, Chapter 5, "The Law That Governs the Manifestation of Supply."

CHAPTER TWELVE

THE DIVINE PARADOXES

INTRODUCTION

A paradox is an assertion that may appear contradictory or opposed to common sense but is nevertheless true. Understanding the concept of paradox helps in becoming more fully aware of the scope of Divine Mind, Oneness or Spirit. Although many people have no difficulty accepting what others may call contradictory or incompatible aspects of Divine Mind, it is appropriate to investigate these apparent paradoxes. For example, how can Divine Mind be both "closer than breathing, and nearer than hands and feet" as the poet Tennyson declared and, at the same time, be impersonal Principle?

The seeming paradoxes of Divine Mind as Principle and personal, transcendent and immanent, father and mother, and Law and Grace will be explored. These aspects of Oneness, or Divine Nature, are, in truth, not indicative of a duality in Divine Mind, but are reflective of the Perfection and Wholeness of Oneness, Beingness, Divine Mind. They are paradoxes only from limited human perception. The more clearly we are able to understand how each of these aspects work together, the more comfortable we will be with the multifaceted Divine Nature, or Oneness.

12A PRINCIPLE/PERSONAL

We shall realize that Being is not only principle so far as its inherent and undeviating laws are concerned, but also personal so far as its relation to each one of us is concerned; that we as individuals do actually become the focus of universal Spirit. (Charles and Cora Fillmore, *Teach Us to Pray*, 2nd ed., Unity House, Unity Village, Mo., 2007, p. 169)

Though God is not a person, yet God is personal. There is nothing impersonal about God Mind in me. It is my mind at the point of God Mind, but it is my mind. (Eric Butterworth, *Discover the Power Within You*, 40th Anniversary Edition, HarperOne, New York, 2008, p. 34)

God is personal to us when we recognize God within us as our indwelling life, intelligence, love and power. There is a difference between a personal God and God personal to us. Since the word personal sometimes leads to misunderstanding, it would probably be better to speak of God individualized in humankind rather than of God personal to humankind. (Charles Fillmore, *The Revealing Word: A Dictionary of Metaphysical Terms,* 2nd ed., Unity House, Unity Village, Mo., 2006, p. 83)

Many have thought of God as a personal being. The statement that God is Principle chills them, and in terror they cry out, "They have taken away my Lord, and I know not where they have laid him" (Jn. 20:13). Broader and more learned minds are always cramped by the thought of God as a person, for personality limits to place and time. God is the name we give to that unchangeable, inexorable principle at the source of all existence. To the individual consciousness God takes on personality, but as the creative underlying cause of all things, He is principle, impersonal; as expressed in each individual, He becomes personal to that one—a personal, loving, all-forgiving Father-Mother. All that we can ever need or desire is the infinite Father-Principle, the great reservoir of unexpressed good. There is no limit to the Source of our being, nor to His willingness to manifest more of Himself through us, when we are willing to do His will. (H. Emilie Cady, *Lessons In Truth,* Centennial Edition, Unity House, Unity Village, Mo., 2003, p. 22)

Where Divine Mind may be realized as unfailing Principle, it is also true that Divine Mind may be experienced as a warm and loving Presence. It is important to emphasize that Divine Mind, the Absolute, is not "personalizing Itself" to us, but rather we are creating the experience of Divine Mind being personal at the point of each one of us. We are aligning our seeming separate consciousness with Divine Mind, the Truth of What "we" are. Divine Mind does not change; it is our awareness of Divine Mind that changes.

There is another paradox presented in the quotation above from Emilie Cady. While she definitely emphasizes that God is not a person, she continues to refer to God as He and Him. We must recognize this usage was usual and customary for her time (she wrote *Lessons In Truth* in the 1890s). Today we would write it differently. We would probably avoid the term "God" altogether and use the pronoun "It" instead of "He" or "Him" as recommended by Myrtle Fillmore in her book *How to Let God Help You*.

12B IMMANENT/TRANSCENDENT

God immanent—this refers to the all-pervading and indwelling presence of God, the life and intelligence permeating the universe. Jesus lovingly revealed that God is within us, forever resident in the invisible side of humankind's nature. (*The Revealing Word*, p. 85)

In the six mind movements, called days, Elohim God creates the Spiritual Universe and Spiritual Man. (Charles Fillmore, *Mysteries of Genesis*, Unity House, Unity Village, Mo., p. 24)

Transcendent God—God above or beyond God's universe, apart from it. God is more than God's universe; God is prior to and is exalted above it, but at once God is in the universe as the very essence of it. God is both transcendent and immanent. (*The Revealing Word*, p. 196)

We realize that Divine Mind creates (ideates) the "Spiritual Universe—the Realm of Divine Ideas," and we also experience Divine Presence, or Oneness, at the point of our very Beingness. Omnipresence must be immanent and transcendent in order to be everywhere present. Jesus said, "Behold, the kingdom of God is within you" (Lk. 17:21 KJV). It is within consciousness. Many people jump to the conclusion that Jesus meant that the Kingdom of God is *only* within them. This view tends to overlook the transcendence of Divine Mind. Only Divine Mind, Oneness, Spirit, can be the immanent/transcendent Presence.

A very important statement is contained within Charles Fillmore's excerpt from *The Revealing Word*: "God is more than God's universe." Divine Mind is truly present within us, within consciousness, and yet is greater than any definition or description from this relative perspective. Divine Mind is unlimited. And, at the same time we must also come to the realization that when we say Divine Mind is everywhere present, we do not mean a piece of Oneness, or Beingness, is here and a piece of It there. We mean that the *totality* of Divine Mind is everywhere present, not simply a piece. So, even though Divine Mind is immanent and Divine Mind is transcendent, we can only have the experience of the totality of God Nature at the point of us, the point of our consciousness. The totality of Oneness, or Divine Ideas, is the Truth of what "we" are. Paradoxically, we are trying to experience and become more aware of That which we already are!

12C AS FATHER AND AS MOTHER

In Scripture the primal ideas in the Mind of Being are called the "sons of God." That the masculine "son" is intended to include both masculine and feminine is borne out by the context, and, in fact, the whole history of the [human] race. Being itself must be masculine and feminine, in order to make humans in its image and likeness, "male and female." (Charles and Cora Fillmore, *The Twelve Powers,* Unity House, Unity Village, Mo., 1999, pp. 52-53)

Just as God has been from the beginning so Spirit substance has been from the beginning. This substance is in fact the Mother side of God, the feminine element in God's nature. It is the universal medium in which we plant all ideas of supply and support.

Just as the earth is the universal matrix in which all vegetation develops so this invisible Spirit substance is the universal matrix in which ideas of prosperity germinate and grow and bring forth according to our faith and trust. (*The Twelve Powers,* p. 39)

Though the term *father-mother* carries the connotation of physical gender or personality traits, when we use it to describe Divine Nature, or Oneness, we are interpreting it metaphysically to represent ideas. We are not saying Divine Mind *is* father or Divine Mind *is* mother. We are saying Divine Mind *as* father and Divine Mind *as* mother. Divine Mind is the source of Principles that *we define* as masculine and feminine. These are labels we put on a subset of Divine Qualities. In Divine Mind, there is neither a box labeled "father" containing those qualities nor a box labeled "mother" containing another subset of qualities. We are speaking of Divine Mind, or Oneness, as having both the masculine and feminine principles of life as determined and labeled from our perception. The masculine principle is the active, energy-generating power. The feminine principle is the more passive, receptive aspect—the matrix from which energy can be generated. Divine Mind is both Wisdom and Love, both Power and Substance. All elements are needed for the full expression of Divine Mind, Oneness or Spirit.

12D LAW/GRACE

Law, divine—Divine law is the orderly working out of the principles of Being, or the divine ideals, into expression and manifestation throughout creation. Humankind, by keeping the law of right thought, works in perfect harmony with divine law, and thus paves the way into spiritual consciousness. Divine law cannot be broken. It holds humankind responsible for the results of its labors. (The Revealing Word, p. 118)

Grace explains the inadequacy of the idea of 'karma,' the endless cycle of cause and effect. It is true that 'as you sow so do you reap.' Yet, God's desire to express completely through you and as you is so great that you never completely reap the harvest of error, and you always reap more good than you sow. This is grace. (Eric Butterworth, *Celebrate Yourself! and Other Inspirational Essays*, Unity House, Unity Village, Mo., 1987, p. 127)

Grace is simply an explanation of a wonderful facet of the activity of God in you. It is not something to work for, to develop. It simply is. (Celebrate Yourself!, pp. 128-129)

To become recipients of that which the Father would bestow, we should take the element of grace into consideration; that even beyond what we ask, seek, earn, or deserve under the law, God is more than willing to give. (Charles Fillmore, *Keep a True Lent*, 2nd ed., Unity House, Unity Village, Mo., 2005, p. 38)

You do not have to earn grace. It is not something that comes only to the good. It comes to all alike, simply because all alike are expressions of God. (Celebrate Yourself!, p.128)

Grace—Good will; favor; disposition to show mercy; aid from God in the process of Regeneration. (The Revealing Word, p. 188)

The paradox of Law/Grace becomes a problem if one thinks solely based on Hebrew Scriptures, the Mosaic Law and a mechanical understanding of the Law of Cause and Effect as the supreme law, with no options or alternatives. This concept is illustrated in the words "eye for eye, tooth for tooth" (Ex. 21:24). Jesus brought a new consciousness of Divine Law. He acknowledged mechanical Law of Cause and Effect, while he knew it was possible to "fulfill the law" by transcending its strictly mechanical repetition. This is only accomplished by certain changes of consciousness. One of these changes is to let go of the insistence on "even exchanges" in life. Another change is to be willing to forgive sin (error) instead of insisting on punishment for sin.

The concept of Grace remains loaded with concepts and ideas that arise from the theological traditions in which we were raised. This is clearly discerned in the excerpts above that would lead one to believe that Grace is something bestowed upon us by a separate God. We do not have to earn it because we *are* It! "Grace" is the name given to the aspect of Divine Law that does not deal in even exchanges. Grace deals with the increase of good through greater giving; It is the unconditional Love of Divine Mind that "we" are and that is always available. Regardless of how negatively we may view ourselves because of what we perceive as our error thoughts, actions and omissions, and regardless of how unworthy we may feel of experiencing Divine Love, Divine Love is always present, always available, because Divine Ideas are always present. And from Divine Love, we can always change our minds and thereby change effects and outcomes. All that is necessary for us to experience Divine Love is our own willingness to become aware of Divine Ideas and change our minds.

SUMMARY STATEMENTS

▼ *Some of the ways we experience Divine Nature, or Oneness, may seem contradictory or paradoxical from our limited human perception.*

▼ *These apparent inconsistencies are not contradictions at all; rather, they are aspects of Divine Wholeness and Oneness.*

▼ *The key to understanding the concept of paradox is learning to acknowledge and accept the apparent opposites as being two aspects of one complete Idea. This can be accomplished through study, prayer and meditation (investing time in the Silence).*

▼ *We may experience Divine Nature as both eternal, immutable Principle as well as create an experience of Divine Nature, or Oneness, as a warm, loving Presence.*

▼ *We may acknowledge both the transcendence and the immanence of Divine Mind "indwelling" or underlying all of physical reality.*

▼ *We may understand Divine Mind as being both the masculine (father) and feminine (mother) principles of life.*

▼ *We may also experience Divine Mind as both unbreakable Law and unconditional Love (Grace)*

TOPICS FOR DISCUSSION

1. *What is your understanding of divine paradox?*

2. *Share a time in your life when you may have experienced Grace. Go into as much detail as you wish.*

THOUGHTS FOR REFLECTION AND MEDITATION

"God is an intelligible sphere whose centre is everywhere and whose circumference is nowhere."

—Corpus Hermeticum

SUPPLEMENTARY READING

Discover the Power Within You by Eric Butterworth, 40th Anniversary Edition, HarperOne, New York, 2008, Chapter 4, "Jesus' Unique Concept of God."

Talks on Truth by Charles Fillmore, Unity House, Unity Village, Mo., 1926, Chapter 1, "Reform Your God Thought."

CHAPTER THIRTEEN

THE TRINITY

INTRODUCTION

The traditional Trinity (God the Father, God the Son and God the Holy Spirit) has been meaningful to Christians in one way or another for centuries. To many individuals it signifies a great mystery. The Trinity of Father, Son and Holy Spirit represents the three primary creative aspects of Beingness that we interpret metaphysically as Mind, Idea and Expression.

In this chapter, we will explore the metaphysical implications of the Trinity so that we may better understand the creative process.

13A **THREE-IN-ONE**

THE HOLY TRINITY is known as the Father, the Son and the Holy Spirit. Metaphysically, we understand the Trinity to refer to mind, idea and expression, or thinker, thought and action. (Charles Fillmore, *Keep a True Lent*, 2nd ed., Unity House, Unity Village, Mo., 2005, p. 14)

Reducing the Trinity to simple numbers takes away much of its mystery. When we say that there is one Being with three attitudes of mind, we have stated in plain terms all that is involved in the intricate theological doctrine of the Trinity. (Charles Fillmore, *Christian Healing*, 2nd ed., Unity House, Unity Village, Mo., 2005, p. 20)

The key to the mystery of the Trinity is to remember that the terms Father (God), Son (the Christ) and Holy Spirit are not separate things, but simply three aspects of Oneness, or Divine Mind. The most practical value of understanding the Trinity is simply that it involves all the orderly energy sequences that result in manifestations, both desirable and undesirable.

Here is the progression of the "Three-In-One" concept from the "original Trinity" to the metaphysical Trinity:

Father - Son - Holy Spirit
God - Christ - Holy Spirit
Mind - Idea - Expression
(Consciousness)

13B FIRST IN THE TRINITY—FATHER, GOD, MIND

God is first in the Trinity. God is mind and is everywhere present. God is principle, law, Being, Spirit, All-Good, omnipotent, omniscient, omnipresent, unchangeable, Creator, Father, cause, and source of all that is. God as Spirit is forever accessible. (Keep a True Lent, p. 14)

First in the Trinity is God, the Absolute—the unlimited, unconditional, transcendent and immanent. God is Mind—Mind consists of and ideates Divine Ideas. Divine Mind includes all the descriptors, as presented in Chapter 10, and more. While in the excerpt above, Fillmore used the terms *omnipotent, omniscient* and *omnipresent*, a strong case was made elsewhere for the use of the terms *omnipotence, omniscience* and *omnipresence*. This adjustment shifts the meaning from Divine Mind *having* these qualities to Divine Mind *being* these qualities.

13C SECOND IN THE TRINITY—SON, THE CHRIST, IDEA

As the son is to the father, so is the idea to the mind. Mind is one with its ideas, so the Father—God Mind—is one with its offspring, the idea—the Son. (Keep a True Lent, p. 173)

An idea is the original, primary, or unlimited thought of Being: in God Mind, the eternal Word or Logos. (Keep a True Lent, p. 172)

Logos—The Word of God; the divine archetype idea that contains all ideas: the Christ, the Son of God, spiritual humankind in manifestation. (Charles Fillmore, The Revealing Word: A Dictionary of Metaphysical Terms, 2nd ed., Unity House, Unity Village, Mo., 2006, p. 123)

The Christ is God's divine idea of humankind, the embodiment of all divine ideas existing in the mind of Being. (Keep a True Lent, p. 10)

In every person the Christ, or the Word of God, is infolded; it is an idea that contains ideas. (Charles Fillmore, Keep a True Lent, 2nd ed., Unity House, Unity Village, Mo., 2005, p. 18)

In the beginning was the Word, and the Word was with God, and the Word was God. He was in the beginning with God. All things came into being through him, and without him not one thing came into being. What has come into being in him was life and the life was the light of all people. (Jn. 1:1-3)

The second aspect of the Trinity is the archetypical, composite Divine Idea that we refer to as the Word of God, the Logos, or the Christ Idea. In John 1, where the concept of Logos is most clearly explained, look closely at verse 3: "All things came into being through him, and without him not one thing came into being." Here is a mystical insight that suggests that through the activity of the Logos, or Christ, all that exists has come into manifestation. Each manifestation is a representation of the creative activity of the Logos. The passage extends into verse 4 with the words "what has come into being in him was life and the life was the light of all people." The activity of the Logos could then be seen as bringing forth into manifestation all of creation as well as the true-life energy of all people. Each person, in Truth, is the consciousness and the fundamental nature of the Divine, the Christ. This is what the Bible means when it says "So God created humankind in his image, in the image of God he created them" (Gen. 1:27).

13D THIRD IN THE TRINITY— HOLY SPIRIT, EXPRESSION

The Holy Spirit is the action or out-pouring or activity of the living Word. This activity produces what may be termed the light of Spirit, the breath of God, the "personality" of Being. (Charles Fillmore, *Mysteries of John,* 2nd ed., Unity House, Unity Village, Mo., 2008, p. 19)

The Holy Spirit is the activity of God-mind in the consciousness of man.

The long way, back to the Father's house is the way of experience; the short cut is being receptive and obedient to the leading of the Holy Spirit in thought word and deed, putting God first in your life. (Myrtle Fillmore, *How to Let God Help You,* p. 86)

The Holy Spirit is ... the whole Spirit of God in action. It is God's word in movement: the working, moving, breathing, brooding [in the sense of a hen setting on a nest, gestating] Spirit. ... The Holy Spirit is the law of God in action; in that action God appears as having individuality. It is the personality of Being. It is neither the all of Being nor the fullness of Christ, but is an emanation, or breath, sent forth to do a definite work. (Charles Fillmore, *Dynamics for Living: A Topical Compilation of Essential Fillmore Teachings,* Unity House, Unity Village, Mo., 1967, p. 39)

To be "filled with the Holy Spirit" is to realize the activities of Spirit in individual consciousness. (*The Revealing Word,* p. 98) *The work of the Holy Spirit is the executive power of Father (mind) and Son (idea), carrying out the creative plan. It is through the help of the Holy Spirit that humankind overcomes. The Holy Spirit reveals, helps and directs in this overcoming.* (Charles Fillmore, *Atom-Smashing Power of Mind,* 2nd ed., Unity House, Unity Village, Mo., 2006, p. 38)

This third aspect of the Trinity refers to the creative activity or the "whole Spirit of God" from which we experience and express Divine Potential in ever-increasing ways. The Holy Spirit is not an entity or person; It is sometimes thought of as the movement of God, or Divine Mind. The Holy Spirit is expression. The Holy Spirit is the term we give to our experience of the activity or expression of Divine Mind at the point of our own awareness. The Holy Spirit is like the wind: While we cannot see the wind we certainly do experience it and we can witness what it does. We may experience this activity as the comforter, guidance, the "still small voice" and the like. As we recognize and live from the awareness of Oneness, or Mind-Idea-Expression, our own expressions become more nearly the expressions of the Divine Mind.

13E UNDERSTANDING THE METAPHYSICAL TRINITY

The Holy Trinity is known as the Father, the Son and the Holy Spirit. Metaphysically, we understand the Trinity to refer to mind, idea and expression. (*Keep a True Lent,* p. 14)

God is the name of the all-encompassing Mind. Christ is the name of the all-loving Mind. Holy Spirit is the all-active manifestation. These three are one fundamental Mind in its three creative aspects. (Charles Fillmore, *Jesus*

Christ Heals, 2nd ed., Unity House, Unity Village, Mo., 1940, p 63)

... there is one underlying law and that through this law all things come into expression; also that there is one universal Mind, the source and sole origin of all real intelligence. First is mind, then mind expresses itself in ideas, then the ideas make themselves manifest. This is a metaphysical statement of the divine Trinity, Father, Son and Holy Spirit. (*Jesus Christ Heals,* pp. 121-122)

If you would know the mystery of Being, see yourself in Being. Know yourself as an integral idea in Divine Mind and all other ideas will recognize you as their fellow worker. Throw yourself out of the Holy Trinity and you become an onlooker. Throw yourself into the Trinity and you become its avenue of expression. (*Christian Healing,* p. 20)

The Trinity describes the reality of the creative process by which a Divine Idea is manifested first in consciousness and then in physicality. The metaphysical interpretation of the Trinity is symbolic of the process whereby invisible and formless Divine Ideas of Absolute Mind become manifest: Mind-Idea-Expression/mind-idea-expression.

We are always using the Trinity to manifest in consciousness as well as in the physical, relative realm. This is because the Trinity, Mind-Idea-Expression/mind-idea-expression, is the universal process by which everything comes into existence. It is one way to define the creative process. Unity co-founder Charles Fillmore also defined this orderly process as "Divine Order" Even though the outcomes may not be so divine.

What we manifest is determined by our seeming individual level of consciousness. Through prayer and meditation, we become increasingly aware of our innate Christ Nature and thereby utilize Divine Ideas at the highest possible levels of consciousness. When we remain in sense consciousness, we utilize the same Divine Ideas and the same process except that it is now from a diminished, limited level of consciousness resulting in outcomes that may be good, bad or ugly.

SUMMARY STATEMENTS

▼ *In Unity, we acknowledge the threefold nature of Divine Mind, or God, and interpret the* Trinity *metaphysically as Mind-Idea-Expression/mind-idea-expression. We refer to this Trinity of Divine Mind as* the creative process.

▼ *First in the Trinity is* Mind—the Absolute, *transcendent and immanent Divine Mind.*

▼ *Second in the Trinity is the* Divine Idea *or Word of God, Logos. It is the aspect of Divine Mind that is the Spiritual Essence, or Fundamental Nature, that is inherent in and underlies everything.*

▼ *Third in the Trinity is* Expression—*The Holy Spirit is our experience of the activity or expression of Divine Mind at the point of our own awareness. We can experience that activity as the comforter, guidance, the "still small voice," and the like.*

▼ *When we speak of the Trinity, we are not referring to three separate beings but* three ways of acknowledging Beingness, *or Divine Mind.*

▼ *We are* always using the Trinity *to manifest in consciousness as well as in the physical, relative realm. This is because the Trinity, Mind-Idea-Expression/mind-idea-expression, is the universal process by which everything comes into existence.*

TOPICS FOR DISCUSSION

1. *What is the purpose of recognizing God as threefold Beingness?*

2. *How does Unity's interpretation of "Son" differ from that of traditional Christianity? How is it similar?*

THOUGHTS FOR REFLECTION AND MEDITATION

"The first chapter [of Genesis] shows two parts of the Trinity: mind, and idea in mind. In the second chapter we have the third part, manifestation. In this illustration all theological mystery about the Trinity is cleared away, for we see that it is simply mind, idea in mind, and manifestation of idea. Since humankind is the offspring of God, made in the image and likeness of Divine Mind, people must express themselves under the laws of this great creative Mind. The law of manifestation for humankind is the law of thought. God ideates: humankind thinks. One is the completion of the other in mind."

(*Mysteries of Genesis*, p. 12)

SUPPLEMENTARY READING

Keep a True Lent by Charles Fillmore, 2nd ed., Unity House, Unity Village, Mo., 2005, Chapter 2, "The Holy Trinity."

CHAPTER FOURTEEN

SIN, EVIL AND THE DEVIL

INTRODUCTION

Divine Mind is Absolute Good. By "Absolute" we mean unchanged, unchanging and unchangeable as well as without opposite. The concept of Good was gleaned from scripture where Jesus said, "Why do you call me good? No one is good but God alone" (Mark 10:18). This is a statement of Good without opposite. Furthermore, we acknowledge that Spiritual Humankind, made in the image and likeness of God, is therefore Good. When we say "image and likeness" we do not mean *form* since Divine Mind is Spirit. Therefore, Spiritual Humankind, in its Essence, is Spirit. Where, then, does evil come from? Who creates it? Why does it seem so powerful?

In this chapter, we explore the exact origin and nature of evil as well as the meaning of sin and its consequences. We will also consider what part our free will plays in the manifestation of sin and evil. As we develop a clearer understanding of the specific cause of sin and evil, we will gain a greater ability to transform their effects on our lives. When we realize that sin and evil are not independent powers outside of ourselves, we can approach them from a standpoint of spiritual strength and poise. Evil is not an enemy we have to constantly fear and fight; it is to be overcome by healing our sense of separation and withdrawing the power we give it.

14A ORIGIN OF SIN AND EVIL

Humankind came out of God, is of the same mind elements, and exists within the mind of God always. Yet by thinking that one is separate from omnipresent Spirit the person has set up a mental state of apartness from his or her source and dwells in ignorance of that which is nearer than hands and feet. (Charles and Cora Fillmore,

Teach Us to Pray, 2nd ed., Unity House, Unity Village, Mo., 2007, p. 160)

By and through the imaging power of thought people can produce illusions that confuse them. This occurs only when they fail to look to Divine Mind for the source and nature of their ideals. Obviously, many are deceived into thinking that they are indeed bound, and the unhappy conditions claimed do show forth in them. This is only consciousness entangled in its own effects. (Charles Fillmore, Keep a True Lent, 2nd ed., Unity House, Unity Village, Mo., 2005, pp. 63-64)

While collective consciousness and individual consciousness exist in Divine Mind, what we perceive as sin and evil does not originate in Divine Mind in Its absolute state. They exist because humankind persists in thinking, feeling and believing in separation from Spirit; this sense of separation is the source of sin and evil. From our sense of separation, we can choose to identify with negative emotions and concepts of ourselves that are lies and illusions, resulting in error thinking, sin and evil. We become entangled in our own effects, first in seeming separate consciousness and then in form.

14B ORIGINAL SIN/ORIGINAL SINLESSNESS (GOODNESS)

Adam in his original creation was in spiritual illumination. Spirit breathed into him continually the necessary inspiration and knowledge to give him superior understanding. But he began eating, or appropriating, ideas of two powers—God and not God, or good and evil. The result, so the allegory relates, was that he fell away from spiritual life and all that it involves. (Charles Fillmore, Metaphysical Bible Dictionary, Unity House, Unity Village, Mo., 1931, p. 23)

Figs, or fig trees, are a symbol of prosperity. Figs are also representative of the seed of humanity. This seed in its original essence is mind energy, and when ideas are related purely to Divine Mind the seed of humanity is the life stream in its original purity. Humankind's original sin is the misappropriation of ideas, which leads to sensation. ... Humankind does not realize the richness of the Christ possibilities that are unfolding within, however, until a person begins uplifting and spiritualizing his or her entire being. ... Until then the inner riches are concealed from that person. If the inner substance and the life that are all the time increasing in consciousness are misappropriated by the individual in fulfillment of carnal desire, inharmonies result. (Metaphysical Bible Dictionary, p. 41)

The whole secret of the demonstration of Christ is that we shall come to realize our original sinlessness. Sin and the consciousness of sin are the cause of all darkness and death. (Charles Fillmore, *Talks on Truth,* Unity House, Unity Village, Mo., 1926, pp. 154-155)

In addition to a definite set of teachings on sin, evil and the devil, Unity has its own view of original sin and sinlessness. Metaphysically, we all have the capacity for original sin in the sense that we can choose, moment by moment, to make the same error(s) as Adam in the biblical allegory. We can and do choose to put limitations upon Divine Ideas, engage in error thinking and the misuse of Divine Ideas. More important, Unity teachings center on original sinlessness, our original Goodness. This belief is based on scripture that states humankind is created in the image and likeness of God (Gen. 1:26 KJV) and that God pronounced humankind Good (Gen. 1:31 KJV). Our opportunity, then, is to turn away from error and embrace Goodness.

14C FREE WILL, SIN AND EVIL

All experience develops personal identity—the consciousness of the powers of Being in the self. This is the bringing forth of free will, which is inherent in all. (Charles Fillmore, *Christian Healing,* 2nd ed., Unity House, Unity Village, Mo., 2005, p. 55)

It is possible for humankind to form states of consciousness that are out of harmony with the God principle, but these do not endure, and through experience we learn to adjust our thought to that of God. ... When we understand this ego-forming capacity of humankind and even of nature, we have the key that unlocks the many mysteries and contradictions that appear in every walk of life. (Charles Fillmore, *The Revealing Word: A Dictionary of Metaphysical Terms,* 2nd ed., Unity House, Unity Village, Mo., 2006, pp. 18-19)

Freedom of choice (in how to think and feel, what to believe, and how to react) gives us a unique place in what we currently know and understand about the universe. Misuse of the freedom of thought, feeling, belief and will is the mainspring of our continuous sojourns into sin, evil and useless, unnecessary suffering (hell). We generate the experience of our own heaven or hell. We may continue to blame Divine Mind for creating heaven and hell, but Divine Mind is simply the source of Divine Ideas, and we have the freedom to use those Divine Ideas in any manner we choose.

14D **SIN**

Missing the mark; that is, falling short of divine perfection. Sin is human-kind's failure to express the attributes of Being—life, love, intelligence, wisdom and the other God qualities. (*The Revealing Word,* p. 179)

Sin is simply the concealment of humankind's son-of-God self. The sin is the changing experience, the failure to express the whole, the divine poten-tial, the changeless reality. (Eric Butterworth, *Celebrate Yourself! and Other Inspirational Essays*, Unity House, Unity Village, Mo., 1984, p. 132)

What theology calls a lost soul is a soul that has lost sight of God's omnipres-ence. … The act of ignorance is the act of sin. (Imelda Octavia Shanklin, *What Are You?*, 2nd ed., Unity House, Unity Village, Mo., 2004, p. 9)

Transgression of the law brings its own punishment. We are not punished for our sins but by them. (*Keep a True Lent*, p. 32)

The New Testament word for sin (*amartia* in Greek) literally means to "miss the mark." An archer may use the same word if he or she missed the bull's eye. While this may seem like a surprisingly benign meaning, it does accurately describe the resulting con-dition of sin, which is a lack of our awareness of perfection.

Sin is failing to accurately identify the True Good; it is also failing to accu-rately assess the consequences of our action or nonaction. Sin results from forgetting Oneness and our Divine Nature. Sin is attempting to negate, distort or limit any Divine idea. We forget What we are (Christ, the Idea that contains Ideas) every time we look to the manifest world using sense or personal consciousness as the source of information and understand-ing. Each of us is capable of becoming distracted and fascinated with the senses, personal power and immediate pleasures we have manifested in the visible realm. We can entangle our-selves in our own effects, resulting in a sense of separation from Divine Source.

14E **SINS OF OMISSION AND COMMISSION**

All the ills of humanity are the effect of broken law, of sin. That word "sin" cov-ers more ground than we have usually granted it. There are sins of omission and commission. If we fail to cultivate the consciousness of the indwelling spiritual life, we commit a sin of omis-sion that eventually devitalizes the organism. (Charles Fillmore, *Jesus Christ Heals*, 2nd ed., Unity House, Unity Village, Mo., 1940, p. 17)

Omission and commission are two methods used to sin (negate, severely limit and/or distort any Divine Ideas):

Sins of omission have an intentional quality. A sin of omission is when we know the righteous thing to do and choose not to do it because we're too committed to an old way of thinking or too lazy to change. It could be called a kind of mental laziness. Sometimes we are unaware or unconcerned about Divine Ideas and their Source. We ignore them, do nothing to learn about them or neglect to experience them.

Sins of commission occur when we are actually very aware of Divine Ideas, Principles and their Source and actively pervert Divine Ideas into harm-causing expressions. They also happen when we choose to satisfy selfishness, cruelty or any negative impulses arising out of sense or personal consciousness and feelings of separation.

An innocent mistake is not a sin. There is no intention to err or misuse Divine Ideas in making a mistake. A mistake may be committed out of pure ignorance of Divine Ideas, Principles and Laws.

14F **EVIL**

That which is not of God; unreality; error thought; a product of the fallen human consciousness; negation. Evil is a parasite. It has no permanent life of itself; its whole existence depends on the life it borrows from its parent, and when its connection with the parent is severed nothing remains. … Apparent evil is the result of ignorance, and when Truth is presented the error disappears. (The Revealing Word, p. 64)

We should not assume that all manifestation is good because the originating idea came from Divine Mind. All ideas have their foundation in Divine Mind, but humankind has put the limitation of his or her negative thought upon them, and sees them "in a mirror, darkly." (Christian Healing, p. 45)

Evil has no permanent or independent existence of its own. Sin and evil result from people using limited beliefs, thoughts, attitudes, feelings and behaviors. In our context, they refer to something being "against" Spiritual Truth and Divine Ideas. Therefore, sin and evil refer to any human *attempt* to negate, severely limit and/or distort any Divine Idea. Evil can be thought of as "sustained sin" or error thinking.

The excerpts above refute the commonly held notion that "it's all God and it's all Good" when the phrase is used to include the relative realm, the realm of thought forms, human feelings and matter. Here, Charles Fillmore clearly makes a distinction between Divine Ideas that are eternally Absolute Good and what we do with them from our limited consciousness. Clearly, all manifestation is not

God and all manifestation is not good. If they were, Myrtle Fillmore would have had no reason to rid herself of her physical ailments.

14G SATAN AND THE DEVIL

In the course of our demonstrations of Being, we arrive at the place where we feel our own ability, and we know that we can exercise it without restraint. "Satan" is the personal mind that tempts humankind to try experience without knowledge. (Christian Healing, pp. 55-56)

Devil—The mass of thoughts that has been built up in human collective consciousness through many generations of earthly experiences and crystallized into what may be termed human personality, or carnal mind, which opposes and rejects God. The "devil" is a state of consciousness adverse to the divine good. ... There is no personal devil. God is the one omnipresent Principle of the universe, and there is no room for any principle of evil, personified or otherwise. (The Revealing Word, p. 54)

Both "Satan" and "the devil" as literal personifications of evil or entities are not part of Unity theology. The devil is a biblical symbol, not a creature that has an independent existence. It is a part of human nature that arises from sense consciousness.

Satan and the devil are valid as metaphysical symbols that represent aspects of our own consciousness that place the human personality (ego) as sovereign in our lives. The devil is a personified symbol of a human tendency toward negativity. In addition to our seeming individual consciousness, there is also a collective phenomenon of the human consciousness (the devil) that can appear to exert considerable influence on the relative plane of existence. However, Satan and the devil have no existence in Spiritual Principle. Sin, evil, Satan and the devil only have the power that we give to them collectively and individually; when we withdraw the power, they will cease to exist.

14H TEMPTATION

We do not encourage those who still have worldly ambitions to take up the development of the twelve powers. You will be disappointed if you seek to use these superpowers to gain money (turn stones into bread), control others ("the kingdoms of the world ... All these things will I give thee"), or make a display of your power ("If thou art the Son of God, cast thyself down"). As recorded in the fourth chapter of Matthew, these are the temptations of the selfish ego which Jesus had to overcome and which all who follow him "in the regeneration" have to overcome.

(Charles and Cora Fillmore, *The Twelve Powers,* Unity House, Unity Village, Mo., 1999, p. 6)

Temptations arise from that level of human nature sometimes called Satan. Tempter, the devil, false personality, egotism, exaggerated sense of self and "me and mine" are other names sometimes used for Satan. When impulses arising from this level reach conscious self-awareness, there is the "moment of temptation," a choice point. Each person has an opportunity to succumb to selfish temptations and lose out, or empower awareness from Christ Nature to overcome the temptation and gain something truly substantial. Each person makes a choice as to whether the personality (ego) or the Individuality (Christ Nature) informs the decision. Each one of us decides from which perspective a decision will be made.

14| REPENTANCE

True repentance means the changing of the mind and all its contents of error belief. (Charles Fillmore, *Mysteries of Genesis,* 2nd ed., Unity House, Unity Village, Mo., 1998, p 340)

True repentance is always followed by forgiveness, which is a complete wiping out of the error thought from consciousness and a full deliverance from the inharmony that the error thought has produced. (Mysteries of Genesis, p. 337)

A turning from a belief in sin and error to a belief in God and righteousness; a reversal of mind and heart in the direction of the All-Good. When we repent, we break with mortal thought and ascend into a spiritual thought realm, the kingdom of God. (The Revealing Word, p. 167)

Sin is a falling short of the divine law, and repentance and forgiveness are the only means that humankind has of getting out of sin and its effect and coming into harmony with the law. ... All sin is first in mind; and the forgiveness is a change of mind or repentance. Some mental attitude, some train of mental energy, must be transformed. We forgive sin in ourselves every time we resolve to think and act according to the divine law. The mind must change from a material to a spiritual base. (Jesus Christ Heals, pp. 58-59)

In overcoming sin, we must choose to let go of error beliefs or transform them so that they reflect the Truth more fully. Even if we have given into temptation, we can always choose again. We can turn from the temptation of the personality to the All-Good, or Divine Mind. Such a correction of our thoughts and feelings enables us to free ourselves from our errors and their consequences. This correction or change of mind concerning some negative mental attitude or train of mental energy is repentance. Furthermore, repentance and *forgiveness* are related, since both repentance and forgiveness involve changing the mind and wiping out error. Forgiveness deals with the change in mind in a certain instance or situation; repentance deals with a more global change of mind and attitude.

14J HELL

People therefore contain within themselves the capacities of Being, and through their words use the creative principle in forming their environment, good or bad. So we make our own heaven or hell. (Charles Fillmore, *Mysteries of John,* 2nd ed., Unity House, Unity Village, Mo., 2008, p. 76)

The fact is that everybody has a soul to save, not from the hypothetical hell after death, but from the sins and the delusions of the sense consciousness that make hell here and now. (*Talks on Truth,* pp. 139-140)

Hell is not a geographic location; hell is a state of consciousness. It results from maintaining beliefs in lack, limitation, loss and pain. Hell is the experience of suffering which we cannot explain or know how to overcome in that moment. In other words, hell is a state of mind that ultimately reflects our sense of separation from the Source of our Good.

14K HELL AS A PURIFYING PROCESS

We have come to think of hell as a sort of reaping what has been sown—not a punishment, but rather a cleansing and purifying process which results in the individual's being brought to face his or her mistakes and being set free from them and their effects. The work of Spirit is thorough, and lasts until we measure up to the Jesus Christ standard of life. So long as there is that in us which needs the refining fire of Spirit, we may be sure we can receive its benefits. (Myrtle Fillmore, *How to Let God Help You,* 4th ed., compiled by Warren Meyer, Unity House, Unity Village, Mo., 2006, p. 54)

We understand hell to be a purifying process, which the soul goes through, to rid it of dross and weakness. The word hell is derived from a word which was used to denote a city incinerator in a valley outside of Jerusalem. Use of the incinerator was a health measure, a means of taking care of the trash of the city. We feel that the Scripture writers were trying to make clear to us the way in which the purifying fire of Spirit continues its work in us until we are free from all that does not measure up to the Christ standard. It is for our good, and does not harm us, except we resist it or do not make the effort to give up and to avoid that which caused the undesirable condition of soul, body or affairs. (How to Let God Help You, p. 64)

Do not brood on things which stir up strife. If it seems that you are in hell, just know that there is a stairway leading from hell to heaven. When there is nothing in you to require the purifying fires, you will rise on the very spiritual atmosphere you have created into a beautiful new realm of life. (How to Let God Help You, p. 58)

This section relates directly back to section 14I on repentance. Our experience of the state of mind called "hell" can be used to begin a corrective, purifying process; otherwise, it is a state of needless and useless suffering. When we realize that our suffering is a result of our error beliefs, we can choose to release those beliefs and remember the Source of our Good, Divine Mind; this is how we emerge from hell. We remain in the hell experience until we choose *heaven consciousness*.

14L HEAVEN

Heaven is everywhere present. It is the orderly, lawful adjustment of God's kingdom in humankind's mind, body and affairs; ... a state of consciousness in harmony with the thoughts of God. Heaven is within every one of us; a place, a conscious sphere of mind, having all the attractions described or imagined as belonging to heaven. (Keep a True Lent, p. 177)

The Kingdom of Heaven is *within consciousness* and is therefore a state of consciousness. It results from our perpetually aligning our thoughts and feelings in and from Divine Ideas such as Life, Love, Order and Wisdom. Such a state of consciousness produces experiences of limitless Good in all areas of our lives.

SUMMARY STATEMENTS

▼ *In Unity, we do not believe that <u>evil</u> exists in Divine Mind or that it has an independent existence.*

▼ *<u>Sin</u> is the result of forgetting Oneness and our Divine Nature. We define sin as "missing the mark" or "falling short of our divine potential."*

▼ *<u>Sins of omission</u> occur when we are indifferent about Divine Ideas and their Source.*

▼ _Sins of commission_ occur when we actively try to pervert Divine Ideas into harm-causing expressions based on sense or personal consciousness and feelings of separation.

▼ _Evil_ originates in _human consciousness_ as a result of the freedom of thought. It is "sustained error."

▼ _Sin and evil_ are the misuse and the negation of Divine Ideas.

▼ _"Satan"_ and "the _devil_" are not literal personifications but metaphysical symbols that represent aspects of the human consciousness in need of transformation.

▼ _Satan_ is the personal mind that tempts humankind to try experience without knowledge.

▼ _The devil_ is "the mass of thoughts that has been built up in race consciousness through many generations of earthly experiences and crystallized into what may be termed human personality, or carnal mind, which opposes and rejects God."

▼ _Temptation_ is when a situation arises where we consciously realize we can choose to act out of personality or out of Individuality.

▼ _Repentance_ and forgiveness are a changing of the mind from error belief to the belief in Divine Mind.

▼ _Heaven_ and _hell_ are not geographic locations; they are states of consciousness.

▼ _Hell_ represents the suffering we experience as the effects of sin and evil. It occurs when we feel a sense of separation from the Source of all Good, Divine Mind.

▼ _Hell_ can be used to begin a corrective, purifying process; otherwise, it is a state of needless and useless suffering.

▼ _Heaven_ is a state of consciousness that is an expanded awareness in harmony with Divine Ideas in Divine Mind.

TOPICS FOR DISCUSSION

1. *If Divine Mind is Absolute Good, why is there evil in the world?*

2. *Define Unity's understanding of Satan and the devil.*

3. *Share your understanding of heaven and hell. Have you ever experienced either of these states of consciousness in your life? Explain.*

THOUGHTS FOR REFLECTION AND MEDITATION

"We don't say that all is evil; that would be mental suicide. We just say it is a 'goat thought.' We do not kill it but transform it. After separating our innocent sheep thoughts, we begin to have fine, high, discriminating judgment."

(Charles Fillmore, *Atom-Smashing Power of Mind*, 2nd ed., Unity House, Unity Village, Mo., 2006, p. 46)

SUPPLEMENTARY READING

Discover the Power Within You by Eric Butterworth, 40th anniversary edition, HarperOne, New York, 2008, Chapter 5, "From Miserable Sinners to Masters."

Know Thyself by Richard Lynch, Unity House, Unity Village, Mo., 1935, Chapter 5, "The Problem of Evil."

CHAPTER FIFTEEN

JESUS, THE CHRIST, JESUS CHRIST, CHRIST JESUS

INTRODUCTION

To more fully comprehend the nature of Jesus Christ, we must interpret his identity metaphysically. If Jesus Christ is truly to function as our Way Shower and supreme model for living the enlightened life, we must be able to discern the elements of his nature that we share in common. The reality of the historical/physical person must be distinguished from the reality of his Universal/Spiritual Essence, Christ. The purpose of this chapter is to provide insight into the basic components that constitute the nature of this illumined individual.

15A **JESUS**

The Man of Nazareth ... Jesus was keenly conscious of the character of God and his own relationship to God. He knew God as unlimited love and as ever-present, abundant life; he knew God as wisdom and supply. He knew God as Father, who is ever ready and willing to supply every need of the human heart. (Charles Fillmore, *The Revealing Word: A Dictionary of Metaphysical Terms*, 2nd ed., Unity House, Unity Village, Mo., 2006, p.111)

He (Jesus) was man on the quest, man making the great discovery of His divinity, man breaking through the psychological barrier between man and God, man proving the Christ in man and his inherent potential for overcoming, for eternal life. (Eric Butterworth, *Discover the Power Within You*, 40th Anniversary Edition, HarperOne, New York, 2008, p.20)

Jesus was himself a parable. His life was an allegory of the experiences that each person passes through in developing from natural to spiritual con-

sciousness. (Charles Fillmore, *Christian Healing*, 2nd ed., Unity House, Unity Village, Mo., 2005, p. 74)

Jesus is the name of the personality. To the metaphysical Christian—that is, to the person who studies the spiritual human—Christ is the name of the supermind and Jesus is the name of the personal consciousness. (Charles Fillmore, *Jesus Christ Heals*, 2nd ed., Unity House, Unity Village, Mo., 1940, p. 10)

"Jesus" is the name of the historical person, the man who was born in Bethlehem and lived in Nazareth and who became our Way Shower. Jesus became aware of the Christ Nature within consciousness that he called the Father. He had a body and a personality just like the rest of humanity.

Metaphysically, Jesus is that aspect of every person which first realizes that he or she is more than a body or a personality. It also discerns that his or her True Nature is Christ Nature and understands the use of the Christ Principle. Jesus represents that part of everyone that is the energy, the wisdom and the understanding to bring forth all that the Christ Potential is. "Jesus is the unfolding and the developing of all the qualities or ideas of Christ. ... Jesus stands for the individual unfoldment and evolution of the Christ." (*Foundations of Unity*, Series Two, Vol. 1, Unity House, Unity Village, Mo., 1973, p. 96)

15B THE CHRIST

Christ abides in each person as ... potential perfection. ... Each person has the Christ Idea within, just as Jesus had. Each person must look to the indwelling Christ in order to recognize ... their divine origin and birth. (*The Revealing Word*, p. 34)

"Christ" is not a person. It is not *Jesus. Christ is a degree of stature that Jesus attained, but a degree of potential stature that dwells in every man.* (*Discover the Power Within You*, p. 12)

Christ in you is your hope of glory, for it is that of you that is of God and is God being projected into visibility as you. Christ in you is your own spiritual unity with the Infinite, the key to your health and success. (*Discover the Power Within You*, p. 45)

In every person the Christ, or the Word of God, is infolded; it is an idea that contains ideas. (Charles Fillmore, *Keep a True Lent*, 2nd ed., Unity House, Unity Village, Mo., 2005, p. 18)

Christ is the pattern, the Divine Idea in Divine Mind for the Spiritual Human; Christ is the Idea that contains Ideas. We speak of Christ as a kind of divine composite: It is Principle, a Divine Idea, a Spiritual Pattern and Spirit. It is the name of the Perfect Pattern of Wholeness that is present in everything. The Christ within consciousness is our True

Essence and our Divine Nature. It is the presence of Divine Mind within consciousness. It is What we really are.

15C JESUS CHRIST

Jesus Christ is a union of the two, the idea and the expression, or in other words, He is the perfect human demonstrated. (The Revealing Word, p. 112)

Jesus Christ, metaphysically, is the perfect fulfillment in humankind that is manifested as the result of the conscious union of the Christ Idea and the Jesus activity in the human consciousness. (Foundations of Unity, Series Two, Vol. 1, p. 96)

The Way would be more difficult for most of us without the Way Shower, for in Him we find the embodiment of what all people truly are and are to be. (Ernest C. Wilson, The Emerging Self, Unity House, Unity Village, Mo., 1970, pp. 56-57)

To say that we are human as Jesus Christ was a human is not exactly true, because He had dropped that personal consciousness by which we separate ourselves from our true God self. ... He proved in His resurrection and ascension that He had no consciousness separate from that of Being, therefore He really was this Being to all intents and purposes. (Charles Fillmore, Atom-Smashing Power of Mind, 2nd ed.,

Unity House, Unity Village, Mo., 2006, pp. 40-41)

Jesus Christ's real name is Jehovah, I AM. The personal man Jesus is merely the veil of mask worn by the spiritual man Christ or Jehovah. We are all, in our personality, wearing the mask that conceals the real, the spiritual, I AM. Jesus shattered that mask and revealed the spiritual man. He also taught the way by which we may all do what He did and thus fulfill the destiny implanted in us by the parent mind. (Jesus Christ Heals, p. 157)

"Jesus Christ" is the name that identifies the individual who perfectly understood his Divine Nature, who fully demonstrated his Divine Potential. Spirit, or Christ Nature, was expressed to Its fullness in him. And when we speak of Jesus Christ, we are simply speaking of the one who revealed Christ through a human form and a human existence. Jesus Christ as our elder brother, teacher and Way Shower, who, by his words and works, teaches us that we, too, have the ability to manifest our own Christ Potential. When we say Jesus *the* Christ, we are intentionally acknowledging that Christ is the name of Jesus' Spiritual Identity, not his earthly last name. Similarly, Christ is also our own Spiritual Identity.

Metaphysically, Jesus Christ represents the union of the Christ Idea and our own potential to manifest the Christ Idea.

Jesus Christ differs from us in that he completely eliminated the mask of personality.

15D CHRIST JESUS

Christ is the divine-idea man. Jesus is the name that represents an individual expression of the Christ Idea. Jesus Christ is the form of the name that is commonly applied to the man of Galilee who demonstrated perfection. Christ Jesus is the idea that is being expressed by individuals as the result of their faith in and understanding of Truth. (The Revealing Word, p. 102)

He [Jesus] has not left us or gone to some faraway heaven, but he may be reached by the humblest of us in a moment's time, if we really aspire in soul for his companionship and help. This is a simple statement of the relation that Jesus of Nazareth bears to us. Yet he was more than Jesus of Nazareth, more than any other human who ever lived on the earth. He was more than human, as we understand the appellation in its everyday use, because there came into his humanness a factor to which most people are strangers. This factor was the Christ consciousness. The unfoldment of this consciousness by Jesus made Him God incarnate, because Christ is the mind

of God individualized, and whoever so loses his or her personality as to be swallowed up in God becomes Christ Jesus, or God man. (Charles Fillmore, Talks on Truth, Unity House, Unity Village, Mo., 1926, p.169)

The Christ within consciousness is our True Essence, our Divine Nature. It is Divine Mind individualized. Jesus is that aspect of every person which understands the use of the Christ Principle, the pattern of perfection. Jesus metaphysically represents that aspect of everyone that is the energy and the understanding to bring forth all that is in the Christ Potential. When we remember these truths with Faith and Understanding, we can then express the Christ; Christ Jesus is the Idea that is being expressed and underlies this expression. We metaphysically and metaphorically "become" Christ Jesus, or Divine Human, when we free ourselves from personality and live exclusively from the Christ Consciousness that we have always been in potential.

Over time, an additional interpretation of Christ Jesus has emerged. This interpretation holds that Christ Jesus is the Ascended Jesus. This Ascended Presence can be our guide and teacher.

15E ATONEMENT

The mind of each individual may be consciously unified with Divine Mind through the indwelling Christ. By affirming at-one-ment with God Mind, we eventually realize the perfect mind which was in Christ Jesus. (Keep a True Lent, p. 178)

Reconciliation between God and humankind through Christ; the uniting of our consciousness with the higher consciousness. (The Revealing Word, p. 18)

Atonement is the spiritual experience in which we as individuals participate in the awareness of conscious Oneness. Though Jesus Christ did not accomplish this *for* us, he showed us by his life and teachings exactly the steps we must take to enter into this state of consciousness. Each individual must come into awareness of Divine Mind through Christ consciousness. By affirming Oneness, we eventually achieve "the mind which was in Christ Jesus."

15F FIRST AND SECOND COMING

The first coming is the receiving of Truth into the conscious mind, and the Second Coming is the awakening and the regeneration of the subconscious mind through the superconscious or Christ Mind. (Talks on Truth, p. 15)

The second coming of Christ is not a point in time but a point in the growth of an individual's consciousness. It is a personal matter, not a group matter. Christ will come out of the depth of your own being when you recognize the presence of your own divinity. And Christ will come into your world through your expression of your divinity. (James E. Sweaney, Practical Christianity for You, Unity House, Unity Village, Mo., 1956, p. 45)

The first and second comings are interpreted metaphysically. We do not expect the physical re-entry of Jesus into the earth plane. The first coming is the coming into awareness of Truth in our conscious mind. The second coming is the awakening and regeneration of the subconscious mind through the Superconscious Mind. This results in our spiritual transformation through the full realization of the Christ Mind within consciousness.

15G SALVATION

Our salvation is in our living by the Christ pattern—not only by the teachings of the man Jesus Christ but by the Christ Mind within us. (Myrtle Fillmore, How to Let God Help You, 3rd ed., Unity House, Unity Village, Mo., 2000, p. 57)

Humankind's salvation from sin, sickness, pain, and death comes by their understanding and conforming to the orderly Mind back of all existence. (*Christian Healing*, p. 42)

"God so loved the world, that he gave his only begotten Son, that whosoever believeth on him should not perish, but have eternal life." This does not mean that a personal man, named Jesus of Nazareth, was sent forth as a special propitiation for the sins of the world, or that the only available route into God's presence lies through such a person. It simply means that God has provided a way by which all humankind may come consciously into God's presence in their own souls. That way is through the only begotten child of God, the Christ consciousness, which Jesus demonstrated. (Charles and Cora Fillmore, *The Twelve Powers,* Unity House, Unity Village, Mo., 1999, p. 118)

Salvation is a process that takes place within our own consciousness, not through the person named Jesus. In addition to living by the teachings and example of the man Jesus Christ, individuals must live by and from the Christ Mind within consciousness. This requires an understanding of the Divine Mind that underlies all existence. Individuals must conform to this Divine Mind in order to achieve their own spiritual transformation just as Jesus did. Salvation results in our being made free *from* ignorance, lack and limitation, and in being made

free *for* wholeness, abundance, peace and fulfillment.

A change of consciousness from literalism and selfishness into spiritual understanding is the salvation taught in Unity. It is the result of individual effort. As individual consciousness rises, so does collective consciousness.

The first effort of an individual is a matter of choice; it engages the thinking and feeling natures: Does the person want it or not? This is followed by:

(1) The desire to realize Oneness or Divine Mind.

(2) The study and application of metaphysical Truth Principles, especially through prayer and meditation, that leads to resting in the Silence and the realization of Truth.

(3) The forgiveness and repentance of sins (the giving up of error thought, repentance—a change of mind).

15H FOLLOWING JESUS

Jesus continually identified himself with and as the Son, and not with the limitations of personality. For he said, "I am the Son of God." This constant identification with God was the secret of his power and of his success in overcoming all adverse conditions, including death, for he thus appropriated in his own consciousness the presence, power, and light of the God Mind. He demonstrated the highest type of embodiment. He is the standard for every individual to follow. (*Foundations of Unity,* Series Two, Vol. 1, p. 97)

It is no idle experiment, this keeping in the mind the words of Jesus. It is a very momentous undertaking and may mark the most important period in the life of an individual. There must be sincerity and earnestness and right motive, and with all a determination to understand the spiritual import. This requires attention, time and patience in the application of the mind to solving the deeper meanings of the sayings that we are urged to keep. (*Talks on Truth,* p. 174)

The language used in the first quotation portrays the traditional image of a child and parent. Since Divine Mind is Spirit, not a person, entity or being, we must keep reminding ourselves that the use of traditional images is metaphorical language. In order to truly "follow" Jesus, we are to proceed on the path of spiritual enlightenment in the ways that he taught us. It is not worshipping the man; it is walking the way of mastery he demonstrated and fulfilling our responsibility to "follow" him. We must constantly identify ourselves by claiming our Christ Nature and, with all sincerity and earnestness, keeping in mind his words.

15| CHRIST MIND/CHRIST CONSCIOUSNESS

One of the laws of mind is that each person becomes like that with which he or she identifies himself or herself. Christ is the one perfect pattern. ... Each should, therefore, be wise and identify himself or herself with the Christ. (*Keep a True Lent,* p. 180)

Consciousness built in accordance with the Christ ideal, or in absolute relationship to God. The perfect mind that was in Christ Jesus. (*The Revealing Word,* p. 42)

This merging of God and humankind does not mean the total obliteration of human-kind's consciousness but its glorification or expansion into that of the divine. (Charles Fillmore, *Mysteries of John,* 2nd ed., Unity House, Unity Village, 2008, p. 151)

By thought, speech, and deed this Christ Mind is brought into manifestation. The new birth is symbolically described in the history of Jesus. (*Christian Healing,* p. 28)

Christian metaphysicians have discovered that man can greatly accelerate the growth in himself of the Christ Mind by using affirmations that identify him with the Christ. These affirmations often are so far beyond the present attainment of the novice as to seem ridiculous, but when it is understood that the statements are grouped about an ideal to be attained, they seem fair and reasonable. (Atom-Smashing Power of Mind, p. 103)

It is your mission to express all that you can imagine God to be. Let this be your standard of achievement; never lower it, nor allow yourself to be belittled by the cry of sacrilege. You can attain to everything you can imagine. If you can imagine that it is possible to God, it is also possible to you. (Talks on Truth, p. 99)

The Christ Mind is the real, innate Essence of every person. The Christ Consciousness is that level of enlightenment we achieve through the process of self-mastery and evolving spiritual awareness, guided by and from the Christ Mind. While instances of Christ Consciousness happen, the attainment of sustained Christ Consciousness is usually not an instantaneous achievement. It is, rather, the result of faithfully following the process of self-mastery and spiritual unfoldment under the guidance of the Christ Mind. We must deny and disempower any thoughts and beliefs that hinder our ability to live from Christ Consciousness. We must claim and affirm the Christ, no matter how ridiculous it may seem at the time and no matter if anyone is crying sacrilege.

Denial: *I give no power to thoughts of limitation and lack.*

Affirmation: *I am Christ, whole and perfect.*

SUMMARY STATEMENTS

▼ *Jesus Christ is spoken of both historically and metaphysically.*

▼ *Jesus is the name of the man from Nazareth, the human personality and body.*

▼ *Jesus, metaphysically, is the capacity within us to realize our Christ Potential.*

▼ *Christ is the universal Divine Idea that is the Spiritual Perfection inherent in Divine Mind.*

▼ *Jesus Christ is the individual who most fully expressed his Christ Potential. He is "the perfect human demonstrated." We often refer to Jesus Christ as our elder brother, teacher and Way Shower.*

▼ We metaphysically become <u>Christ Jesus</u>, or Divine Human, when we lose our personality and be the Christ.

▼ <u>Christ Jesus</u> is the name given to the Ascended Jesus.

▼ <u>Atonement</u>—at-one-ment—is the awareness of conscious Oneness.

▼ <u>The second coming</u> is the full awareness and acceptance of our Divine Nature at every level of our being.

▼ The man Jesus does not accomplish <u>salvation</u> for us. Salvation is accomplished by our ongoing identification of the Christ Presence within consciousness.

▼ <u>Following Jesus</u> means to follow his teachings and his example.

▼ The <u>Christ Mind</u> is the absolute Reality of our Beingness. The <u>Christ Consciousness</u> is the result of a process of self-mastery and spiritual unfoldment.

▼ We must deny and disempower any thoughts and beliefs that hinder our ability to live from Christ Consciousness. We must claim and affirm the Christ, no matter how ridiculous it may seem at the time and no matter if anyone is crying sacrilege.

TOPICS FOR DISCUSSION

1. *Explain your understanding of the terms* Jesus, Christ *and* Jesus Christ. *What does this awareness mean to you?*

2. *Are you "saved"? Have you been "born again"? Explain.*

3. *Share what it means for you to "follow Jesus." Be specific.*

THOUGHTS FOR REFLECTION AND MEDITATION

"From the metaphysical or the spiritual standpoint, the terms Christ, Jesus and Jesus Christ represent spiritual principles and laws that are eternal and omnipresent. They were active and they found fulfillment in the man Jesus of Nazareth. They are in every human being and will find fulfillment in everyone, when the same spirit of devotion and obedience is cultivated in the mind and heart of each individual."

(*Foundations of Unity*, Series Two, Vol. 1, p. 95)

SUPPLEMENTARY READING

Christian Healing by Charles Fillmore, 2nd ed., Unity House, Unity Village, Mo., 2005, Chapter 2, "Being's Perfect Idea."

How to Let God Help You by Myrtle Fillmore, 3rd ed., Unity House, Unity Village, Mo., 2000, Chapter 13, "The Christ Spirit."

The Emerging Self by Ernest C. Wilson, Unity House, Unity Village, Mo., 1970, Chapter 6, "Jesus Christ."

CHAPTER SIXTEEN

THE THREEFOLD NATURE OF HUMANKIND— SPIRIT, SOUL AND BODY

INTRODUCTION

In Chapter 13, we discussed the metaphysical Trinity: Father (God, Divine Mind), Son (Christ, Idea) and Holy Spirit (Expression). There is also a corresponding trinity, the threefold nature of humankind: Spirit, soul and body. The trinity in humankind is a framework to better understand the creative process inherent within each individual as well as to understand our Spiritual, mental and physical natures. This creative process may be better stated as a creative sequence.

16A THE TRINITY

If you would know the mystery of Being, see yourself in Being. Know yourself as an integral idea in Divine Mind, and all other ideas will recognize you as their fellow worker. Throw yourself out of the Holy Trinity, and you become an onlooker. Throw yourself into the Trinity, and you become its avenue of expression. The Trinity is known commonly as Father, Son, and Holy Spirit; metaphysically it is known as mind, idea, expression. These three are one. Each sees itself as including

the other two, yet in creation separate. (Charles Fillmore, *Christian Healing*, 2nd ed., Unity House, Unity Village, Mo., 2005, p. 20)

The mind of God is Spirit, soul, body; that is, mind, idea, expression. The mind of humankind is Spirit, soul, body—not separate from God Mind, but existing in it and making it manifest in an identity peculiar to the individual. Every person is building into his or her consciousness the three departments of God Mind, and success in the process is evidenced by the harmony, in consciousness, of Spirit, soul and body. (Christian Healing, p. 21)

The relationship of the metaphysical Trinity to the trinity in humankind illustrates an aspect of the Law of Correspondence which states "as above, so below," or "as in Heaven (Spiritual Consciousness), so on Earth (sense or personal consciousness)." This gives a deeper insight into the metaphysical meaning of the scriptural reference that humankind is "made in the image and likeness of God." Divine Mind is Spirit, Soul, Body (Mind-Idea-Expression), so we, too, are Spirit, soul, body (mind-idea-expression); this threefold nature is in consciousness. Furthermore, the threefold nature of humankind— Spirit, soul, body (mind-idea-expression)—is not separate from God-Mind; it "exists" in God-Mind. This creative sequence is also known as Divine Order.

In summary, there is the Absolute Level of Mind (Spirit/Mind-Soul/Idea-Body/Expression); the relative level of mind (Spirit/mind-soul/idea-body/expression); and physical manifestation. The physical body is the manifestation of mind-idea-expression. Mind-Idea-Expression/mind-idea-expression are statements of our threefold nature, described in detail below.

16B OUR THREEFOLD NATURE

An analysis of humankind in our threefold nature reveals that on every plane there is a certain reflective and discerning power of the mind and its thoughts. In the body, conclusions are reached through experience; in intellect, reason is the assumed arbiter of every question; in Spirit, intuition and inspiration bring the quick and sure answer to all the problems of life. (Charles and Cora Fillmore, *The Twelve Powers,* Unity House, Unity Village, Mo., 1999, p. 45)

Our threefold nature relates to how information and answers to questions are discerned.

When questions arise, the answers are processed in the following ways:

1. The body provides answers by gleaning information from the five senses and experience.

2. The mind provides answers using the intellect and reason.

3. Spirit (Divine Mind) provides quick and sure answers through intuition and inspiration.

16C INCREASING AWARENESS OF THE TRINITY OF HUMANKIND

Humankind sets into action any of the three realms of being, Spirit, soul and body, by concentrating thought on them. If we think of the body, the physical senses encompass all our existence. If mind and emotion are cultivated we add soul to our consciousness. If we rise to the Absolute and comprehend Spirit, we round out the God-person. (Charles Fillmore, *Jesus Christ Heals*, 2nd ed., Unity House, Unity Village, Mo., 1940, p. 71)

In his right relation, man is the inlet and the outlet of an everywhere present life, substance, and intelligence. When his "I" recognizes this fact and adjusts itself to the invisible expressions of the one Mind, man's mind becomes harmonious; his life, vigorous and perpetual; his body, healthy. It is imperative that the individual understand this relation in order to grow naturally. It must not only be understood as an abstract proposition, but it is necessary that he blend his life consciously with God life, his intelligence with God intelligence, and his body with the "God body." Conscious identification must prevail in the whole man before he can be in right relation. This involves not only a recognition of the universal intelligence, life and substance, but also their various combinations in man's consciousness. These combinations are, in the individual world, dependent for perfect expression upon man's recognition of and his loyalty to his origin— God-Mind. Man is in God-Mind as a perfect idea. God-Mind is constantly trying to express in every man its perfect idea, the real and only man. (*Christian Healing*, p. 22)

Prior to increasing our consciousness, it may seem that the body and its senses are the totality of awareness. However, awareness must be expanded by mind and emotion in order to add "soul" to our consciousness. It is only when we rise to the awareness of Spirit, Oneness or Divine Mind that we complete the components of consciousness. We therefore want to enhance our awareness of all three realms of our beingness, our trinity. We must activate all three realms (Spirit, soul and body) by concentrating on each of them. The method is simple: (1) acknowledge, (2) concentrate and (3) affirm.

Conscious identification with the Absolute by putting Oneness (Divine Mind) first is essential to the realization of Oneness ("in right relation"). This allows Divine Ideas to express without limitation. Putting Oneness first requires the ending of the seeming sense of separation as well as the "blending" of our life with Divine Life, intelligence with Divine Intelligence, and the body with the Spiritual Body.

16D SPIRIT

In its higher functioning the mind of humankind deals with spiritual ideas, and we can truthfully say that everyone is a spiritual being. (Jesus Christ Heals, p. 74)

Spirit in you is you. You are Spirit. It is the whole of you which you may be expressing in part. (Eric Butterworth, *Celebrate Yourself! and Other Inspirational Essays,* Unity House, Unity Village, Mo., 1984, p. 55)

You are Spirit, the Son of God, and your place is at the right hand of the Father. To realize this is to call down upon yourself the baptism of the Holy Spirit, after which baptism you no longer labor as a carpenter, or as a fisher, but begin to gather together your disciples—powers of mind. This gathering together of your powers is an orderly process, and you will find that it proceeds right along the lines laid down in Jesus' choosing of His disciples, as recorded in Matthew 4:18 and Mark 1:16. Your first power is the hearing faculty, Simon, and with him is strength, "Andrew his brother." You discover that hearing gives direction to your thinking faculty and that obedience increases your power to control your thoughts and to make your world conform to your ideas. Then you disentangle the I AM from the thinking faculty; you take control of the thinking and direct its power according to your wisdom. But wisdom is of Spirit. (Charles Fillmore, *Talks on Truth,* Unity House, Unity Village, Mo., 1926, pp. 90-91)

We are Spirit, "Son of God," Christ. We are not a Spiritual entity or being, but Beingness Itself. Spirit is invisible and eternal. Spirit is What we really are. One of the ways in which we develop our awareness and expression of Spirit, or Christ Nature, is through the regeneration of the Twelve Powers. This is metaphysically represented by the way Jesus called his disciples. The first one he called was Simon Peter, who represents the Power of Faith—the ability to spiritually intuit, believe, to "hear." The second one called was Andrew, representing Strength—the ability to stay the course, be steadfast and obedient to Truth. Our "hearing the Truth" is coupled with our ability to stick with it and be obedient, resulting in gaining control over the thinking nature. In this way, we begin to make our world conform to our ideas. This process also helps to disentangle our thinking faculty from sense consciousness/personal consciousness.

16E SOUL

Humankind's consciousness; the underlying idea back of any expression. In humankind, the soul is the many accumulated ideas back of his or her present expression. In its original and true sense, the soul of each person is the expressed idea of humankind in Divine Mind ... soul includes the conscious and subconscious minds. (Charles Fillmore, *The Revealing Word: A Dictionary of Metaphysical Terms,* 2nd ed., Unity House, Unity Village, Mo., 2006, p. 182)

Soul unfoldment means the bringing forth of divine ideas in the soul or consciousness of humankind and the bringing of these ideas into expression in the body. (Charles Fillmore, *The Mysteries of John,* 2nd ed., Unity House, Unity Village, Mo., 2008, p. 124)

The one and only object of a person's existence is the development of his or her soul, and any attainment, whether mental or material, that cannot be associated with and counted as an aid toward that end will ultimately be refused. (Charles and Cora Fillmore, *Teach Us to Pray*, 2nd ed., Unity House, Unity Village, Mo., 2007, p. 130)

Notice that "soul" is used differently than how it is generally used as a synonym for "spirit." While the terms "soul" and "consciousness" are often used somewhat interchangeably, this usage is not quite precise. Soul describes the entire spectrum of our awareness, including the conscious and subconscious minds. It is the sum total of all our beliefs, thoughts and attitudes, both conscious and subconscious minds. Contained within our soul is individual awareness of both our Spiritual Nature through intuition and inspiration, and the physical body via the senses and experience. Subconscious is not the same as unconscious since unconscious is being unaware. A person is unconscious or unaware of what is in the subconscious and Superconscious minds.

16F THE THREE ELEMENTS OF SOUL

[The] soul realm includes the sum total of consciousness, all that the individual has experienced. In analyzing the soul realm we have first the animal soul.

The animal soul comprises all sensations and all thoughts that we entertain with reference to animal life. Through man's thought the animal soul forms the animal man.

The second element in the soul realm, the human soul, is one step higher than the animal, and comprises all the thoughts and emotions we entertain on the human plane of consciousness: thoughts of family, of friends, of business associates, or personal possessions.

The third and highest element of soul is the spiritual. This phase of the soul is the depository of all thoughts and aspirations we have ever had about God and things spiritual. Here also we find a consciousness that relates us to God and forms the connecting link between the human and the divine. When through prayers, meditations, and good works man has built spiritual qualities into his soul to the point of dominance over the animal and human natures, he is ready for the regeneration with Jesus Christ.

The soul has three element or natures: animal, human and spiritual. The animal element or nature of soul pertains to the sensation and thoughts of our physical existence. The human element or nature of soul pertains to thoughts and emotions concerning our the human or personality/ego plane of consciousness. This would include thoughts about family, friends and associates. The spiritual element or nature of soul pertains to our thoughts and aspirations about God, or Divine Mind. It is the link between the human and the Divine. Prayers, meditations and good works build spiritual qualities into our souls that we use to have dominance over the animal and human natures or elements of the soul.

16G BODY

The outer expression of consciousness. (*The Revealing Word*, p. 26)

The body of a person is the visible record of his or her thoughts. (Sue Sikking, *Beyond a Miracle,* Unity School of Christianity, Unity Village, Mo., 1973, p. 19)

Your body is the blossom of your mind. (Imelda Octavia Shanklin, *What Are You?* 2nd ed., Unity House, Unity Village, Mo., 2004, p. 15)

Body—The outer expression of consciousness; the precipitation of the thinking part of man. God created the idea of the body of man as a self-perpetuating, self-renewing organism, which man reconstructs into his personal body. God creates the body idea, or divine idea, and man, by his thinking, makes it manifest. As God created man in His image and likeness by the power of His word, so man, as God's image and likeness, projects his body by the same power. (The Revealing Word, p. 27)

Our Real Body, the Spiritual Body, is the expression of Divine Idea in Divine Mind; It is formless and timeless. Divine Mind does not manifest the physical body, humankind does. The physical body manifests from this formless and timeless Divine Idea of Body; however, it has been limited by both the collective human consciousness and individual consciousness. We function in a physical form that is an outpicturing of our current level of consciousness; this includes consciousness of matter, or physicality, as well as collective consciousness. Regardless of what happens to the physical body, the Perfect Body Idea is always present and available; Its perfection can be brought forth and expressed. All healing is based on claiming this Perfection, or Wholeness, that eternally exists in Divine Mind. It is good to remember that healing is always first of the error beliefs, thoughts and feelings in mind/consciousness. Error is released as the awareness and realization of Wholeness takes its place resulting in effects like peace of mind, centeredness etc. This Wholeness in consciousness may or may not find its way into the physical realm; the physical realm is sometimes slow to change.

16H **WHOLENESS**

In thinking of ourselves, we must not separate Spirit, soul and body, but rather hold all as one, if we would be strong and powerful. (H. Emilie Cady, *Lessons in Truth*, Centennial Edition, Unity House, Unity Village, Mo., 2003, p. 28)

Even though we have a threefold nature, in Truth, we are describing Oneness and Wholeness. These aspects are separated as a way to understand them; in Truth, they operate as one. The physical body is the effect of soul; there is no body without soul. Nor can we have soul without Spirit because everything in the relative realm has its basis in the Absolute Realm. The Absolute Realm of Superconscious Mind does not change; soul, including conscious and subconscious minds, does change according to the limitations and interpretations placed on Divine Ideas. These limitations and interpretations arise from the beliefs, attitudes and ideas held in the sense/personal consciousness as well as the collective consciousness of humankind.

SUMMARY STATEMENTS

▼ *The <u>relationship of the metaphysical Trinity to the trinity</u> in humankind gives meaning to the scriptural reference that we are ". . . made in the image and likeness of God."*

▼ *In the Absolute, <u>Mind, Idea and Expression</u> each "knows itself" as including the other two. From a limited human perspective, we tend to perceive mind, idea and expression as separate.*

▼ *The <u>threefold nature</u> (trinity) in humankind is also referred to as Spirit, soul and body.*

▼ *Spirit, Soul, Body/Spirit, soul, body is Mind-Idea-Expression/mind-idea-expression. These represent the creative process or sequence that is also known as Divine Order.*

▼ *Spirit is what we really are, our True Nature that is invisible and eternal.*

Soul is the sum total of conscious and subconscious minds, the entire spectrum of our awareness.

▼ *Soul has three natures or elements: animal, human and spiritual.*

▼ *Prayer, meditation and good works build up the spiritual nature of the soul so that there may be dominion over the animal and human natures.*

▼ *Body is the outer expression of consciousness. Its first level of expression is in consciousness.*

▼ *As we continue on our path of spiritual unfoldment, we must remember to devote the proper time and attention to balancing the trinity of our humanness (Spirit, soul and body) in order to cultivate Wholeness in our lives.*

TOPICS FOR DISCUSSION

1. *What is the relationship between the metaphysical Trinity and the trinity in humankind? What meaning does this relationship have for you?*

2. *How is the concept of our threefold nature useful and practical?*

THOUGHTS FOR REFLECTION AND MEDITATION

"Daily declare that your spiritual life and world, your mental life and world, your physical life and world are unified and that you are expressing harmoniously the ideas of the Christ Mind on these three planes."

(Myrtle Fillmore, *Myrtle Fillmore's Healing Letters*, revised paperback edition, Unity House, Unity Village, Mo., 2006, p. 66)

SUPPLEMENTARY READING

Christian Healing by Charles Fillmore, 2nd ed., Unity House, Unity Village, Mo., 2005, Chapter 2, "Being's Perfect Idea."

How to Let God Help You by Myrtle Fillmore, 3rd ed., Unity House, Unity Village, Mo., 2000, Chapter 3, "Life Is a School."

Lessons in Truth by H. Emilie Cady, Centennial Edition, Unity House, Unity Village, Mo., 2003, Chapter 3, "Thinking."

-

CHAPTER SEVENTEEN

THE THREE PHASES OF MIND

INTRODUCTION

While there is only one Mind, Divine Mind, our individual experience of It seems to include a collective consciousness and our own individual consciousness. Each of us is consciousness individualized in the one Divine Mind. In this chapter, we examine the three phases of mind: conscious, subconscious and Superconscious. We explore the purpose of these phases of mind and how each interacts with the others. We will learn how habits are formed and stored in our subconscious mind.

17A CONSCIOUSNESS

The sense of awareness, of knowing. The knowledge or realization of any idea, object or condition. The sum total of all ideas accumulated in and affecting a person's present being. The composite of ideas, thoughts, emotions, sensation and knowledge that makes up the conscious, subconscious and superconscious phases of mind. It includes all that humankind is aware of—spirit, soul and body. (Charles Fillmore, *The Revealing Word: A Dictionary of Metaphysical Terms*, 2nd ed., Unity House, Unity Village, Mo., 2006, p. 41)

Consciousness means more than conscious awareness. It includes all three phases of mind: conscious, subconscious and Superconscious. Consciousness is made up of all that we are and can be aware of: Spirit, soul and body.

17B EVOLUTION OF CONSCIOUSNESS

When people evolve spiritually to a certain degree, they open up inner faculties that connect them with cosmic Mind, and attain results that are sometimes so startling that they seem to be miracle workers. What seems miraculous is the action of forces on planes of consciousness not previously understood. When people release the powers of their souls, they do marvels in the sight of the material-minded, but they have not departed from the law. They are merely functioning in a consciousness that has been sporadically manifested by great people in all ages. (Charles Fillmore, *Prosperity,* Unity House, Unity Village, Mo., 1936, p. 64)

Evolution of consciousness seems to be individual, not collective. However, collective consciousness, also called "race" or "mass" consciousness, benefits from these evolutionary changes. The evolution of the collective consciousness becomes "available" to everyone as each one appropriates the "inner faculties" and seemingly miraculous results mentioned above.

Miracles are not the result of breaking Spiritual Laws and Principles; miracles are the result of the operation of unknown Laws and Principles. Higher levels of consciousness generate higher awareness of these unknown Divine Ideas, Principles and Laws. Higher levels of consciousness can accomplish things on lower levels that are described as miraculous.

17C THE ONE MIND

In truth there is but one Mind; in it all things exist. Accurately speaking, people do not have three minds, nor do they have even one mind; but they express the one Mind in a multitude of ways. (Charles Fillmore, *Christian Healing,* 2nd ed., Unity House, Unity Village, Mo., 2005, p. 97)

The greatest and most important discovery for any and every person is the realization that we are an "eachness" within the allness of God or Divine Mind. (Eric Butterworth, "You and Your Mind," *Unity Magazine*, Vol. 161, November 1981, p. 9)

When we speak of the One Mind, or Divine Mind, we are referring to the Divine Source of all intelligence. Although we perceive that our minds function independently, in Truth, our minds have consciousness in the One Mind. Like nesting dolls, seeming individual consciousness has its existence in seeming collective consciousness, which has its existence in the One Mind.

17D CONSCIOUS MIND

The mind that makes one know of one's mental operations and states of consciousness; that phase of mind in which one is actively aware of one's thoughts. The mind through which one establishes one's identity. (The Revealing Word, p. 41)

We are all well acquainted with the conscious mind. Through its use we establish our relations with the outer realm and recognize our individual entities. The conscious mind makes one know of one's mental operations. It is that phase of mind in which one is actively aware of one's thoughts. It is the mind through which we establish our identity. The conscious mind should look ever to the superconscious for all direction and instruction. The Spirit of wisdom rests in the superconscious. (Charles Fillmore, *Dynamics for Living: A Topical Compilation of Essential Fillmore Teachings,* Unity House, Unity Village, Mo, pp. 50-51)

The conscious mind is the phase of our mind from which we function rationally and are cognizant of our mental processes. The conscious mind shifts and changes. It consists of our current awareness of the internal thinking process as well as our perceptions of the world around us. The conscious mind consists solely of current perceptions, opinions, thoughts, beliefs and ideas; these components may be about the present, past or future. It is from the conscious mind that we choose to access the Superconscious Mind for direction and instruction.

17E SUBCONSCIOUS MIND

The subconscious mind is the vast, silent realm that lies back of the conscious mind and between it and the superconscious. (Charles Fillmore, *Keep a True Lent,* 2nd ed., Unity House, Unity Village, Mo., 2005, p. 87)

The subconscious mind, or subjective consciousness, is the sum of all humankind's past thinking. It may be called memory. The subconscious sometimes acts separately from the conscious mind; for instance, in dreams and in its work of carrying on bodily functions, such as breathing and digestion. The subconscious mind has no power to do original thinking. It acts upon what is given it through the conscious or the Superconscious mind. All our involuntary, or automatic, activities are of the subconscious mind; they are the result of our having trained ourselves by the conscious mind to form certain habits and do certain things without having to center our thought upon them consciously. (Charles Fillmore, *Metaphysical Bible Dictionary,* Unity House, Unity Village, Mo., 1931, p. 155)

The subconscious realm of mind is the realm that contains all past thoughts. First, we think consciously and this thought becomes subconscious, carrying on its work of building up or tearing down, according to its character. The subconscious mind cannot take the initiative, but depends on the conscious mind for direction. When one is quickened of Spirit, one's true thoughts are set to work and the subconscious states of error are broken up and dissolved. In one's daily silence and communion with God, thoughts from the subconsciousness come into the conscious realm of mind to be forgiven and redeemed. Flesh heredity is denied and inheritance from God affirmed, which enables man consciously to draw divine ideas from the one Mind. These ideas are established in consciousness and the whole mentality is at one with Christ, the divine-man idea. (Charles Fillmore, *Atom-Smashing Power of Mind,* 2nd ed., Unity House, Unity Village, Mo., 2006, pp. 76-77)

The subconscious mind stores memories, past thoughts and feelings. It stores whatever we are holding in mind at any given time, without a choice-making process. It has no ability to discern the difference between Truth/truth and error. Recent research has shown that the subconscious mind actually records in pictures and images and not in words as was commonly thought. Contrary to the last excerpt above, the subconscious mind does "take the initiative" in influencing our conscious thoughts and actions; it drives our habits. It also directs all the subconscious activity of the body.

Subconscious beliefs, thoughts and feelings that were stored sometime in the past are actually present in every now moment. They are present beliefs, thoughts and feelings in the subconscious about past events. The specific contents of the subconscious mind are unknown; therefore, it is important that its contents be brought into the conscious activity of mind so that any error beliefs, thoughts and feelings may be identified and transformed. One way we become aware of these unknown subconscious thoughts is through daily practice of the Silence and the realization of Oneness. Another way is to examine our habits and our lives to become aware of these subconscious memories—for example, when we have strong reactions to people we meet for the first time it is probably because of some similarity to a person from our past that has been stored in the subconscious mind.

17F SUBCONSCIOUS IMPRESSIONS

The subconscious may be called the sensitive plate of mind. Its true office is to receive impressions from the superconscious and to reproduce them upon the canvas of the conscious mind. Humankind, however, having lost the consciousness of the indwelling God as an ever present reality, has reversed the process and impresses the subconscious from the conscious mind. In this way the former is made to register impressions of both good and evil, according to the thought held in conscious mind at the time the impression is made. (Keep a True Lent, p. 87)

Each person determines how to respond or react to life's situations and conditions. Repeated reactions and responses to specific situations impress the subconscious mind and can give rise to patterns and habits, some of which are desirable while others are not. Through self-observation, patterns and habits can be discerned, including how they manifest in the present. Further discernment can eventually uncover the beliefs, thoughts and feelings giving rise to these patterns and habits; then, through denials and affirmations, they can be transformed. Denials disempower error beliefs, thoughts and feelings; affirmations claim Truth rooted in the Oneness, from the Superconscious Mind

17G **SUPERCONSCIOUS MIND**

The superconsciousness is the realm of divine ideas. Its character is impersonal. It therefore has no personal ambitions; knows no condemnation; but is always pure, innocent, loving and obedient to the call of God. (Atom-Smashing Power of Mind, p. 36)

The superconscious mind, Christ consciousness or spiritual consciousness, is a state of consciousness that is based upon true ideas, upon an understanding and realization of spiritual Truth. (Metaphysical Bible Dictionary, p. 155)

The Superconscious Mind is also known as I AM, the Christ Mind, and is that phase of mind in which we realize the Divine Ideas of Divine Mind. The Superconscious Mind can inform both the conscious and subconscious minds. It is through the activity of the Superconscious phase of mind that our whole consciousness is spiritualized. From the conscious mind, the Superconscious Mind is accessed for guidance and direction. The error beliefs, thoughts and feelings of the subconscious mind are cleared or transformed by investing time in prayer and the Silence, a practice that accesses the Superconscious Mind and infuses the subconscious mind with Divine Ideas.

17H **UNEXPLORED CONSCIOUSNESS**

This Spirit of wisdom is right now a part of the consciousness of everyone. It is in you and about you, and you will come into conscious relations with it when you believe on it and its powers. If you ignore it and thereby deny that it exists in you and for you, you remain in the darkness of ignorance. It is exactly as if a person lived in the basement of a large house and refused to go upstairs, declaring that because the upper rooms did not come down to him or her they were not there. (Keep a True Lent, p. 57)

The Spirit of Wisdom is an aspect of the Superconscious Mind. For the most part, the Superconsciousness remains a glorious mystery. When we're aware of It, the experience is unforgettable. Even though we may experience the Superconsciousness "communicating" in words, It does not always occur in the form of words. Very often It simply imparts pure knowing without us being aware of exactly how we learned it. We have a wordless sense of It. We simply need to "believe on It and Its powers" in order to make use of Its illumination. A prayer that claims illumination is swiftly and surely answered with Divine Ideas because the Superconscious Mind is Divine Mind.

17| **THE TRANSFORMATION PROCESS**

The connection between the superconscious mind and the conscious mind is established within—by meditation, by going into the silence, and by speaking the word. (The Revealing Word, p. 188)

The work of overcoming is carried on largely in the subconscious mind. All

past thinking must be redeemed and the whole person, conscious and subconscious, brought into the harmony of the Christ consciousness. (The Revealing Word, p. 186)

The superconscious mind lifts up, or regenerates, both the subconscious and the conscious, transforming them into the true image and likeness of God. The conscious mind must be faithful during this transformation. It must look ever to the superconscious for all direction and instruction. It can of itself do nothing with assurance, because the Spirit of wisdom rests in the superconscious. (Keep a True Lent, p. 89)

What you are about is the releasing of your divine potential, stirring up the gifts of God within you … Thus the prayer treatment is not to make the potential but to awaken and remember that true image that was yours before the world was. (Eric Butterworth, "You and Your Mind," Unity Magazine, Vol. 161, November 1981, p. 9)

Whether we are aware of it or not, the Superconscious Mind is always impressing and informing the conscious and subconscious minds with Truth, or Divine Ideas. In order to demonstrate our Spiritual Nature, Christ, on all levels of consciousness, we must be intentional and disciplined in directing the work of our conscious phase of mind. We must use the conscious mind to choose the inspirations of Truth from the Superconscious so that our whole mind will be illumined by Divine Mind. One way to accomplish this is to become aware of our habits and patterns, then use denials and affirmations to transform those we no longer desire. The subconscious mind is cleansed by Superconscious Mind through prayer and meditation. The Superconscious Mind informs and transforms the subconscious mind so that it eventually contains only impressions from the Superconscious Mind. Ultimately, each individual chooses whether to heed Its inspiration or not.

SUMMARY STATEMENTS

▼ *In Truth there is only <u>One Mind, Divine Mind,</u> and humankind has its consciousness in and expresses this Mind in a multitude of ways.*

▼ *When we speak of our <u>conscious mind</u>, we are referring to the phase of mind that is cognizant of our mental processes.*

▼ *Our <u>subconscious phase of mind</u> is the storehouse or receptacle of all memories and experiences.*

▼ *The <u>subconscious mind</u> originally was impressed solely from the Superconscious Mind. Humankind has reversed the process and impresses the subconscious from the conscious mind.*

▼ *The <u>Superconscious Mind</u> is the I AM, the Christ Mind.*

▼ *The <u>Superconscious Mind</u> is always impressing and informing the conscious and subconscious minds with Truth, or Divine Ideas.*

▼ *Through <u>conscious choice</u>, each of us has the ability to access the Superconscious Mind for guidance and direction. Only in this way can we transform the undesirable beliefs held in the conscious and subconscious minds.*

▼ *The <u>Superconscious Mind infuses the subconscious mind with Divine Ideas, thereby</u> clearing and transforming its contents. Prayer and meditation are tools that enhance the process.*

TOPICS FOR DISCUSSION

1. *Describe the relationships between and among the three phases of mind.*

2. *Why is it important to bring the content of the subconscious mind to conscious awareness?*

THOUGHTS FOR REFLECTION AND MEDITATION

"We must begin at once to rejoice in the light that is come to redeem our subconsciousness from the shadows of error and fear and superstition and mistakes."

(Myrtle Fillmore, *Myrtle Fillmore's Healing Letters*, revised paperback edition, Unity House, UnityVillage Mo., 2006, p. 58)

SUPPLEMENTARY READING

Atom-Smashing Power of Mind by Charles Fillmore, 2nd ed., Unity House, Unity Village, Mo., 2006, Chapter 4, "I AM, or Superconsciousness."

Keep a True Lent by Charles Fillmore, 2nd ed., Unity House, Unity Village, Mo., 2005, Chapter 12, "Conscious Mind and Subconscious Mind."

Myrtle Fillmore's Healing Letters by Myrtle Fillmore, revised paperback edition, Unity House, Unity Village Mo., 2006, Chapter 11, "The Subconsciousness."

CHAPTER EIGHTEEN

PERSONALITY/INDIVIDUALITY

INTRODUCTION

There are two basic attitudes of mind that make up our identity: personality and Individuality. Personality is a perception of ourselves that is made up of the characteristics that we have invented to distinguish ourselves from others. Personality is who we think and feel we are. Individuality, our True Identity, consists of the characteristics that reflect our unique expression of the Christ Mind. Individuality is What we are.

In this chapter, we explore personality and Individuality as well as the ways this framework serves to remind us of the importance of true self-awareness and self-expression.

18A **PERSONALITY**

The sum total of characteristics that each person has personalized as distinct of himself or herself, independent of others or of divine principle. ... Personality is what people seem to be when they think in their three-dimensional consciousness. (Charles Fillmore, *The Revealing Word: A Dictionary of Metaphysical Terms*, 2nd ed., Unity House, Unity Village, Mo., 2006, pp. 148-149)

Personality applies to the human part of you—the person, the external. ... When you say that you dislike anyone, you mean that you dislike his or her personality—that exterior something that presents itself from the outside. It is the outer, changeable human, in contradistinction to the inner or real human. (H. Emilie Cady, *Lessons In Truth*, Centennial Edition, Unity House, Unity Village, Mo., 2003, p. 88)

Personality is who we think and feel we are. It is the attitude of mind that has distorted our True Uniqueness into a sense of separateness. Personality consists of elements that make up our earthly persona, our ever-changing sense of self. Personality is the sum total of characteristics, opinions and beliefs which compose a fragmented, separated sense of self. In today's language we would call this the "ego."

18B MORE CONCERNING THE EGO

The personal self is the ego around which revolve all thoughts that bind us to error. We cannot cross all out at once, but little by little we cast out the specific thoughts that have accumulated and built up the false state of consciousness termed Judas. In the life of Jesus, Judas represents the false ego that error thought has generated. (Charles Fillmore, *Christian Healing*, 2nd ed., Unity House, Unity Village, Mo., 2005, p. 58)

Ego—The I. The ego is man/woman, and by reason of our divinity we make and remake at will In this lie our greatest strength and our greatest weakness. The ego of itself is possessed of nothing. It is a mere ignorant child of innocence floating in the Mind of Being, but through the door of its consciousness must pass all the treasures of God. (The Revealing Word, p. 61)

ego, adverse—When the ego attaches itself to sense consciousness, it builds the antichrist man/woman, who has no basis in reality. This is known as the adverse ego. It is the adverse ego that causes all the trouble in the world. Its selfishness and greed make us grovel in the mire of materiality, when we might soar in the heavens of spirituality. (The Revealing Word, p. 61)

ego, spiritual—The true self; an individualized center of God consciousness; I AM; conscious identity. (The Revealing Word, p. 61)

It is interesting to note that in some historic texts what is called Individuality today was at one time called the "spiritual ego." Today, the focus has been more on the "adverse ego" based on sense consciousness and error thought. The adverse ego is mired in materiality, selfishness and greed. It is from the adverse ego that error and trouble arise in personal lives and the world.

Paradoxically, it is from the ego that we choose to begin the process of awakening to Christ Consciousness. While the ego, the personal self, is our greatest weakness, it is also our greatest strength because "all the treasures of God," the treasures of Oneness (Divine Ideas), must pass through this ego consciousness. We must use our ego to wake up to the awareness of Oneness and develop our Twelve Powers, or Divine Faculties/Abilities (see Chapters 23 and 24).

18C OUR MANY SELVES

The Adam human being exists in the subconsciousness as a multitude of people: The wise person and the foolish person, the kind person and the cruel person, the loving person and the hateful person, the stingy person and the generous person, the weak person and the strong person, the hungry person and the full person, the happy person and the troubled person, the good person and the bad person, the live person and the dead person, the poor person and the rich person, the timid person and the courageous person, the sick person and the healthy person, the erratic person and the sane person— these, and a thousand other types of people as active personalities occupy the consciousness of every human being. (Charles and Cora Fillmore, *The Twelve Powers,* Unity House, Unity Village, Mo., 1999, p. 35)

Every thought we loose in our mind carries with it a certain substance, life and intelligence. So we might call our thoughts our "thought people." (Charles Fillmore, *Jesus Christ Heals,* 2nd ed., Unity House, Unity Village, Mo., 1940, p.138)

Personality expresses in such a variety of ways that we sometimes experience ourselves as being many different "people." Personality is always shifting and changing. Our self-concept is composed of many "subpersonalities," or aspects of personality; these many aspects and concepts of self are strands that combine to form our unique personality. We are inconsistent and unpredictable when our lives are dominated by personality. From the awareness of "many selves," we realize that the confusing changes we experience are more than likely products of the fragmented nature of personality.

18D INDIVIDUALITY

... individuality is what we really are when we think in our unlimited spiritual consciousness. (*The Revealing Word,* p. 149)

The true self; that which is undivided from God; our spiritual identity .... That which characterizes one as a distinct entity or particular manifestation of divine Principle. Individuality is eternal; it can never be destroyed. (*The Revealing Word,* p. 106)

One's individuality is that part of one that never changes its identity. It is the God self. (*Lessons in Truth,* p. 89*

Individuality is What we truly are and will always be; It is our unique and individual expression of the Christ Idea. Individuality is composed of the attributes of our Spiritual Nature that is our eternal True Identity; It is the Real Self. The degree or "amount" of the Christ Idea we are able to express is equal to the degree to which we have realized ourselves to be the One Mind, or Divine Mind. Individuality is that amount of the Christ Idea (the Idea that contains Ideas) that we are able to express from our current level of consciousness.

18E REVEALING INDIVIDUALITY

The cry goes up: "This is foolish, sacrilegious, to put humankind beside Jesus Christ and claim that they are equals." The claim is not that mortals, in their present consciousness, are equal with Jesus, but that they must be equal with him before they will emerge from the sense of delusion in which they now wander. (Charles Fillmore, *Talks on Truth,* Unity House, Unity Village, Mo., 1926, p.143)

When Jesus spoke again to the people, he said, "I am the light of the world" (Jn. 8:12). You are the light of the world (Mt. 5:14).

This perfect-idea-of-God human is your true self. God Mind is, under the law of thought, constantly seeking to release its perfection in you. It is your spirit, and when you ask for its guidance and place yourself, by prayer and affirmation, in mental touch with it, there is a great increase of its manifestation in your life. (*Christian Healing,* p. 23)

Right here we should appeal to the supreme reason of Spirit and proclaim what we perceive as the highest truth, regardless of precedent or tradition, mental ignorance or physical limitation; I AM is the "image of God," the "only begotten Son" (the expressed, or pressed out, *Mind) of the Most High. This is our true estate, and we shall never realize it until we enter into it in mind, because there it is, and nowhere else.* (*Christian Healing,* p. 25)

As the true Christ self emerges, personality decreases. The real self, the individuality, begins to express. "He must increase, but I must decrease" (Jn. 3:30). (*The Revealing Word,* p. 149)

Some think it foolish or sacrilege to equate ourselves with Jesus; yet Jesus equated us with him when he called himself "the light of the world" and referred to us in the same words. A heart-centered metaphysician achieves this by heartfelt self-observation, which helps us be aware of whether we are living from our personality or our Individuality. If we find we are living from our personality, we can choose again to express our Individuality. As we do this, the personality decreases, while our Individuality increases.

Realization of our Individuality comes through prayer, meditation and listening to the "still small voice." We are created/ideated in the "image and likeness of God," or Divine Mind. Divine

Mind is Spirit; we are Spirit, the Christ Revealing, expressing and living more and more of our Individuality happens by claiming the Truth of What we really are by the power of the Word, including the use of denials and affirmations.

18F SERVICE

Much is heard about giving ourselves to service to the world, but how important is the self that we are offering? If we have found our real self the offer will be worthwhile, but if we are offering personality alone we shall never set the world afire. (Charles and Cora Fillmore, *Teach Us to Pray*, 2nd ed., Unity House, Unity Village, Mo., 2007, p. 161)

When we feel compelled to give in service to the world, as heart-centered metaphysicians we must examine ourselves to discern which attitude is uppermost in our minds. If we give only from our personality, our motives will be selfish—we will expect great rewards and appreciation for our work and we will often resent what is asked of us. This type of service leads to burn-out. However, when we serve from our Individuality, we will give freely without expectation of particular results, and what we give will always be a blessing.

SUMMARY STATEMENTS

▼ *Personality/Individuality is a framework that provides us with the opportunity to examine the nature of our True Identity and release the erroneous assumptions and opinions that may currently comprise our sense of identity.*

▼ *Personality is the sum total of the characteristics and opinions that comprise our current beliefs about who we are. Our personality, or sense of self, is inconsistent and often unreliable because it is based primarily on appearances.*

▼ *Personality is not to be confused with the concept of personal identity. When we choose to transform our limited human awareness (personality) into an awareness of our unique spiritual origin and purpose (Individuality), we do not lose our personal identity—we gain it. We become more our True Self and more able to express Christ Potential.*

▼ *The <u>adverse ego</u> is based on sense consciousness and error thought.*

▼ *While the ego, the personal self, is our greatest weakness, it is also our <u>greatest strength. This is</u> because "all the treasures of God," the treasures of Oneness, or Divine Mind, must pass through this ego consciousness.*

▼ *<u>Individuality</u> is our Real Spiritual Self. Individuality is the name for the unique manner in which each individual expresses the universal Christ Idea.*

▼ *Personality and Individuality are <u>attitudes of mind</u>. Our goal is to realize that every one of our attitudes can be spiritualized so that we are able to fully demonstrate the truth of Christ Nature.*

▼ *Through <u>self-observation</u> we are able to recognize which attitude of mind we are expressing at any given time and realize that we always have the opportunity to act from Individuality instead of personality.*

▼ *When we give <u>service to the world,</u> it is alwayss a blessing when we give it from Individuality and not from personality.*

TOPICS FOR DISCUSSION

1. *How can an understanding of "our many selves" contribute to your quest for self-knowledge?*

2. *Share a time in your life when you first became aware of your Divine Identity.*

THOUGHTS FOR REFLECTION AND MEDITATION

"... we live and move and have our being in an infinite ocean of intelligence and life and substance, and we are a wave within that ocean in which intelligence and life and substance are projected into livingness as the person we are. When we become aware of this unity, we are transformed from personality to individuality."

(Eric Butterworth, *Discover the Power Within You*, 40th Anniversary Edition, HarperOne, New York, 2008, p. 36)

SUPPLEMENTARY READING

Lessons in Truth by H. Emilie Cady, Centennial Edition, Unity House, Unity Village, Mo., 2003, Chapter 7, "Definition of Terms: Chemicalization, Personality, and Individuality."

Listen, Beloved, by Martha Smock, Unity House, Unity Village, Mo., 1980, Chapter 4, "You Are Needed."

The Basic Tool Kit for Living

There are some basic tools that are components of heart-centered metaphysics. We use these tools to change our thoughts, feelings and beliefs in order to elevate our consciousness so that we can be heart-centered metaphysicians.

CHAPTER NINETEEN

THE FOUR FUNCTIONS OF CONSCIOUSNESS

INTRODUCTION

Our consciousness is made up of all the dimensions of our awareness. It consists of our innate capacity to sense, to think, to feel and to intuit. As we engage in the process of heartfelt self-observation, we learn to see ourselves as spiritual, mental, emotional and physical. In this chapter, we will explore the meaning and dynamics of each of these functions of consciousness. A heart-centered metaphysician expresses them in a more complete and balanced way.

19A **SENSING**

The five senses are simply avenues of one great central desire—sensation. The I AM desired experience in sensation, and the five senses are the five formulated avenues through which It enjoys that experience. (Charles Fillmore, *Talks on Truth,* Unity House, Unity Village, Mo., 1926, p. 82)

The senses are accurate within their own ranges, but their ranges are so circumscribed that you cannot from the senses alone gain any appreciable knowledge of Reality. There are vast universes of being that the senses do not touch, and in order not to be deceived you must have a more capable

guide, a more comprehensive reporter of events than the senses ever can be. (Imelda Shanklin, *What Are You?* 2nd ed., Unity House, Unity Village, Mo., 2004, p. 57)

In the flesh, the sensation of humankind was turned outward through feeling and we were bound to the eternally rolling wheels of birth and death by physical generation. When a person is born into the Spirit, he or she cuts off the indulgence of the external and is delighted to learn that sensation finds an interior faculty through which it expresses itself in perpetual ecstasy. Had the person continued to indulge the desires of the flesh in the external, he or she would never have discovered the enduring faculty of the internal. (Talks on Truth, p. 84)

What is termed "sense consciousness" in humankind is not to be condemned but lifted up to its rightful place. ... If you are bound to the flesh, the cords that hold you are words. If you want to be unbound, it must be accomplished by words. The cords are states of consciousness that you must dissolve. This dissolving process is accomplished by words that express denial—negations. (Talks on Truth, p. 82)

Sensing is the function of consciousness by which we experience the external physical world. In other words, it is how we obtain direct outer knowing. We use our five senses to appreciate and participate in outer knowing and to appreciate and participate in the beauty and energy of manifestation. However, if our five senses become the only source of information about what appears to be real and true in the physical world of manifestation, then we will be using our function of sensation erroneously. It will not serve its highest purpose in our lives, which is also to be an avenue of expression of the I AM.

The I AM is the "name of God in humankind" and presumably began in Divine Mind (Divine Consciousness) as a "Self-conscious" Divine Idea. As the I AM became "involved and wrapped up" in Its own creations, desire for sensation arose. The I AM

forgot Source and began to believe that It was and is sourced from the outer. Thus, the I AM desired experience in sensation, which occurs by experiencing the physical/ phenomenal world through the senses alone rather than through thought or intuition.

Our words give rise to states of consciousness that bind us to the world of the senses. These bindings are also dissolved through words—through the use of "denials." We *deny* the power we have given to those words which have bolstered sense consciousness and dissolve reliance solely on this limited consciousness.

19B THINKING

The formulating process of mind. ... The thinking faculty is the inlet and outlet of all your ideas. ... The thinking faculty in you makes you a free agent, because it is your creative center; in and through this one power you establish your consciousness—you build your world. (Charles Fillmore, *The Revealing Word: A Dictionary of Metaphysical Terms,* 2nd ed., Unity House, Unity Village, Mo., 2006, pp. 192-193)

Think; do not be content in playing at thinking. Your brain will enjoy the exercise involved in real thinking. ... Search. Delve into the matter that interests you; do not be satisfied with skimming the surface. ... Use your full mental equipment. (What Are You?, p. 109)

Thinking is the function of consciousness by which we develop ideas into concepts or rational patterns of thought. We use our intellect to observe, record, arrange and evaluate the input we receive both from our intuition and from the sense world. Thoughts are either very clearly based on Divine Ideas or on Divine Ideas that have been diluted, filtered and/or limited by sense consciousness. Thoughts clearly based on Divine Ideas are always True. However, thoughts that are primarily based upon sense impressions can be risky; they do not reflect Truth as clearly, because thoughts based on sense consciousness are really thoughts based on the *effects* of Divine Ideas rather than Cause. It is important for each of us to invest our attention and energy in the process of thinking and unfold our powerful mental capacity so that we can make the fullest use of Divine Ideas.

Thinking should not be equated with such terms as Understanding, Wisdom or Divine Ideas. Understanding is a Divine Idea, and thinking does not change it. In *Keep a True Lent* (p. 155), Unity co-founder Charles Fillmore defines Spiritual Understanding as "the ability to apprehend and realize the laws of thought and the relation of ideas one to another." Wisdom is the ability to discern the meaning in conjunction with the ability to discern how to use any knowledge. In *The Revealing Word*, Fillmore said this about Wisdom and Understanding: "The price that we must pay for the conscious attainment of divine wisdom and understanding is the letting go of the personal self with its limited beliefs" (p. 211). In other words, Understanding is the comprehension of Divine Ideas, while Wisdom is the faculty that we use to put our Understanding to work. Divine Ideas just *are* and have no dependency on thinking.

19C FEELING

Feeling is external to thought; behind every feeling or emotion there lies thought, which is its direct cause. To erase a feeling, a change of thought is required. (The Revealing Word, pp. 73-74)

Feeling is mental reaction to things recognized or unrecognized. ... Your ideals are the parents of your impulses and your feelings. Whatever your ideals may have been in the past, the impulses and the feelings generated by them will be supplanted by the offspring of more sublime ideals, as these are adopted and cherished by you. (What Are You?, p. 24)

In one of the most telling discoveries about emotions of the last decade, LeDoux's work revealed how the architecture of the brain gives the amygdala a privileged position as an emotional sentinel, able to hijack the brain. His research has shown that sensory signals from eye or ear travel first in the brain to the thalamus, and then— across a single synapse—the amygdala; a second signal from the thalamus is routed to the neocortex—the thinking brain. This branching allows the amygdala to begin to respond before the neocortex, which mulls information through several levels of brain circuits before it fully perceives and finally initiates its more finely tailored response. (Daniel Goleman, *Emotional Intelligence,* Bantam House, New York, 1997, p. 17)

... I finally asked the Lord[1] [our Divine Consciousness] just why I did not get well. I explained that I had gone all through my consciousness to see what it was that held me, and that I had tried to find the fault.

The Spirit said to me, "You have looked among your faults; now look among your virtues." I thought that strange, but soon it came to me that I had tried to keep my feelings to myself, taking great pride in the fact that I never let anyone know just how I felt when anything displeased me or hurt me. I found that I did not feel as sweet and poised on the inside as I seemed out-

wardly. I began to watch and to redeem this state of mind. I determined to handle all that came to me, before I "swallowed it" and allowed it to irritate, cut, and weaken my nerves and organs. As I gained real poise and the ability to keep my thoughts and feelings truly free, I was healed and restored to strength and normal functioning. (Myrtle Fillmore, *How to Let God Help You*, 3rd ed., Unity House, Unity Village, Mo., 2000, p. 187)

For decades it has been assumed and taught that thoughts always precede feelings. Much of the Unity teachings have been based on this premise; the first two excerpts above express this notion. Knowing that thoughts can sometimes precede feelings is useful to our awakening awareness of Oneness. Feeling is the function of consciousness by which thoughts are empowered and made personal. Feelings reflect our thoughts, and they are the avenues by which we express the energy generated by these thoughts. Observing feelings can be a way to discern the character of our thoughts. Feelings that reflect error thought will be destructive and uncomfortable, whereas feelings that reflect inspired thinking will be constructive and fulfilling.

The excerpt from *Emotional Intelligence* clearly indicates that emotions (feelings) can and do precede thoughts. Research has also shown that even though information is passed in both directions between the parts of the brain called the "amygdala" (associated with feelings) and the "neocortex" (associated with thinking), there are many more neurons running from the amygdala to the neocortex, than there are from the neocortex to the amygdala. Further, there is a cascade of responses from the amygdala that includes the autonomic nervous system and the release of hormones. Therefore, simply thinking positively is sometimes not enough in the face of an emotional reaction arising from the amygdala. It is important to note that Unity does not teach simple positive thinking; it teaches "realization thinking." This is where both thinking and feeling natures are engaged to such depth that a person knows and feels that he or she knows and feels some Truth.

Here are some examples of feelings preceding thoughts.

1. Whenever we have invested time in the Silence we first are aware of the feeling or experience. Then we think about the experience arriving at conclusions and assumptions that we can express in words.

2. A similar process occurs as the result of a mystical experience. A mystical experience is beyond words and difficult to put into thoughts and words that adequately convey the experience.

3. The first of time we experience anything in the relative realm seems to have feelings arising before thoughts. Some examples would be riding a roller coaster, skiing or even burning your fingers for the first time on a stove. First the event occurs, we have an emotional reaction and then we formulate thoughts to understand and communicate about the experience.

Other research has found that some of these responses from the amygdala result from relevant emotional history stored in memories. So, it very well may be that thought and feeling are a kind of unity, two sides of one coin. Perhaps people who tend to be "feelers" become aware of a feeling before a thought, while people who tend to be "thinkers" become aware of a thought before a feeling. It would seem that there is only a feeling in the case of memories imbedded in the subconscious mind (a subconscious thought/belief).

Finally, as the excerpt from Unity cofounder Myrtle Fillmore indicates, it is important that we recognize the difference between stuffing our feelings and erasing them. Stuffed or ignored feelings lead to more unproductive and uncomfortable results. Working to change and eliminate feelings implies that we acknowledge they are there and that they may be generating thoughts. Through *realization* (thinking and feeling generated from the

Silence) feelings can be changed or eliminated.

19D **INTUITING**

The natural knowing capacity. Inner knowing; the immediate apprehension of spiritual Truth without resort to intellectual means. ... Through the power of intuition, humankind has direct access to all knowledge and the wisdom of God. (The Revealing Word, pp. 108-109)

If you ask me about the language I use in communicating with God, I am not able to tell you; because you are talking from the standpoint of using words to convey ideas, while in the language of God ideas in their original purity are the vehicles of communication. (Charles Fillmore, *Jesus Christ Heals,* 2nd ed., Unity House, Unity Village, Mo., 1940, p. 32)

Compared with audible language, communion in mind can be said to be without sound. It is the "still small voice," the voice that is not a voice, the voice using words that are not words. Yet its language is more definite and certain than that of words and sounds, because it has none of their limitations. (Jesus Christ Heals, p. 33)

Intuiting is inherent in all humankind and is the highest function of consciousness. Using intuition in its highest form, we become aware of Divine Ideas in "our" Divine Mind. We intuitively perceive Spiritual Truth. It comes in the "language of Spirit" that is not in words. In consciousness, when the language of Spirit arises from our True Nature into human consciousness, it becomes pure knowing and feeling. Intuition is the faculty that translates pure knowing and feeling into word language for the intellect. We need to cultivate an awareness of the perpetual activity of intuition in our lives so that we are able to recognize and discern Divine Guidance (Chapter 5) from *human* intuition, or simple human thought. We develop this capacity to recognize and discern Divine Guidance by investing time in the Silence.

Human intuition is based on sense consciousness and experience remembered or stored in the subconscious mind; it is frequently erroneous. The hallmarks of human intuition are a sense of rush, fear or even dread. There is also the sense that if we do not follow it, something bad will happen.

19E **CULTIVATING BALANCE**

SENSING

Your mind will accept the reports of the senses until you have trained it to distinguish between permanence and impermanence. (What Are You?, p. 27)

THINKING

Do not let your thoughts riot ... Put all the force of order into your thinking. (*What Are You?*, p. 33)

FEELING

Harness your moods. Make them work for you. They embody great power. (*What Are You?*, p. 34)

INTUITING

You do not have to wait on time or on inspiration. ... Time always is yours; inspiration is continuous. (*What Are You?*, p. 34)

Each of these functions can be used from human/collective consciousness or empowered from our True Nature, Christ. Through conscious awareness, each of the four functions must be developed and utilized to its full potential so we are able to achieve a balanced state of consciousness. It is ironic and seemingly paradoxical that we must use Christ Nature to achieve the balanced state of mind that is also understood as a prerequisite to the development of Christ Consciousness. This is resolved, little by little, as we make use of choices from our Individuality—the amount of Christ consciousness that we have already realized.

SUMMARY STATEMENTS

▼ *The <u>four functions of consciousness</u> are a framework by which we become aware of our spiritual, mental, emotional and physical natures.*

▼ *<u>Sensing</u> refers to the use we make of our five senses in order to experience the external or physical world. Sensing is direct outer knowing.*

▼ *"... sensation finds an interior faculty through which it expresses itself in perpetual ecstasy." (Talks on Truth, p. 84)*

▼ *<u>Thinking</u> is the formulating process of mind known as the intellect that translates Divine Inspiration into mental concepts.*

▼ *<u>Feeling</u> is the function of consciousness by which thoughts are empowered and made personal.*

▼ *<u>Feelings</u> may precede thoughts, and thoughts may precede feelings. They intercommunicate through neural pathways between the amygdala and the neocortex in the brain.*

▼ *<u>Intuiting</u> is direct inner knowing. It is the function of consciousness by which we become aware of Divine Ideas directly from Divine Mind.*

▼ *It is important to make right use of our functions of consciousness and develop them to the fullest in order to achieve a <u>balanced</u> state of consciousness.*

TOPICS FOR DISCUSSION

1. *What are some of the ways in which our intellect can deceive us? How can we develop our intellect so that it serves to enhance our process of spiritual evolution?*

2. *What are some ways in which we can cultivate a greater awareness of our intuitive function of consciousness? How can we recognize true guidance?*

THOUGHTS FOR REFLECTION AND MEDITATION

"Clothe your mind with the garments of Truth, and let your thoughts yield to you their wealth of spiritual power. Think from the Truth standpoint when you think about the outer, material world. It is by your spiritual thinking that you build up your spiritual consciousness."

(Myrtle Fillmore, *How to Let God Help You*, 3rd ed., Unity House, Unity Village, Mo., 2000, p. 119)

SUPPLEMENTARY READING

Atom-Smashing Power of Mind by Charles Fillmore, 2nd ed., Unity House, Unity Village, Mo., 2006, Chapter 11, "The Only Mind."

God Is the Answer by Dana Gatlin, revised paperback edition, Unity House, Unity Village, Mo., 1995, Chapter 2, "Buried Talents."

CHAPTER TWENTY

THOUGHT/FEELING

INTRODUCTION

This chapter focuses on the Law of Cause and Effect and the Law of Mind Action by which Divine Mind ideates (creates) and mind thinks. By mind is meant consciousness and not the physical structure, the brain. When we use the term *thought* in Unity, we almost always mean the combined energies of thought and feeling. We will develop our understanding of how Divine Ideas are translated into thoughts and images in our minds for the purpose of manifestation. We will discover that we contribute in a profound way to the forming of our physical, mental and emotional realities. As we come to understand more about these Laws, we will become aware of our ability to consciously use them to create and form our lives.

20A DOMINION

Humankind is given authority and dominion over all ideas. (Charles Fillmore, *Mysteries of Genesis,* 2nd ed., Unity House, Unity Village, Mo., 1998, p. 28)

The dominion given you as your divine right is over your own thoughts only. When you fully apprehend this and begin to exercise your God-given dominion, you begin to find the way to God, the only door to God, the door of mind and thought. (Charles Fillmore, *Prosperity,* Unity House, Unity Village, Mo., 1936, p. 92)

Our dominion is over our own thoughts, emotions, and passions. (Charles and Cora Fillmore, *The Twelve Powers,* Unity House, Unity Village, Mo., 1999, p.140)

Dominion is an inner consciousness obtained only through mind discipline. (Charles Fillmore, *The Revealing Word: A Dictionary of Metaphysical Terms,* 2nd ed., Unity House, Unity Village, Mo., 2006, p. 57)

Dominion is one of the Twelve Powers and is more commonly known as the Power of Power. It is our ability to master, have dominion and control. In

Genesis 1:26 humankind is said to have dominion over the fish, birds, cattle, wild animals and every creeping thing. This is more commonly understood to mean that we have dominion over physicality. Metaphysically, it is dominion over our own ideas, thoughts, feelings and passions; dominion over the earth is dominion over human sense consciousness. We claim Dominion by controlling our own consciousness and by making choices from Superconscious Mind. We use Divine Ideas from Superconscious Mind to inform our expression of "God's image and likeness," the Christ (the Divine Idea made up of Ideas).

In exercising Dominion as heart-centered metaphysicians, we must be good stewards as well as have good will or good intention so that we are not hard on ourselves.

20B CAUSE AND EFFECT

All true action is governed by law. Nothing just happens. There are no miracles. There is no such thing as luck. Nothing comes by chance. All happenings are the result of cause and can be explained under the law of cause and effect. (*Prosperity,* p. 58)

Effects and causes are inseparable. They are a balanced equation. Most of us begin with effects and try to work from them, but the true metaphysician *begins with causes.* (Ernest C. Wilson, *Many Mansions: A Book of Sermons,* Christ Church, Los Angeles, 1946, p. 18)

The outer acts are secondary; the primal world of causes is within, and it is to this inner realm that we must look for the transforming power of each individual and of the word about him or her as well. (Charles Fillmore, *Jesus Christ Heals,* 2nd ed., Unity House, Unity Village, Mo., 1940, p. 16)

In Spirit, cause and effect are one. They appear as one, and the ultimate is just as clear as the inception. (Charles Fillmore, *Keep a True Lent,* 2nd ed., Unity House, Unity Village, Mo., 2005, p. 46)

All ideation, creation and formation are based on the Law of Cause and Effect. All cause is in the realm of mind (consciousness), whether we are referring to Divine Mind or the human mind, Divine Consciousness or human consciousness. Effects are the result of thoughts held in mind (not brain) with feeling. This insight helps us become aware of the power of our thoughts/feelings to shape and form our world.

At the level of consciousness as well as Spirit, cause and effect are never separate; they are always one. When you have a thought, you have the *effect* of that thought at the same time accompanied by a feeling. The tendency is to erroneously separate cause and effect in time and space. Cause and effect are mistakenly separated in time by saying, "I am feeling the way I am because of something that happened in the past or might happen in the future." In fact, what is truly happening is a *present* thought/feeling *about* the past or future that is giving rise to the *present* effect. Cause and effect are inaccurately separated in the present by *space*. I say, "I am feeling the way I am because of what you (over there) are saying to me right now." In fact, it is what I am thinking or believing and feeling about what you are saying that is giving rise to the effect. We are not saying the events in the past, present or future did not occur; we are saying that the effects we feel and experience in our own consciousness are the result of a present cause in our own minds. Cause and effect are not separated.

20C THE POWER OF THOUGHT

Humankind is the power of God in action. To humankind is given the highest power in the universe, the conscious power of thought. (*The Twelve Powers*, p. 68)

We have no independent mind—there is only universal Mind—but we have consciousness in that Mind, and we have control over that consciousness. We have control over our own thoughts, *and our thoughts fill our consciousness.* (Charles and Cora Fillmore, *Teach Us to Pray*, 2nd ed., Unity House, Unity Village, Mo., 2007, p. 138)

The thinking faculty in humankind makes each person a free agent, because it is our creative center; in and through this one power, we establish our consciousness—we build our world. (*Keep a True Lent,* p. 114)

In Reality we have no independent mind (consciousness). There is only one universal Divine Mind (Oneness, Beingness), and we seem to have independent and separate consciousness within that Mind (Consciousness). In this seeming separate consciousness we have our own thoughts/feelings and we have control over them. These thoughts/feelings fill our consciousness and awareness.

It is by our thoughts and feelings that we transform our inner world as well as the seeming outer world. It is important to remember that when we use the term *thought* we are referring to the combined energies of both thinking and feeling natures.

20D THE LAW OF MIND ACTION

There is a chain of mind action connecting cause and effect in all the activities of life. This chain is forged by humankind, and its links are thoughts, words. (Jesus Christ Heals, pp. 132-133)

We must realize all the while, however, that whatever we put as seed into the subconscious soil will eventually bring forth after its kind ... (Prosperity, p. 67)

Whatever the seed word is that is implanted in omnipresent Spirit substance, this seed word will germinate and grow and bring forth fruit "after its kind." Just as the farmer therefore selects the very best seed corn for planting, so we must choose the words that will bring forth the rich harvest of plenty. (Teach Us to Pray, p. 40)

The Law of Mind Action is usually phrased "thoughts held in mind produce after their kind." It is more accurate to say, "thoughts and feelings or thought/feelings held in mind produce after their kind. This is because thoughts without feelings carry little energy and tend to have fewer effects. If we are talking about producing after their kind in physicality, it is more accurate to say that "thoughts/feelings held in mind *tend* to produce after their kind." Evidence of this is all around us. Most people have had the experience of holding a thought with feeling that resulted in no outward expression. Therefore, it is useful to look at the Law of Mind Action in several ways: in consciousness, in experience, in the body and in the physical world beyond the body.

- *In consciousness:* The thoughts held with feeling tend to give rise to like thoughts. These thoughts/feelings do not change until we choose to change our thinking/feeling.

- *In experience:* Our thoughts, beliefs and ideas create our experience of the world which includes our feelings. Our thinking is the *cause,* and the experience is the *effect.* Cause and effect are inseparable.

- *In the body:* At the level of the physical body, scientific research is catching up with metaphysical thinking. It is now known that the mind-body connection is hardwired. There is a mind-body connection that results in our thoughts, feelings and emotions affecting our bodies. Our thoughts, feelings and emotions have a direct influence on our bodies, most notably the immune system.

- *In the physical world:* Our thoughts/feelings, beliefs and ideas do not necessarily create the events in the world around us. Many of us have known a hypochondriac who thinks and feels that he or she has some dreadful disease, but it never occurs. However, the experience of the disease does occur in consciousness, in the mind of the person. In order to have events and activities in the outer realm, there must be an originating thought somewhere by someone charged with feeling and emotion.

Regardless of whether thought/feeling has an effect on the outer realm, thought/feeling always has effects at the level of consciousness. This is sufficient reason for each person to be vigilant of the thoughts and feelings being held. Dominion over these thoughts/feelings can lead to the disempowering of an unwanted thought/feeling or belief in the personality (ego), and the heightened awareness of Oneness, or Divine Mind (Divine Consciousness).

20E **METAPHYSICAL GUILT AND MALPRACTICE**

Metaphysical guilt has no place in heart-centered metaphysics. It can arise when people use the Law of Mind Action to beat themselves up for some event or physical distress in their lives. We humbly suggest that each person use this Law productively, knowing that thoughts, feelings and emotions held in mind (consciousness) related to Divine Ideas, such as Wholeness and Abundance, produce life-enhancing results.

Nor does metaphysical malpractice have a place in heart-centered metaphysics. It occurs when someone misuses the Law of Mind Action or uses it in unkind ways. Frequently this malpractice shows up as saying to someone who is ill, "What have you been holding in consciousness to produce this illness?" Sometimes a person cannot know if it was his or her own thought/feeling or a thought/feeling held in collective consciousness having its way. Therefore, we would do well to ask, "What is the most supportive and positive response can I make to this situation?" Part of that response will always be to hold the situation and all concerned in prayer, knowing the Truth that everyone is already whole and perfect.

20F **COLLECTIVE CONSCIOUSNESS**

The beliefs that you and your ancestors have held in mind have become thought currents so strong that their course in you can be changed only by your resolute decision to entertain them no longer. They will not be turned out unless the ego through whose domain they run decides positively to adopt means of casting them out of consciousness, and at the same time erect gates that will prevent their inflow from external sources. This is done by denial and affirmation; the denial always comes first. (The Twelve Powers, p. 154)

The work that the overcomer does for the world is to help establish a new race consciousness, "new heavens and a new earth, wherein dwelleth righteousness." By being true to his highest understanding of Truth the overcomer never swerves to the right nor left for any reason. (Charles Fillmore, Atom-Smashing Power of Mind, 2nd ed., Unity House, Unity Village, Mo., 2006, p. 39)

Spiritual harmony in humankind depends largely on the right relation of the inner and the outer realms of our consciousness. Expression is the law of life. Whatever is expressed becomes manifest. I realize that as an overcomer, I am working also for the whole world, establishing a new race consciousness, "new heavens and a new earth." (Keep a True Lent, p. 190)

"Collective consciousness" is the current terminology that replaces "race consciousness" found in Unity's early writings. Some are advocating for the term "mass consciousness" because the word "collective" has the connotation of a collection of consciousnesses when all it is a collection of beliefs. Not all of collective consciousness is negative or undesirable. There are good beliefs and ideas within it, such as the belief in the goodness of humankind; we want to maintain and nurture the desirable content. However, as the first excerpt indicates, the undesirable content of collective consciousness needs to be detected and transformed. An example of undesirable content is the collective belief in illness. Spiritual discrimination and good judgment (the Power of Wisdom) enable us to discern the difference between true and false,

positive and negative. The use of our illumined Power of Will (the ability to choose) enables us to make positive and productive choices. Our conscious mind is able to say *no* to the unwanted elements in collective consciousness (denial/release/The Power of Elimination) and *yes* to that which is creative and useful (affirmation/The Power of Faith). The concept of collective consciousness in relation to the human condition must be considered seriously; however, it poses no permanent barrier to one who is functioning in awakened spiritual awareness.

The collective consciousness can be the cause of the events or illnesses in an individual's life. This is why metaphysical guilt and malpractice are to be avoided. One may become ill or have other untoward circumstances due to the subconscious thoughts held in the collective consciousness. Certainly, Jesus' life demonstrates how collective consciousness as well as seeming individual consciousness resulted in persecution during much of his life, ending in crucifixion. Whether an illness or untoward circumstance is due to seeming individual or collective consciousness, the conscious work is always the same: use the Law of Mind Action. Use denials to declare that no power is being given to these thoughts and feelings in personal or collective consciousness. Use affirmations with feeling to claim, hold and realize thoughts that affirm Truth.

Finally, each of us must do our own work in consciousness to establish a new Heaven (an elevated state of consciousness) and new Earth (sense consciousness), to establish new and higher states of consciousness. As this is accomplished, the entire collective consciousness is affected and elevated. Individuals overcoming the undesirable content of the collective consciousness must use the Power of Strength, the ability to stay the course and endure, and swerve neither left nor right; this is accomplished by being true to our highest understanding of Truth. As seeming individual consciousness is raised, so, too, is collective consciousness.

SUMMARY STATEMENTS

▼ *Humankind, including each individual, has <u>dominion</u> over thoughts, emotions and passions.*

▼ *All <u>cause</u> is in the realm of mind (consciousness. <u>Effects</u> are the results of thoughts held in mind. This holds true for Divine Mind and the human mind. Divine Consciousness and human consciousness.*

▼ *Through the <u>power of thought</u>, we have the ability to shape and form our consciousness and our world.*

▼ *<u>"Thought"</u> is generally used as an overarching term that means both thinking and feeling nature.*

▼ *The <u>Law of Mind Action</u> says that thoughts held in mind produce after their kind. This is absolutely true as it pertains to consciousness. What we think, especially in utilizing both our thinking and feeling natures, increases in consciousness and shapes our experience of the world—but not necessarily the events.*

▼ *The <u>collective consciousness</u> (race consciousness) of humankind contains a mixture of both truth and error beliefs accumulated throughout the history of the human race.*

▼ *As individuals take dominion (the Power of Power/Dominion) over their own error thoughts, feelings and beliefs while being true to the highest understanding of Truth, their own seeming individual consciousness is raised. This also transforms error thoughts, feelings and beliefs held in collective consciousness.*

TOPICS FOR DISCUSSION

1. *Share a time in your life when you demonstrated your dominion.*

2. *Share a time in your life that you demonstrated the Law of Mind Action.*

3. *What is the relationship of our individual consciousness to collective (race) consciousness? How do we go about transforming the error beliefs held in race consciousness?*

THOUGHTS FOR REFLECTION AND MEDITATION

"Your mind is your kingdom. It has no boundaries. The free flow of ideas and creativity is your inheritance. ...It is a wellspring that is inexhaustible."

(Eric Butterworth, *In the Flow of Life*, revised paperback edition, Unity House, Unity Village, Mo., 1994, p. 78)

SUPPLEMENTARY READING

Atom-Smashing Power of Mind by Charles Fillmore, 2nd ed., Unity House, Unity Village, Mo., 2006, Chapter 11, "The Only Mind."

The Emerging Self by Ernest C. Wilson, Unity House, Unity Village, Mo., 1970, Chapter 4, "Thinking."

CHAPTER TWENTY-ONE

THE WORD

INTRODUCTION

Many are familiar with the expression "the Word of God." In this chapter, we will focus on the meaning of the Word, or Logos, which is Christ (not Jesus) as well as the power of the word and the power of the spoken word. It is important to realize that the power is not in the words alone, but also in the intention, thought and feeling behind the words.

21A LOGOS

In pure metaphysics there is but one word, the Word of God. This is the original creative Word, or thought, of Being. It is the "God said" of Genesis. It is referred to in the first chapter of John as the Logos. It cannot be adequately translated into English. In the original it includes wisdom, judgment, power, and, in fact, all the inherent potentialities of Being. This divine Logos was and always is in God; in fact, it is God as creative power. (Charles Fillmore, *Christian Healing*, 2nd ed., Unity House, Unity Village, Mo., 2005, p. 61)

An understanding of the Logos reveals to us the law under which all things are brought forth, the law of mind action. Divine Mind creates by thought, through ideas. (Charles Fillmore, *The Revealing Word: A Dictionary of Metaphysical Terms*, 2nd ed., Unity House, Unity Village, Mo., 2006, p. 124)

Logos is a Greek word translated into English as "Word" with a capital "W." There seems to be no clear single definition or interpretation of this Greek word. The metaphysical meaning of Logos is not something concrete, literal and finished. The general consensus seems to be that Logos denotes Creative Principle in action. Logos originates *in* and *is* God, or Divine Mind.

21B THE WORD OF GOD

The Word of God is immanent in humankind and all the universe. All creation is carried forward by and through humankind's conscious recognition of this mighty One. Humankind is the consummation of the Word. God's spirit has within it the concentration of all that is contained within the Word. God being perfect, God's idea, thought and word must be perfect. Jesus expresses this perfect Word of God as spiritual human being. "The word became flesh, and dwelt among us" (Jn. 1:14). (The Revealing Word, p. 213)

The seed is the symbol of the Word of God, and in its generative qualities it represents the apparent insignificance of the Word as it goes forth from its invisibility and silence. But this Word is a generative center with all the possibilities of God at its call. It is the idea of God, the image and likeness. It is just like God in its essentials, and needs only to be planted in fertile ground to produce the living picture of which it is the image. In its highest degree of expression this is humankind. Christ is the Word of God. It was in the beginning with God, and is now with God. It came forth from God. ... So the "seed," that is, "the word of God," is humankind; not the external thinking personality that has a consciousness of separation, but the internal spiritual germ. The central

seed is the generative center from which the personal man forms himself. (Charles Fillmore, *Atom-Smashing Power of Mind*, 2nd ed., Unity House, Unity Village, Mo., 2006, p. 136)

In the beginning was the Word, and the Word was with God, and the Word was God. He was in the beginning with God. All things came into being through him, and without him not one thing came into being (Jn. 1:1-3).

The Word of God, or Divine Mind, is Creative Principle in action, meaning all creation proceeds from and through the Word. This concept is first presented in the book of Genesis. The symbolic imagery is that of a gigantic "person" who literally speaks words that instantly come true. This makes for an interesting story, but it raises a number of unanswerable questions on the strictly literal level. Taken as allegory, however, it illustrates the action of the Creative Principle of God in the form of the Word (Logos). This is the metaphysical meaning of "And God said ..." (Gen. 1:6).

From John 1:1 we learn that the Word was *with* God and *is* God. In traditional Christian theologies the Word is Jesus Christ. For Unity, the Word is the Christ. To be a bit more precise, Divine Mind is made up of Divine Ideas. Christ is the Divine Idea that is made up of Ideas. So we can think of Christ being a kind of Master Divine Idea, or the Divine Idea. Essentially, then, we have the Word=Christ=the Divine Idea=Divine Mind=God.

From the excerpts above, we can see that, according to Unity co-founder Charles Fillmore, the Word may also refer to "man" or "humankind." Fillmore is definitely not saying that the Word refers to the personality or the body. More accurately, we experience the Word at first as the seed of Christ Potential, a seed in consciousness. It is from this Christ Potential, the seed Idea, from which "the personal man forms himself." Thus, the physical body and the "external thinking personality" are actually effects of the seed Idea, which is limited by the consciousness of the individual.

21C **WHAT ARE WORDS?**

The vehicles through which ideas make themselves manifest. Words that have in them the realization of perfect, everywhere-present, always present divine life, and our oneness with this life, are dominant in the restoration of life and health.

When spiritual words abide in one's consciousness, the word or thought formed in intellectual and sense mind must give way to the higher principles of Being. The whole consciousness is then raised to a more spiritual plane. Affirmation of words of Truth realized in consciousness brings the mind into just the right attitude to receive light, and power, and guidance from Spirit. (The Revealing Word, pp. 213-214)

Words bring forth after their kind. Words from the Inner Realm of Divine Life/Oneness manifest good, including the restoration of our realization of Life and Health.

Words are the means by which we express ideas and thoughts. Realization of the power of words will not come if they are viewed as only sounds or as a combination of letters on a printed page. Like ambassadors who have a mandate to carry the power and authority of their governments, words carry the power and authority of their originating consciousness. Words are really expressions of consciousness, and consciousness is the ruling factor. Words may either be based on sense consciousness and the outer realm, or on Oneness, Divine Mind and the Inner Realm.

21D **POWER OF THE WORD**

Everybody realizes to some degree the effect of words. Every word has a three-fold power: first, the force of the primal idea; second, what has been put into it by collective use; and third, the intelligence and feeling given to it by the speaker. Analyze your words, because every word produces a result. (Unity

Correspondence School Lessons, Series 2, Lesson 6, pp. 14-15)

The power of the word comes from three sources:

1) The Primal Idea(s) or the Divine Idea(s) in Superconscious Mind, or Divine Mind.

2) The addition and coloring of the Divine Idea(s) from thoughts, feelings and beliefs in collective consciousness that primarily reside in the subconscious mind.

3) The intelligence and feeling added by the speaker from the conscious mind.

The wise heart-centered metaphysician observes, evaluates and chooses words with care. They reflect our individual consciousness with corresponding effects.

21E THE SPOKEN WORD

The spoken word carries vibrations through the universal ether, and also moves the intelligence inherent in every form, animate or inanimate. (Christian Healing, p. 68)

Thus, he who realizes most thoroughly that God is the supreme perfection and that in God there can be no imperfection, and speaks forth that realization with conviction, will cause all things to arrange themselves in divine order

[Mind-Idea-Expression]. (Charles and Cora Fillmore, *Teach Us to Pray*, 2nd ed., Unity House, Unity Village, Mo., 2007, p. 172)

When spiritual words abide in one's consciousness, the word or thought formed in intellectual and sense mind must give way to the higher principles of Being. The whole consciousness is then raised to a more spiritual plane. Affirmation of words of Truth realized in consciousness brings the mind into just the right attitude to receive light, and power, and guidance from Spirit. (Revealing Word, pp. 213-214)

The spoken word is much more than just the audible sound of the word; it includes the consciousness of the person who speaks it. When words of Truth are consciously spoken, Truth Consciousness energizes those words and mighty things are accomplished. These are spoken words that have spiritual intention and motivation behind them and carry great power. If a word is consciously spoken with the sole intention of expressing a Divine Idea, it is called an "affirmation of Truth" and it carries the greatest power of all words.

Words used and empowered from the awareness of Oneness are *spiritual* words based on higher principles of Beingness. They have the power to supplant words from the intellect and sense consciousness so that the entire consciousness is raised to a more spiritual plane. This enables a greater awareness of Divine Ideas arising from Spirit.

21F **SONG AND SINGING**

Everybody can sing. Cultivate the singing soul. Through the vibrations of the voice joined with high thinking, every cell in the body is set into action, and not only in the body but out into the environing thought atmosphere the vibrations go and break up all crystallized conditions. The whole universe is in vibration. Vibration is under law. Each particular thing has its rate of vibration. What causes vibration? We answer: Mind. (Charles Fillmore, *Dynamics for Living: A Topical Compilation of Essential Fillmore Teachings,* Unity Books, Unity Village, Mo., p. 1967, 158)

By going to the Source of power, and affirming your oneness with it. Declare that you have power to express in all its fullness your Christ mastery and dominion. Think of all the power of the universe centered at your throat. Sing songs of victory. Raise your voice in praise, and you will lift your whole organism into high, harmonious spiritual radiation. (*Dynamics for Living,* p. 172)

Bring harmony into your life by singing and praising. Everybody should play and sing. We should rejoice in the divine harmony. We should sing songs of joy and of love and of peace and of the unity of the Spirit, the Spirit of Jesus Christ, the supreme Man expressed. (*Dynamics for Living,* p. 175)

You can drive away the gloom of disappointment by resolutely singing a sunshine song. I believe that we could cultivate the power of music in connection with the understanding of Truth and thus rend all the bonds of sin, sickness, and death. The world needs a new hymnal, with words of Truth only and music so strong and powerful that it will penetrate to the very center of the soul. (Charles Fillmore, *Jesus Christ Heals,* 2nd ed., Unity Books, Unity Village, Mo., 1940, p. 173.)

Some people think it almost a sacrilege to sing when they feel bad. They think that that is the time to groan, and they usually do. That is the way the mortal looks at it, and that is the way you may happen to feel, but you can quickly be released from the prison of pain or grief if you will sing and praise and pray.

First sing in your soul [conscious and subconscious mind]—you can sing way down inside of yourself—then you will soon be singing with your voice. So we lay down the metaphysical law that everybody should know how to sing. Everybody can sing. It does not make any difference what your previous thoughts have been about your ability to sing, it does not make any difference what you think about it at present, and it does not make any difference whether you can sing or not; cultivate the singing soul and you will some day break forth into a singing voice.

"Nothing accesses the inner world of feelings, sensation, memories and associations as directly as music does," says Diane Austin, adjunct associate professor of music therapy at New York University and executive director of music at the Psychotherapy Center in New York. *"The voice is like a bridge from your heart to your head. Singing freely releases what's locked up in your body."* A pilot study published in the British Journal of Nursing *found that singing therapy could greatly reduce the anxiety and depression patients can experience following a major surgery. The effect was strong enough that authors suggested doctors prescribe therapy before trying antidepressants.* (Sari Harrar, "Sing Two Songs and Call Me in the Morning," *O, The Oprah Magazine*, May 2008, pp. 191-192)

Singing is a very powerful use of the word. It is a means to cut through gloom and to bring harmony to the body. When we sing, we tend to add more feeling nature to our words, thus further empowering them. Singing penetrates into the center of the soul (conscious and subconscious minds).

We actually drive the thoughts, feelings and beliefs expressed by the lyrics of the song deeper and deeper into the subconscious mind. It is therefore important that we sing songs with lyrics that express Truth as clearly as possible.

When we sing songs based on ego belief and thought systems, we are empowering those words and driving them deeper and deeper into the conscious and subconscious minds (the soul). Similarly, when we sing songs based on beliefs from the spiritual traditions in which we were raised, we reinforce that theology in our soul. Unfortunately, singing such songs ensures that we keep one foot firmly rooted in the embedded theology of our childhood while trying to get traction with the other foot in the Truth that Unity teaches.

The following are three effective ways to use and improve your voice:

1. Lie on your back, relax and simply breathe in. As you exhale, make a sound, any sound.

2. Sing a long sustained tone, a vowel sound. Continue this for at least 10 minutes and allow yourself to change the pitch and tone as you go.

3. As you go about your day, sing a happy song. In Unity, these have traditionally been called "joy songs." Remember to use lyrics that reflect the beliefs you want to reinforce.

21G JESUS' USE OF WORDS IN HEALING

Whatever these various theories of Jesus' remarkable healing power may be, no one disputes one point: He used words as the vehicle of the healing potency. He always spoke to the patient "as one having authority." He had a certain assurance, an inner conviction, that he was speaking the truth when he said, "Thou art made whole"; and the result of his understanding carried conviction to the mind of the patient and opened the way for the "virtue" that went forth from the speaker. (Teach Us to Pray, p. 165)

Jesus laid great stress on the power of the word. The word has two activities: One is that of the still small voice in the silence, and the other is that of the "loud voice" that was used by Jesus when he raised Lazarus from the dead. In the beginning "God said, let there be" … and there was. We are the off-spring of God, and our words have power proportionate to our realization of our indwelling spiritual kingdom. (Atom-Smashing Power of Mind, p. 148)

Jesus is a prime example of Logos reaching its final stage as conscious speech. Jesus exemplified this to such an extent that he is sometimes referred to as "the Word become flesh." The words of Jesus came from a consciousness that most of us have not yet attained and may even find difficult to comprehend. This consciousness energized his words and caused them to have overwhelming power. He spoke words from an inner conviction—a deep "realization." Jesus himself constantly called attention to the importance of his words, which remain one form of his presence with us today. Perhaps this form gives new meaning to the "second coming" of Jesus Christ, and it happens every time we use his words.

21H FORMING AND CREATING

Every individual makes his or her own world, and does this through the word. Only to the extent that the individual knows the qualities or attributes of Being, such as life, love, wisdom, power, faith order and so forth, does he or she use them righteously. Humankind in mortal consciousness only partly realized the wisdom, substance, life and power of God, and therefore does not create; one merely forms, and his or her work is not enduring. (Correspondence School Lessons, Series 2, Lesson 6, pp. 6-7)

The Word is the creative idea in Divine Mind, which may be expressed by an individual when he or she has fulfilled the law of expression. All words are formative but not all words are creative. The creative word lays hold of spirit substance and power. (Dynamics for Living, p. 133)

Creative, enduring words are spoken out of the Christ consciousness and not out of the personal consciousness. The personal consciousness [personality] is barren of life-giving substance. The Word is the voice of the indwelling Christ, the immanent or personal God of each individual [individuality]. (Correspondence School Lessons, Series 2, Lesson 6, p. 15)

There is a difference between words that are formative and words that are creative. Formative and creative words have the same starting point: a Divine Idea that is manifested by means of the creative process (Divine Order) of Mind, Idea, Expression (Manifestation, Consciousness). However, we each decide the world we want to form or create based on our own level of consciousness.

We shape our world using feeling infused formative words when, primarily from our personality (intellect and sense consciousness), we couple the power of the word with a limited understanding of a Divine Idea like Wisdom, Substance, Life, etc. When we engage our personalities, our words are formative and their results are less enduring. In a sense, we form our world from a "warped" or at least limited understanding of the Divine Idea.

When we remember and are aware of our Higher Nature, our Individuality, our words infused with feeling are creative. We "lay hold of" (become aware of) a Divine Idea in as pure a state as possible. We then use the power of the word to create our experience of the world.

211 THE EFFECTS OF FORMATIVE WORDS

The use of words without wisdom makes and maintains ignorance in the world. We find it literally true that "every idle word that people shall speak, they shall give account thereof in the day of judgment." Idle words are words that do not measure up to the standard of the Word of God. This warning of Jesus would be better heeded if one realized that every day is a day of judgment; that every day some of his or her word seeds come to fruition as pain and suffering in some form or other, for every word of ignorance makes its mark in the body. Ignorant words cast a shadow over one's path, and one cannot see the way; they dull a person's ears until he or she cannot hear the counsel and guidance of Spirit. (Correspondence School Lessons, Series 2, Lesson 6, p. 14)

Words that do not carry the consciousness of divine power, Christ power, produce negative conditions; and the result of their use is failure to manifest the Christ dominion and mastery. Words lacking the substance of Spirit are "empty words" and produce conditions of hunger, lack and poverty. Much of what is called sickness and disease in the world comes from feeding on empty words. Empty words are words that are void of Truth. Such words leave a vacuum in the mind, and the sensation of emptiness is reflected into the body and the affairs. (Correspondence School Lessons, Series 2, Lesson 6, p. 13)

All words that a person uses carelessly in regard to life, words that do not carry the realization of divine life in one's consciousness, fail to bring forth the manifestation of perfect life and health, and this falling short makes many of the conditions called sickness and disease. (Correspondence School Lessons, Series 2, Lesson 6, p. 13)

Every word that has in it no consciousness of divine love makes discord, because love is the great attracting, harmonizing power, and the Word of God is not expressed in its fullness so long as this unifying power of Being is omitted. This understanding will do away with the use of all condemning, criticizing, faultfinding, and angry words. (Correspondence School Lessons, Series 2, Lesson 6, p. 10)

When formative words are used that are not wholly based in Christ con-sciousness, there are all kinds of unpleasant results: conditions of discord, hunger, lack, poverty and sickness. Therefore, we want to avoid words that arise from the limited awareness of our personality. We want to avoid words that condemn, criticize, find fault and/or are angry. We want to be careful not to put the limitations of intellect and sense consciousness on Divine Ideas, resulting in words that merely form and do not create.

21J RESTORING HARMONY

Harmony and rightful conditions are restored only by an awakening to Truth and by putting Truth into expression by the Word. (Correspondence School Lessons, Series 2, Lesson 6, p. 12)

The soul needs to be fed with the very substance of Spirit in order to satisfy its longings and desires. "Man shall not live by bread alone, but by every word that proceedeth out of the mouth of God" (Mt. 4:4).] We must realize that words of Truth have power to nourish the soul, the body, and the affairs. "Thy words were found, and I did eat them; and thy words were unto me a joy and the rejoicing of my heart." (Correspondence School Lessons, Series 2, Lesson 6, pp. 13-14)

Once we become aware of error thinking and the erroneous use of the power of the word, we have the free will to change our minds and restore harmony. This is accomplished by being still, resting in the Silence, and then, from the Silence, realizing the Truth. We allow this Truth to nourish our souls (conscious and subconscious minds), bodies and affairs. We use this Truth to spiritually empower our words.

21K HOW TO BEGIN SPEAKING THE WORD

A person cannot bring into expression divine, unlimited qualities of Being until one first becomes conscious of the Christ Spirit within. A person cannot manifest that which one does not possess in some degree in one's own mind. (Correspondence School Lessons, Series 2, Lesson 6, p. 13)

When one wishes to speak the word of power, one should become very still and make union with one's Christ power through realizing in this stillness, "I am power." Thus the student unites with the Source of power, he or she has become one with the divine idea, power. When through this communion with the Source one is filled with the consciousness of power, he or she can speak the word that will have in it the very power of God. ... When one thinks and feels this union with the one life, he or she will be able to speak healing, lifegiving words. (Correspondence School Lessons, Series 2, Lesson 6, p. 16)

Let us see then what God does that we may do likewise. As recorded in Genesis, the first fiat of creation is "Let there be light" [Gen. 1:3]. Light means intelligence. Darkness is ignorance. An individual's first word in bringing forth his or her world should be "Let there be light." Instead of saying, "I don't know," thus making darkness, say, "I am illumined with divine intelligence." By your word your world will be lighted with divine understanding. (Correspondence School Lessons, Series 2, Lesson 6, p. 9)

Suppose you are not wholly illumined at once: suppose the darkness does not at once comprehend the light; be sincere, patient and persistent in declaring, "I am the light of the world" [Jn. 9:5], and have faith that your word, being Truth, is Spirit and life and shall bring forth its fruit. (Correspondence School Lessons, Series 2, Lesson 6, p. 9)

When Jesus said, "The words that I have spoken unto you are spirit, and are life" [Jn. 6:63], he knew that in his Words of Truth there were the life, the power, the substance of God. Understanding the power of his words we realize the force of his counsel: "If you abide in me, and my words abide in you, ask whatsoever you will, and it shall be done unto you" [Jn. 15:7]. (Correspondence School Lessons, Series 2, Lesson 6, p. 10)

Our part is to understand how to keep Jesus' words, and the only way this can be done is to so write them on our heart that they will be embodied in the flesh. To write them on our heart is not merely to give an intellectual assent that they are true, but it is to repeat them over and over with the realization that they are words of Truth, containing life, substance, intelligence, power. By consciously understanding, laying hold of them in this way, the truths gradually settle down into the subconscious phase of mind—the heart. It is the subconscious that brings forth our body and affairs. Just committing them to memory does not "keep" them, for we must consciously live them until they are so established in our subconsciousness that spontaneously and effortlessly they are manifested in our daily life. (Correspondence School Lessons, Series 2, Lesson 6, p. 10)

One of the ideas in Divine Mind is substance, and its scriptural name is "the earth." "In the beginning, God created the heavens and the earth. And the earth was waste and void" [Gen. 1:1]. This substance idea must be formed in the mind of a person and established through faith. This forming of the substance is symbolized by the appearance of "dry land" as recorded in Genesis. Out of the substance idea the personal ego has conceived matter, which is the unreal and transient in the structures that mortal humankind has formed.

Humankind has creative power and uses it to make substance into form. Every thought and every word works in the universal ether and out of it humankind makes his or her body and environment. (Correspondence School Lessons, Series 2, Lesson 6, p. 17)

Each of us has creative power and uses it to turn Substance into form and matter. Every thought and every word, especially those charged with feeling, works in the universal "ether" and out of it we form our bodies and our environment. Here is an overview of the process outlined in the quotes above. This is simply a framework from which to work. Please do not be rigid stick to these particular words; rather, see them as a model.

1. Remember that Jesus said, "If you abide in me, and my words abide in you, ask whatsoever you will, and it shall be done unto you."

2. Become conscious of the Christ Spirit within consciousness by entering the Silence and realize Oneness, Christ, Divine Mind.

3. From the Oneness, realize Christ Power and declare:

I am Christ. I am Power.

4. Your first words in bringing forth your world should be *Let there be light,* then declare:

I am illumined with Divine Intelligence.

5. Be sincere, patient and persistent in declaring:

I am the light of the world,

and have faith that your word, being Truth, is Spirit and Life and shall bring forth its fruit.

"By consciously understanding, laying hold of Jesus' words" means to repeat them over and over with the realization (feeling infused thought)that they are words of Truth, containing Life, Substance, Intelligence and Power. In this way, the Truth gradually settles into the subconscious phase of mind. It is the subconscious that brings forth our body and affairs.

21L HOW TO SPEAK THE WORD OF ABUNDANCE

One can overcome belief in poverty by entering into a realization of the omnipresent substance of Spirit and from this realization speaking the word of abundance. First make union with the substance idea by claiming, "I am substance," and become conscious of your identity as one and the same as the very substance of God. You are the substance of all that you can ask or think. A person cannot bring into expression divine, unlimited qualities of Being until one first becomes conscious of the Christ Spirit within. A person cannot manifest that which one does not possess in some degree in one's own mind. (Correspondence School Lessons, Series 2, Lesson 6, pp. 17-19)

Follow the general instruction in section 21L. Then in the stillness and from the awareness of Oneness, realize you are Substance and claim It. Repeatedly affirm *I am Substance* until the realization of this Truth occurs. Next take the following steps for speaking the word of abundance:

1. Remember that Jesus said, "If you abide in me, and my words abide in you, ask whatsoever you will, and it shall be done unto you."

2. Become conscious of the Christ Spirit within by becoming very still and realize Oneness, Christ, Divine Mind.

3. From the Oneness, realize Christ Power and declare:

I am Christ. I am Power.

4. Your first words in bringing forth your world should be *Let there be light, then* declare:

I am illumined with Divine Intelligence.

5. Be sincere, patient, and persistent in declaring:

I am the light of the world,

and have faith that your word, being Truth, is Spirit and Life and shall bring forth its fruit.

6. Repeatedly affirm:

I Am Substance

until the realization of this Truth occurs. Keep doing this until you know that you know, despite outer circumstances, that this is the Truth.

21M HOW TO SPEAK THE WORD FOR HEALING AND STRENGTHENING THE BODY

You must consciously free the life center from all the ignorant thoughts that have been stored there. Tell it that it is not limited to threescore years and ten of imperfect manifestation, but is one with universal, omnipresent, unchanging, perfect, eternal Life. Tell it that it is not carnal and evil, but pure with the purity of Spirit. Tell it that it is not material, but that it is the pure substance of Spirit. The Word will set it free, quicken it to activity, and promote an inflow of the pure, rich, spiritual substance of life.

Speak to the power center at the root of the tongue. Deny all inefficiency and declare, "All power is given unto me in mind and in body."

Go in consciousness to the love center near the heart and tell it the truth. It is not filled with selfishness, but with the substance of divine love, pure universal love.

Quicken the substance center, back of the pit of the stomach, with the word that there is one pure, spiritual substance, and that out of it your body is formed in perfection.

In the strength center, at the small of the back, speak words of strength.

Think of the intelligence manifested in every organ and every function of the body.

Whether you are awake or asleep, the blood is busy carrying on a work that requires intelligence greater than humankind has yet consciously understood. If humankind's ignorance did not interfere with these processes they would build a perfect body and keep it in perfect order. This they will do when, by the power of the Word, the old error states [that] are established in the subconsciousness are dissolved and perfect union is made between the conscious, the subconscious, and the superconscious phases of mind. (Correspondence School Lessons, Series 2, Lesson 6, pp. 21-22)

Again, follow the general instruction in 21K, take the following steps (based on the excerpt above):

1. Remember that Jesus said, "If you abide in me, and my words abide in you, ask whatsoever you will, and it shall be done unto you."

2. Become conscious of the Christ Spirit within consciousness by becoming very still and realize Oneness, Christ, Divine Mind.

3. From the Oneness, realize Christ Power and declare:

I am Christ. I am Power.

4. Your first words in bringing forth your world should be *Let there be light,* then declare:

I am illumined with Divine Intelligence.

5. Be sincere, patient and persistent in declaring:

I am the light of the world

and have faith that your word, being Truth, is Spirit and Life and shall bring forth its fruit.

6. Declare:

I give no power to (fill in your current age) years of imperfect manifestation. I AM universal, omnipresent, unchanging, perfect, eternal Life.

7. Focus awareness to the love center located back of the heart and declare:

I give no power to selfishness. I am filled with the substance of Divine Love, pure universal Love.

8. Focus more awareness to the back of the pit of the stomach. Declare:

There is one pure, spiritual Substance and I form my perfect body out of it.

SUMMARY STATEMENTS

▼ *Logos denotes Creative Principle in action as it relates to the universe. Logos originates in God, Divine Mind. Logos reaches its later stage in us, where it is expressed through us as conscious speech.*

▼ *The Word of God, or Divine Mind, is Creative Principle in action.*

▼ *Words are really expressions of consciousness; and in our world, consciousness is the ruling factor. Words, especially those infused with feeling, carry the power and authority of their originating consciousness.*

▼ *The power of the word comes from the Divine Idea that the word expresses; it also comes from the sense of I AM of the person who speaks the word.*

▼ *The power of the word comes from three sources: Divine Ideas, the additions and coloring from seeming collective consciousness, and the intelligence and feeling added from seeming individual consciousness.*

▼ When words of Truth are consciously spoken, the Truth consciousness is in those words and mighty things are accomplished. The most powerful of all _spoken words_ are affirmations of Truth.

▼ As one use of the power of the word, _singing_ can change gloomy thinking and bring harmony to the body. Therefore, we should be very conscious of the words we are singing.

▼ _Jesus_ is the prime example of Logos reaching its final stage as conscious speech. His words are one form of his presence with us today, giving new meaning to the "second coming" of Jesus Christ, which is happening now.

▼ _Formative words_ are words empowered primarily by our personality (intellect and sense consciousness including the feeling nature). We couple the power of the word with a limited understanding of a Divine Idea like Wisdom, Substance, Life, etc.

▼ _Creative words_ are primarily empowered by our Higher Nature, our Individuality. We couple the power of the word with awareness of a Divine Idea in as pure a state as possible.

▼ We _form our world_ when, from our personality, we couple the power of the word with a limited understanding of a Divine Idea like Wisdom, Substance, Life, etc. When we remember and are aware of our Higher Nature, our Individuality, we then lay hold of a Divine Idea in an unadulterated state and use the power of the word to _create our world_.

▼ When we use words that are not in Christ consciousness, there are _unpleasant results_.

▼ _Restore harmony_ after the formative use of words by remembering Oneness, being still, and realizing the Truth.

TOPICS FOR DISCUSSION

1. What is the Word and where does Its power come from?

2. What is the difference between words being formative and words being creative?

3. *What do you see as your biggest obstacle to using words creatively?*

4. *What are some strategies you might employ in order to use your words creatively?*

THOUGHTS FOR REFLECTION AND MEDITATION

"Every idea originating in Divine Mind is expressed in the mind of individual men and women; through thought the Divine Mind idea is brought to the outer plane of consciousness. In the organism of each individual are centers that respond to the divine ideas, as a musical instrument sympathetically responds to musical vibrations. Then through another movement on what is termed the conscious, or most outer, plane of action, the thought takes expression as the spoken word."

(*Christian Healing*, p. 63)

SUPPLEMENTARY READING

Christian Healing by Charles Fillmore, 2nd ed., Unity House, Unity Village, Mo., 2005, Chapter 6, "The Word," and Chapter 7, "The Power of Words."

Keep a True Lent by Charles Fillmore, 2nd ed., Unity House, Unity Village, Mo., 2005, Chapter 10, "The Affirmative Word.."

CHAPTER TWENTY-TWO

DENIALS AND AFFIRMATIONS

INTRODUCTION

Thoughts have their beginnings in Divine Ideas. The use of denials and affirmations is a key tool in heart-centered metaphysics. Denials and affirmations are thoughts that are both a form of prayer and a tool in the transformation of consciousness. In this chapter, we will explore what denials and affirmations are and are not, as well as how to use them to transform consciousness.

22A **THOUGHTS ARE THINGS**

Thoughts are things; they occupy space in the mental field. A healthy state of mind is attained and continued when the thinker willingly lets go the old thoughts and takes on the new. This is illustrated by the inlet and the outlet of a pool of water. Stop the inlet, and the pool goes dry. Close the natural outlet, and the pool stagnates, or, like the Dead Sea, it crystallizes its salts until they preserve everything that they touch. (Charles and Cora Fillmore, *The Twelve Powers,* Unity House, Unity Village, Mo., 1999, p. 144)

It is because thoughts are *things* that we can observe and talk about the Law of Mind Action and the formative power of thought. As things, thoughts and their associated feelings come and go; some are life-affirming, while others are not. Error and negative thoughts/feelings are harmful to our consciousness; when we hang onto them they get "lodged" in the subconscious mind. These thoughts can then outpicture in the world around us in unpleasant ways. When we let these thoughts go, they cease causing harm. We can choose to think new and better thoughts that will generate more positive feelings and attitudes and elevate our consciousness.

22B **KEYS TO THE KINGDOM**

Whatever we bind or limit in earth, in the conscious mind, shall be bound or limited in the ideal or heavenly realm, and whatever we loose and set free in the conscious mind (earth) shall be loosed and set free in the ideal, the heavenly. In other words, whatever you affirm or deny in your conscious mind determines the character of the super-mind activities. All power is given unto you, both in heaven and in earth, through your thought. (Charles Fillmore, *Prosperity*, Unity House, Unity Village, Mo., 1936, pp. 176-177)

The work done on the conscious level of mind is important because this level actually holds the keys to two states of consciousness—Heaven and hell. The keys to the Kingdom of Heaven are two significant abilities not found on other levels of the mind: the abilities to *consent* and to *refuse*. This is where trouble starts and ends; it is also where all improvement begins. The first step to Heaven consciousness is developing self-awareness and focusing more attention on what is going on at the conscious level of mind. We do this by giving attention to what we are thinking. What are our thoughts?

all the intricate thought forms of the universe it becomes complex. The law of mental denial and affirmation will prove its truth to all those who persist-ently make use of it. (Charles Fillmore, *Christian Healing*, 2nd ed., Unity House, Unity Village, Mo., 2005, p. 51)

Denial and affirmation are two parts of one process for the cleansing and rebuilding of consciousness. We use them to evolve consciousness into alignment with Spiritual Law. *Denial* is the ability to let go and release old, outworn, negative thoughts, feelings, attitudes or incorrect beliefs; it is also the ability to refuse or to reject. Denial is the great "no, no" power of the mind. *Affirmation* is the ability to claim, accept and realize the newer, truer, higher, more correct thoughts, feel-ings, attitudes and beliefs. It is the great "yes, yes" power of the mind. Affirmations produce thoughts, feel-ings, attitudes and beliefs more closely aligned with Divine Ideas. (Matthew 5:37: "Let your word be 'Yes, Yes' or 'No, No'; anything more than this comes from the evil one.")

22C DENIAL AND AFFIRMATION

It is found that, by the use of these mind forces, humanity can dissolve things by denying their existence, and that humanity can build them up by affirming their presence. This is a sim-ple statement, but when it is applied in

22D DENIALS

To deny oneself, then, is not to withhold comfort or happiness from the external person, much less to inflict torture upon oneself, but it is to deny the claims of error consciousness, to declare these claims to be untrue. (H.

Emilie Cady, *Lessons in Truth*, Centennial Edition, Unity House, Unity Village, Mo., 2003, pp. 47-48)

What people form that is evil they must unform before they can take the coveted step up the mountain of the ideal. Here enters the factor that dissolves the structures that are no longer useful; this factor in metaphysics is known as denial. Denial is not, strictly speaking, an attribute of Being as principle, but it is simply the absence of the impulse that constructs and sustains. (*The Twelve Powers,* p. 150)

Denial is not the mere wishing or hoping something will go away, nor is it the withholding of comfort or happiness. Denial is not an attribute of Being as Principle. It is more "the absence of the impulse that constructs and sustains."

We have the power to disassociate ourselves, completely and permanently, from any sin, evil, error, false beliefs, thoughts, feelings and attitudes. If we discover that we have empowered destructive thoughts and feelings and allowed them to remain in our consciousness, we have the ability to transform them with statements of denial and affirmation. A denial requires a decision followed by a certain effort of mind, beginning with the deep realization (inner conviction) that the beliefs, thoughts and feelings are truly false. It is an effort made in mind to bring about an "absence." It is

the effort required to say "no," to let go, to refuse or reject. It is the "absence of the impulse that constructs or sustains."

It is important to point out that by the term *denial* we do not mean suppressing or ignoring the challenges in our lives. In fact, in order to successfully utilize the tools of denial and affirmation, we must first *admit* or recognize our present state of affairs that includes the facts as well as our thoughts and feelings about the facts; this is a healthy use of self-awareness and self-knowledge. Then, if we choose to release a belief that is not for our highest good, we refuse to give it any more power. Remember, correct use of denial does not *repress* error belief, thoughts or feelings; rather it *releases* the energy or power we have invested in them. Then, using affirmations, we are ready to bring to awareness those Divine Ideas we will utilize to bring good into all aspects of our lives.

22E HOW DENIALS WORK

In all actual transformation of mind and body a dissolving, breaking-up process necessarily takes place, because thought force and substance have been built into the errors that appear. In each individual these errors have the power that humankind has given to them by his or her thought concerning them. These thought structures must be broken up and eliminated from consciousness. The simplest, most direct, and most effective method is to withdraw from them the life and substance that have been going to feed them, and to let them shrivel away into their own nothingness. This withdrawal is best accomplished by denial of the power and reality of evil and affirmation of the allness of Spirit. Nothing is destroyed, because "nothing" can't be destroyed. The change that takes place is merely a transference of power from an error belief to faith in the Truth, through the recognition that God is good and is all that in reality exists. (Charles Fillmore, *Jesus Christ Heals*, 2nd ed., Unity House, Unity Village, Mo., 1940, p. 63)

Denial is primarily a process concerned with eliminating errors found in one's own consciousness. It is based one of the Twelve Powers—the Power of Elimination/Renunciation. It is a built-in process that supports life-enhancing decisions and choices. It involves thinking and feeling, resulting in the realization that the error is not the Truth. In the spiritual sense, denial is based on the idea that all error thought has no basis in Reality. Therefore, these conditions have no power in and of themselves. They simply have the power, thought force, life and substance that we give them. We use denials to release ourselves from the error thoughts by denying power, life and substance to them. We release ourselves from a belief in the power or reality of anything other than Divine Mind, which is Absolute Reality.

22F HOW TO USE AND CONSTRUCT A DENIAL

Denials may be spoken silently or audibly, but not in a manner to call forth antagonism and discussion. (*Lessons in Truth*, p. 55)

Almost hourly little vexations and fears come up in your life. Meet each one with a denial. ... Do not fight it vigorously but let your denial be the denial of any thought of its superiority over you, as you would deny the power of ants on their little hill to disturb you. (*Lessons in Truth*, p. 53)

Human consciousness is made up of a multitude of false personal and collective beliefs. Denial is the mental process of erasing from consciousness the false beliefs. It clears away belief in evil as reality and thus makes room for the establishing of Truth. Through it we get rid of the shadows. We cleanse the mind. A denial is a relinquishment and should not be made with vehemence. Make denials as though you were gently sweeping away cobwebs. (Charles Fillmore, *Dynamics for Living: A Topical Compilation of Essential Fillmore Teachings,* Unity House, Unity Village, Mo., 1967, p. 66)

Denials are used each time a person becomes aware of a thought, feeling, belief or attitude that is not in alignment with their good and what is desired. They are used each time there is awareness of a thought, feeling, belief or attitude that denies one's True Nature, Christ. Denials are constructed in the present tense and in the first person. While they are spoken silently or audibly, they are never used to "fight" against an erroneous thought; in other words, never speak a denial with a great deal of power or energy. For example, if you become aware of thoughts about not having enough money, you could gently say, "I give no power to thoughts of not having enough money," or "I give no power, life or substance to the thought of lack."

22G AFFIRMATIONS

The affirmation is not to make a thing true, but to prepare in consciousness the way of releasing what is already an eternal reality in the superconsciousness. (Eric Butterworth, "You and Your Mind," *Unity Magazine*, Vol. 161, November 1981, p. 16)

To affirm anything is to assert positively that it is so, even in the face of all contrary evidence. We may not be able to see how, by our simply affirming a thing to be true, a thing that to all human reasoning or sight does not seem to be true at all, that we can bring this thing to pass; but we can compel ourselves to cease all futile quibbling and go to work to prove the rule, each one in his or her own life. (*Lessons in Truth,* p. 60)

There are two uses or purposes for affirmations. One is to educate our minds in positive habits and ways of thinking; the other is to bring Divine Ideas from the unformed to the formed, from the invisible to the visible. Affirmations that identify oneself with the Christ serve to raise personal consciousness, yet they also indirectly raise collective consciousness and demonstrate the Christ Mind to the world.

Affirmations are more than "positive thinking." Affirmations are more than "possibility thinking." Affirmations are *realization thinking*. Realization is when we know that we know something is True regardless of outer appearances or circumstances. Realization is a state of inner conviction that involves thinking and feeling the Truth.

After error beliefs are erased by denials, affirmations train our minds into right thinking and feeling. An affirmation is the process whereby we claim and declare what is already True at the level of Divine Mind, the Absolute Realm; it is a statement of Truth. An affirmation establishes the Truth about Oneness, or Beingness, in our seemingly limited consciousness in the relative realm, regardless of outer appearance or any previous beliefs or attitudes. If possible, a heart-centered metaphysician uses the Power of Imagination with affirmations. Visualize the Truth; see it outpicturing into your experience and the world. Using affirmations build ups, strengthens and empowers a higher, more elevated state of consciousness. For example, after denying power, life and substance to thoughts of lack, one could claim: *"I am Christ, I am abundance*; or *I am Christ, I am prosperous"* while visualizing what that prosperity may look like.

22H **IDEA-THOUGHT-WORD**

Ability to pick up the life current and through it perpetually to vitalize the body is based on the right relation of ideas, thoughts, and words. (Jesus Christ Heals, Foreword)

It is a metaphysical law that there are three steps in every demonstration: the recognition of Truth as it is in principle; holding the idea; and acknowledging fulfillment. Pray believing that you have received, and you shall receive. (Jesus Christ Heals, p. 109)

The metaphysical sequence of idea-thought-word is a form of the law of the Trinity (Mind-Idea-Expression) in its most personal aspect. Involving ourselves with this Trinity, we experience remarkable, even miraculous results. The formula is clear and easy: *Idea* (the Divine Idea), *thought* (our thought or idea, including feeling, about or from the Divine Idea), and *word* (affirmation).

There are three steps in demonstrating the good we desire:

1. Recognize Truth as it is in Principle. For example, having the realization of abundance.

2. Create an affirmation and hold it in consciousness. For example: *I am Christ; I am abundant.* Visualize it.

3. Have Faith; believe you have received—not blind Faith, but understanding Faith, the Power of Faith. "Faith is a deep inner knowing that that which is sought is already ours for the taking" (Charles Fillmore, *The Revealing Word: A Dictionary of Metaphysical Terms,* 2nd ed., Unity House, Unity Village, Mo., 2006, p. 67).

Faith is "the perceiving power of mind linked with the ability to shape substance" (*Dynamics for Living,* p. 52). "Faith is more than mere belief. It is the very substance of that which is believed. Faith working in spiritual substance accomplishes all things" *Dynamics for Living,* p. 53).

22I HOW AFFIRMATIONS WORK

One who knows Principle has a certain inner security given him or her by the understanding of God Mind. Our affirmations are for the purpose of establishing in our consciousness a broad understanding of the principles on which all life and existence depend. (*Prosperity,* p. 56)

In order to demonstrate Principle we must keep establishing ourselves in certain statements of the law. The more often you present to your mind a proposition that is logical and true, the stronger becomes that inner feeling of security to you. (*Prosperity,* p. 57)

Affirmations play an important part in the process of Divine Ideas becoming facts and experiences in our lives. Like denial, affirmation is a process of thinking and feeling, with Faith playing a key role. The affirmation process leads to realization; it is an act of Faith to affirm Truth in the face of contrary appearances. Affirmations work by retraining and enriching our minds to establish the awareness of Divine Ideas in our consciousness; they require repetition by the conscious mind so that the subconscious mind is transformed. Affirmations do not work by changing Divine Mind, which is absolute, unchanged, unchanging, unchangeable. They work by changing our seemingly separate consciousness, including our subconscious and conscious minds (soul). Affirmations change both our thinking and feeling natures by building a consciousness of Oneness, or Christ Nature, and therefore a consciousness of Truth. However, when the feeling nature is not engaged, the words of affirmation, while they have some effect, are merely hollow shells of the Truth—they lack the "spirit" or meaning underlying the words.

22J HOW TO USE AND CONSTRUCT AN AFFIRMATION

In some way, which it is not easy to put into words—for spiritual laws cannot always be compassed in words, and yet they are nonetheless infallible, immutable laws that work with precision and certainty—there is power in our word of faith to bring all good things right into our everyday life. (*Lessons in Truth,* p. 61)

They who have carefully studied spiritual laws find that, besides denying the reality and power of apparent evil, which denying frees them from it, they also can bring any desired good into their lives by persistently affirming it is there already. (*Lessons in Truth,* p. 61)

We use affirmations to renew the mind with Truth. We can also use them to bring desired good into our lives by repeating our affirmations silently or audibly, with Power and Faith, using our thinking and feeling natures. Like denials, affirmations are in the present tense and first person. They are positive statements or realizations of Truth. We do not affirm for things in the future; we affirm that whatever good we desire is already here and now. We affirm what is already true in Divine Mind by establishing it in our seemingly separate consciousness. For example: *I am Christ, whole and perfect.*

SUMMARY STATEMENTS

▼ *Through our* <u>*conscious choice,*</u> *each of us has the ability to look to the Superconscious Mind for guidance and direction. Only in this way can we transform the undesirable beliefs held in the subconscious mind.*

▼ *The "tools" for cleansing the conscious and subconscious minds (soul) are* <u>*denial*</u> *and* <u>*affirmation.*</u>

▼ *The use of denials and affirmation is a process that engages thinking and feeling.*

▼ <u>*Denial*</u> *is our ability to release the energy and the power we have invested in negative (error) thoughts, feelings and beliefs.*

▼ <u>*Denials*</u> *are repeated silently or audibly and are in the present tense. While spoken gently with conviction, they are not used in the sense of fighting against.*

▼ <u>*Affirmations*</u> *confirm the conscious recognition of the eternal Reality of Oneness and Divine Ideas. They are spoken from the realization of Truth.*

▼ <u>*Affirmations*</u> *are repeated silently or audibly, with power. They are in the present tense, the first person and are positive realization statements.*

▼ <u>*Affirmations*</u> *are used to raise consciousness and bring Divine Ideas from the Superconscious Mind to the subconscious and conscious minds (soul) and ultimately to the visible world.*

TOPICS FOR DISCUSSION

1. *Why is it important not to use a denial in an antagonizing or "fighting against" manner?*

2. *Why is it important to follow a denial with an affirmation?*

THOUGHTS FOR REFLECTION AND MEDITATION

"Christian metaphysicians have discovered that people can greatly accelerate the formation of the Christ Mind in themselves by using affirmations that identify themselves with the Christ. These affirmations often are so far beyond the present attainment of the novice as to seem ridiculous, but when it is understood that the statements are grouped about an ideal to be attained, they seem fair and reasonable."

(Charles Fillmore, *Keep a True Lent*, 2nd ed., Unity House, Unity Village, Mo., 2005, p. 71)

SUPPLEMENTARY READING

Lessons in Truth by H. Emilie Cady, Centennial Edition, Unity House, Unity Village, MO, 2003, Chapter 4, "Denials" and Chapter 5, "Affirmations."

Foundations of Unity, Series Two, Vol. 2, Lesson II, "Denials," and Lesson III, "Affirmations."

CHAPTER TWENTY-THREE

CREATION

INTRODUCTION

To the heart-centered metaphysician, creation is an orderly and divine process or formula that is perpetually available, much like the laws and equations of electricity. In this chapter, we will focus on the process by which all creative activity occurs from Divine Mind, beginning in consciousness and then into physical manifestation.

While we speak of Divine Mind and "our mind," it is important to remember that our minds have consciousness in Divine Mind. We will develop our understanding of how Divine Ideas translate into thoughts and images in our minds for the purpose of manifestation. We will discover that we are essential to the forming of our mental, emotional and physical realities by using the Law of Cause and Effect. This Law is particularized in the Law of Mind Action and Divine Order to actively create in this world through the power of our thoughts and words.

23A THE FUNDAMENTALS OF CREATION

The truth is then: That God is Principle, Law, Being, Mind, Spirit, All-Good, omnipotent, omniscient, omnipresent, unchangeable, Creator, Father, Cause and Source of all that is;

That God is individually formed in consciousness in each of us, and is known to us as "Father" when we recognize God within us as our Creator, as our mind, as our life, as our very being;

…

That to bring forth or to manifest the harmony of Divine Mind, or the "kingdom of heaven," all our ideas must be one with divine ideas, and must be expressed in the divine order of Divine Mind. (Charles Fillmore, *Christian Healing*, 2nd ed., Unity House, Unity Village, Mo., 2005, p. 16)

God idealized two universal planes of consciousness, the heaven and the earth, or more properly, 'the heavens and the earth.' One is the realm of pure ideals; the other, of thought forms. (Charles Fillmore, *Keep a True Lent*, 2nd ed., Unity House, Unity Village, Mo., 2005, p. 176)

The fundamental starting point of creation is Divine Mind, also called Principle, Law, Being, Mind, Spirit, All Good, Creator, Father, First Cause and Source. We become aware of the Truth of Mind, and from our relative existence may create the experience of It as "Father," "Mother" or "Creator" when we have the realization that this Oneness is the Source of Mind/mind, our Life/life and our very Beingness/beingness. The starting point is always Oneness, or Divine Mind, and Divine Ideas that are expressed in an orderly process or sequence. The clarity and purity by which Divine Ideas are expressed are determined by our level of consciousness. In order for each of us to consciously participate fully in this process, we need to integrate these insights into every level of our being.

In the original creation (the Spiritual Universe), there is only Divine Mind as Creative Principle. Divine Mind's original creation/ideation is the omnipresent Realm of Divine Ideas (Pure Ideals), out of which all possible thought forms may be brought forth.

Physical forms are an effect of these thought forms.

In the first excerpt above, Charles Fillmore uses the terms *omnipotent*, *omniscient* and *omnipresent* to describe God. This usage is not accurate as described by Fillmore and Emilie Cady in other places. Their preference is to use the terms *omnipotence*, *omniscience* and *omnipresence* in describing Divine Mind, or God. Divine Mind does not *possess* these qualities; Divine Mind *is* these qualities. Walter Starke in his book, *It's All God*, explains it this way: "The most common mistake that a well-meaning spiritual student will make in trying to think of God subjectively is to refer to God as being omnipresent, omniscient or omnipotent. By the addition of the 't' at the end of those words, God is objectified and made into something apart from ourselves. There has to be a thing or a being in order for it be omnipresent, omniscient and omnipotent. Take away the 't' and add a 'ce' and the whole meaning changes. The words become plural, infinite, all inclusive and impersonal."

23B DIVINE IDEAS

The ideas of Divine Mind are whole and complete in their capacity to unfold perpetually greater and more beautiful forms according to the thinking capacity in humankind. (Charles

Fillmore, *Atom-Smashing Power of Mind*, 2nd ed., Unity House, Unity Village, Mo., 2006, p. 94)

Divine ideas are humankind's inheritance; they are pregnant with all possibility, because ideas are the foundation and cause of all that humankind desires. (Christian Healing, p. 13)

Divine Ideas are the most important "things" in the Spiritual Universe. All possibilities that exist and could exist in the relative realm are enfolded in Divine Ideas. Humankind gives form to these Divine Ideas by accepting them and giving them whatever expression we are capable of at our current level of consciousness. As we invest time in meditation and ultimately rest in the Silence, we access levels of consciousness above our current level and therefore are able to utilize Divine Ideas from more elevated states of consciousness.

23C THE PROCESS OF CREATION/DIVINE ORDER

... there is one underlying law and ... through this law all things come into expression; also ... there is one universal Mind, the source and sole origin of all real intelligence. First is mind, then mind expresses itself in ideas, then the ideas make themselves manifest. (Charles Fillmore, *Jesus Christ Heals,*

2nd ed., Unity House, Unity Village, Mo., 1940, pp. 121-122)

... divine order, which is mind, idea and manifestation. (Charles and Cora Fillmore, *The Twelve Powers,* Unity House, Unity Village, Mo., 1999, p. 113)

The movement of every mind in bringing forth the simplest thought is a key to the great creative process of universal Mind. In every act [are] involved mind, idea, and manifestation. The mind is neither seen nor felt; the idea is not seen, but it is felt; and the manifestation appears. (Jesus Christ Heals, p. 54)

Substance is first given form in the mind, and as it becomes manifest it goes through a threefold activity. In laying hold of substance in the mind and bringing it into manifestation, we play a most important part. (Charles Fillmore, *Prosperity,* Unity House, Unity Village, Mo., 1936, p. 15)

All creative processes involve a realm of ideas and a realm of patterns or expressions of those ideas. The patterns arrest or "bottle up" the free electric units that sustain the visible thing. Thus creation is in its processes a trinity, and back of the visible universe are both the original creative idea and the cosmic rays that crystallize into earthly things. (Prosperity, Foreword)

Spiritual creating is ideation in Truth. (Charles Fillmore, *Mysteries of*

Genesis, Unity Classic Library edition, Unity House, Unity Village, Mo., 1998, p. 133*)*

Mind-Idea-Expression is the process of creation/ideation as it unfolds within Divine Mind. This is also how we form or create in the relative realm. Each Idea that exists in Divine Mind is whole and perfect; It manifests first as a thought in consciousness and then, sometimes, in time and space as form.

This orderly sequence is also the definition of Divine Order (Mind-Idea-Expression/mind-idea-manifestation). While the process is Divine and orderly, the outcomes may or may not be. At the level of Divine Mind, the Absolute Realm, it may be useful to think of this as Mind-Idea-*Consciousness.* "Consciousness" is the closest term we use to express the Idea of expression and manifestation in Divine Mind. Mind-Idea-Consciousness is the Principle, Divine Process and Divine Law (the Law of the Trinity) underlying all ideation, creation and formation. Without this sequence there can be no such thing as existence as we know it. It is the orderly sequence and process of the Law of Cause and Effect in action. To understand this Law is to add new awareness of the power of consciousness.

Divine Ideas, like ordinary ideas, are not seen; they are "known" with the thinking nature and "felt" with the feeling nature. First, there are Divine Ideas; then there are thoughts, ideas and feelings about Divine Ideas—the *effects* of Divine Ideas. These thoughts, ideas and feelings are the first level of manifestation and occur entirely in mind, or consciousness. They are first experienced in consciousness, and they may or may not be manifest in the outer realm.

23D CO-CREATION

The ideas of Divine Mind are whole and complete in their capacity to unfold perpetually greater and more beautiful forms according to the thinking capacity in humankind. A person catches mental sight of an idea in Divine Mind and proceeds to put it in terms comprehensible to the person on his or her plane of consciousness. All ideas have their origin in Divine Mind, but their character as unfolded by each person depends entirely upon his or her acquaintance with God. (Atom-Smashing Power of Mind, p. 94)

Some metaphysicians teach that humankind makes itself, others teach that God makes humankind, and still others hold that the creative process is a cooperation between God and humankind. The latter is proved true by those who have had the deepest spiritual experiences. Jesus recognized this dual creative process, as is shown in many statements relative to his work and God's work. "My Father worketh even until now, and I work." God creates in the ideal, and humankind carries out in the manifest what God has idealized. (Christian Healing, pp. 42-43)

The ideas of God are potential forces waiting to be set in motion through proper formative vehicles. The thinking faculty in humankind is such a vehicle, and it is through this that the visible universe has existence. Humankind does not "create" anything if by this term is meant the producing of something from nothing; but he or she does make the formless up into form; or rather it is through his or her conscious cooperation that the one Mind forms its universe. (Atom-Smashing Power of Mind, p. 93)

The traditional term as noted here is *co-creation*. Why this term has been used over the decades is clarified in the second quote above. We recognize the paradox in believing in Oneness and the concept of co-creation that implies more than one. While there does seem to be an "us" (humankind) and Divine Mind, a deeper awareness and understanding of Oneness would show that, in Truth, there is only One and therefore there can only be creation. After all, the seeming individual consciousness has its existence in the collective (race, mass) consciousness and it has its seeming existence with the Oneness. Humankind, collectively and individually, are the *conscious*

transformers of Divine Ideas into form and the "facts of manifest life." We always have the freedom to choose the character and configuration of what those Divine Ideas are transformed into.

It is humankind's thinking and feeling faculties by which Divine Ideas are given form and shape, first in consciousness (mind) and then in outer form. Humankind turns the formless Divine Ideas into form. This is how the physical universe came into existence and has its existence. (See Chapter 11, "The Spiritual Universe and the Physical Universe.")

23E THE WORD/LOGOS

The living Word of God is spiritual principle. It is omnipresent, like the air we breathe, and anyone may apply it. Its premise is that God is good and that God's offspring is like God. You have only to recognize this premise in all that you think and do, and then speak it forth to get the results promised. (Connie Fillmore Strickland, The Unity Guide to Healing, Unity, Unity Village, Mo., 1982, p. 35)

This divine Logos was and always is in God; in fact it is God as creative power. (Charles Fillmore, Mysteries of John, 2nd ed., Unity House, Unity Village, Mo., 2008, p. 11)

The Word of God is immanent in humankind and all the universe. All creation is carried forward by and through humankind's conscious recognition of this mighty One.

Humankind is the consummation of the Word. His or her spirit has within it the concentration of all that is contained within the Word. ... Jesus expresses this perfect Word of God as spiritual humankind. "The Word became flesh and dwelt among us" (Jn. 1:14 RSV). (Charles Fillmore, *The Revealing Word: A Dictionary of Metaphysical Terms,* 2nd ed., Unity House, Unity Village, Mo., 2006, p. 213)

An understanding of the Logos reveals to us the law under which all things are brought forth, the law of mind action. Divine Mind creates by thought, through ideas. (*The Revealing Word,* p. 124)

The Word, or Logos, is a mystical concept—a metaphor that refers to Divine Mind as Creative Principle. Each of us has the ability to express this Creative Principle through our spoken word. The more aware we are of its Source and Nature, the more powerful our word will be. It is important to recall from the chapter on the Word (Chapter 21) that the power of the word comes from three sources:

1) The Primal Idea(s) or the Divine Idea(s) from Superconscious Mind (Divine Mind, or Oneness).

2) The addition and coloring of the word from thoughts, feelings and beliefs in collective consciousness that primarily reside in the subconscious mind.

3) The intelligence and feeling added by the speaker from the conscious mind.

It is wise to observe and analyze the words we use because all words have an effect or result, especially those with the energetic charge of the feeling nature.

23F CREATION—AN ONGOING PROCESS

God is thinking the [spiritual] universe into manifestation right now. Even God cannot create without law. The law of the divine creation is the order and harmony of perfect thought. (*Christian Healing,* p. 18)

... Elohim God creates the spiritual universe and spiritual man. He then rests. He has created the ideas or patterns of the formed universe that is to follow. (*Mysteries of Genesis,* p. 28)

Elohim is God in His capacity as creative power. Create means ideate. Elohim creates the spiritual idea which is afterward made manifest.

God created not the earth as it appears but that which produced the earth.' (Charles Fillmore, *Dynamics for Living: A Topical Compilation of Essential Fillmore Teachings,* Unity House, Unity Village, Mo, 1967, p. *37*)

God creates in the ideal, and man carries out in the manifest what God has idealized. (Christian Healing, p. 43)

It is therefore true, in logic and in inspiration, that humankind and the universe are within God Mind as living, acting thoughts. God Mind is giving itself to its creations, and those creations thus are evolving an independence that has the power to cooperate with, or to oppose, the original God will. It is then of vital importance to study the mind and understand its laws, because the starting point of every form in the universe is an idea. (*Christian Healing,* p. 19)

When we speak of creation as an ongoing process, it does not mean that each creative occurrence is a brand-new creation. When we read, "God is thinking the universe into manifestation right now," it is important to remember that this "universe" is the Spiritual Universe. Divine Mind created (ideated) the Spiritual Universe of Divine Ideas and it is finished in the sense that it is eternally whole and complete with no parts missing. From this creation in the Spiritual Universe/the Realm of Divine Ideas, a process of expression and manifestation continues at all times. This process does not continue because of things being added to the Realm of Divine Ideas, but by means of humankind using those Divine Ideas in various combinations to produce ideas and thoughts and ultimately the manifest realm. What Divine Mind created (ideated) is finished, and the outpicturing of Divine Ideas from humankind is living, growing, unfolding and expanding.

SUMMARY STATEMENTS

▼ *The starting point is always* <u>Oneness, or Divine Mind</u> *and the awareness of Divine Ideas.*

▼ *When we speak of the* <u>creative process</u>, *we are referring to the process by which abstract and formless Divine Ideas become manifest form.*

▼ *We refer to the metaphysical trinity of* <u>mind, idea</u> *and* <u>expression</u> *(manifestation, consciousness) as the creative process. It is also a definition of* <u>Divine Order</u>. *"First is mind, then mind expresses itself in ideas, then the ideas make themselves manifest" (Jesus Christ Heals, pp. 121-122). It is the orderly process or sequence by which everything comes into existence.*

▼ *Humankind creates from the awareness of Oneness and Divine Ideas. Humankind creates from these Divine Ideas putting limits upon them, molding and shaping them according to collective and individual consciousness.*

▼ *The <u>Word</u>, or <u>Logos</u>, is a metaphor that refers to Divine Mind as Creative Principle. Our spoken words are vehicles through which this Creative Principle becomes manifest.*

▼ *<u>What Divine Mind created (ideated) is finished</u>, and the outpicturing of Divine Ideas from humankind is living, growing, unfolding and expanding. <u>Affirmations</u> are used to raise consciousness and bring Divine Ideas from the Superconscious Mind to the subconscious and conscious minds (soul) and ultimately to the visible world.*

TOPICS FOR DISCUSSION

1. *Describe your understanding of how Divine Mind/humankind creates and tell how this process has meaning in your life.*

2. *Share a time in your life when you were aware of your power of thought. What did you learn from this experience?*

THOUGHTS FOR REFLECTION AND MEDITATION

"Dwell much on this concept that life is lived from the inside-out, and that you are a dynamic center in the creative flow which is God [Divine Mind], and that you have a built-in capacity for health and success. You can be more, you can do more, and you can have more in life because you are inexorably linked to the transcendent flow of life."

(Eric Butterworth, *In the Flow of Life*, revised paperback edition, Unity House, Unity Village, Mo., 1994, pp. 26-27)

SUPPLEMENTARY READING

Atom-Smashing Power of Mind by Charles Fillmore, 2nd ed., Unity House, Unity Village, Mo., 2006, Chapter 11, "The Only Mind."

The Emerging Self by Ernest C. Wilson, Unity House, Unity Village, Mo., 1970, Chapter 4, "Thinking."

CHAPTER TWENTY-FOUR

THE TWELVE POWERS

INTRODUCTION

There are 12 inherent Spiritual Faculties (Abilities) that reflect Divine Nature and compose "our own" Divine Nature. By affirming their presence and calling them into expression, we will quicken and develop them into realized Powers within us. The ultimate goal of a heart-centered metaphysician is to exercise and regenerate these Faculties from the awareness of Oneness, Christ Nature may be realized.

Each faculty will be described as it exists within consciousness as well as within the body. These Twelve Powers work together in the process of regeneration as we develop Christ consciousness. *Regeneration* is the process by which we re-establish the awareness of our True Identity, our Christ Consciousness, through the quickening (enlivening) of our innate Powers, or Abilities. (See Chapter 25 for more on regeneration.)

In this chapter, we will be making an important distinction in the use of the Twelve Powers, and we will do this through capitalization. When a power is being used from sense consciousness/personal consciousness, it will not be capitalized. But if it's being used from higher consciousness, that Power will be capitalized.

Charles Fillmore frequently used the term *faculty* in relation to the Powers. The online *Encarta Dictionary* defines faculty as "a capacity or ability that somebody is born with or learns." While the more traditional term *Power* will still be used in this text, we will also be heavily relying on the term *Abilities* because this term is better understood in today's language. Each Power is an Ability to do something. For example, the Power of Will is the ability to choose.

An easy way to remember the Twelve Powers is to use the phrase LIP JUZE FLOWS, in which each letter is the first letter of one of the Powers.

L	I	P
Love	Imagination	Power

J	U	Z	E
Judgment	Understanding	Zeal	Elimination

F	L	O	W	S
Faith	Life	Order	Will	Strength

24A THE TWELVE POWERS

Inherent in the Mind of Being are 12 fundamental ideas, which in action appear as primal creative forces. It is possible for a person to ally with and to use these original forces and thereby cooperate with the creative law, but in order to do this he or she must detach from the forces and enter into the consciousness of the idea lying back of them. (Charles and Cora Fillmore, *The Twelve Powers,* Unity House, Unity Village, Mo., 1999, p. 52)

The subconscious realm in humankind has 12 great centers of action, with twelve presiding egos or identities. When Jesus had attained a certain soul development, he called his twelve apostles to him. This means that when humankind is developing out of mere personal consciousness into spiritual consciousness, they begin to train deeper and larger powers; they send their thoughts down into the inner centers of their organisms, and through their words quicken them [the powers] to life. Where before his powers have worked in the personal, now they begin to expand and work in the universal. This is the First and Second Coming of Christ, spoken of in the Scriptures. The First Coming is the receiving of Truth in the conscious mind, and the Second Coming is the awakening and the regeneration of the subconscious mind through the superconscious or Christ Mind. (The Twelve Powers, p. 15)

The Twelve Powers are the Twelve Fundamental Aspects of our Divine Nature, the Twelve Components of God's "image and likeness" in humankind, the Twelve Disciples of our Christ Mind. They are Divine Ideas that constitute the pattern for perfection within us. At our present level of spiritual evolution, these powers are incomplete in their development and expression. Most are using these abilities from mere personal consciousness. As we come to a fuller realization of our True Nature, we become more able to fully demonstrate our Divine Potential, Christ.

"He [Jesus] went up the mountain and called to him those whom he wanted, and they came to him. And he appointed twelve, whom he also named apostles, to be with him, and to be sent out to proclaim the message" (Mk. 3:13-14).

24B OVERVIEW OF THE TWELVE POWERS

Each of these 12 department heads has control of a certain function in soul [conscious and subconscious mind] or body. Each of these heads works through an aggregation of cells that physiology calls a "ganglionic center." Jesus, the I AM or central entity, has his throne in the top head, where phrenology locates spirituality. This is the mountain where he so often went to pray. The outline gives a list of the Twelve, the faculties that they represent, and the nerve centers at which they preside. (The Twelve Powers, p. 16) (A portion of this excerpt has been printed in chart form on page 251 to increase its usefulness.

The Twelve Faculties exist spiritually as realities in Mind/mind, symbolically as the 12 disciples of Jesus Christ, and as 12 centers of energy within the physical body of every individual. This is not meant to imply that the body centers are the Twelve Powers. We might even say that the locations are the outpicturing of the Powers in the body; in other words, the Powers are expressed through the body from these centers. The choice of body center for each Power was the result of Fillmore's own prayer, meditation and inner self-observation.

Some people do have difficulty understanding all of the pairings of the Powers with the 12 disciples; some of the pairings make more sense than others. Many students challenge the third phase of the listings—the body locations or nerve centers—often asking if these locations/centers are necessary. Fillmore did not teach that it was necessary to know about them, but he did recommend it. Also, he did not invent this idea of the Twelve Powers; it existed long before Fillmore wrote about it. Investigation will reveal that this idea is found in many systems of religions, esoteric schools and branches of more occult teachings. Fillmore simply updated the idea and connected it with his understanding of Christianity. (See the Twelve Powers Chart on page 251.

24C **FAITH**

The faith center, the pineal gland, opens the mind of humankind to spiritual faith. (*The Twelve Powers*, p. 31)

The first and greatest disciple of Jesus was Peter, who has been universally accepted by the followers of Jesus the Christ as a type representing faith. Before he met Jesus, Peter was called Simon. Simon means "hearing," which represents receptivity. We understand from this that listening to the Truth in a receptive state of mind opens the way for receiving the next degree in the divine order, which is Faith. (*The Twelve Powers*, p. 28)

Faith is the perceiving power of the mind linked with a power to shape substance. It is spiritual assurance, the power to do the seemingly impossible. It is a force that draws to us our heart's desire right out of the invisible spiritual substance. It is a deep inner knowing that that which is sought is already ours for the taking, the "assurance of things hoped for" (Heb. 11:1). (Charles Fillmore, *Keep a True Lent*, 2nd ed.,

Unity House, Unity Village, Mo., 2005, p. 148)

Faith is that quality in us which enables us to look past appearances of lack, limitation or difficulty, to take hold of the divine idea and believe in it even though we do not see any evidence of it except in our mind. Through faith we know with an inner knowing the Truth that has not yet expressed in our manifest world. (Winifred Wilkinson Hausmann, *Your God-Given Potential: Unfolding the Twelve Spiritual Powers,* revised paperback edition, Unity House, Unity Village, Mo., 1999, p. 38)

Faith is more than mere belief. It is the very substance of that which is believed. Faith working in spiritual substance accomplishes all things. This is the faith that cooperates with creative law. When it is exercised deep in spiritual consciousness, it finds its abode. Here it works under divine law, without variation. It brings results that are seemingly miraculous. (Charles Fillmore, *Dynamics for Living: A Topical Compilation of Essential Fillmore Teachings,* Unity House, Unity Village, Mo, 1967, p. 53)

Peter represents the Power of Faith, located in the pineal gland. It is our Ability to perceive the reality of Divine Mind's Kingdom of Good, despite evidence to the contrary. It is the Faculty of positive expectation and definite assurance that the power, presence and promise of Divine Mind are real, here and now. In the words of the Indian writer-philosopher Rabindranath Tagore, "Faith is the bird that feels the light when the dawn is still dark." Said another way, faith is the bird that feels the dawn and sings before first light.

Faith in the absolute realm: the Ability to believe, intuit, perceive, to have conviction, to hear.

From sense consciousness and personal consciousness: the ability to believe erroneously based on sense consciousness, error thoughts and feelings; believing in things of the outer realm. "Belief, human intuition, conviction, opinion."

From Spiritual Awareness/Higher Consciousness: the Ability to believe and perceive the Reality of Divine Ideas, Truths, Principles and Laws. "Conviction, Spiritual Intuition."

Affirmation: *I claim my Power of Faith. I perceive and spiritually intuit Divine Ideas.*

Scripture: "Now faith is the assurance of things hoped for, the conviction of things not seen. Indeed, by faith our ancestors received approval. By faith we understand that the worlds were prepared by the word of God, so that what is seen was made from things that are not visible" (Heb. 11:1-3).

24D STRENGTH, STABILITY AND STEADFASTNESS

Among the apostles of Jesus, the strong man is designated as Andrew, brother of Peter. The Greek meaning of Andrew is "strong man." (The Twelve Powers, p. 34)

Gaza means a "citadel of strength." It refers to the nerve center in the loins, where Andrew (strength) reigns. (The Twelve Powers, p. 18)

In the Mind of God, strength is an idea of enduring power, which to us means the continuous and sustained energies with which creation is projected and maintained. (Ella Pomeroy, *Powers of the Soul and How to Use Them,* Island Press, New York, 1948, p. 13)

Strength—The energy of God. Freedom from weakness; stability of character; power to withstand temptation; capacity to accomplish. (Charles Fillmore, *The Revealing Word: A Dictionary of Metaphysical Terms,* 2nd ed., Unity House, Unity Village, Mo., 2006, p. 186)

The strength discussed here is not physical strength alone, but mental and spiritual strength. All strength originates in Spirit; and the thought and the word spiritually expressed bring the manifestation. (The Twelve Powers, pp. 37-38)

Andrew represents the Power of Strength, which is physically located in the loins (lower back). It is the faculty of steadfastness, dependability, stability and capacity for endurance. More than a physical endowment, it is also a degree of Spiritual awareness. The Power of Strength is not force, manipulation or defensiveness; it is spiritual courage and confidence. Nonresistance is the highest expression of strength; it does not mean non-action, but is an effective, calm, single-minded, Divine Mind-centered attitude of mind.

Strength in the Absolute Realm: the Ability to endure, stay the course, last, be persistent, persevere; to be stable.

From sense and personal consciousness: the ability to endure and hold on, based on sense consciousness, error thoughts and feelings; hanging on to things in the outer realm. "Stubbornness, forcefulness, obsessive compulsiveness."

From Spiritual Awareness/Higher Consciousness: the Ability to persevere and hold on to Divine Ideas, Truths, Principles and Laws. "Endurance, Perseverance."

Affirmation: *I claim my Power of Strength. I stay the course based on Divine Ideas, despite outer appearances.*

Scripture: "Finally, be strong in the Lord and in the strength of his power" (Eph. 6:10).

24E JUDGMENT, WISDOM, DISCERNMENT

James, the son of Zebedee, represents discrimination and good judgment in dealing with substantial things. James is the faculty in humankind that wisely chooses and determines. (The Twelve Powers, p. 19)

The house or throne of this wise judge is at the nerve center called the solar plexus. The natural person refers to it as the pit of the stomach. (The Twelve Powers, p. 49)

Judgment—Mental act of evaluation through comparison or contrast. Spiritual discernment; the inner voice through whose expression we come into larger realization of ourselves.

Judgment is a faculty of the mind that can be exercised in two ways—from sense perception or spiritual understanding. If its action be based on sense perception its conclusions are fallible and often condemnatory; if based on spiritual understanding, they are safe. (The Revealing Word, p. 113)

When we awaken to the reality of our being, the light begins to break upon us from within and we know the truth; this is the quickening of our James or judgment faculty. When this quickening occurs, we find ourselves discriminating between the good and the evil. We no longer accept the race standards or the teachings of the worldly wise, but we "judge righteous judgment" (Jn. 7:24); we know with an inner intuition, and we judge people and events from a new viewpoint. (The Twelve Powers, p. 44)

James, the son of Zebedee, represents Judgment, which is located at the pit of the stomach or solar plexus. It is the faculty by which we appraise, evaluate and discern in order to make correct decisions. "Wisdom includes judgment, discrimination [discernment], intuition, and all the departments of mind that come under the head of knowing" (*The Twelve Powers,* p. 49). Judgment, discernment and wisdom make up our ability to maintain enlightened objectivity about our life and our world.

The judgment faculty can be used in two ways. When we allow our sense consciousness, our personalities, to inform this faculty, its conclusions are erroneous and condemning. When we allow our Spiritual Understanding, our Individuality, to inform this Faculty, Its conclusions are Spirit-filled and safe. We no longer let collective (race) standards or worldly "wisdom" have influence. We can clearly discriminate between good and evil through our Divine Inner Intuition. We see and evaluate people and events from a new perspective.

Judgment/Discernment/Wisdom in the Absolute Realm: the Ability to judge, evaluate, discern, be wise, appraise; to know how to.

From sense and personal consciousness: the ability to judge and evaluate based on sense consciousness, error thoughts and feelings; judging based on worldly standards. "Judging, judgmental, discrimination, shrewdness."

From Spiritual Awareness/Higher Consciousness: the Ability to discern and be wise based on Divine Ideas, Truths, Principles and Laws; the Ability to know how to use what we Spiritually Understand. "Discerning, Being Wise."

Affirmation: *I claim my Power of Wisdom now. I wisely know how to use Divine Ideas.*

Scripture: "Do not judge by appearances, but judge with right judgment" (Jn. 7:24).

24F LOVE

Among the apostles of Jesus, John represents love—he laid his head on the Master's bosom. (Charles Fillmore, *Christian Healing*, 2nd ed., Unity House, Unity Village, Mo., 2005, p. 132)

Among the faculties of the mind, love is pivotal. Its center of mentation in the body is the cardiac plexus [back of the heart]. (Christian Healing, p. 130)

Love, in Divine Mind, is the idea of universal unity. In expression, it is the power that joins and binds together the universe and everything in it. Love is a harmonizing, constructive power. When it is made active in consciousness, it conserves substance and reconstructs, rebuilds and restores everyone and his or her world. (Keep a True Lent, pp. 151-152)

Divine love is impersonal; it loves for the sake of loving. It is not concerned with what or who it loves, nor with a return of love. Like the sun, its joy is in the shining forth of its nature. ... Love is an inner quality that sees good everywhere and in everybody. It insists that all is good, and by refusing to see anything but good it causes that quality finally to appear in the uppermost in itself, and in all things. ... Love is the great harmonizer and healer. (The Revealing Word, p. 125)

[Love] is a faculty native to humankind, existent in every soul, which may be used at all times to bring about harmony and unity among those who have been disunited through misunderstandings, contentions or selfishness. (Christian Healing, p. 133)

The Spectrum of Love has nine ingredients, viz.: Patience—"Love suffereth long." Kindness—"And is kind." Generosity—"Love envieth not." Humility—"Love vaunteth not itself, is not puffed up." Courtesy—"Doth not behave itself unseemly.) Unselfishness—"Seeketh not her own." Good Temper—"Is not easily provoked." Guilelessness—"Thinketh no evil."

Sincerity—"Rejoiceth not in iniquity, but rejoiceth in the truth." (1 Cor. 13). (Christian Healing, pp. 133-134)

John represents the Power of Love, located at the back of the heart, the cardiac plexus. It is the attracting, harmonizing, unifying Faculty of mind. The constructive, building force of Spirit, It is our Power to comprehend Oneness. Spiritual Love is the total, unconditional acceptance of everyone and everything. Love is patient, kind, humble, courteous, unselfish, good-tempered, guileless and sincere.

There is an aspect of Love that is definitely of the "affectional" nature—the feeling side. When we love someone, we desire that person; love is the ability to desire. When we love something or someone, we attract ourselves to it or them. Charles Fillmore is clear that Love does not care what it loves. It is indiscriminate and impersonal, "seeing" everything as good. This includes the good, the bad and the ugly.

There is another side of Love that is Principle, the thinking side. Whatever we are focusing on or attracting ourselves to, we are "loving." If we are angry at something or someone we are, in a negative way, desiring or attracting ourselves to and focusing on that in the moment. The Power of Love will then harmonize and unify whatever it can to match that anger. Therefore, you can see that this is the main power through which the Law of Mind Action works. The thoughts that we hold in our mind are "loving, desiring, attracting ourselves to that thought." The Power of Love, then, harmonizes and unifies other thoughts to match the thought being held in mind.

Love in the Absolute Realm: the Ability to harmonize, unify, desire, feel affection for.

From sense and personal consciousness: the ability to attract ourselves to the ideas, thoughts and things based on sense consciousness, erroneous thoughts and feelings; the ability to harmonize and unify everything to match what we attract ourselves to based on sense consciousness; attracting ourselves to things and people in the outer realm; the ability to harmonize and unify everything to match erroneous thoughts and feelings; the ability to desire or feel affection for another person, object or situation based on the senses. "Craving, needing, neediness, 'fatal attraction,' obsession."

From Spiritual Awareness/Higher Consciousness: the Ability to attract ourselves to Divine Ideas, Truths, Principles and Laws; the Ability to harmonize and balance everything to match Divine Ideas and or thoughts related to Divine Ideas.

Affirmation: *I claim my Power of Love now. I harmonize and unify my life from Divine Ideas.*

Scripture: "Love is patient; love is kind; love is not envious or boastful or arrogant or rude. It does not insist on its own way, it is not irritable or resentful; it does not rejoice in wrongdoing, but rejoices in the truth. It bears all things, believes all things, hopes all things, endures all things.

Love never ends. ... And now faith, hope and love abide, these three; and the greatest of these is love" (1 Cor. 13:4-8, 13).

24G POWER, DOMINION AND MASTERY

Among the apostles of Jesus, Philip represents the power faculty of the mind. The word "Philip" means "a lover of horses." In physical activity the horse represents power; the ox, strength. (The Twelve Powers, p. 62)

The power center in the throat controls all the vibratory energies of the organism. (The Twelve Powers, p. 62)

From Divine Mind a person inherits power over the forces of his or her mind—in truth, power over all ideas. A quickening from on high must precede a person's realization of his or her innate control of thought and feelings. (The Twelve Powers, p. 61)

The mind and the body of a person have the power of transforming energy from one plane of consciousness to another. This is the power and dominion implanted in humankind from the beginning. (The Twelve Powers, p. 63)

Power, we must understand, is not an end in itself, not a goal to be sought. Rather, it is simply a means that enables us to attain the end of bringing forth God ideas on earth. It is not to be used for selfish gain or satisfaction of the personal ego, but for the forward spiritual movement of the whole. It is to be exercised not for the purpose of controlling others, but for the purpose of taking dominion over our own thoughts and feelings in order to come into a greater God awareness. (Your God-Given Potential, p. 95)

In the kingdom of God within a person's consciousness, the power faculty plays an important part in controlling the expression of the many emotions, inspirations and thoughts. The voice is the most direct avenue of this expression, when a person has dominion over the emotions and feelings from which the original impulse arises. (The Twelve Powers, p. 64)

A person can never exercise dominion until that person knows who and what he or she is and, knowing, brings forth that knowledge into the external by exercising it in divine order, which is

mind, idea and manifestation." (The Twelve Powers, p. 113)

Philip represents Power (Dominion and Mastery), which is located in the throat. It is the Faculty that enables us to have authority over our own emotions (feelings), inspirations and thoughts, not for controlling others. Our greatest creative power is generated by our realization of the Power of Divine Mind within consciousness. Our spoken words are vehicles through which this Power manifests in our lives. Power, or Dominion, Mastery, is the means of bringing forth Divine Ideas on earth through Divine Order (mind, idea and manifestation). (For more on the Power of Word, see Chapter 21.)

Power/Dominion/Mastery in the Absolute Realm: The Ability to master, dominate, control.

From sense and personal consciousness: the ability to master and dominate thoughts and feelings based on sense consciousness, erroneous thoughts and feelings; dominating based on the outer realm. "Domineering, controlling."

From Spiritual Awareness/Higher Consciousness: the Ability to have dominion and master thoughts and feelings based on Divine Ideas, Truths, Principles and Laws.

Affirmation: *I claim my Power of Dominion now. I have dominion over all my beliefs, ideas, thoughts and actions based on Divine Ideas.*

Scripture: "Then God said, 'Let us make humankind in our image, according to our likeness; and let them have dominion over the fish of the sea, and over the birds of the air, and over the cattle, and over all the wild animals of the earth, and over every creeping thing that creeps upon the earth" (Gen. 1:26). (Note: Metaphysically, these animals and creatures represent thoughts and feelings.)

24H IMAGINATION

Among the apostles, Bartholomew represents the imagination. He is called Nathanael in the first chapter of John, where it is recorded that Jesus saw him under the fig tree—the inference being that Jesus discerned Nathanael's presence before the latter came into visibility. This would indicate that images of people and things are projected into the imaging chamber of the mind and then by giving them attention one can understand their relation to outer things. (The Twelve Powers, p. 72)

The imagination has its center of action directly between the eyes. (The Twelve Powers, p. 20)

When the faculties of mind are understood in their threefold relation—spirit, soul, body—it will be found that every form and shape originated in the imagination. It is through the imagination that the formless takes form. ... Humankind and the universe are a series of pictures in the Mind of Being. God made people in His image and likeness. People, in their turn, are continually making and sending forth into their minds, their bodies, and the world about them living thought forms embodied and [imbued] with their whole character. (The Twelve Powers, p. 71)

The idea is first projected into mind substance, and afterward formed in consciousness. The mind of humankind sees all things through thought forms made by the imagination. (Christian Healing, p. 103)

Bartholomew represents the Power of Imagination, which has its center directly between the eyes. It is our conceiving, picturing and conceptualizing faculty. It is the formative power of mind that shapes thoughts into mental images, which have color, variety and dimension. The highest use of Imagination is to shape thoughts into images that most fully reflect the nature of the original Divine Idea. Imagination gives form to the formless.

Imagination in the Absolute Realm: the Ability to image, picture, conceptualize, envision, dream.

From sense and personal consciousness: the ability to envision all sorts of errors and horrors based on sense consciousness, erroneous thoughts and feelings; envisioning based on the outer realm. "Waking nightmares, fantasy, delusion."

From Spiritual Awareness/Higher Consciousness: the Ability to envision and conceptualize Divine Ideas, Truths, Principles and Laws. (Linked with Faith.)

Affirmation: *I claim my Power of Imagination now. I give form and shape to Divine Ideas and Substance.*

Scripture—In this verse, Paul referred to the power of imagination: "And all of us, with unveiled faces, seeing the glory of the Lord as though reflected in a mirror, are being transformed into the same image from one degree of glory to another; for this comes from the Lord, the Spirit" (2 Cor. 3:18).

24| UNDERSTANDING

Thomas represents the understanding power of humankind. He is called the doubter because he wants to know about everything. Thomas is in the front brain, and his collaborator, Matthew, the will, occupies the same brain area. (The Twelve Powers, p. 21)

Understanding—God is supreme knowing. That in us which comprehends is understanding; it knows and comprehends [compares] in wisdom. Its comparisons are not made in the realm of form, but in the realm of ideas. It knows how to accomplish things. Spiritual discernment reveals that knowledge and intelligence are auxiliary to understanding. (The Revealing Word, p. 201)

There are two ways of getting understanding. One is by following the guidance of Spirit that dwells within, and the other is to go blindly ahead and learn by hard experience. ... Spiritual understanding is the ability of the mind to apprehend and realize the laws of thought and the relation of ideas one to another. (The Revealing Word, pp. 201-202)

So we find that there is in humankind a knowing capacity transcending intellectual knowledge. (The Twelve Powers, p. 88)

Thomas represents the Power of Understanding, which is located, along with the Power of Will represented by Matthew, in the front brain. Understanding is the Faculty by which we receive enlightenment and insight; It is our Capacity to gain direct perceptions of Truth and our Faculty of Spiritual Intelligence. According to Charles Fillmore, "*Will* and *know* designate the faculties of mind that we term will and understanding" (*Christian Healing*, p. 108).

Understanding and Will work hand in hand in one's spiritual development.

Understanding in the Absolute Realm: the Ability to know, perceive, comprehend and apprehend.

From sense and personal consciousness: the ability to know and comprehend based on sense consciousness, error thoughts and feelings; the ability to know based on the outer, relative realm. "Human knowledge, human knowing."

From Spiritual Awareness /Higher Consciousness: the Ability to know, comprehend and apprehend the laws of thought and the relation of ideas (Divine Ideas, Truths, Principle and Laws), one to the other. "Spiritual Knowledge."

Affirmation: *I claim my Power of Understanding now. I know Divine Ideas.*

Scripture: "Think over what I say, for the Lord will give you understanding in all things" (2 Tim. 2:7).

24J WILL

Thomas is in the front brain, and his collaborator, Matthew, the will, occupies the same brain area. (The Twelve Powers, p. 21)

... the will is the executive faculty of the mind, the determining factor in

humankind. (The Revealing Word, p. 209)

The will moves to action all the other faculties of the mind. (The Twelve Powers, p. 97)

The perfect person is produced by rounding out the will and joining it to the understanding. The idea of giving up the will to God's will should not include the thought of weakening it, or causing it to become in any way less; it properly means that the will is being instructed how to act for the best. Do not act until you know how to act. "Look before you leap." This does not imply that one should be inactive or indefinite, waiting for understanding, as do many persons who are afraid to act because they may possibly do the wrong thing; it means that understanding will be quickened and the will strengthened by the confidence that comes as a result of knowledge. (Christian Healing, pp.109-110)

Matthew represents the Power of Will, which is centered, along with the Power of Understanding, in the front brain. It moves all the other Powers (Faculties, Abilities) to action. Will is the decision-making, directing, choosing, determining Faculty of the mind. It is our capacity to say yes or no to opportunities and options. It works in conjunction with the faculty of understanding. The highest expression of human will is willingness.

Will in the Absolute: the Ability to choose, decide, command, lead, determine.

From sense and personal consciousness: the ability to choose and lead based on sense consciousness, the "outer realm." "Willfulness, wrong-headedness, obstinacy."

From Spiritual Awareness/Higher Consciousness: the Ability to choose and lead based on Divine Ideas, Truths, Principles and Laws. "Will."

Affirmation: *I claim my Power of Will now. I choose, decide and lead based on Divine Ideas.*

Scripture: "Again he went away for the second time and prayed, 'My Father, if this cannot pass unless I drink it, your will be done'" (Mt. 26:42).

24K ORDER AND SPIRITUAL LAW

James, the son of Alphaeus, represents divine order. His center is at the navel. (The Twelve Powers, p. 22)

Order in the Mind of God is an idea of harmonious progress, evolution. Order in humankind is humankind's ability to perceive and cooperate with the law of growth. (Powers of the Soul, p. 138)

The divine idea of order is the idea of adjustment, and as this is established in a person's thought, his or her mind and affairs will be at one with the uni-versal harmony. (The Revealing Word, p. 143)

To develop divine order in our life, we must learn to cooperate with spiritual law. (Your God-Given Potential, p. 123)

A person can never exercise dominion until he or she knows who and what he or she is and, knowing, brings forth that knowledge into the external by exercising it in divine order, which is mind, idea and manifestation. (The Twelve Powers, p. 113)

James, the son of Alphaeus, represents the Power of Order, located at the navel. It is the faculty by which we establish harmony, balance, right adjustment, right sequence and adjustment in our lives. Order is the one underlying Law of Manifestation, and we each must learn to participate consciously in that process which enables growth without struggle. Divine Order (mind, idea, manifestation) is a Universal Law. Each one of us is always using it to manifest everything. Each person determines how it will be used. When used in accordance with Spiritual Principle, *good* results. When used out of alignment with Spiritual Principle, we miss the mark (sin) and *error* results.

Order in the Absolute Realm is the Ability to organize, balance, sequence, adjust.

From sense and personal consciousness: the ability to organize, sequence, balance and/or adjust based on sense consciousness, erroneous ideas, thoughts, beliefs and feelings; organization based on the outer realm. "Obsessive about orderliness, obsessive about details, anal retentive." As Divine Order (mind-idea-expression), it forms based on sense and personal consciousness.

From Spiritual Awareness/Higher Consciousness: the Ability to organize, balance, sequence and/or adjust according to and based on Divine Ideas, Truths, Principles and Laws. As Divine Order (mind-idea-expression), it is creating based on pure Divine Ideas from Spiritual Awareness/Higher Consciousness.

Affirmation: *I claim my Power of Order now. I organize and balance my life according to Divine Ideas.*

Scripture: "But all things should be done decently and in order" (1 Cor. 14:40).

24L ZEAL, ENTHUSIASM

Simon, the Canaanean, represents zeal; his center is at the medulla, at the base of the brain. (The Twelve Powers, p. 22)

Zeal is the great universal force that impels humankind to spring forward in a field of endeavor and accomplish the seemingly miraculous. (Atom-Smashing Power of the Mind, p. 26)

To be without zeal is to be without the zest of living. Zeal and enthusiasm incite to glorious achievement in every aim and ideal that the mind conceives. Zeal is the impulse to go forward, the urge behind all things. (The Twelve Powers, p. 130)

Zeal—Intensity, ardor, enthusiasm; the inward fire of the soul that urges humankind onward, regardless of the intellectual mind of caution and conservatism. (The Revealing Word, p. 216)

Zeal is the mighty force that incites the winds, the tides, the storms; it urges the planet on its course, and spurs the ant to greater exertion. To be without zeal is to be without the zest of living. Zeal and enthusiasm incite to glorious achievement in every aim and ideal that the mind conceives. (The Twelve Powers, p. 130)

Turn a portion of your zeal to do God's will, to the establishing of the kingdom within you. Do not put all your enthusiasm into teaching, preaching, healing and helping others; help yourself. Do not let your zeal run away with your judgment. When zeal and judgment work together great things can be accomplished. (The Revealing Word, p. 216)

Simon, the Canaanean, represents the Power of Zeal, which is located at the medulla, the base of the brain. It is the Faculty of enthusiasm, intensity, and exuberance. It provides our inner urge to progress; it is our motivation to achieve. The highest expression of Zeal is an unflagging, fervent interest in knowing, speaking, and doing good. Understanding and Wisdom help to temper Zeal so that its enthusiasm and intensity are directed to grow spiritually and express the Christ Nature.

Zeal in the Absolute Realm: the Ability to be enthusiastic and passionate, to start and motivate. It is the urge and impulse behind all things.

From sense and personal consciousness: The ability to be enthusiastic and passionate based on sense consciousness, error thoughts and feelings. "Zealous, impulsive, overly ambitious, ruthless, compulsive."

From Spiritual Awareness/Higher Consciousness: The Ability to be passionate and enthusiastic about Divine Ideas, Truths, Principles and Laws. "Passionate."

Affirmation: *I claim my Power of Zeal now. I am passionate and enthusiastic about Divine Ideas.*

Scripture: "He [Jesus Christ] it is who gave himself for us that he might redeem us from all iniquity and purify for himself a people of his own who are zealous for good deeds" (Titus 2:14).

24M ELIMINATION, RENUNCIATION

People have faculties of elimination, as well as appropriation. If you know how to handle them you can expel error from your thought body. The denial apostle is Thaddaeus, presiding in the abdominal region, the great renunciator of the mind and the body. (The Twelve Powers, p. 21)

A letting go of old thoughts in order that new thoughts may find place in consciousness. A healthy state of mind is attained when the thinker willingly lets go [of] the old thoughts and takes on the new. This is illustrated by the inlet and outlet of a pool of water. (The Revealing Word, p. 167)

Thoughts are things; they occupy space in the mental field. A healthy state of mind is attained and continued when the thinker willingly lets go [of] the old thoughts and takes on the new. (The Twelve Powers, p. 144)

Thaddaeus represents Elimination, the Power centered in the abdominal region. It is the Faculty by which we release false beliefs and accomplish a mental cleansing. Elimination enables us to surrender to our inner Spirit any thought that is not for our highest good so that transformation and purification of consciousness can take place.

Elimination/Renunciation in the Absolute Realm: the Ability to release, remove, denounce, deny, let go.

From sense and personal consciousness: the ability to release, deny and let go based on sense consciousness, error thoughts and feelings; releasing based on the outer realm. "Purging, eradication, wasteful."

From Spiritual Awareness/Higher Consciousness: The Ability to release, deny and let go of false ideas, error thoughts, old thoughts and thoughts that are of a lesser good.

Affirmation: *I claim my Power of Elimination now. I deny and eliminate any limiting beliefs, ideas, thoughts, feelings and attitudes.*

Scripture: "Above all, my beloved, do not swear, either by heaven or by earth or by any other oath, but let your 'Yes' be yes and your 'No' be no, so that you may not fall under condemnation" (Jas. 5:12).

24N LIFE

Judas, who betrayed Jesus, has his throne in the generative center. Judas governs the life consciousness in the body. (The Twelve Powers, p. 22)

In the phenomenal world, life is the energy that propels all forms to action. (The Twelve Powers, p. 161)

Life in people is their increasing consciousness of their world, their inner activities, the forces and movements about them. It is their power to express the eternal activity of God. (Powers of the Soul, p. 144)

Life—That expression of Being which manifests as animation, activity, vigor. Life and substance are ideas in Divine Mind. Life is the acting principle; substance is the thing acted upon. In the phenomenal world, life is the energy that propels all forms to action. Life is not in itself intelligent; it requires the directive power of an entity that knows where and how to apply its force in order to get the best results." (The Revealing Word, p. 121)

Life is divine, spiritual, and its source is God, Spirit. The river of life is within all in their spiritual consciousness. They come into consciousness of the river of life through the quickening of Spirit. They can be truly quickened with new life and vitalized in mind and body only by consciously contacting Spirit. This contact is made through prayer, meditation and good works." (The Revealing Word, p. 122)

Judas represents the Power of Life, located in the generative center (external sex organs). It is the Faculty of movement, vitality, wholeness and creativity. It is the expression of the pure, eternal Life of Divine Mind within consciousness. Life, much like the

Faculty of Love, is indiscriminant and requires direction. When it is directed from sense consciousness, it degenerates into a seeking to satisfy the senses. When the Faculties of Wisdom, Understanding and Judgment direct it, it enhances one's spiritual life.

Life in the Absolute Realm: the Ability to energize, vitalize, enliven, animate, invigorate.

From sense and personal consciousness: the ability to vitalize and energize erroneous ideas and thoughts based on sense consciousness, error thoughts and feelings; energizing based on the outer realm. "Frenetic, hectic, feverish, chaotic."

From Spiritual Awareness/Higher Consciousness: the Ability to enliven and energize Divine Ideas, Truths, Principles and Laws.

Affirmation: *I claim my Power of Life now. I vitalize and energize all that I think and do based on Divine Ideas.*

Scripture: "I came that they may have life, and have it abundantly" (Jn. 10:10).

The Twelve Powers

Power	Ability to	Location	Disciple	Color
Faith	believe, intuit	Pineal Gland	Peter	Blue
Strength	endure, stay the course, last, be persistent, persevere, be stable	Small of the back	Andrew	Spring Green
Judgment	evaluate, discern, be wise, appraise	Pit of the stomach	James (son of Zebedee)	Yellow
Love	harmonize, unify, attract	Back of the heart	John	Pink
Power	master, dominate, control	Base of tongue, voice box	Philip	Purple
Imagination	image, conceptualize, envision	Between the eyes	Bartholomew	Light Blue
Understanding	know, perceive	Front brain	Thomas	Gold
Will	choose, decide	Front brain	Matthew	Silver
Order	organize, sequence, adjust	Navel	James (son of Alphaeus)	Olive Green
Zeal	start, motivate, be passionate, be enthusiastic	Medulla, brain stem	Simon (the Canaanean)	Orange
Elimination	release, remove, denounce	Lower abdominal region	Thaddeus	Russet
Life	energize, vitalize, enliven	Generative center, external reproductive organs	Judas	Red

SUMMARY STATEMENTS

▼ *The Twelve Powers are the 12 fundamental aspects of our Divine Nature which comprise the pattern for perfection within us.*

▼ *Spiritually, the Powers exist in our minds as Divine Ideas. Symbolically, they are the 12 disciples of Jesus. They are represented as 12 centers of energy within each individual.*

▼ *The Twelve Powers are Faith, Strength, Judgment, Love, Power, Imagination, Understanding, Will, Order, Zeal, Elimination and Life*

▼ Please refer to the supplementary charts and diagrams that are part of this chapter for an overview of the Powers and their locations.

TOPICS FOR DISCUSSION

1. *Name each of the Twelve Powers and describe its function.*

2. *Relate your understanding of the Twelve Powers to your current concept of regeneration.*

THOUGHTS FOR REFLECTION AND MEDITATION

"In order to command our powers and to bring them into unity of action, we must know what they are and their respective places on the staff of Being. The Grand Man, Christ, has 12 powers of fundamental ideas, represented in the history of Jesus by the Twelve Apostles. So each of us has 12 faculties or fundamental ideas to make manifest, to bring out, and to use in the attainment of his ideals. There are innumerable other ideas, but each one stems from some one of these fundamental ideas."

(Charles Fillmore, *Keep a True Lent*, pp. 112–113)

SUPPLEMENTARY READING

Christian Healing by Charles Fillmore, 2nd ed., Unity House, Unity Village, Mo., 2005, Lesson 8, "Faith," Lesson 9, "Imagination," Lesson 10, "Will and Understanding," Lesson 11, "Judgment and Justice," Lesson 12, "Love."

How to Use Your Twelve Gifts From God by William A. Warch, DeVorss, Marina del Rey, Calif, 1976.

The Twelve Powers by Charles and Cora Fillmore, Unity House, Unity Village, Mo., 1999.

Twelve Powers in You by David Williamson, Gay Lynn Williamson and Robert H. Knapp, Health Communications, Deerfield Beach, Fla., 2000.

Your God-Given Potential: Unfolding the Twelve Spiritual Powers by Winifred Wilkinson Hausmann, revised paperback edition, Unity House, Unity Village, Mo.,1999, Chapter 1, "From Primordial Cell to Christ Oriented Man," and Chapter 2, "Discover a New World Within."

CHAPTER TWENTY-FIVE

DEVELOPING AND EXPRESSING THE TWELVE POWERS

INTRODUCTION

The previous chapter laid the groundwork for this chapter, which focuses on how to actually develop each of the Twelve Powers. In Unity heart-centered metaphysics, this process is a work of the head and the heart. As in the last chapter, this text is based on our commonly held first and second Unity principles: (1) Divine Mind is Absolute Good, everywhere present, and (2) Humanity's True Nature is Divine—the Christ, or Divine Mind. Since Divine Mind is Good, humankind's True Nature must be Good.

In the development of the Twelve Powers, please see Cora Fillmore's book *Christ Enthroned in Man*, which is currently published as the second half of *The Twelve Powers* by Charles and Cora Fillmore. The book gives a further understanding of each of the Powers as well as meditations that are specifically designed to develop each of them. While the language is outdated, the teaching remains strong.

25A DEGENERATION, GENERATION AND REGENERATION

When the Adamic race reached a point in their evolution where they had personal-will volition, they began to think and act independently of the Jehovah or Christ Mind. Then the sense consciousness began to rule and the mate- *rialization of the body resulted. Degeneration of the whole man followed. Loss of ability to draw constantly on the one and only source of life threw the whole race into an anemic condition. Their bodies began to disintegrate, and death came into the world. Then Satan, the mind of sense, began to rule; sin was in the saddle. The people like sheep had gone astray; they were lost in the wilderness of sense; they were in the throes of race extinction.* (Charles Fillmore, *Keep a True Lent*, 2nd ed., Unity House, Unity Village, Mo., 2005, p. 131)

Regeneration follows generation in the development of humankind. Generation sustains and perpetuates the human; regeneration unfolds and glorifies the divine. (Charles and Cora Fillmore, *The Twelve Powers*, Unity House, Unity Village, Mo., 1999, p. 3)

When people begin to follow Jesus in the regeneration, they find that they must cooperate with the work of their disciples or faculties. Heretofore they have been under the natural law; they have been fishers in the natural world. Through their recognition of their relation as the Children of God, they cooperate in the original creative law. They call their faculties out of their materiality into their spirituality. This process is symbolized by Jesus' calling his apostles. (*The Twelve Powers,* p. 50)

In order to follow Jesus in the regeneration, we must become better acquainted with the various phases of mind and how they function in and through the body. (Charles Fillmore, *Atom-Smashing Power of Mind*, 2nd ed., Unity House, Unity Village, Mo., 2006, p. 42)

Fillmore's plan for the regeneration of "humankind" was based on the individual development of innate powers

and abilities expressing themselves through ganglionic centers in the human body. These centers are to be activated as the qualities are developed in mind, all under the supervision of the Christ or God-self of each person. (Winifred Wilkinson Hausmann, *Your God-Given Potential: Unfolding the Twelve Spiritual Powers,* revised paperback edition, Unity House, Unity Village, Mo., 1999, pp. 18-19)

Degeneration:
Degeneration resulted from the use of free will to think independently of Christ Mind, or Divine Mind. Sense mind began to be in control, resulting in the materialization of the body. Degeneration continued and included the loss of the ability to draw from the one Source, Divine Mind. "Bodies began to disintegrate and death came into the world." In the degenerate state, sense mind rules and sin, or error, is in control.

Generation:
"Generation sustains and perpetuates the human." Generation deals with the birth of the physical, human body.

Regeneration:
Regeneration is the way we rise above sense consciousness and the body, and begin to reassert the power of the Christ Mind. Any person who makes a serious commitment to follow the teachings of spiritual Truth immediately comes under the ministration of Laws that are higher and finer than

before. Up to this point, most people are almost entirely dominated by what we call the laws of nature and also by the most mechanical level of cause and effect. Until a certain level of spiritual consciousness is attained, our Twelve Powers are in an unregenerate state and we use them to serve mostly selfish purposes. As the Twelve Powers are regenerating, we begin to use them to serve those higher purposes. We begin to express the Twelve Powers in cooperation with Laws that are higher and finer than natural law, and our life becomes directly affected by the laws of inner Divine Guidance and Protection.

The recognition that each of us is the Christ, together with a commitment made to Spirit, or Divine Mind, results in the building of consciousness and spiritual evolution. Once regeneration, or transformation in consciousness, begins to occur and the Twelve Powers/Faculties/Abilities are regenerating within us, we begin to experience the manifestation of purity and wholeness in our consciousness as well as our bodies.

25B OUR WORK/OUR GOAL

Our work is to transmute the natural powers (starting where we are in consciousness and spiritual growth) into the spiritual powers we are designed to express for the fulfillment of our Christ potential. Each faculty is discovered first as an intellectual concept. This concept is explored and nurtured through prayer as it gradually grows into the spiritual idea from which it came. Finally we have no sense of separateness, but rather a realization of our oneness with the God-power itself, expressing through us entirely under the guidance and direction of the Christ. (Your God-Given Potential, pp. 20-21)

Transformation into fully conscious and enlightened beings occurs through the development of our Twelve Spiritual Faculties. The goal is to express our Christ potential unselfishly, lovingly and powerfully.

25C TEMPTATION

We do not encourage those who still have worldly ambitions to take up the development of the Twelve Powers of man. You will be disappointed if you seek to use these superpowers to gain money ("turn stones into bread"), control others ("the kingdoms of the world ... all these things I will give thee"), or make a display of your power ("If thou art the Son of God, cast thyself down"). These are the temptations of the selfish ego, as recorded in the fourth chapter of Matthew, which Jesus had to overcome, and which all who follow Him "in the regeneration" have to overcome. (The Twelve Powers, p. 6)

Temptations come to everyone. We are tempted to use the Powers to gain money, control others or make a display of power. Perhaps, in some ways, we are already using them in these ways as we use them from sense or personal consciousness. However and whenever the temptations appear, they come from the level of human nature that is the personality, ego, exaggerated sense of self, "me and mine," etc. The moment of temptation occurs when the impulses arising from this level reach the level of conscious self-awareness. At this point we have an opportunity for choice; if we allow spiritual awareness to overcome the temptation, we gain immeasurably in the long run.

25D JESUS THE WAY SHOWER

You are Spirit, the Child of God, and your place is at the right hand of God. To realize this is to call upon yourself the baptism of the Holy Spirit, after which baptism you no longer labor as a carpenter or as a fisher, but begin to gather together your disciples—powers of mind. This gathering together of your powers is an orderly process, and you will find that it proceeds right along the lines laid down in Jesus' choosing of his disciples, as recorded in Matthew 4:28 and Mark 1:16. (Charles Fillmore, *Talks on Truth,* Unity House, Unity Village, Mo., 1926, p. 90)

The metaphysical interpretation of Jesus calling the 12 disciples symbolizes a turning point in an individual's spiritual unfoldment. Jesus assuming leadership in a Christ ministry symbolizes that point where spiritual awareness becomes the guiding, motivating factor in an individual's life. Metaphysically, Jesus is that aspect of every person that understands the use of the Christ principle, the pattern of perfection. He represents that part of everyone which is the energy and the understanding to bring forth all that is in the Christ potential.

25E DEVELOPING OUR TWELVE POWERS

Humankind is a focal point in God-consciousness and expresses God. Therefore humankind must understand the processes that bring about that expression. Infinite Mind is here with all its ideas as a resource for humankind, and what we are or become is the result of our efforts to accumulate in our own consciousness all the attributes of infinite Mind. (Charles Fillmore, *Prosperity,* Unity House, Unity Village, Mo., 1936, p. 29)

Our work here now is to awaken to the divine powers with which God has endowed us, to encourage and develop them under God's direction and to get about the business of becoming that which Jesus demonstrated in his life and told us we could become. (Your God-Given Potential, p. 17)

Within each person there is a new world awaiting discovery, a world in which there are capabilities of unlimited strength, perfect knowing, radiant life, and other latent abilities beyond our greatest present capacity to conceive. (Your God-Given Potential, p. 24)

All that a person really needs is the quickening and rounding out of the thinking centers in consciousness; that having been done, Divine Mind will think through the person. This supreme Mind holds humankind at its center, a perfect instrument through which to express its possibilities. (Charles Fillmore, *Christian Healing*, 2nd ed., Unity House, Unity Village, Mo., 2005, p. 98)

The increasing awareness of our Twelve Spiritual Faculties/Abilities will enable us to call them forth into dynamic expression. This regeneration process requires discipline, dedication and a conscious recognition of our Divine Nature. The development and regeneration of the Twelve Powers is a fundamental practice of the heart-centered metaphysician.

(See Chapter 24 for a more extensive discussion of each of the Twelve Powers.)

25F EXPRESSING THE TWELVE POWERS

These Twelve Powers are all expressed and developed under the guidance of Divine Mind. "Not by might, nor by power, but by my Spirit, saith Jehovah of hosts" (Zech. 4:6). You must keep the equipoise; you must, in all the bringing forth of the Twelve Powers of humankind, realize that they come from God: that they are directed by the Word of God, and that man (Jesus) is their head. (The Twelve Powers, p. 23)

"I am the vine, ye are the branches." In this symbol Jesus illustrated a law universal to organisms. The vine-building law holds good in a person's body. The center of identity is in the head, and its activities are distributed through the nerves and the nerve fluids to the various parts of the body. The Twelve Apostles of Jesus Christ represent the 12 primal subcenters in a person's organism. A study of a person's mind and body reveals this law. (The Twelve Powers, p. 48)

Development and expression of a given Power may entail meditating and focusing upon that Power for a period of time. However, the proper expression of the Twelve Powers is that of balance and integration instead of individual development and expression. In other words, the Twelve Powers are a sort of "team" designed to work together instead of independently. In the last excerpt above, the Powers are described by Jesus as the branches of a vine. Jesus is the symbol of spiritual awareness generated by the Christ-within consciousness. The Twelve Powers (branches) express spiritual awareness.

25G GENERAL APPROACH

To call a disciple is mentally to recognize that power; it is to identify oneself with the intelligence working at a center—for example, judgment, at the solar plexus. To make this identification, one must realize one's unity with God through Christ, Christ being the Child of God idea always existing in humankind's higher consciousness. This recognition of one's [kinship] and unity with God is fundamental in all true growth. ... We can call our Twelve Powers into spiritual activity only through Christ. If we try to effect this end by any other means, we shall have an abnormal, chaotic and unlawful soul unfoldment. (The Twelve Powers, p. 50)

Humankind's development is not primarily under the physical law, because the physical law is secondary. There is a law of Spirit, and the earthly is but the showing forth of some of the results of that law. We begin our existence as ideas in Divine Mind; those ideas are expressed and developed and brought

to fruitage, and the expression is the important part of the soul's growth. (The Twelve Powers, pp. 38-39)

The power of the spoken word is but slightly understood, because the law of the Word is not rightly observed. The Word is the creative idea in Divine Mind, which may be expressed by a person when he or she has fulfilled the law of expression. All words are formative but not all words are creative. The creative word lays hold of Spirit substance and power. (The Twelve Powers, p. 29)

Our disciples will do what we tell them and continue to do it after they have been sufficiently instructed and assisted in the use of the Word. Remember the mind rules both the within and the without, the visible and the invisible, the high and the low. (The Twelve Powers, p.140)

Everything has origin in thought, and material thoughts will bring forth material things. So you should baptize and cleanse with your spiritual word every center, as Philip baptized the eunuch of Gaza. Baptism is cleansing. It always represents the erasing power of the mind.

When the baptizing power of the word is poured upon a center, it cleanses all material thought; impotence is vitalized with new life, and the whole subconscious is awakened and quickened. (The Twelve Powers, p. 19)

We grow to be like that which we idealize. Affirming or naming a mighty spiritual principle identifies the mind with that principle; then all that the principle stands for in the realm of ideas is poured out upon the one who affirms. (*The Twelve Powers*, p. 38)

This is the general approach to developing each of the Twelve Powers:

1. The starting point of all spiritual growth is always Divine Mind. We must first recognize and realize the Truth of Oneness, or Divine Mind, Beingness, Christ, in higher consciousness.

2. Divine Ideas make up Divine Mind. It is the expression and development of these Divine Ideas that are important in the growth of the soul (conscious and subconscious minds) and therefore spiritual evolution.

3. The Divine Ideas we are working with are the Twelve Powers.

4. The Power of the Word and the spoken word engaging both thinking and feeling natures, develops each of the Twelve Powers.

5. Denials baptize and cleanse consciousness. The baptizing power of the Word cleanses each center of material thought (sense consciousness and personal consciousness), awakening and quickening the entire subconscious mind.

6. Affirming a "Spiritual Principle" identifies the human mind with that Principle. Affirming a given Power identifies the mind with that Power.

7. Naming a "Spiritual Principle" claims that Principle for us. We must name and claim each of the Twelve Powers.

25H FAITH

People who live wholly in the intellect deny that humankind can know anything about God, because they do not have quickened faith. The way to bring forth the God presence, to make oneself conscious of God, is to say: "I have faith in God; I have faith in Spirit; I have faith in things invisible." Such affirmations of faith, such praise to the invisible God, the unknown god, will make God visible to the mind and will strengthen the faith faculty. Thus faith (Peter) is called and instructed spiritually. (*The Twelve Powers*, p. 18)

Faith words should be expressed both silently and audibly. (*The Twelve Powers*, p. 29)

The faith center, the pineal gland, opens the mind of humankind to spiritual faith. Merely affirming the activity of this superpower will quicken it in consciousness. (*The Twelve Powers*, p. 31)

... Paul, who said, "Have this mind in you, which was also in Christ Jesus" (Phil. 2:5). It was not Jesus but the mind in Jesus that did the great works. He was the center of faith that transformed the mighty creative force of Being (which are active in the universe through the mind and brain of humankind) into a form of force usable in his environment. Tap this inner reservoir of faith, and you can do what Jesus did. That was his promise; its fulfillment is the test of a true follower. (The Twelve Powers, p. 32)

Quicken Faith through the spiritual activity of the Christ, focusing your attention on the pineal gland, denying and affirming:

Denial:

I give no power to doubt and fear.

Affirmations:

I have Faith in [Divine Mind]; I have Faith in Oneness; I have Faith in things invisible. (The Twelve Powers, p. 18)

Jesus Christ is now here, raising me to his consciousness of unfailing Faith, and I abide in him. (The Twelve Powers, p. 217)

25I STRENGTH, STABILITY, STEADFASTNESS

Be steadfast, strong, and steady in thought, and you will establish strength in mind and body. Never let the thought of weakness enter your consciousness, but always ignore the suggestion and affirm yourself to be a tower of strength, within and without. (The Twelve Powers, p. 38)

Quicken Strength through the spiritual activity of the Christ. Focus your attention on the lower back (the loins) as you deny and affirm:

Denial:

I give no power to weakness, helplessness or despair.

Affirmations:

I am strong in Divine Nature and in the strength of Divine Might. (Modified from The Twelve Powers, p. 38)

Jesus Christ is now here, raising me to his consciousness of sustaining Strength, and I rest in joy and peace. (The Twelve Powers, p. 225)

25J JUDGMENT, WISDOM, DISCERNMENT

A quickening of our divine judgment arouses in us the judge of all the world. ... When we call this righteous judge into action, we may find our standards of right and wrong undergoing rapid changes, but if we hold steadily to the Lord as our supreme guide, we shall be led into all righteousness. (The Twelve Powers, p. 47)

Having identified oneself with God through Christ, one should center one's attention at the pit of the stomach [solar plexus] and affirm: "The wisdom of the Christ Mind here, active, is through my recognition of Christ identified and unified with God. Wisdom, judgment, discrimination, purity and power are here now expressing themselves in the beauty of holiness. The justice, righteousness and peace of the Christ Mind now harmonize, wisely direct and surely establish the kingdom of God in God's temple, my body. There are no more warring, contentious thoughts in me, for the peace of God is here established, and the lion and the lamb (courage and innocence) sit on the throne of dominion with wisdom and love." (The Twelve Powers, p. 51)

Quicken Judgment, Wisdom and Discernment through the spiritual activity of the Christ. Focus your attention on the pit of the stomach (solar plexus) as you use the denial and affirmations below:

Denial:

> *I give no power to judgmental thoughts and feelings.*

Affirmations:

> *Wisdom, Judgment, Discrimination, purity, and power are now here, expressing themselves in the beauty of holiness. (The Twelve Powers, p. 51)*

Jesus Christ is now here, raising me to his consciousness of Divine Judgment, and the Wisdom of [Divine Mind] is expressed in all that I think, say and do. (The Twelve Powers, p. 231)

25K LOVE

When this apostle is "called," love is quickened in consciousness. The calling of this apostle consists in bringing into one's consciousness a right understanding of the true character of love, also in exercising love in all the relations of life. One should make it a practice to meditate regularly on the love idea in universal Mind, with the prayer, Divine love, manifest thyself in me. *Then there should be periods of mental concentration on the love center in the cardiac plexus near the heart. It is not necessary to know the exact location of this aggregation of love cells. Think about love with the attention drawn within the breast, and a quickening will follow; all the ideas that go to make up love will be set into motion. (Christian Healing, p. 132)*

Quicken Love through the spiritual activity of the Christ. Keep your attention centered on the cardiac plexus (or simply the breast) as you deny and affirm:

Denials:

I give no power to thoughts and feelings of separation.

I give no power to selfish desires.

Affirmations:

Divine Love manifests in me. (Adapted from *Christian Healing*, p. 132)

Divine Love fills my heart and I am tender and kind. (Adapted from *Christian Healing*, p. 138)

Jesus Christ is now here, raising me to his consciousness of infinite Love, and my soul is filled and satisfied. (*The Twelve Powers*, p. 237)

25L **POWER, DOMINION, MASTERY**

If a person binds or controls the appetites, passions and emotions in the body (earth), he or she establishes ability and power to control the same forces in the realms universal, out of which the heavens are formed. (*The Twelve Powers*, p. 69)

No disciple can do any great overcoming work without a certain realization of spiritual Power, Dominion and Mastery. Without power, one easily gives up to temporal laws, man-made. (*The Twelve Powers*, p. 66)

Through the vibrations of power in the throat, one can feel the power of unity with the higher self more quickly than in any other way. This reveals that ideas rule the person. Jesus affirmed: "All power is given unto me in heaven [mind] and in earth [body]" (Mt. 28:18 KJV). When Jesus made this affirmation, he undoubtedly realized his innate spiritual dominion, and when he consciously attuned his spiritual identity to mind and body, there was a conscious influx of power, and his hearers said that he "taught them as having authority, and not as the scribes" (Mt. 7:29). (*The Twelve Powers*, pp. 64-65)

Quicken Power (Dominion and Mastery) through the spiritual activity of the Christ, focusing your attention on the throat as you deny and affirm:

Denial:

I give no power to thoughts and feelings about not being in control.

Affirmations:

I use Divine Power and Dominion to master my thoughts and feelings.

All Power is given unto me in heaven and in earth. (Mt. 28:18 KJV)

Jesus Christ is now here, raising me to his consciousness of Divine Power, and I am established in the Mastery and Dominion of Spirit. (*The Twelve Powers*, p. 242)

25M **IMAGINATION**

All things, including the mind, work from center to circumference. A knowledge of this fact puts a person on his or her guard and causes him or her to direct that his or her Imagination shall not create things in his or her mind that have been impressed upon him or her from without. (Christian Healing, p. 100)

As a person develops in Understanding, the Imagination is the first of the latent faculties to quicken. (Christian Healing, p. 101)

The highest and best work of the Imagination is the marvelous transformation that it works in character. Imagine that you are one with the Principle of Good, and you will become truly good. To imagine oneself perfect fixes the idea of perfection in the invisible mind substance, and the mind forces at once begin the work of bringing forth perfection. (Christian Healing, pp. 105-106)

Quicken Imagination through the spiritual activity of the Christ. Keep your attention centered between the eyes as you deny and affirm:

Denial:

I give no power to erroneous images of seeing myself as only an ego.

Affirmations:

> *I use Divine Imagination to be the best Christ I can be.*

> *I am the image and likeness of [Divine Mind]. (The Twelve Powers, p. 255)*

> *Jesus Christ is now here, raising me to his consciousness of Divine Imagination, and I see spiritual perfection everywhere. (The Twelve Powers, p. 249)*

25N **UNDERSTANDING**

Never say, "I don't know," "I don't understand." Claim your Christ understanding at all times and declare: I am not under any spell of human ignorance. I am one with infinite Understanding. (Christian Healing, pp. 113-114)

No one ever attained spiritual consciousness without striving for it. The first step is to ask. "Ask, and it shall be given you; seek, and ye shall find; knock, and it shall be opened unto you" (Mt. 7:7). Prayer is one form of asking, seeking and knocking. Then make your mind receptive to the higher understanding, through silent meditations and affirmations of truth. The earnest desire to understand spiritual things will open the way, and revelation within and without will follow. (The Twelve Powers, p. 93)

Quicken Understanding through the spiritual activity of the Christ. Focus your attention on the front brain as you deny and affirm:

Denials:

I give no power based entirely upon what I think I know from my senses.

I give no power to thoughts of ignorance.

Affirmations:

I am one in infinite Understanding. (Adapted from *Christian Healing*, pp. 113-114)

Jesus Christ is now here, raising me to his consciousness of Divine Understanding, and all my mental activities are spiritual. (The Twelve Powers, p. 256)

25O **WILL**

The Will must be strengthened by being constantly used in divine Understanding. (Christian Healing, p. 113)

The problem of self-control is never settled until all that a person is comes into touch with the divine Will and Understanding. You must understand all your forces before you can establish them in harmony. This overcoming is easy if you go about it in the right way. But if you try to take dominion through will, force and suppression, you will find it hard and will never accomplish any permanent results. Get your I AM centered in God, and from that place of

Truth speak true words. (Christian Healing, p. 115)

"Not my will, but thine, be done" (Lk. 22:42) is one of the most far-reaching affirmations of Jesus, and those who follow him and keep his sayings are finding great peace and relaxation of mind and body. (The Twelve Powers, p. 109)

Quicken Will through the spiritual activity of the Christ. Keep your attention centered on the front brain as you deny and affirm:

Denial:

I give no power to choices and decisions made entirely from sense consciousness.

Affirmations:

I use Divine Will to make wise choices and decisions.

Not my ego-based will, but Divine Mind-Will be done. (adapted from Lk. 22:42)

Jesus Christ is now here, raising me to his consciousness of Divine Will, and I continually will to do [the Will of Divine Mind]. (The Twelve Powers, p. 262)

25P **ORDER AND SPIRITUAL LAW**

Law and Order are back of all manifestation. All creation is working through an evolutionary process under Law.

Especially is this true of humans in whom and through whom God carries forth creative law.

The perfect person is created as a perfect idea, which is to be manifested under the Law of Divine Order. This perfect pattern (Christ) is working itself out through the flesh, coming into perfect manifestation under Law and Order. (The Twelve Powers, pp. 267-268)

The center of Order in the body is located at a nerve center back of the navel. By employing prayer and meditation, one may quicken the ganglionic nerve cells at the order center ... so it is through this order center that the soul, spiritually quickened, receives the divine manna from the Father-Mother God. Through our meditation and consecration, the spiritual laws are unfolded to us from within. (The Twelve Powers, p. 270)

Quicken Order and Spiritual Law through the spiritual activity of the Christ, keeping your attention centered on the ganglionic center behind the navel. Deny and affirm:

Denial:

I give no power to chaos and disorder in my thinking, body or my affairs.

Affirmations:

Divine Order is active in my mind, body and affairs, and I am working

all things together for my good. (The Twelve Powers, p. 271)

Jesus Christ is now here, raising me to his consciousness of Divine Order, and I realize that the Law of [Divine Mind] is fulfilled in me. (The Twelve Powers, p. 267)

25Q **ZEAL, ENTHUSIASM**

To help Simon the Zealot do his work, center your attention for a moment at the base of your brain and quietly affirm that infinite energy and intelligence are pouring forth in Zeal—Enthusiasm. Then follow in imagination a set of motor nerves that leads out from the medulla to the eyes, affirming all the time the presence and power of energy and intelligence now manifesting in your eyes.

For the ears, affirm energy and intelligence, adding, "Be you open."

For the nose, affirm energy and intelligence, adding, "The purity of Spirit infolds you."

For the mouth, carry the life current to the root of the tongue, with the thought of freedom.

At the root of the tongue is situated the throne of another disciple, Philip. When you carry the zeal current from its medulla center and connect it with the throne of Philip, a mighty vibration is set up that affects the whole sympathetic nervous system. (*The Twelve Powers,* pp. 140-141)

Quicken Zeal and Enthusiasm through the spiritual activity of the Christ, your attention centered on the medulla at the base of the brain. Now deny and affirm:

Denial:

> *I give no power to thoughts and feelings of listlessness or apathy.*

Affirmations:

> *I am Infinite energy and intelligence pouring forth in Zeal.* (*The Twelve Powers,* p. 140)

> *Jesus Christ is now here, raising me to his consciousness of Divine Zeal, and I enthusiastically express the inner spiritual urge.* (*The Twelve Powers,* p. 273)

25R ELIMINATION, RENUNCIATION

It is found by metaphysicians that praise and thanksgiving are laxatives of efficiency and that their cleansing work not only frees the mind of egotism but also cleanses the body of effete matter.

Thoughts are things; they occupy space in the mental field. A healthy state of mind is attained and continued when the thinker willingly lets go the old

thoughts and takes on the new. (*The Twelve Powers,* p. 144)

No one can play fast and loose with God. What one builds, one must care for. What a person forms that is evil, he or she must unform before he or she can take the coveted step up the mountain of the ideal. Here enters the factor that dissolves the structures that are no longer useful; this factor in metaphysics is known as denial. Denial is not, strictly speaking, an attribute of Being as principle, but it is simply the absence of the impulse that constructs and sustains. When the ego consciously lets go and willingly gives up its cherished ideals and loves, it has fulfilled the law of denial and is again restored to God's house.

As all desire is fulfilled through the formative word, so all denial must be accomplished in word or conscious thought. (*The Twelve Powers,* p. 150)

Quicken elimination and renunciation through the spiritual activity of the Christ, keeping attention centered on the lower abdomen as you deny and affirm:

Denial:

> *I give no power to limiting thoughts and feelings.*

Affirmations:

> *My Divine Power of Elimination is now working to remove and*

renounce anything unlike the Christ Nature I am.

My spiritual center of Elimination is quickened in me. "I gladly let go of the old. My whole being expands with the new life in Christ Jesus." (The Twelve Powers, p. 285)

Jesus Christ is now here, raising me to His consciousness of self-denial, and I realize that the cleansing, purifying power of the Holy Spirit, the activity of Divine Mind, is active in me. (The Twelve Powers, p. 279)

25S **LIFE**

Whenever the desire for the material stimulant manifests itself, say to it: "You are nothing. You have no power over me or over anybody else. I am Spirit, and I am wholly satisfied by the great flood of spiritual Life that now fills my being." (The Twelve Powers, p. 169)

It is through persistent realizations of perfect life, through broadening the vision and keeping the Imagination stayed on the perfect patterns of life, that the false concepts are erased and spiritual Faculties are established. In your deeper meditations you have attained wonderful realizations of Divine Life. For instance, you have been able to take a statement such as: The purifying Power of Divine Life is active in me through Jesus Christ, *and*

to concentrate upon it until the living Truth contained in the word became so alive that it was resolved back into formless essence, in which state it was dispensed throughout the soul and body consciousness, awakening every function and organ to a greater degree of power and life. (The Twelve Powers, pp. 290-291)

Quicken Life through the spiritual activity of the Christ, with attention centered on the generative function, as you deny and affirm:

Denials:

I give no power to any thought or feeling that I have of lifelessness or lack of energy.

I give no life to thoughts, feelings and projects based entirely from sense consciousness.

Affirmations:

I am Spirit, and I am wholly satisfied by the great flood of spiritual Life that now fills my mind and body. (The Twelve Powers, p. 169)

Jesus Christ is now here, raising me to his consciousness of everlasting Life, and I am filled with vitalizing energy and power. (The Twelve Powers, p. 287)

25T WAYS TO USE THE TWELVE POWERS

Use the Twelve Powers in the following ways:

1. Use the above affirmations to quicken a selected Power in your daily meditations as well as throughout the day. Focus on the Power that you feel needs quickening or awakening in your life.

2. You can use the Powers as a way to prepare for your day, a meeting or any activity. Sitting still, ask yourself which Power(s) would be especially useful today. Call the Power(s) forth by quickening it/them as above. It could be as simple as focusing on your medulla and affirming: *The power of*

Zeal is quickened in me now through the activity and presence of the Christ.

3. When you notice that a particular meeting or activity did not go quite as you would have liked, you can become still and ask yourself which Power(s) you did not quicken, or enliven, in that situation. Then you can make that Power(s) a focus of your future meditations.

4. Notice how the Powers can be used from sense/personal consciousness and then from Spiritual/Higher Consciousness. Here is an example of using the Powers to hold on to a negative thought, such as "I am not worthy," then how to use the Powers to replace that thought (the Law of Substitution) with a higher thought, such as *I am Christ*.

power/Power	sense consciousness / personal consciousness	Spiritual Consciousness / Higher consciousness
Faith	Use this ability to believe "I am not worthy."	Use this Ability to more than believe, to realize that *I am Christ*.
Strength	Use this ability to stick with and hold on to the belief that "I am not worthy."	Use this Ability to preserve and stay the course with the belief that *I am Christ*.
Judgment/ Wisdom	Use this ability to appraise that "I am not worthy" as well as know how to be not worthy.	Use this Ability to discern that *I am Christ* as well as to know how to be the best Christ you can be.

power/Power 	sense consciousness personal consciousness	Spiritual Consciousness Higher consciousness
Love	Use this ability to "desire" to not be worthy and so attract yourself to evidence that "I am not worthy."	Use this Ability to desire the Truth that "I am Christ" and therefore harmonize and balance everything to match the belief that *I am Christ*.
Power/Dominion	Use this ability to dominate your thinking such that you are only thinking about how unworthy you are.	Use this Ability to master and have dominion over all your thoughts such that you support only the belief that *I am Christ*.
Imagination	Use this ability to picture how unworthy you are and therefore demonstrate it more.	Use this Ability to imagine, picture or conceptualize how it looks to be the best Christ you can be.
Understanding	Use this ability to know what it is like to be unworthy.	Use this Ability to know and deeply perceive what it is like to be Christ.
Will	Use this ability to constantly choose the belief that "I am not worthy."	Use this Ability to choose, command and lead the way to being the best Christ you can be.
Order	Use this ability to sequence and organize your thinking to support the belief in unworthiness.	Use this Ability to organize and sequence your thinking so that you support the belief in *I am Christ*.
Zeal	Use this ability to aggressively and zealously empower the belief "I am not worthy."	Use this Ability to passionately and enthusiastically empower the belief *I am Christ*.
Elimination/ Renunciation	Use this ability to eliminate any thoughts that contradict or negate the belief in unworthiness.	Use this Ability to renounce and deny any beliefs, thoughts or feelings that are contrary to the Truth, *I am Christ*.
Life	Use this ability to enliven and vitalize your belief in unworthiness.	Use this Ability to energize and vitalize the belief, the realization, that *I am Christ*.

SUMMARY STATEMENTS

▼ _Degeneration_ resulted from the use of free will to think independently of Christ Mind, or Divine Mind. Sense mind began to be in control, resulting in the materialization of the body.

▼ _Generation_ deals with the birth of the physical, human body.

▼ _Regeneration_ of the Twelve Powers is the transformation process that takes place by bringing all the forces of mind and body to the support of the Christ idea. Both thinking and feeling natures are fully engaged in this process.

▼ _Our goal_ is to express our Christ potential unselfishly, lovingly and powerfully through the development of the Twelve Powers.

▼ Our _work_ is to develop our Twelve Spiritual Faculties so that we become the full expression of our Christ nature.

▼ Avoid _temptation_. The Powers are not for outer gain. They are for raising consciousness.

▼ _Jesus,_ assuming leadership in a Christ ministry, symbolizes that point where spiritual awareness becomes the guiding, motivating factor in an individual's life.

▼ Our increasing _awareness_ of our Twelve Faculties/Abilities will enable us to express them in creative and useful ways.

▼ _Development and expression_ of a given power may entail meditating and focusing on it for a period of time. The Twelve Powers are a sort of "team" designed to work together instead of independently.

▼ The _general approach_ to developing each of the Twelve Powers utilizes denials and affirmations through the power of the spoken word.

▼ One _model for a focused meditation_ to quicken a particular Power is to use the following affirmation: The Power of [name Power] is quickened in me now through the activity and presence of the Christ.

▼ Please refer to the individual Powers in this chapter, sections 24H-24S, for specific denials and affirmations.

TOPICS FOR DISCUSSION

1. *What are some strategies or plans you could create to help you regenerate each of your Twelve Powers?*

2. *What are some of the obstacles you might encounter while putting this plan or strategy into action?*

3. *What are the potential benefits of regenerating your Twelve Powers?*

4. *Think of a time when you were in a difficult situation or experience. Which of your regenerated Twelve Powers could have made this situation or experience different?*

THOUGHTS FOR REFLECTION AND MEDITATION

"Generation sustains and perpetuates the human; regeneration unfolds and glorifies the divine."

(Charles and Cora Fillmore, *The Twelve Powers*, Unity House, Unity Village, Mo., 1999, p. 3)

SUPPLEMENTARY READING

The Twelve Powers by Charles and Cora Fillmore, Unity House, Unity Village, Mo., 1999, Chapter 1, "The Twelve Powers of Man."

Christ Enthroned in Man by Cora Fillmore, 2nd ed., Unity School of Christianity, Unity Village, Mo., 1981, Chapter 14, "Twelve Power Exercise."

How to Use Your Twelve Gifts From God by William A. Warch, Christian Living Publishing, Anaheim, Calif., 1976.

Twelve Powers in You by David Williamson, Gay Lynn Williamson and Robert H. Knapp, Health Communications, Deerfield Beach, Fla., 2000.

Section 4:

Proving the Truth We Know

Demonstration is one of the goals of heart-centered metaphysics. Spiritual demonstration is a spiritual realization followed by the manifestation of Divine Ideas, Laws and Principles in the outer realm, first in mind and then in form. A heart-centered metaphysician consistently and compassionately lives from a higher state of awareness and consciousness, demonstrating the application of Divine Laws and Principles in everyday life.

CHAPTER TWENTY-SIX

THE KINGDOM OF HEAVEN— THE FOURTH DIMENSION

INTRODUCTION

The Kingdom of Heaven, a key teaching of Jesus, is called the "Fourth Dimension" as well as the "Garden of Eden" in some Unity writings. The Fourth and other dimensions mentioned in this chapter are not necessarily related to the many dimensions that science has postulated. W.I. Hoshover wrote, "In metaphysical circles much is said about a Fourth Dimension of Consciousness, a Realm in which humankind as well as everything else exists in a state of unconditioned freedom" (*Unity Magazine*, Oct. 1926, "Some Thought on Faith," p. 313). Charles Fillmore said, "... in considering this subject [the Fourth Dimension] we should bear in mind that the Garden of Eden, the Kingdom of the Heavens and the universal Cosmic Ethers are all synonymous" (unpublished notes of L.E. Meyer of Training School class taught by Charles and Cora Fillmore, 1935). Whatever it is called, the Kingdom of Heaven is a fundamental teaching because it is the Dimension from which everything is manifested. The heart-centered metaphysician uses the thinking and feeling natures to consciously manifest from this Dimension. From here, everything seen is formed out of that which is unseen and unformed.

In this chapter, the phrase "Kingdom of God" will be retained, as it is from the Bible. However, we must keep in mind that what we really mean is the Kingdom of Divine Mind, or the Realm of the Absolute.

26A KINGDOM OF HEAVEN

The kingdom of heaven is the orderly adjustment of divine ideas in humankind's mind and body. (Charles Fillmore, *Metaphysical Bible Dictionary,* Unity House, Unity Village, Mo., 1931, p. 387)

The kingdom of heaven is the realm of divine ideas, producing their expression, perfect harmony. (Charles Fillmore, *The Revealing Word: A Dictionary of Metaphysical Terms,* 2nd ed., Unity House, Unity Village, Mo., 2006, p. 115)

The Kingdom of Heaven, the Fourth Dimension, is the Realm of Divine Ideas as well as the orderly adjustment of Divine Ideas in the mind and body of humankind. The "Field of Divine Ideas" underlies everything; the body and relative thoughts in mind are effects of these Divine Ideas.

26B KINGDOM OF GOD AND KINGDOM OF HEAVEN

I have found that the kingdom of God is within man and that we are wasting our time and defeating the work of the Spirit if we look for it anywhere else. (Charles Fillmore, *Atom-Smashing Power of Mind,* 2nd ed., Unity House, Unity Village, Mo., 2006, p. 26)

He [Jesus] understood exactly what the conditions were on the invisible side of life, which is termed in His teaching the "kingdom of God" or the "kingdom of the heavens. (*Atom-Smashing Power of Mind,* p. 27)

We know that the kingdom of the heavens or kingdom of God is not a place in the skies but an ideal state in creative mind, ready to be ushered into the minds of men. (Charles Fillmore, *Dynamics for Living: A Topical Compilation of Essential Fillmore Teachings,* Unity House, Unity Village, Mo, p. 58)

The kingdom of the heavens, or the kingdom of God, is within us. It is a kingdom of substance [Substance] and of Mind. (*Dynamics for Living,* p. 189)

Heaven is everywhere present. It is the orderly, lawful adjustment of God's kingdom in humankind's mind, body and affairs; it is the Christ consciousness, the realm of divine ideas, a state of consciousness in harmony with the thoughts of God. Heaven is within every one of us; a place, a conscious sphere of mind, having all the attractions described or imagined as belonging to heaven. (Charles Fillmore, *Keep a True Lent,* 2nd ed., Unity House, Unity Village, Mo., 2005, p. 177)

As mentioned in Chapter 14, Heaven is a State of Consciousness. In Unity literature it is clear that the Kingdom of Heaven and the Kingdom of God are the same and are also equated with the Christ Consciousness.

Metaphysically interpreted, the Kingdom of God and the Kingdom of Heaven are not exactly the same things. The Kingdom of God is the Absolute. It is Omnipresence, Omniscience, Omnipotence; It is limitless, changeless and pure Beingness. The Kingdom of Heaven is based on our relative perception of the Kingdom of God, and It encompasses the very highest levels of our Beingness based on our current level of consciousness; It is our growing and unfolding consciousness of Truth and Oneness. The Kingdom of Heaven is in different stages of realization for each person; It is not a fixed Absolute as is the Kingdom of God.

26C RECOGNITION OF THE KINGDOM

It is not a question of geographical locality but of mental recognition. Seeking the kingdom of God within changes our whole mental viewpoint. We find ourselves right in the presence of creative Mind, and seeking to cooperate with this Mind, we receive spiritual inspiration and are guided in even the most minute details of life. (Charles and Cora Fillmore, *Teach Us to Pray*, 2nd ed., Unity House, Unity Village, Mo., 2007, p. 87)

The Divine Mind we know is the kingdom of the heavens which is everywhere present. Jesus located the kingdom of heaven within everyone and said that it was at hand, meaning it is omnipresent. (unpublished notes of L.E. Meyer of Training School class taught by Charles and Cora Fillmore, 1935: Lesson One)

The Kingdom of God is within us, within Consciousness/consciousness, but more accurately, we have consciousness "within" It. The Kingdom of God is a term used by Jesus that has the same meaning as Omnipresence. Every person has his or her consciousness and beingness within the very heart of Omnipresence. Since Divine Mind is beyond all dimensions and limitations of space and time, the very center of Omnipresence is wherever anyone becomes centered in the awareness of that Oneness. A person can become centered only "within" consciousness. Hence, Jesus states, "Behold, the kingdom of God is within you" (Lk. 17:21 KJV).

As Charles Fillmore said, "Seeking the kingdom of God within changes our whole mental viewpoint." A person's mental viewpoint before seeking the inner Kingdom might be mediocre, or even lacking. However, by making the sincere effort to center in and from the Consciousness of Omnipresence, wonderful changes of consciousness will occur. These changes in consciousness manifest in thoughts and feelings as well as in the physical realm, beginning with the health of the body, then into the many affairs of daily existence.

26D KINGDOM OF HEAVEN ON EARTH

The real of the universe is held in the mind of Being as ideas of life, love, substance, intelligence, Truth and so forth. These ideas may be combined in a multitude of ways, producing infinite variety in the realm of forms. There is a right combination, which constitutes the divine order, the kingdom of heaven on earth. This right relation of ideas and the science of right thought is practical Christianity. (Charles Fillmore, *Christian Healing*, 2nd ed., Unity House, Unity Village, Mo., 2005, p. 14)

The real universe is not the physical universe; it is the Spiritual Universe where Divine Ideas constitute the Kingdom of Heaven. They are formless and intangible as long as they remain as Ideas in God Mind. As our minds appropriate these Divine Ideas, we give them form and location in time and space, and therefore have the possibility of manifesting the Kingdom of Heaven on earth. This first happens by a transformation of "earth," which is a transformation of sense consciousness. Then through the Law of Mind Action, the process of Divine Order (Mind-Idea-Expression), these Ideas are given form and character. We

transform their energies into our own experiences according to our own level of consciousness.

26E THE FOURTH DIMENSION

The fourth dimension is the realm of forces and powers which are invisible and unexplainable to humankind of [the] three-dimensional world. It is a realm which interpenetrates the other dimensions yet is not bound by them. It is the realm of mental perception. (unpublished notes of L.E. Meyer of Training School class taught by Charles and Cora Fillmore, 1935: Lesson One)

The fourth dimension is the free, unconfined dimension, and the means or process by which the three dimensions were determined. (E. V. Ingraham, *The Fourth Dimension Plus*, DeVorss, Los Angeles, Calif., 1931, p. 14)

A transcendent realm that Jesus called the "kingdom of the heavens." Here one can discern the trend of spiritual forces and see with the spiritual vision of the Christ Mind. (*The Revealing Word*, p. 78)

The fourth dimension (which encompasses the other three dimensions) is also realization, the doing away with time and space and all conditions. The human mind, with its limited reasoning faculties, is bound by time, space and conditions and can get no farther into the spiritual than reason will take it, but when we go beyond reason into the realm of realization, then we have attained the consciousness of pure being, the fourth-dimension mind. (*The Revealing Word*, p. 78)

The Fourth Dimension, the Kingdom of Heaven, is a transcendent Realm that encompasses the three-dimensional realm of length, width and depth in that It interpenetrates them and yet is not bound by them. The Fourth Dimension does away with time and space and all other conditions, as It is the Realm of Pure Beingness where we have the realization of the Truth. It is the Realm from which one can see with the "Spiritual Eyes" of the Christ Mind; It is the Realm out of which we manifest our good.

26F GARDEN OF EDEN

[Eden] A pleasant, harmonious, productive state of consciousness in which are all possibilities of growth. When someone is expressing in harmony with Divine Mind, bringing forth the qualities of Being in divine order, he or she dwells in Eden, or in a state of bliss in a harmonious body. ... The Garden of Eden is the divine consciousness. (*Metaphysical Bible Dictionary*, p. 181)

Represents a region of Being in which are provided all primal ideas for the production of the beautiful. As described in Genesis, it represents, allegorically, the elemental life and intelligence placed at the disposal of humankind and through which humankind is to evolve both mind and body. (*The Revealing Word*, p. 60)

The Garden of Eden is the finer force of our mind and body. In our spiritual understanding we are the light of our minds and the strength of our bodies. (unpublished notes of L.E. Meyer of Training School class taught by Charles and Cora Fillmore, 1935: Lesson Three)

These definitions of Eden and the Garden of Eden give further insight into the Fourth Dimension. It is the State of Consciousness where all the possibilities of growth reside. It is the Realm from which we express Divine Ideas from Divine Mind by utilizing the Process of Divine Order (Mind-Idea-Expression/mind-idea-expression), thus creating an experience of harmony and beauty according to our level of consciousness.

26G THE FOURTH DIMENSION IN RELATIONSHIP TO OTHER DIMENSIONS

The seventh dimension is the universal mass, or the great whole wherein is contained everything in potential nature. If you would like also to take the Scriptures for it, you will find the seventh dimension described in the statement that "God is all." The first chapter of Genesis gives it as: "In the beginning God." In other words, in the beginning God was the Universal All, but without form, and was void of manifestation. (The Fourth Dimension Plus, p. 17)

Now the first thing which we recognize of Universal Mass is that it is not immovable in its nature, but is capable of motion. Universal Mass moves, and this is its first capacity or first attribute in departing from its mere state of being. The Bible describes this condition as "and the spirit of God moved." Therefore motion is the sixth dimension, or the next in line following the seventh. This dimension is also retained in all formed things, for all things have motion. The sixth dimension or condition of everything, formed and unformed, is therefore motion. (The Fourth Dimension Plus, p. 18)

But the Universal Mass is capable of more than motion, for it can be divided into its component parts. "And God divided the waters from the waters." This process of dividing the Universal Mass into its component parts is the fifth capacity of the universe, therefore the fifth dimension. Therefore the fact that Universal Mass can be divided into its component parts, together with

the process by which they are so separated or isolated, is the fifth dimension. (The Fourth Dimension Plus, pp. 18-19)

The next condition which is possible in this process is that elements once separated from the Universal Mass can be brought together in other combinations and in other proportions. Such combinations cause a precipitate. This recombining of various elements previously separated out of Universal Mass, in such combinations and proportions as cause a precipitation to result and which comprises the world of three-dimensional form, is the fourth dimension. (The Fourth Dimension Plus, pp. 19-20)

The three-dimensional world is but the precipitate caused by various combinations of elements which formerly existed as a part of the Universal Mass. Though separated from the Universal Mass and combined in other relationships, they are not taken outside of it, and therefore all the former relationship is retained except their previous freedom within it. (The Fourth Dimension Plus, p. 20)

The dimensions put forth in these quotes do not necessarily correspond with the dimensions that science is discovering today. Therefore, it is important to understand the ideas and concepts that lie behind these metaphorical dimensional constructs. In *The Fourth Dimension Plus,* 14 instead of seven are advocated—seven of mind and seven of form and matter. In the hierarchy of dimensions, in the movement from the seventh dimension to the three-dimensional world, each successive Dimension moving toward the three-dimensional realm includes all those preceding it. One might conceive of these as a flow of consciousness from the formless basis of everything, the Universal Mass, into form.

The Seventh Dimension is the Basis of everything, the Universal Mass, the Absolute Field of Infinite Potential and Possibilities out of which everything flows. It is Divine Mind; It is Source; It is the Kingdom of God. We could conceive of it as unformed Substance, the amorphous Potential for Divine Ideas.

The Sixth Dimension is the "movement that takes place in the Universal Mass, whether in proceeding from the Universal Mass toward form, or the return of form to Universal Mass" (*The Fourth Dimension Plus*, p. 23). This perhaps describes something akin to what we might call "energetic potential" in the relative realm.

The Fifth Dimension is the separation of Elements from Universal Mass, or in their return to It. This Dimension could be conceived as Divine Ideas "taking form" in Consciousness.

The Fourth Dimension is all that takes place in the combining of Elements (Divine Ideas) that have "separated out" (taken form) from the Universal Mass so as to cause or give rise to the "precipitated" three-dimensional world. It is all that takes place in the expansion of the three-dimensional world as well as resolving it back into its component parts. The form that is precipitated into the three-dimensional realm is dependent on the level of the precipitating consciousness. This first emergence into form is in consciousness, where the thoughts and ideas that derive from the combining of the Elements (Divine Ideas) create their effects.

"The three-dimensional realm is but the precipitate caused by various combinations of elements which formerly existed as part of the Universal Mass" (*The Fourth Dimension Plus*, p. 20). It "is the world of form having length, breadth, and thickness" (unpublished notes of L.E. Meyer of Training School class taught by Charles and Cora Fillmore, 1935: Lesson One)

26H THE TWO PATHS OF PROGRESS

Two paths of progress open up before us in thus considering the ultimate relationship of all things. First there is the path from Universal Mass to its precipitated form. Second, the path of the precipitated form back to its origin in Universal Mass. One is contraction and the other is expansion. Creation is from the whole or Universal Mass to form, and resurrection is from form to Universal Mass. The progress of Universal Mass from its state of Absolute Being is toward form, but the progress of form is back to its state in Universal Mass. Form only loses its limitation when it begins its return to its primal elements. (The Fourth Dimension Plus, p. 22)

In the ultimate relationship of all things, "they" are either progressing from the Universal Mass, where the potential and possibilities are limitless, into form, where there are limitations based on the consciousness of the one(s) laying hold of the Divine Ideas. Or, as form loses its limitations, it can ultimately resolve back into the Universal Mass.

261 THE SEEN AND UNSEEN

All things were first in the invisible before they came forth into manifestation. (unpublished notes of L.E. Meyer of Training School class taught by Charles and Cora Fillmore, 1935: Lesson One)

Every person, and every being, as well as every form, has a relationship to the universal whole; a relationship which irrevocably exists in spite of our forgetfulness of the fact. Yet we know that we can achieve advancement only when we are able to reinforce our own apparent nature with elements and forces beyond ourselves. "Form" is possible only as greater forces and elements have contributed to the form, and this form is capable of transcending itself only when linked with those same elements which produced the form in the first place. (The Fourth Dimension Plus, p. 6)

Each person lives in a world of his or her own comprehension. Your world is different from the world of those about you just to the degree that our outlook upon life is different. You see and note certain things, while those most closely associated with you may note things of quite a different character. Our worlds differ just to the degree that this mental variance, or awareness, exists. To live in different worlds, we have only to become aware of different things. (The Fourth Dimension Plus, p. 6)

Everything that exists comes out of the unseen Universal Mass. Before something is seen, it was first unseen. Equally, each experience of the seen is different based on individual perception. For each unique event there are as many experiences of it as the number of people observing and/or participating in it.

26J OUR WORK

The important fact for us is not to attempt to understand these dimensions in their entirety, but to understand that we have within ourselves a greater capacity, an infinitely greater magnitude that stretches back to infinity itself, that we can form new combinations, rearrange the three-dimensional world, and thereby continue indefinitely to develop new possibilities from an inexhaustible storehouse of elements. (The Fourth Dimension Plus, p. 25)

Our work is to learn how to release and use the forces of the fourth-dimensional world. We consider God as Mind with ideas inhering in it which are its medium of expression. Ideas are the basis of all things that appear, and back of ideas there are forces which Jesus Christ knew how to lay hold of and use. These powers are for our use when we understand how to release them and direct them aright. God is Mind. God Mind is within and around everyone. (unpublished notes of L.E. Meyer of Training School class taught by Charles and Cora Fillmore, 1935: Lesson One)

Whether these dimensions exist or not, they provide a useful concept. It is from the perspective of the Fourth Dimension that we give rise to shape and form, first in consciousness and then in the three-dimensional realm.

The most fundamental elements are Divine Ideas; everything else is based on these Divine Ideas. Humankind has the capacity to combine and recombine Divine Ideas as well as resolve them back into Divine Mind (Universal Mass). It is at the level of the Fourth Dimension that the Elements exist, having arisen "out of" the Universal Mass (Seventh Dimension) through its capacities of motion (Sixth Dimension) and separation from Universal Mass and return to Universal Mass. It is from the Kingdom of Heaven Consciousness, or Christ Consciousness, that we can create in the most harmonious, loving and peaceful way ... or not. In E.V. Ingraham's words, *"that we can form new combinations, rearrange the three-dimensional world, and thereby continue indefinitely to develop new possibilities from an inexhaustible storehouse of elements."* Ingraham is clearly stating that Divine Mind, Universal Mass, did not create the three-dimensional realm; *we* "form new combinations" and "rearrange the three-dimensional world." God is the Mind, the Universal Mass, from which *we* manifest the three-dimensional realm.

26K OUR PURPOSE: RAISING CONSCIOUSNESS

We know that there is Divine Mind back of all things, and through direct contact with it we can learn how to use righteously the powers of being, to the glory of God and the service and edification of humankind. (unpublished notes of L.E. Meyer of Training School class taught by Charles and Cora Fillmore, 1935: Lesson Two)

Everyone who loses confinement in the three-dimensional world of limitation when he or she takes on more of the fundamental magnitude in and with the Universal Mass, thereby ascending into conscious relationship with the ALL. This has ever been the way of progress employed by those of humanity who have achieved greatness, and it will ever be the way of progress for this and future generations. (*The Fourth Dimension Plus*, pp. 29-30)

Everything is manifest from the Fourth Dimension, good and bad (error), depending on the manifesting consciousness. Awareness of the Fourth Dimension from higher levels of consciousness manifests more and more good. This is accomplished by first realizing our fundamental Magnitude (Christ, Oneness) in the Universal Mass, or Divine Mind. Ultimately, as more Truth is realized, the glory of Oneness is brought to awareness, resulting in more Power (Omnipotence) and Presence (Omniscience) being placed into the service and edification of humankind. As seeming individual consciousness rises, so does the collective conscious-ness. The totality of humankind spirals up in consciousness as increasing numbers of people come into the realization of Truth.

26L **ATTENTION**

When we unfold our fourth-dimensional consciousness we shall see into Omnipresence, and there will be nothing hidden from us. When we refine and spiritualize our consciousness and the temple in and through which it finds expression, we shall be able to think of the most distant point in the universe, and immediately be there. There is no time or space to one who has unfolded the Christ consciousness to the degree that Jesus had. (Myrtle Fillmore as quoted in *Torch-Bearer to Light the Way: The Life of Myrtle Fillmore* by Neal Vahle, Open View Press, Mill Valley, Calif., 1996, p. 96)

That which we concentrate attention upon we become like. As Adam concentrated his attention upon the external and descended in consciousness, so in Christ we focus our attention upon the inner Power and Presence and ascend in consciousness. That which is pure and true is the Christ consciousness. (unpublished notes of L.E. Meyer of Training School class taught by Charles and Cora Fillmore, 1935: Lesson One)

Everyone is bound only by his or her attention upon the apparently fixed dimensions or magnitude of the world. When the attention is free from the apparently fixed dimensions of time, space and form, there is an infinite realm of freedom and opportunity available. (The Fourth Dimension Plus, p. 11)

Each person decides where attention is focused, determining what grows in consciousness. If the focus is on the outer realm, as reported by the five senses, consciousness becomes increasingly limited and spirals down, increasing sense consciousness. If the focus is on the Inner Realm of the Fourth Kingdom of Heaven, the fixed, finite realm reported by the senses is transcended and consciousness elevates into the Infinite Field of Potential and Possibilities. As consciousness spirals ever higher, understanding increases, resulting in demonstrating more and more Christ Consciousness.

26M **HOW TO**

We entered into the silence to realize the presence of the universal Cosmic Ether, the kingdom of the heavens in which we live, move and have our being. (unpublished notes of L.E. Meyer of Training School class taught by Charles and Cora Fillmore, 1935: Lesson Two)

Individuals and their world are not primarily individual manifestations of form, but combinations of energies and forces, all of which may be reinforced, expanded, and amplified by an expanse of its nature to include more of the forces and elements which comprise their being, and which exist endlessly within the Universal Mass. (The Fourth Dimension Plus, p. 29)

All who enter the realm of elements back of [form], back in the realm of new elements, new things and new ideas, immediately step out of their confinement in three-dimensional form and include in their nature the freedom of the fourth. As they continue this process, they liberate themselves more and more, for they feel the increased ability through the greater magnitude of the fourth-dimensional field. Even to consider new powers and new possibilities with respect to any situation, condition, or thing is to start, immediately, the expansion of your nature and your ability in the fourth-dimensional state. (The Fourth Dimension Plus, pp. 14-15)

As in Adam consciousness we have named all things that have been brought before us, some good and some not good, so in Christ we must characterize all things that come before us as God did in the beginning when God looked upon all things that God had created [Divine Ideas] and made and beheld they were very good. To *enlighten, to preach, to heal, to embody God in all ways and show forth God's creation is our work. (*unpublished notes of L.E. Meyer of Training School class taught by Charles and Cora Fillmore, 1935: Lesson Three)

*If all people apply themselves to know the unknown, attaining the as yet unattained, progressing into the realm of new powers, new possibilities, new discoveries, they are truly functioning in their rightful estates expanding themselves more and more in their fundamental relationships with the Universal Mass, the source from which all form, including themselves. All people are circumscribed only by their thoughts, their measure of life and events. When their thoughts are uncircumscribed, their progress into absolute freedom begins. (*The Fourth Dimension Plus, pp. 28-29)

Utilizing the Fourth Dimension is multifaceted. At first, manifestation and expression are unconscious and primarily based on sense consciousness. Then comes the realization that all manifestation and expression are brought forth from the Fourth Dimension (the good, the bad and the ugly). As the possibility of the existence of more than the three-dimensional world of the senses is considered, there is the awakening and expansion of awareness of Christ Consciousness. Investing more and more time in the Silence enables the conscious use of the Fourth-Dimensional State. Next, by monitoring where attention is focused, uncompromising choices to see the Good regardless of the outer appearance can be made. Energies and forces are reinforced, expanded and amplified to include more of the True Forces and Elements that comprise Beingness and exist endlessly within the Universal Mass. In short, it is by consciously working from the Fourth-Dimensional State that more and more of the Christ Potential is realized. Embodying Divine Mind in all ways results in the ability to enlighten and heal.

SUMMARY STATEMENTS

▼ *There is the essence of Oneness that binds, blends and harmonizes all things.*

▼ *The* <u>*Kingdom of Heaven*</u> *is the Realm of Divine Ideas as well as the orderly adjustment of these Ideas in the mind and body of humankind.*

▼ *Metaphysically, the* <u>*Kingdom of God*</u> *is the Absolute. It is omnipresent, limitless, changeless and pure Being.* <u>*The Kingdom of Heaven*</u> *is relative to us; It is our growing and unfolding consciousness of Truth and Oneness.*

▼ *The Kingdom of Heaven, the* <u>*Fourth Dimension*</u>*, is a State of Consciousness. As our minds appropriate Divine Ideas (the Kingdom of Heaven), we give them form and location in time and space according to the level of our own consciousness. Therefore, it is possible to manifest the Kingdom of Heaven on earth, or sense consciousness.*

▼ *The* <u>*Fourth Dimension*</u>*, the Garden of Eden, the Kingdom of Heaven, and the universal Cosmic Ethers are all synonymous.*

▼ *The* <u>*Fourth Dimension*</u> *is the Realm of mental perception from which one can see with the Spiritual Eyes of the Christ Mind. It is the Realm out of which we can manifest our good.*

▼ *The* <u>*Garden of Eden*</u> *is the State of Consciousness where all the possibilities of growth reside. It is the Realm from which Divine Ideas are expressed through the orderly adjustment and process of Divine Order (Mind-Idea-Expression in the Absolute and it is "reflected" in the relative as mind-idea-expression).*

▼ *The* <u>*Seventh Dimension*</u> *is the Universal Mass of infinite potential and possibility. The* <u>*Sixth Dimension*</u> *is motion. The* <u>*Fifth Dimension*</u> *is the separation of elements from Universal Mass, or their return to it. The* <u>*Fourth Dimension*</u> *is all that takes place in the expansion of the three-dimensional world as well as resolving it back into its component parts. The remaining* <u>*three dimensions*</u> *are width, length and breadth.*

▼ *Everything that is* <u>*seen*</u> *comes out of the* <u>*unseen*</u> *Universal Mass.*

▼ *Everything is either* <u>*progressing*</u> *from or* <u>*resolving*</u> *into the Universal Mass.*

▼ <u>*Our work*</u> *is to learn how to consciously release and use the Elements and Forces of the Fourth Dimension.*

▼ <u>*Our purpose*</u> *is to utilize our Power and Presence that is the glory of Divine Mind in the service and edification of humankind.*

▼ *What we focus our <u>attention</u> upon grows in our consciousness. When we focus attention on our Fourth-Dimensional State, we transcend the fixed realm of form and limitation and enter into the Infinite Field of Potential and Possibilities.*

▼ *The way to more fully realize the Fourth-Dimensional State and eventually Christ Consciousness is to (1) begin to consider that there is more than the three-dimensional world of the senses; (2) focus attention on the Fourth-Dimensional State and uncompromisingly choose to see Good everywhere regardless of appearance; and (3) devote time in the Silence.*

▼ *We can move beyond creating for our individual needs. We are then more able to enlighten, to heal and to embody God in all ways.*

TOPICS FOR DISCUSSION

1. *What is the Kingdom of Heaven—the Fourth Dimension?*

2. *Describe ways in which realizing the Kingdom of Heaven—the Fourth Dimension—impacts your everyday life.*

3. *What might hinder your realization of the Kingdom of Heaven, or Fourth Dimension?*

THOUGHTS FOR REFLECTION AND MEDITATION

"There is absolutely no limit to anything in the heavens above or in the earth below. That which seems to be a limitation is but the limit of the individual perception."

(E.V. Ingraham, *The Fourth Dimension Plus*)

SUPPLEMENTARY READING

Fourth Dimension by L. E. Meyer, unpublished notes of class taught by Charles and Cora Fillmore, 1935 Unity Training School. housed in Unity Archives.

The Fourth Dimension Plus by E.V. Ingraham, DeVorss, Los Angeles, 1931.

CHAPTER TWENTY-SEVEN

THE CREATIVE PROCESS

INTRODUCTION

The Bible plays a very important role in the Unity teachings; it is seen as both a record of historical events and an account of the evolving of spiritual awareness, in both collective and individual consciousness. For this reason, we interpret the Bible metaphysically, with its characters and events representing various aspects of our own consciousness. We use these insights and increased awareness to transform our lives.

Charles Fillmore had a distinct way of metaphysically interpreting the creation stories in the Book of Genesis. In his book *Mysteries of Genesis*, Fillmore interpreted the first creation story, found in Genesis 1, to mean that the creative process begins first in consciousness and includes a balance of both thinking and feeling natures; it takes place entirely in mind. His interpretation of the second creation story, found in Genesis 2, is that we take an idea in consciousness and clothe it in form. In this chapter, we will focus on gaining deeper insights into this process.

27A DIVINE IDEAS

The first chapter [of Genesis] shows two parts of the Trinity: mind, and idea in mind. In the second chapter we have the third part, manifestation. In this illustration all theological mystery about the Trinity is cleared away, for we see that it is simply mind, idea in mind, and manifestation of idea. Since humankind is the offspring of God, made in the image and likeness of Divine Mind, humankind must express itself under the laws of this great creative Mind. The law of manifestation for humankind is the law of thought. God ideates; humankind thinks. One is the completion of the other in mind. (Charles Fillmore, Mysteries of

Genesis, 2nd ed., Unity House, Unity Village, Mo., 1998, p. 12)

God is mind, and all God's works are created in mind as perfect ideas. (Mysteries of Genesis, p. 25)

God creates through the action of God Mind, and all things rest on ideas. (Mysteries of Genesis, p. 14)

The idea is the directing and controlling power. Every idea has a specific function to perform. (Mysteries of Genesis, p. 21)

Mental activity in Divine Mind represents two phases: first, conception of the idea; and second, expression of the idea. In every idea conceived in mind there is first the quickening spirit of life, followed by the increase of the idea in substance. Wisdom is the "masculine" nature or expressive side of Being, while love is the "feminine" or receptive side of Being. Wisdom is the father quality of God, and love is the mother quality. In every idea there exist these two qualities of mind, which unite in order to increase and bring forth under divine law. (Mysteries of Genesis, p. 27)

Every idea is a seed that, sown in the substance of mind, becomes the real food on which humankind is nourished. Humankind has access to the seed ideas of Divine Mind, and through prayer and meditation, one quickens and appropriates the substance of those ideas, which were originally planted in his or her I AM by the

parent mind. (Mysteries of Genesis, p. 27)

God, or Divine Mind, creates/ideates through the action of Mind. Everything in the Spiritual Universe (the Realm of Divine Ideas) and the material universe is based on Divine Ideas in Divine Mind. Operating under the Laws of Divine Mind are Mind, idea in mind, and manifestation (expression). The first chapter of Genesis metaphysically shows Mind and Idea in mind. The second chapter of Genesis symbolically represents the manifestation of Idea. Humankind manifests through the law of thought. "God ideates; humankind thinks."

There are two phases of mental activity in Divine Mind. First, the Idea quickens the Spirit of Life; and second, this quickening is followed by an increase of the impact of Idea in Substance. (There is always the Idea and always Substance. Neither actually increases or decreases, as this would imply some sort of change in the Absolute, which, of course, is not possible because the Absolute does not change.) In order to increase and bring forth according to Divine Law, two qualities must be present: Wisdom and Love. Wisdom is the expressive side of Beingness, while Love is the receptive side. Humankind has access to Divine Ideas (seed ideas) in the I AM. Through prayer and meditation,

Substance is quickened and appropriated for these seed ideas.

27B STAGES OF CREATION

The key to the operation of mind is symbolically set forth in the Genesis account of the six days of creation. One's mind goes through the identical steps in bringing an idea into manifestation. Between the perception of an idea and its manifestation, there are six definite, positive movements, followed by a (seventh) "day" of rest, in which the mind relaxes and sees its work in a process of fulfillment. (Charles Fillmore, *Prosperity,* Unity House, Unity Village, Mo., 1936, p. 83)

In the first chapter of Genesis it is the great creative Mind that is at work. The record portrays just how divine ideas were brought into expression. As a person must have an idea before he or she can bring an idea into manifestation, so it is with the creations of God. When a person builds a house, he or she builds it first in the mind. One has the idea of a house, completes the plan in the mind, and then works it out in manifestation. (*Mysteries of Genesis*, p. 12)

All things are created first in mind. This is involution. *Next comes evolution; ideas take form and shape. The realm of pure ideas and the realm of thought forms are two universal planes*

of consciousness. We have said that God's creations are always spiritual. However, humankind's creations are both spiritual and material. The law of thought is, for us, the law of manifestation. (*The Creative Process: Learner's Workbook,* Unity School for Religious Studies, 1998, pp. 112-113)

Charles Fillmore sees a distinct analogy in the first chapter of Genesis between God, or Divine Mind, and creation/ideation, and between humankind and the process of manifestation. This is the reason for metaphysically interpreting the allegory in a step-by-step manner. Charles Fillmore understood the great importance of becoming acquainted with our Twelve Spiritual Faculties/Powers/Abilities; he viewed the creation allegory as the earliest example we have of humankind's dawning awareness of these Powers. In the Bible, numbers have symbolic meanings, and seven is the symbol of completion in the manifest realm.

27C CHAOS

We begin by acknowledging the need for and accepting the presence of the chaos, darkness, that may be present in our experience right now ... darkness preceded each day of creation. Our choice is to affirm that God's good is present in the chaos, to see beyond the outer appearances to the inner truth. (*The Creative Process*, pp. 140-141)

God, or Divine Mind, created/ideated out of the "chaos, darkness." Chaos here does not mean a disorderly or confused mess; it is more like the void of infinite potential and possibilities. Before light, there was darkness. Therefore, it is important that we acknowledge the chaos and the darkness in our lives and begin to see how this can be used for good and for expressing more Divine Will. We can use the chaos and darkness in our lives to break up our crystallized thinking, thus opening up the full range of infinite potential and possibility.

"In the beginning when God created the heavens and the earth, the earth was a formless void and darkness covered the face of the deep, while a wind from God swept over the face of the waters." (Gen. 1:1-2)

27D FIRST STEP—LIGHT

In bringing forth a manifestation of God's abundant supply, take the first step by saying, "Let there be light"; that is, let there be understanding. You must have a clear perception of the principle back of the proposition "God will provide." The one universal, eternal, substance of God, which is the source of all, must be discerned and relied on, while dependence on material things must be eliminated from thought. ... If you have established that light, you have begun your demonstration and can go to the second step. (*Prosperity*, p. 83)

"Light" is intelligence, a spiritual quality. It corresponds to understanding and should precede all activity. At the beginning of any of our creating, we should declare for light. (Mysteries of Genesis, p. 16)

The first step to turn chaos into blessing is the awakening of light, divine illumination, in our minds. In prayer, we quiet the concerns of our human mind and invite Divine Mind to illumine our thoughts with spiritual light. We cannot move forward in a positive way without the clarity and guidance that God's light provides us. (The Creative Process, p. 141)

"Let there be light" is an affirmation of illumination and of Understanding. Light is a symbol with many meanings in the Bible, one of the most important of which is "intelligent awareness." In the Silent Unity® prayer ministry, the prayer for illumination is always spoken first. The most illuminating insight we can realize is that Divine Mind is our Source. From Divine Mind we are illumined with Understanding.

"Then God said, 'Let there be light'; and there was light. And God saw that the light was good; and God separated the light from the darkness. God called the light Day, and the darkness he called Night. And there was evening and there was morning, the first day." (Gen. 1:3-5)

27E **SECOND STEP—FAITH**

The second step in creation is the development of faith or the 'firmament.' (*Mysteries of Genesis*, p. 16)

A "firmament" must be established; that is, a firm place in the mind, a dividing of the true from the apparent. This is done through affirmation. As you affirm God as your supply and support, your words will in due season become substance to you, the substance of faith. (Prosperity, p. 83)

We next establish a firm base on which our illumined thoughts will rest by having unshakable faith in them. Faith commits us totally to the spiritual truth, despite all appearance. We know that all is well because we have faith in God's unfailing good. (The Creative Process, p. 141)

Faith is our supreme affirmative Faculty. It is interesting to note that the first Bible symbol for Faith is "a firmament"; also worth noting is the similarity between the words "affirmation" and "a firmament." Through our faculty of Faith, we affirm the reality of Divine Ideas as our Divine Inheritance. Faith is our ability to believe, which goes beyond simple belief: Faith is more like *perceiving* the Truth without external evidence of it.

"And God said, 'Let there be a dome in the midst of the waters, and let it separate the waters from the waters.' So God made the dome and separated the waters that were under the dome from the waters that were above the dome. And it was so. God called the dome Sky. And there was evening and there was morning, the second day." (Gen. 1:6-8)

27F **THIRD STEP—IMAGINATION**

The third step is the forming of this substance into tangibility. "Let the dry land appear." Out of the omnipresent substance your mind forms whatever it wants by the power of imagination. ... If you have already taken the other steps, you can picture in mind the things you desire and bring them into your manifest world. (Prosperity, p. 84)

The first day's creation reveals the light or inspiration of Spirit. The second day establishes faith in our possibilities to bring forth the invisible. The third day's creation or third movement of Divine Mind pictures the activity of ideas in mind. (Mysteries of Genesis, p. 18)

Our imagination holds the key to shaping our illumined thoughts by envisioning their material results. Instead of letting our imagination wander to possible negative consequences, we image only the highest good that we know God has in store. (The Creative Process, p. 141)

It is through our Imagination that we form and shape our desired good from the invisible Substance that is everywhere available. The Imagination does not *cause* manifestation; It produces the mental image that usually has an associated feeling of that which is to be made manifest, even if it is only in mind. The Imagination does, however, perform the important step of determining the general *form* of the desired good.

"And God said, 'Let the waters under the sky be gathered together into one place, and let the dry land appear.' And it was so. God called the dry land Earth, and the waters that were gathered together he called Seas. And God saw that it was good. Then God said, 'Let the earth put forth vegetation: plants yielding seed, and fruit trees of every kind on earth that bear fruit with the seed in it.' And it was so. The earth brought forth vegetation: plants yielding seed of every kind, and trees of every kind bearing fruit with the seed in it. And God saw that it was good. And there was evening and there was morning, the third day." (Gen. 1:9-13)

27G FOURTH STEP— UNDERSTANDING AND WILL

The fourth step in creation is the development of the "two great lights," the will and the understanding, or the sun (the spiritual I AM) and the moon (the intellect). These are but reflectors of the true light; for God had said, "Let there be light: and there was light"—before the sun and the moon were created. (Mysteries of Genesis, p. 19)

The "greater light," in mind, is understanding and the "lesser light" is the will. The greater light rules "the day," that realm of consciousness which has been illumined by Spirit. The lesser light rules "the night," that is, the will; which has no illumination ("light" or "day") but whose office is to execute the demands of understanding. (Mysteries of Genesis, p. 20)

The Creative Process continues as we let go [of] personal desires and surrender ourselves to God's spiritual will and understanding. We pray for an understanding heart, and this spiritual understanding increases our desire to follow divine will. Following God's guidance is becoming natural to us. (The Creative Process, p. 141)

Will and Understanding are symbolized in the fourth day of the creation allegory. When we develop our spiritual *Understanding*, we then use *Will* to choose what to manifest as well as become *willing* to do what is required to manifest our highest good.

"And God said, 'Let there be lights in the dome of the sky to separate the day from the night; and let them be for signs and for seasons and for days and years, and let them be lights in the dome of the sky to give light upon the earth.' And it was so. God made the two great lights—the greater light to rule the day and the lesser light to rule the night—and the stars. God set them in the dome of the sky to give light upon the earth, to rule over the day and over the night, and to separate the light from the darkness. And God saw that it was good. And there was evening and there was morning, the fourth day." (Gen. 1:14-19)

27H **FIFTH STEP—JUDGMENT**

In the fifth day's creation, ideas of discrimination and judgment are developed. The fishes and fowls represent ideas of life working in mind, but they must be properly related to the unformed (seas) and the formed (earth) worlds of mind. When an individual is well balanced in mind and body, there is an equalizing force flowing in the consciousness, and harmony is in evidence. (Mysteries of Genesis, p. 23)

Human judgment is the mental act of evaluation through comparison or contrast. ... Divine judgment is of spiri-

tual consciousness. ... This faculty may be exercised in two ways: [either] from sense perception or [from] spiritual understanding. If its action be based on sense, its conclusions are fallible and often condemnatory; if on spiritual understanding, they are safe. (Charles Fillmore, Keep a True Lent, 2nd ed., Unity House, Unity Village, Mo., 2005, p. 182)

With our faculty of judgment, we discern the difference between the human and the spiritual. Our judgments are ground firmly in Principle. These decisions keep us moving in the right direction along our spiritual path. (The Creative Process, p. 141)

The fifth day symbolizes the Judgment Faculty. Judgment is our ability to discern, evaluate and come to decisions. It is most important that our judgments are based on Spiritual Understanding. We use our Judgment Faculty to separate the wheat from the chaff, the useful thoughts from the not-useful error thoughts. The Power of Judgment helps us know how to use what we know.

"And God said, 'Let the waters bring forth swarms of living creatures, and let birds fly above the earth across the dome of the sky.' So God created the great sea monsters and every living creature that moves, of every kind, with which the waters swarm, and every winged bird of every kind. And God saw that it was good. God blessed them, saying, 'Be fruitful and multiply and fill the waters in the seas, and let birds multiply on the earth.' And there was evening and there was morning, the fifth day." (Gen. 1:20-23)

271 SIXTH STEP—WISDOM AND LOVE

The sixth step in creation is the bringing forth of ideas after their kind. ... Wisdom and love are the two qualities of Being that, communing together, declare, "Let us make humankind in our image, after our likeness." (*Mysteries of Genesis,* pp. 24-25)

Wisdom is the "masculine" or expressive side of Being, while love is the "feminine" or receptive side of Being. Wisdom is the father quality of God and love is the mother quality. In every idea there exist these two qualities of mind, which unite in order to increase and bring forth under divine law. Divine Mind blessed the union of wisdom and love and pronounced on them the increase of Spirit. When wisdom and love are unified in the individual consciousness, a person is a master of ideas and brings forth under the original creative law. (*Mysteries of Genesis,* p. 27)

Our next step is to add love to everything we think, do, and say. When we can truly express love toward all, without regard to what the physical world seems to tell us, we are completing our work in consciousness. (*The Creative Process,* p. 141)

The mastery of Divine Ideas comes through the awareness that every Idea has the qualities of Wisdom and Love. The masculine nature, Wisdom, and feminine nature, Love, metaphysically interpreted from the sixth day in the allegory are symbolic of wholeness in each individual's Spiritual Nature. The whole person is both masculine and feminine—that is, thinking and feeling, expressive and receptive, wise and loving. These need to become united and used together within our own consciousness if we are to have our desires manifested.

Love also has the aspect of desire. What we desire and focus on grows in consciousness. Since Love is indiscriminate about what it loves, it needs Wisdom to direct and guide it.

"And God said, 'Let the earth bring forth living creatures of every kind: cattle and creeping things and wild animals of the earth of every kind.' And it was so. God made the wild animals of the earth of every kind, and the cattle of every kind, and everything that creeps upon the ground of every kind. And God saw that it was good.

"Then God said, 'Let us make humankind in our image, according to our likeness; and let them have dominion over the fish of the sea, and over the birds of the air, and over the cattle, and over all the wild animals of the earth, and over every creeping thing that creeps upon the earth.'

"So God created humankind in his image, in the image of God he created them; male and female he created them. God blessed them, and God said to them, 'Be fruitful and multiply, and fill the earth and subdue it; and have dominion over the fish of the sea and over the birds of the air and over every living thing that moves upon the earth.' God said, 'See, I have given you every plant yielding seed that is upon the face of the earth, and every tree with seed in its fruit; you shall have them for food. And to every beast of the earth, and to every bird of the air, and to everything that creeps on the earth, everything that has the breath of life, I have given every green plant for food.' And it was so. God saw everything that he had made, and indeed, it was very good. And there was evening and there was morning, the sixth day." (Gen. 1:24-31)

27J SEVENTH STEP—THE SABBATH

All is finished first in consciousness and mind then rests, in faith, from further mental activity. This "rest" precedes manifestation. The seventh day refers to the mind's realization of ful-

fillment, its resting in the assurance that all that has been imaged in it will come forth in expression. (Mysteries of Genesis, p. 31)

Sabbath—The true Sabbath is that state of spiritual attainment where humankind ceases from all personal effort and all belief in their own words, and rests in the consciousness that "the Father abiding in me doeth his works" (Jn. 14:10). ... We rest from outer work, cease daily occupation, and give ourselves up to meditation or the study of things spiritual.

The Sabbath is kept any time we enter into spiritual consciousness and rest from thought of temporal things. (Charles Fillmore, The Revealing Word: A Dictionary of Metaphysical Terms, 2nd ed., Unity House, Unity Village, Mo., 2006, p. 172)

It is now time to let go of the work we have done and to rest in the Sabbath, trusting God to complete the process of manifestation. Our part in the creating is done and we know that all is well. This is the final step in the Creative Process. (The Creative Process, p. 142)

The Sabbath type of rest is a rest of the mind, not necessarily of the physical body. The true Sabbath occurs when we become quiet and still *within*; it is the realization and assurance that manifestation is forthcoming. Sabbath sometimes lasts no longer than a moment, and it is necessary for the good of the whole person as well as for the right outworking of the entire creative process. To maintain the supply of creative energy, a person needs to take time out from constant expenditure of that energy. All is now prepared in consciousness for manifestation to occur. Manifestation is metaphysically represented in the second chapter of Genesis.

"Thus the heavens and the earth were finished, and all their multitude. And on the seventh day God finished the work that he had done, and he rested on the seventh day from all the work that he had done. So God blessed the seventh day and hallowed it, because on it God rested from all the work that he had done in creation." (Gen. 2:1-3)

SUMMARY STATEMENTS

▼ *God* <u>*creates/ideates*</u> *through the action of Mind.*

▼ *The* <u>*Spiritual Universe*</u> *is made up of Divine Ideas.*

▼ *Everything in the material universe is based on* <u>*Divine Ideas*</u> *in the Spiritual Universe, or Divine Mind.*

▼ <u>*Humankind has "access" to Divine Ideas*</u>*, seed ideas, in the I AM. Through prayer and meditation, Substance is quickened and appropriated for those Divine Ideas.*

▼ *The* <u>*creation/ideation*</u> *as depicted in the first chapter of Genesis* <u>*is entirely spiritual*</u> *and should not be confused with manifestation. It is Elohim God that creates the Spiritual Universe and the Spiritual Human, Christ.*

▼ *The* <u>*"Image-and-Likeness Human" is the Spiritual Human,*</u> *also referred to as the Christ, the Lord God, the Jehovah, the I AM. The Spiritual Human is made up of Twelve Faculties, Powers or Divine Ideas.*

▼ *The* <u>*Image-and-Likeness Human, the Spiritual Human*</u>*, "pours forth" Divine Ideas from the Absolute into the relative. Each individual then arranges these Ideas into thoughts, forms and life.*

▼ <u>*God created/ideated the Spiritual Universe*</u> *and the Divine Ideas that make the material (physical) universe possible. It is the* <u>*Christ*</u>*, I AM, Jehovah, or God that* <u>*uses these Ideas to manifest the physical universe.*</u>

▼ *Humankind has become* <u>*entangled with materiality.*</u> *Some manifestation is not necessarily good because the manifestation of Divine Ideas is related to the level of consciousness of the individual as well as collective consciousness.*

▼ *We in Unity believe there is an orderly process of manifestation by which we are able to bring forth* <u>*ideal creation.*</u> *An example of this process can be understood when we interpret the first chapter of Genesis metaphysically.*

▼ *The first step is* <u>*Light, Illumination and Understanding*</u>*, which allows us to recognize Oneness, God, or Divine Mind as the Source of our supply.*

▼ *The second step is* <u>*Faith,*</u> *through which we affirm the reality of Divine Ideas as our Divine Inheritance.*

▼ *The third step is* <u>*Imagination,*</u> *through which we form and shape our desired good from omnipresent Substance in consciousness.*

▼ *The fourth step is* <u>*Will and Understanding.*</u> *As we develop our spiritual Understanding, we then use* Will *to choose what to manifest as well as become* willing *to do what is required to manifest our highest good.*

▼ *The fifth step is* <u>*Discrimination*</u> *(Judgment), through which we are able to make wise and appropriate decisions concerning our demonstration process.*

▼ *Every* <u>*Divine Idea*</u> *is imbued with Wisdom, the masculine, expressive side, and Love, the receptive side.*

▼ *The sixth step,* <u>*Wisdom and Love,*</u> *is symbolic of the wholeness inherent in our Spiritual Nature. We must become united within our own consciousness in order to have our desires manifested.*

▼ *The seventh step is the* <u>*Sabbath.*</u> *It is the realization and assurance that our manifestation is forthcoming.*

TOPICS FOR DISCUSSION

1. *Why is it important to begin the seven-step process with "illumination"?*

2. *Why is the Sabbath necessary to the seven-step demonstration process? How has it been meaningful in your own life?*

THOUGHTS FOR REFLECTION AND MEDITATION

"God creates through the action of His mind,
and all things rest on ideas. ...
Evolution is the working out in manifestation
of what mind has involved.
Whatever mind commands to be brought forth
will be brought forth by and through
the law of evolution inherent in being.
This applies to the great and the small.
In mind there is but one."

(Charles Fillmore, *Mysteries of Genesis*, p. 14)

SUPPLEMENTARY READING

Mysteries of Genesis by Charles Fillmore, Unity Classic Library edition, Unity House, Unity Village, Mo., 1998, Chapter 1, "Spiritual Man."

Prosperity by Charles Fillmore, Unity House, Unity Village, Mo., 1936, Chapter 5, "The Law That Governs the Manifestation of Supply."

CHAPTER TWENTY-EIGHT

STUMBLING BLOCKS AND KEYS TO DEMONSTRATION

INTRODUCTION

In our metaphysical studies, we have explored the Divine Ideas that make up Truth as we teach it in Unity. These Divine Ideas are the most basic elements utilized in all demonstration. In this chapter, we will summarize the essential elements involved in demonstration; these elements are explored in more detail in other chapters. Some of the sections of this text focus on one or more of the Twelve Powers, all of which can be and are used in demonstration. There is much more about the Twelve Powers in Chapters 24 and 25.

Keep in mind that the most important demonstration we can have is the unfolding of our Divine Nature, or Christ Nature, in a creative and fulfilling way. May this be your own experience as you grow into being a heart-centered metaphysician.

DEMONSTRATION

Demonstration—The proving of a Truth principle in one's body or affairs. The manifestation of an ideal with its accomplishment has been brought about by one's conformity to thought, word, and act to the creative Principle of God. (Charles Fillmore, *The Revealing Word: A Dictionary of Metaphysical Terms,* 2nd ed., Unity House, Unity Village, Mo., 2006, p. 52)

You may rest in the assurance that the principles that you mentally perceive as true of God are inviolate, and that, if there seems to be error in their out-working, it is because of some misapplication on the part of the demonstrator. By holding to the principle and insisting upon its accuracy, you open the way to a fuller understanding of it; you will also be shown the errors in the demonstration. (Charles Fillmore,

Christian Healing, 2nd ed., Unity House, Unity Village, Mo., 2005, p. 9)

It is a metaphysical law that there are three steps in every demonstration: the recognition of Truth as it is in Principle; holding an idea; and acknowledging fulfillment. "Whatsoever ye shall ask in prayer, believing, ye shall receive" (Mt. 21:22). (*The Revealing Word*, p. 52)

Demonstration, spiritual—a spiritual realization followed by the manifestation in the outer of the Truth that has been realized within. (*The Revealing Word,* p. 52)

The secret of demonstration is to conceive what is true in Being and to carry out the concept in thought, word, and act. If I can conceive a truth, there must be a way by which I can make that truth apparent. (Charles Fillmore, *Prosperity,* Unity House, Unity Village, Mo., 1936, p. 37)

KEY IDEA: Demonstration is always occurring whether the results are liked or not. Therefore, conscious demonstration is the goal.

Unity focuses on the conscious application and practice of the Laws, Principles and Divine Ideas of Divine Mind. This is what is meant by "practical Christianity"; this is demonstration. Whether it happens consciously or unconsciously, demonstration is always occurring from different levels of consciousness. What's most impor-tant in demonstration is the level of consciousness from which it occurs—the higher the level, the better the result. But sometimes there is "misapplication on the part of the demonstrator." By holding true to Principle and its accuracy, a fuller understanding arises that illuminates the errors in the demonstration. Where's the proof in any demonstration? The late management consultant and "social ecologist" Peter F. Drucker said, "The knowledge that we consider knowledge proves itself in action."

As stated above from *The Revealing Word*, "There are three steps in every demonstration: the recognition of Truth as it is in Principle; holding an idea; and acknowledging fulfillment." Further, demonstration occurs when something is realized in consciousness and then manifests in the outer. Conceive and realize what is True in Beingness, or Divine Mind, and then carry It out in thought, feeling, word and act.

BLOCKS TO DEMONSTRATION AND WAYS TO RESOLVE THEM

28A STUMBLING BLOCKS

You are mind. Your consciousness is formed of thoughts. Thoughts form barriers about the thinker, and when contended for as true they are impregnable to other thoughts. So you are compassed about with thought barriers, the result of your heredity, your education, and your own thinking. (Charles Fillmore, *Jesus Christ Heals*, 2nd ed., Unity House, Unity Village, Mo., 1940, p. 33)

Stumbling blocks at first may seem to be in the physical environment, but closer discernment reveals that they are primarily in the mind. Therefore, we should not put additional weight into the already existing obstacles by filling them with the thought-stuff of condemnation. (The Revealing Word, p. 186)

We usually judge zeal by the noise it makes. But noise is not characteristic of the zeal that overcomes seemingly insurmountable obstacles and wheels them into line with its quiet yet mighty energy of purpose. (Charles and Cora Fillmore, *Teach Us to Pray*, 2nd ed., Unity House, Unity Village, Mo., 2007, p. 126)

One who exercises his thought powers discovers that there is a steady growth with proper use. The powers of the mind are developed in much the same way that the muscles of the body are. Persistent affirmation of a certain desire in the silence concentrates the mental energies and beats down all barriers. (Jesus Christ Heals, p. 70)

KEY IDEA: Stumbling blocks and obstacles that seem to be in the outer are primarily in the mind as thoughts and feelings. Zeal's quiet passion, coupled with Dominion's power to master and control, helps to bring all thoughts and feelings into line in order to demonstrate good.

Everything in the physical, or relative realm, begins first in thought and feeling. Therefore, all seeming stumbling blocks and obstacles that are in the physical realm are primarily in mind. One must exercise the power of the mind much like a body must be exercised. Mind exercise is accomplished through the use of affirmations clustered around a desire that includes the feeling nature; this clustering concentrates the mental energies that will knock down the blocks in mind which are holding back demonstration.

Each person can use the Powers of Zeal and Dominion to overcome the stumbling blocks and obstacles in mind. Zeal's quiet passion, coupled with Dominion's power to master and control, helps to bring all thoughts and feelings into line in order to demonstrate good.

28B FEAR, LACK AND THE NEGATIVE SIDE

When Peter tried to walk on the water to meet Jesus, he went down in the sea of doubt. He saw too much wetness in the water. He saw the negative side of the proposition, and it weakened his demonstration. If you want to demonstrate, never consider the negative side. (*Jesus Christ Heals*, p. 106)

The only lack is the fear of lack in the mind. We do not need to overcome any lack, but we must overcome the fear of lack. (*Prosperity*, p. 53)

KEY IDEA: Focusing on the negative and/or dwelling in fear increases what is feared in consciousness and can result in its outpicturing in the physical realm.

Do not give attention to the negative side or become fearful because of it. Peter did not sink simply because he saw the wetness of the water; he sank because he became afraid. Identifying with the negative side or becoming fearful of the negative hinders demonstration. Focusing on the negative and/or dwelling in fear increases what is feared in consciousness. The first step out of negativity and fear is becoming aware of them. Once negativity and fear are identified, then denials can be used to withdraw the power given them. After this withdrawal of power, affirmations can be used to raise consciousness from fear to Love, from the false to the True. Both denials and affirmations are created from the awareness of Oneness; they are realization statements derived from Truth.

28C JOY/CHEERFULNESS

We should all practice delightful, happy, joyous states of mind. It is such thoughts that open the way for ever-present God Mind to pour out its splendid resources into our mind and through us into all our affairs. (*Jesus Christ Heals*, p. 177)

Those who persistently exercise faith in God find there is generated in their mind a condition that gradually grows into a conviction of the permanent presence of divine substance within, and this gives rise to the most exquisite joy. (Charles Fillmore, *Mysteries of Genesis*, Unity Classic Library edition, Unity House, Unity Village, Mo., 1998, p. 175)

Joy sends its shining beams throughout consciousness. It dissipates all discouraged, doubting states of mind, all fears and apprehension. It lifts one on the wings of the morning to the spiritual heights where all things are seen in their right relation. (Myrtle Fillmore, quoted in *Torch-Bearer to Light the Way: The Life of Myrtle Fillmore* by Neal Vahle, Open View Press, Mill Valley, Calif., 1996, p. 74)

We should sing songs of joy and of love and of peace and of the unity of the Spirit, the Spirit of Jesus Christ, the supreme Man expressed. (Charles Fillmore, *Dynamics for Living: A Topical Compilation of Essential Fillmore Teachings*, compiled by

Warren Meyer, Unity House, Unity Village, Mo., 1967, p. 175)

You can drive away the gloom of disappointment by resolutely singing a sunshine song. (Jesus Christ Heals, p. 173)

KEY IDEA: Joy dissolves the blocks to demonstration: uneasiness, fears, doubts and discouraged states of mind.

The awareness of joy and cheerfulness is evidence that our free and open minds are stayed on Divine Mind. Faith in Oneness, or Divine Mind, increases the conviction of Divine Ideas and Substance—the keys to manifesting our desires, resulting in joy. Joy dissolves the blocks to demonstration, including uneasiness, fears, doubts and discouraged states of mind.

Singing "joy songs," a Unity tradition, fills one with the awareness of joy and peace. Even if one is feeling gloomy or sad, one can sing to re-establish the awareness of joy.

28D ATTACHMENT AND NONATTACHMENT

One must give up personal attachments before one can receive the universal. (Charles and Cora Fillmore, The Twelve Powers, Unity House, Unity Village, Mo., 1999, p. 126)

When we deny our attachment to matter and material conditions and affirm our Unity with spiritual substance, we

enter the new consciousness of real substance. (Mysteries of Genesis, p. 127)

If the mind is free from attachment to money or love of it, and lovingly concentrated on the divine substance, there is never failure in the demonstration. (Charles Fillmore, Keep a True Lent, 2nd ed., Unity House, Unity Village, Mo., 2005, p. 106)

KEY IDEA: Attachment to the outer realm and outer outcomes inhibits demonstration by hindering awareness of the Oneness and Substance. Nonattachment smoothes the path to demonstration.

Attachments to the outer realm and outer results hinder demonstration. They must be given up; an attitude of nonattachment smoothes the path to demonstration. Deny attachments to matter and material conditions and affirm Oneness to become aware of Divine Ideas, especially Divine Substance.

28E RESISTANCE AND NONRESISTANCE

The greatest disintegrating element in the human consciousness is resistance. Beware of every form of fighting and all thoughts of destructive character. By the law of Mind Action these will work in your mind and body in an adverse way and tear down the good you desire to build up. (Weekly Unity,

February 16, 1922, "Establishing Spiritual Consciousness")

In nonresistance there is no misuse of power through combativeness or through defensive tactics. The strength of all your gifts can be turned to the creation of harmonies. (Imelda Shanklin, *What Are You?* 2nd ed., Unity House, Unity Village, Mo., 2004, p. 147)

Jesus went back to the very source of all discord, and showed how all resistance and antagonism must cease. He did not stop to argue whether the cause was just or not, but He said, "Agree with thine adversary quickly" [Mt. 5:25]; "And if any man will sue thee at the law, and take away thy coat, let him have thy cloak also" [Mt. 5:40]. To the mortal mind, this seems like foolishness, but Jesus knows that it is dangerous to allow any kind of opposing thoughts to form in consciousness. He knew that the universal law of justice would adjust all matters, if people would trust it and cease fighting mentally for their rights. (*Keep a True Lent*, p. 175)

KEY IDEA: Through the Law of Mind Action, resisting, fighting and opposing unwanted thoughts hinder demonstration by increasing them in consciousness. Nonresistance eliminates an oppositional attitude; however, nonresistance does not mean nonaction.

The practice of nonresistance is solely about thoughts and feelings being held in mind. Through the Law of Mind Action, resisting, fighting and opposing unwanted thoughts hinder demonstration by increasing them in consciousness. In addition, resisting, resenting and fighting are the very antithesis of Oneness. It is from Oneness that the highest demonstration occurs.

Nonresistance eliminates an oppositional attitude; however, nonresistance does not mean nonaction. Instead of focusing on what we don't want through resistance and opposition, we actively focus on what we desire. Also, we have an opportunity to choose to learn something from all situations in life, resulting in the greater awareness of the inner Presence and Power of Divine Mind.

28F UNFORGIVENENESS, FORGIVENESS—THE CHANGE OF MIND/REPENTANCE

The forgiveness of sin is an erasure of mortal thought from consciousness. (*Christian Healing*, p. 57)

But what shall we do with the appearance of evil? Forgive and forget it, and thus take away its power. Only the good is true. This means that in every experience you have, you should try to find the good. If you do not understand the law, you will pronounce conditions evil because they seem adverse. You will be saying that you have a hard time and that things are all against you. That is not the way to forgive evil [error consciousness]. You will get out of everything just what you put into it. Then put the thought of good into everything you meet, and you will get good out of it. (*Weekly Unity,* May 4, 1911, "Praise the Good and Forgive the Evil")

Forgiveness really means the giving up of something. When you forgive yourself, you cease doing the thing that you ought not to do. Jesus was correct in assuming that humankind has power to forgive sin [error]. Sin is a falling short of the divine law, and repentance and forgiveness are the only means that humankind has of getting out of sin and its effect and coming into harmony with the law. ... All sin is first in mind; and the forgiveness is a change of mind, or repentance. Some mental attitude, some train of mental energy, must be transformed. We forgive sin in ourselves every time we resolve to think and act according to the divine law. The mind must change from a material to a spiritual base. (*Jesus Christ Heals,* pp. 58-59)

Forgiveness is not silent consent, the negative appearance of making the best of a situation while underneath there is resentment. Forgiveness is the art of putting something else in place of the thing forgiven. You put the positive

realization of the Truth of Being in place of the appearance of negation and adversity which your sense and your intellectual training report. It does not matter that there is no immediate transformation; you have made use of your God-power to erase the appearance and to establish Truth. Such an attitude invites only the best from other souls. (Myrtle Fillmore, *How to Let God Help You,* 3rd ed., Unity House, Unity Village, Mo., 2000, pp. 69-70)

Here is a mental treatment that is guaranteed to cure every ill that flesh is heir to: Sit for half an hour every night and mentally forgive everyone against whom you have any ill will or antipathy. (*Book of Silent Prayer,* 2nd ed., Unity School of Christianity, Unity Village, Mo., 1966, p. 16, "A Sure Remedy")

KEY IDEA: Forgiveness and repentance clear the blocks to demonstration by moving the awareness from the outer realm to the inner realm of Truth and Oneness.

Any unforgiveness can be a block to demonstration. The things we hold against ourselves and others keep us focused on the outer and not on the inner. By the Law of Mind Action, what we focus on in consciousness *grows* in consciousness. When Peter asked Jesus, "How often should I forgive?" Jesus replied, "Not seven times, but, I tell you, seventy-seven times"

(Mt. 18:21-22). Jesus also offers this instruction in Matthew 5:23-24: "So when you are offering your gift at the altar, if you remember that your brother or sister has something against you, leave your gift there before the altar and go; first be reconciled to your brother or sister, and then come and offer your gift." It is incumbent on us to be reconciled in our relationships. Forgiveness/repentance is about changing the mind and resolving to think and act according to Divine Law. Replace error with the realization of Truth. Make the conscious choice to replace the appearance of negation and adversity arising from sense consciousness with the positive realization of Truth. Every night before going to sleep, consciously forgive and repent of any thoughts you have had of ill will or antipathy.

KEYS TO DEMONSTRATION

28G **CONSCIOUSNESS**

The sense of awareness, of knowing. The knowledge or realization of any idea, object or condition. The sum total of all ideas accumulated in and affecting a person's present being. The composite of ideas, thoughts, emotions, sensation, and knowledge that makes up the conscious, subconscious, and superconscious phases of mind. It includes all that a person is aware of— spirit, soul and body.

It is very important to understand the importance of our consciousness in spiritual growth. Divine ideas must be incorporated into our consciousness before they can mean anything to us. An intellectual concept does not suffice. To be satisfied with an intellectual understanding leaves us subject to sin, sickness, poverty and death. To assure continuity of spirit, soul and body as whole, we must ever seek to incorporate divine ideas into our mind. (Charles Fillmore, *The Revealing Word: A Dictionary of Metaphysical Terms,* 2nd ed., Unity House, Unity Village, Mo., 2006, p. 41)

KEY IDEA: As consciousness rises, it becomes easier and easier to consciously demonstrate good.

Life is consciousness (See Chapter 2). Consciousness must be developed, raising it to higher and higher levels of understanding. This increased understanding comes through the appropriation of Divine Ideas and the realization of them beyond intellectual concepts. As consciousness rises, it becomes easier and easier to consciously demonstrate. One aspect of raising consciousness is becoming aware of beliefs and attitudes that may be hindering the evolution of spiritual awareness.

28H DIVINE MIND—ONENESS

Therefore do not worry, saying, "What will we eat?" or "What will we drink?" or "What will we wear?" For it is the Gentiles who strive for all these things; and indeed your heavenly Father knows that you need all these things. But strive first for the kingdom of God and his righteousness, and all these things will be given to you as well. (Mt. 6:31-33)

It is impossible that in this universal Mind that fills everything there can be any such thing as absence. There is no lack of anything anywhere in reality. (Charles Fillmore, *Prosperity,* Unity House, Unity Village, Mo., 1936, p. 52)

KEY IDEA: Begin all demonstration from the awareness of Divine Mind, or the Oneness. Divine Mind is the Source of Divine Ideas.

In all things, we must put Truth, or Divine Mind, first. Divine Mind is the Source of Divine Ideas that are utilized to demonstrate anything. Our attention is focused on the consciousness of Oneness, or the Kingdom. In this way, Divine Potential is increasingly realized, making possible decisions from the awareness of Oneness that bring about good for all concerned. This also helps to objectively look at any fears, resistance or unforgiveness so that they may be cleared from consciousness.

28I DIVINE IDEAS

The superconsciousness is the realm of divine ideas. Its character is impersonal. (Charles Fillmore, *Atom-Smashing Power of Mind*, 2nd ed., Unity House, Unity Village, Mo., 2006, p. 36)

The real of the universe [the Spiritual Universe] is held in the mind of Being as ideas of life, love, substance, intelligence, Truth and so forth. These ideas may be combined in a multitude of ways, producing infinite variety in the realm of forms. There is a right combination, which constitutes the divine order, the kingdom of heaven on earth. This right relation of ideas and the science of right thought is practical Christianity. (*Christian Healing,* p. 14)

Divine ideas are man's inheritance; they are pregnant with all possibility, because ideas are the foundation and cause of all that man desires. With this understanding as a foundation, we easily perceive how "all ... mine are thine." All the ideas contained in the one Father-Mind are at the mental command of its offspring. Get behind a thing into the mental realm where it exists as an inexhaustible idea, and you can draw upon it perpetually and never deplete the source. (*Christian Healing,* p. 13)

KEY IDEA: Everything in the physical or manifest realms has its basis in Divine Ideas. Divine Ideas are the beginning point of all demonstration.

Divine Ideas constitute the Divine Mind, or the Superconscious Mind. They are formless and intangible as long as they remain Ideas in the higher levels of Beingness. Under the Law of Mind Action, these Ideas are able to penetrate the relative realm where they take on form and character. We can experience any Divine Idea directly by (1) believing in the Idea, and (2) becoming totally willing to accept the Idea, claiming and affirming it. The Idea becomes our experience. Demonstration occurs when Divine Ideas are appropriated and are given "form" first in consciousness as thoughts and feelings and then in time and space.

28J MEDITATION/THE SILENCE

By meditation people light up the inner mind, and they receive more than they can put into words. Only those who have strengthened their interior faculties can appreciate the wonderful undeveloped possibilities in humankind. (Christian Healing, p. 86)

We get our most vivid revelations when in a meditative state of mind. This proves that when we make the mind trustful and confident, we put it in harmony with creative Mind; then its force flows to us in accordance with the law of like attracting like. (Jesus Christ Heals, pp. 82-83)

In true meditation one becomes joined with the Giver, contact is made with the Source of all good, and such faith, harmony, and peace are established in mind that through it the body and affairs are opened to receive. (Frances W. Foulks, Effectual Prayer, 3rd ed., Unity House, Unity Village, Mo., 2000, p. 78)

When we are endeavoring to listen, to understand, and to follow our divine guidance from the spiritual center of our own soul, we find that every wind that blows (whether it appears at first to be good or ill) does fill us with the spirit of plenty—because the winds are evidence of God's ideas and substance, and plenty is the one reality. (How to Let God Help You, p. 145)

KEY IDEA: Meditation allows the Silence to arise, resulting in the awareness of Divine Ideas as well as thoughts, illumination, guidance and viewpoints related to Them.

The need for the type of daily meditation that allows the Silence to arise is imperative for evolving spiritual awareness. When we invest time in the Silence, we know Oneness. Investing time, intention and attention in meditation/the Silence will keep us in a state of receptivity to the Divine Ideas from our True Nature. Meditation becomes more enjoyable and beneficial as practice continues. It is actually after investing time in the Silence that we become aware of thoughts and ideas related to Divine Ideas—illuminations, expanded viewpoints, guidance and many other important insights. (For more on the Silence see Chapter 6; for more on meditation see Chapter 7.)

28K PRAYER

Do not supplicate or beg God to give you what you need, but get still and think about the inexhaustible resources of infinite Mind, its presence in all its fullness, and its constant readiness to manifest itself when its laws are complied with. This is what Jesus meant when He said, "But seek ye first the kingdom of God, and his righteousness; and all these things shall be added unto you" [Mt. 6:33]. (*Jesus Christ Heals*, pp. 77-78)

Pray with persistence and pray with understanding. Be insistent in prayer, and never allow anything to keep you from having your daily quiet hour of communion with God, your own indwelling Father. (*Atom-Smashing Power of Mind*, p. 32)

KEY IDEA: Prayer focuses intention and attention on what is desired. Prayer results in the realization of Divine Ideas that are then claimed and from which good is manifested.

Prayer is a continual process of praise, thanksgiving and claiming what is already True in Divine Mind. Jesus taught that Divine Mind is always more willing to give than we are willing to receive. This means that our Divine Nature is always available with Its infinite supply of Divine Ideas. Our personalities simply have to learn to become aware of them. When we realize this, prayer becomes a joyous experience. In prayer we can fulfill the law of the Word by (1) being in a state of gratitude and praise in advance, (2) claiming the Truth, and (3) affirming it. This claiming is not for things (or anything for that matter) in the outer, relative realm. It is about claiming the awareness of Divine Ideas that are then used to manifest by clothing them in Substance and thought. (For more on prayer, see Chapters 8 and 9. For more on the Power of the Word, see Chapter 21.)

28L CONCENTRATION

Every thought that goes forth from the brain sends vibrations into the surrounding atmosphere and moves the realm of things to action. The effect is in proportion to the ability of the thinker to concentrate his or her mental forces. The average thought vibration produces but temporary results, but under intense mind activity, conditions more or less permanent are impressed upon the sensitive plate of the universal ether, and through this activity they are brought into physical manifestation. (*Christian Healing,* p. 63)

Concentrate thoughts, feelings, words, [and] actions on constructive projects. What you can conceive, you can achieve. When desire becomes conviction, results are well on the way. (Ernest C. Wilson, *The Emerging Self,* Unity House, Unity Village, Mo., 1970, p. 122)

KEY IDEA: Concentration focuses intention and attention on the ideas and thoughts of what is desired, gathering the thought forces used to manifest it. Then the outer resources for manifesting what is desired begin to be perceived.

True concentration means that we keep an idea like prosperity or wholeness securely in mind and based on Faith. We should be careful not to confuse true concentration with strained attention. This form of concentration can be quite relaxed, yet it leads to realization. Frivolous or erratic changes of mind can interfere with concentration, while intelligent changes of mind can actually be part of it. True concentration simply has to be genuine and it will bring about good results. It focuses intention and attention on the ideas, thoughts and feelings about what is desired, a process that gathers the thought forces used in manifestation. Outer resources then begin to be perceived and used to manifest what is desired.

28M REALIZATION

It [realization] is the dawning of Truth in the consciousness. When realization takes place, one abides in the light of God Mind. It is the inner conviction that prayer has been answered, although there is yet no outer manifestation. (*The Revealing Word,* p. 164)

Metaphysically, realization is expectancy objectified. The mind conceives a proposition and then marshals all its forces to make that conception a reality in the objective world. (*Jesus Christ Heals,* p. 50)

KEY IDEA: Realization is an inner conviction and a knowing that what is desired will be demonstrated, despite outer appearances.

To demonstrate, one must invest time in meditation/the Silence and prayer so that realization may occur. Whatever it is that we wish to demonstrate, we must first realize it as a Divine Idea, resulting in thoughts, ideas and feelings that "see" it accomplished in consciousness. When we realize something in consciousness, we know that we know that it is done. Realization is an inner conviction, despite any appearance to the contrary.

28N **SUBSTANCE AND SUPPLY**

This [Substance] does not mean matter, because matter is formed while God is the formless. The substance that God is lies back of all matter and all forms. It is that which is the basis of all form yet enters not into any form as finality. It cannot be seen, tasted or touched. Yet it is the only enduring substance in the universe. (The Revealing Word, p. 85)

In comparing substance and matter as regards their relative reality, one scientific writer says that matter is merely a crack in the universal substance. It is universal substance that man is handling all the time with his spiritual mind. Through your thoughts you deal with the wonderful spiritual substance, and it takes form in your consciousness according to your thought about it. That is why we must hold the thought of divine wisdom and understanding: so that we may use these creative mind powers righteously. We use them all the time either consciously or unconsciously and we should use them to our advantage and blessing. (Prosperity, p. 52)

You want a larger supply, not a limited supply of substance. Therefore it is important to watch your thoughts so that the larger supply may come through your mind and into your affairs. (Prosperity, p. 52)

KEY IDEA: Substance is our supply; our supply is Divine Ideas. Substance is molded in consciousness to manifest what is desired.

Divine Substance is not matter; It is our supply. Our supply is Divine Ideas. Out of Divine Substance we form whatever we choose according to our faith and understanding. We become conscious of Divine Substance from the awareness of Oneness that comes from investing time in the Silence. Spiritual realization enriches our awareness of the Omnipresence of invisible Substance. It is ever ready to take form in accordance with the mental pattern based on our present consciousness and understanding of the Divine Idea.

28O **THE TWELVE POWERS**

So in the demonstration of spiritual powers as they are expressed through humankind, we must be willing to follow the directions of someone [Jesus] who has proved his understanding of the law by his demonstrations. (Prosperity, p. 37)

When a person releases the powers of his or her soul, that person does marvels in the sight of the material-minded, but has not departed from the law. He or she is merely functioning in a consciousness that has been sporadically manifested by great individuals in all ages. (Prosperity, p. 64)

KEY IDEA: All of the Twelve Powers are used to manifest and demonstrate.

Faith—The Ability to believe in the final outcome of demonstration, despite all outer evidence to the contrary. The Power behind affirmations. Understanding and Faith are the Powers behind realization.

Strength—The Ability to stay the course during the process of demonstration. The Power behind patience.

Judgment/Wisdom—The Ability to evaluate, discern and be wise about what to demonstrate. It is also used to evaluate what to eliminate.

Love—The Ability to desire what to demonstrate. Love and Order are the Powers behind harmony.

Power/Dominion—The Ability to master and have dominion over the process of demonstration. The Power behind the spoken word. Strength and Power are the Powers behind concentration.

Imagination—The Ability to visualize and conceptualize what to demonstrate. The Power behind visualization and seeing the Good.

Understanding—The Ability to know and understand what to demonstrate. Understanding and Faith are the Powers behind realization.

Will—The Ability to decide or choose what to demonstrate as well as to make choices in the process of demonstration.

Order—The Ability to demonstrate in an orderly fashion, first in mind using the process of Divine Order (Mind-Idea-Expression/mind-idea-expression). Order and Love are the Powers behind harmony.

Zeal—The Ability to start the process of demonstration as well as the Ability to be passionate about what to demonstrate.

Elimination/Renunciation—The Ability to eliminate what gets in the way of demonstration. It is the Power behind denials.

Life—The Ability to vitalize and enliven the process of demonstration.

28P MORE ON THE POWERS OF FAITH AND IMAGINATION

But free faith has power to do, and power to bring about results in the affairs of those who cultivate it. (Christian Healing, p. 86)

It is when faith is exercised deep in spiritual consciousness that it finds its right place, and under divine law, without variation or disappointment, it brings results that are seemingly miraculous. (Christian Healing, p. 87)

KEY IDEA: Faith linked with Imagination are the impetus for moving Divine Ideas from the unseen to the seen.

"Now faith is the assurance of things hoped for, the conviction of things not seen" (Heb. 11:1). "Faith is the perceiving power of the mind linked with the power to shape substance" (*The Revealing Word*, p. 67). Faith is key to demonstration because it is the Ability to believe, spiritually intuit and "hear." It is the activating Faculty that is the impetus of moving Divine Ideas from the unseen to the seen. Faith is linked with the Power of Imagination, the Ability to shape Substance. We must have Faith that what we want to demonstrate is already ours in Divine Mind as Divine Ideas. These Divine Ideas are in consciousness and we can manifest Them in this relative realm. We give the Divine Ideas shape and form through the Power of Imagination. (Faith and Imagination are two of the Twelve Powers; see Chapters 24 and 25 for more information on all of the Powers.)

28Q MORE ON THE POWERS OF LOVE, WISDOM AND UNDERSTANDING

Love is good will in action. It holds the universe together by its constructive, dynamic, unifying power. It is the great solvent of every limitation and every problem. (Richard Lynch, *The Secret of Health,* Unity House, Unity Village, Mo., 1975, p. 133)

Wisdom is the "masculine" or expressive side of Being, while love is the "feminine" or receptive side of Being. Wisdom is the father quality of God and love is the mother quality. In every idea there exist these two qualities of mind, which unite in order to increase and bring forth under divine law. Divine Mind blessed the union of wisdom and love and pronounced on them the increase of Spirit. When wisdom and love are unified in the individual consciousness, a person is a master of ideas and brings forth under the original creative law. (*Mysteries of Genesis,* p. 27)

Through your thoughts you deal with the wonderful spiritual substance, and it takes form in your consciousness according to your thought about it. That is why we must hold the thought of divine wisdom and understanding: so that we may use these creative mind powers righteously. We use them all the time either consciously or unconsciously and we should use them to our advantage and blessing. (*Prosperity,* p. 52)

KEY IDEA: Love (the Ability to desire) must be utilized with Understanding (the Ability to know) and Wisdom (the Ability to apply what is known) so that good for everyone is demonstrated. Love without Understanding and Wisdom leads to the desire of erroneous demonstrations and undesirable outcomes.

The Powers of Love, Wisdom and Understanding work in unison. The all-important presence of Love is essential in all demonstration, including Spiritual demonstration. Without it, the possibility of failure is great. The affectional side of Love should permeate all our human desires and efforts. Love should be a part of all motivation; It is the harmonizing, unifying Power that heals and transforms all situations.

The law side of the Power of Love is the Ability to harmonize, unify, desire and attract oneself to whatever is desired—that is, whatever one "loves" in the moment. Then the Power of Love harmonizes and unifies everything to match what one desires. Whatever we are giving our attention to is what we are loving, desiring, in the moment. That is why we also need the Powers of Wisdom and Understanding working with the Power of Love. The Power of Wisdom is the Ability to discern, judge, evaluate and apply, based on what is known through the Power of Understanding. Love without Wisdom and Understanding is indiscriminate, resulting in the use of Love to desire and attract ourselves to thoughts and things based on sense consciousness. The highest and wisest use of the Powers of Love, Wisdom and Understanding is to desire to be the best Christ we can be. (See Chapters 24 and 25 for more on the Twelve Powers.)

28R HARMONY—THE POWERS OF LOVE AND ORDER

Resolve to become one with God through Christ. Harmonize yourself with Christ [Mind] and all your world will be in harmony. Be on the alert to see harmony everywhere. Do not magnify seeming difference. Do not keep up any petty divisions but continually declare the one universal harmony. This will ensure perfect order and wholeness. The Christ Mind is here as the unifying principle of humankind, and we must believe in this Mind working in us and through us and know that through it we are joined to the God Mind. (Jesus Christ Heals, p. 131)

Bring harmony into your life by singing and praising. Everybody should play and sing. We should rejoice in the divine harmony. (Dynamics for Living, p. 175)

KEY IDEA: The Powers of Love and Order harmonize all aspects of demonstration. Desire (Love) is linked with Mind-Idea-Expression (Order).

Harmony is an attribute of the Powers of Love and Order. Harmonize yourself with the Christ Mind and be determined to see only harmony everywhere. Give no power to any difference and give up any attachments to divisions. Believe in harmony, and be totally willing toward harmony—affirm it and claim it. Harmony is used to ensure that what is desired is demonstrated. Through the Powers of Love and Order, harmony ensures that everything works together to achieve the demonstration through Divine Order (Mind-Idea-Expression/mind-idea-expression). One way to bring harmony into our lives is through singing and praising (see section 28C on Joy).

28S PEACE

Humankind's dominion over the forces of Being is exercised in peace and harmony. Peace and harmony are the focalizing ideas that chord with the divine nature of love, and when they are associated in the mind there is no limit to humankind's power. (Charles Fillmore, *Talks on Truth*, Unity House, Unity Village, Mo., 1926, p. 59)

When a person becomes so at-one with the Divine Mind as to feel it consciously, she or he also recognizes this eternal peace, in which all things are accomplished. The person then knows that she or he is not subject to any condition whatsoever and is "lord even of the sabbath." (Charles and Cora Fillmore, *The*

Twelve Powers, Unity House, Unity Village, Mo., 1999, p. 113)

KEY IDEA: Peace and harmony create a receptive condition of the mind that assures demonstration.

Peace and harmony help focus ideas that align with Divine Ideas in Divine Mind, leading to unlimited power. As consciousness is elevated, the mind becomes more receptive by creating a peaceful state through affirmations of peace. This instills confidence that demonstration will occur and that our wholeness and vitality will be restored.

28T THE CREATIVE POWER OF THOUGHTS AND FEELINGS

Constructive thought-force is a great and mighty power, but when it is realized in the silence, it becomes the one and only power in all the earth. The understanding of this makes one an adept in the domain of scientific prayer. (*Dynamics for Living*, p. 103)

Our affairs are just an extension of our consciousness; as a person thinketh in the heart, so is that person—in mind, body and affairs. ... It all sums up this way; whatever we think of ourselves, others, and the world in general, makes conditions and draws them to us. (Myrtle Fillmore, quoted in *Torch-Bearer to Light the Way: The Life of Myrtle Fillmore* by Neal Vahle, Open

View Press, Mill Valley, Calif., 1996, p. 235)

KEY IDEA: Thoughts and feelings create a mental atmosphere from which a person perceives the world. Use thoughts and feelings to focus on what is desired; this results in perceiving what is needed in the outer world to accomplish what is desired.

The power of thoughts and feelings cannot be overestimated; it is through thoughts and feelings that the experience of the world is created. The power of thought and feelings linked with the power of the word through denials and affirmations creates a mighty tool to change the experience of the world as well as to demonstrate what is desired. The power of thought and feelings work with the Law of Cause and Effect and the Law of Mind Action. (For more on thought/feeling, see Chapter 20.)

From the above quote of Unity co-founder Myrtle Fillmore, it seems that conditions are drawn to us by the power of our thought. However, current thinking and observation show that it is through our thoughts that we attract *ourselves* to conditions, things and people. For example, when a person desires a new car, he or she begins to see that car everywhere. The cars were not drawn to the person, the person was drawn to the cars.

28U THE WORD AND THE SPOKEN WORD

One of the first lessons to be learned by the student of metaphysics is the "seed is the word." The next is that this kind of seed is hidden in the darkness of the mind where it germinates, sprouts and comes into visibility with all the scientific accuracy of detail of the ordinary plant. The fruit is a living organism, too, and has the power to throw off seeds that find lodgment and produce crops in other receptive minds. (Atom-Smashing Power of Mind, pp. 140-142)

In Divine Mind the idea is referred to as the Word. (Christian Healing, p. 61)

All the metaphysicians recognize that certain words, used persistently, mold and transform conditions in mind, body and affairs. (Christian Healing, p. 137)

When one understands the power of words spoken in spiritual consciousness, the results are in fulfillment of divine law. (Jesus Christ Heals, p. 14)

KEY IDEA: The spoken word, based on thoughts and feelings closely aligned with Divine Ideas, has the power to manifest desires according to the level of consciousness of the speaker.

The Word is the Christ as implied in John 1:1-3: It was "with God and is God." The Word, Christ, is the Truth of What we are. We want to use words drawn from the Word. The words we use are linked to our thoughts, feelings and intentions. In demonstration, we choose words that are the seeds of what we want to manifest. These seed thoughts and their associated feelings are closely related to Divine Ideas. We speak these words with power, authority and dominion. The power of the spoken word is infused with intention from 1) Divine Ideas, 2) thoughts and beliefs in collective consciousness, and 3) thoughts, beliefs, attitudes and feelings in personal consciousness. (For more on the Power of the Word, see Chapter 21.)

28V DENIALS AND AFFIRMATIONS

Day and night, heat and cold, sunshine and shadow, intelligence and ignorance, good and evil, saint and sinner—all are the reflections of mental affirmations and denials. The constructive or destructive factor in all manifestation is "yes" or "no." (*Christian Healing*, p. 51)

KEY IDEA: Use denials to disempower and brush away any obstacles to demonstrating your good. Use affirmations to claim that which is already True in consciousness.

Denials and affirmations are specific ways to use the power of our thought, the word and the spoken word. We deny giving power to any negative or untoward appearance. We affirm the Truth that has been realized in consciousness. In the process of demonstrating and manifesting in this relative realm, we use denials to brush away obstacles and affirmations to claim that which is already ours in consciousness. (For more on denials and affirmations, see Chapter 22.)

28W GRATITUDE, PRAISE AND BLESSING

Metaphysicians have discovered that words which express thanks, gratitude, and praise release mind energy of mind and Soul; and their use is usually followed by effects so pronounced that they are quickly identified with the words that provoke them.

Let your words of praise and thanksgiving be to Spirit, and the increase will be even greater than when they are addressed to a human being. (*Jesus Christ Heals*, p. 137)

We open the way for great demonstrations by recognizing the Presence and praising it, by thanking God for Spiritual quickening. We quicken our life by affirming that we are alive with the life of Spirit; our intelligence by affirming our oneness with divine intelligence; and we quicken the indwelling, interpenetrating substance by recognizing and claiming it as our own. We should meditate in this understanding and give sincere thanks to the God of this omnipresent realm of ideas because we can think God thoughts after God. We can thank God that its thoughts are our thoughts and that our natural mind is illumined by Spirit. (*Prosperity,* p. 35)

As you come out of the silence, count your blessings and give thanks for them. Realize that only the good exists in you and in your world, that the power you contacted in the silence may have opportunity to multiply and increase your blessings. Give thanks that you have already received the good for which you looked to God in the silence, feeling the assurance "Before they call, I will answer; and while they are yet speaking, I will hear." (Myrtle Fillmore, *Myrtle Fillmore's Healing Letters,* revised paperback edition, Unity House, Unity Village, Mo., 2006, p. 32)

KEY IDEA: Praise, bless and be grateful for the Oneness that we are in Truth. Praise, bless and be grateful for what you want to demonstrate.

Before praying, Jesus often gave thanks for what he wanted to demonstrate. We, too, should adopt this method because what we praise, bless and express gratitude for increases in our awareness. We praise, bless and are grateful for the Oneness, Spirit, or Divine Mind that is quickening within us, and for the Truth that our Divine Nature is always present and available. This is not so much being grateful *to* as it is being grateful *from* the awareness of Oneness.

28X THE LAW OF VISUALIZATION/SEEING THE GOOD

When something in your world is awry ... normally the first concern is to set things right. However, when you understand the law of visualization, you will realize that the greatest need is not to set it right but to see it rightly. Right seeing is one of the most important keys to the effective demonstration of Truth. More important than changing things 'out there' is changing the way you see them. (Eric Butterworth, *Spiritual Economics: The Principles and Process of True Prosperity,* 2nd revised paperback ed., Unity House, Unity Village, Mo, 1998, p. 50)

If you will start right now with the idea of universal and eternal goodness uppermost in your mind, talk only about the good, and see with the mind's eye everything and everybody as good, then you will soon be demonstrating all kinds of good. Good thoughts will become a habit, and good will manifest itself to you. You will see it everywhere. (*Prosperity,* p. 60)

Pronounce every experience good, and of God, and by that mental attitude you will call forth only the good. What seemed error will disappear and only the good will remain. This is the law, and one can not break it. The adversary always flees before the mind that is fixed on the pure, the just and the upright. There is no error in all the universe that can stand for one moment in the presence of the innocent mind. Innocence is its own defense, and he who invokes God with pure motive and upright heart need not fear any experience. (Charles Fillmore, *Talks on Truth,* Unity House, Unity Village, Mo., 1926, pp. 107-108)

Remember that you behold only the good, only the perfect, for this is what you desire to see brought forth. (Silent Unity, *The Art of Healing,* Unity Village, Mo., 1965, p. 6)

KEY IDEA: The Power of Imagination is used to visualize the desire to be demonstrated; see only good in place of the error that may be blocking demonstration. Couple your visualization with the Power of the Word, affirming and talking only about Good.

There is the Universal Principle of Good. Use the mind and affirm the presence of the Good at all times and under all circumstances. Good is always present since everything in the relative realm is based in the Absolute Realm of Divine Ideas. This does not mean that *everything* is good or that *every event* is good or that *every personality* is always good in the relative

realm. It does mean that the Principle of Good is always present. Even if one cannot see any trace of it, the potential for Good is there because Divine Ideas are the fundamental basis of everything. Since everyone is Christ in Truth, then there is always the potential and power to manifest Good from any situation. Affirm the presence of Good and give thanks in advance for Its revelation, and Good will result. Use the Power of Imagination to see or visualize the Good.

28Y **PATIENCE**

Patience—An attitude of mind characterized by poise, inner calmness and quiet endurance, especially in the face of trying conditions. Patience has its foundation in faith, and it is perfected only in those who have unwavering faith in God. "The trying of your faith worketh patience" [Jas. 1:3]. (*The Revealing Word,* p. 146)

The first requisite in the development of patience is spiritual understanding. The larger our vision of life, the more freedom we feel, and we are spared the friction and frettings that come to those who are centered in personality. (*Keep a True Lent,* p. 181)

An understanding faith functions from Principle. It is based on knowledge of Truth. It understands the law of Mind Action. Therefore, it has great strength.

To know that certain causes produce certain results gives a bedrock foundation for faith. (*Dynamics for Living*, p. 53)

Patience gives self-control. We unfold the capacity to direct our behavior in right ways, a result of spirituality. (*Keep a True Lent*, p. 182)

KEY IDEA: Patience based on Faith, Understanding and Strength is needed if demonstration does not come quickly.

We must be patient and not become discouraged when demonstration does not come quickly. Working things out into physicality can take time. Patience has its foundation in Faith and Understanding and Strength. Understanding Faith deals with knowledge of Principles and Truth; therefore, in all demonstration, it is important to trust and be patient. Patience and trust help us remain focused on the Truth that Divine Mind is our Source and Supply. We can use our Power of Strength to stay the course until the demonstration is ours.

SUMMARY STATEMENTS

▼ *Demonstration is always occurring whether the results are liked or not. Therefore, conscious demonstration is the goal.*

▼ *Stumbling blocks and obstacles that seem to be in the outer are primarily in the mind as thoughts and feelings.*

▼ *Zeal's quiet passion, coupled with Dominion's power to master and control, helps to bring all thoughts and feelings into line to demonstrate good.*

▼ *Focusing on the negative and/or dwelling in fear increases this negativity and fear in consciousness and can result in outpicturing them in the physical realm.*

▼ *Joy dissolves the blocks to demonstration: uneasiness, fears, doubts and discouraged states of mind.*

▼ *Attachment to the outer realm and outer outcomes inhibits demonstration by hindering awareness of the Oneness and Substance.*

▼ *Nonattachment smoothes the path to demonstration.*

▼ *Through the Law of Mind Action, <u>resisting</u>, fighting and opposing unwanted thoughts hinder demonstration by increasing them in consciousness.*

▼ *<u>Nonresistance</u> eliminates an oppositional attitude. However, nonresistance does not mean nonaction.*

▼ *<u>Forgiveness and repentance</u> clear the blocks to demonstration by moving the awareness from the outer realm to the inner realm of Truth and Oneness.*

▼ *As <u>consciousness</u> rises, it becomes easier and easier to consciously demonstrate good.*

▼ *Begin all demonstration from the awareness of <u>Divine Mind</u>, or the Oneness. Divine Mind is the source of Divine Ideas.*

▼ *Everything in the physical or manifest realms has its basis in <u>Divine Ideas, which</u> are the beginning point of all demonstration.*

▼ *<u>Meditation allows the Silence</u> to arise, resulting in the awareness of Divine Ideas as well as related thoughts, illumination, guidance and viewpoints.*

▼ *<u>Prayer</u> focuses intention and attention on what is desired. Prayer results in the realization of Divine Ideas, which are then claimed and from which good is manifested.*

▼ *<u>Concentration</u> focuses intention and attention on the ideas and thoughts of what is desired, gathering the thought forces used in manifestation. Then the outer resources begin to be perceived for manifesting what is desired.*

▼ *<u>Realization</u> is an inner conviction and knowing that what is desired will be demonstrated, despite outer appearances.*

▼ *<u>Substance is our supply</u>; our supply is Divine Ideas. Substance is molded in consciousness to manifest what is desired.*

▼ *All of the <u>Twelve Powers</u> are used to manifest and demonstrate.*

▼ *<u>Faith linked with Imagination</u> is the impetus for moving Divine Ideas from the unseen to the seen.*

▼ *Love (the ability to desire) must be utilized <u>with Understanding</u> (the ability to know) <u>and Wisdom</u> (the ability to apply what is known) so that good for everyone is demonstrated.*

▼ *<u>Love without Understanding and Wisdom</u> leads to the desire of erroneous demonstrations and undesirable outcomes.*

▼ *The <u>Powers of Love and Order harmonize</u> all aspects of demonstration. Desire (Love) is linked with Mind-Idea-Expression (Order).*

▼ *<u>Peace</u> and harmony create a receptive condition of the mind that assures demonstration.*

▼ *<u>Thoughts and feelings</u> create a mental atmosphere from which a person perceives the world. Use thoughts and feelings to focus on what is desired; this results in perceiving what is needed in the outer world to accomplish what is desired.*

▼ *<u>The spoken word</u> based on thoughts closely aligned with Divine Ideas has the power to manifest desires according to the level of consciousness of the speaker.*

▼ *Use <u>denials</u> to disempower and brush away any obstacles to demonstrating your good. Use <u>affirmations</u> to claim that which is already True in consciousness.*

▼ *<u>Praise, bless and be grateful</u> for the Oneness that we are in Truth. Praise, bless and be grateful for what you want to demonstrate.*

▼ *The <u>spoken word,</u> based on thoughts closely aligned with Divine Ideas, has the power to manifest desires according to the level of consciousness of the speaker.*

▼ *Couple your <u>visualization with the Power of the Word,</u> affirming and talking only about good.*

▼ *<u>Patience,</u> based on Faith, Understanding and Strength, is needed if demonstration does not come quickly.*

TOPICS FOR DISCUSSION

1. *Why is nonresistance so important to demonstration?*

2. *Think of a time when you saw the good despite appearances. What did you do?*

THOUGHTS FOR REFLECTION AND MEDITATION

"Just in proportion as a person yields willingly and obediently to the transforming process does he demonstrate truth.

All that pertains to self must be put away as fast as it is revealed, and that which is of the universal, the Christ, must take its place."

(Charles Fillmore, *Atom-Smashing Power of Mind*, pp. 73-74)

SUPPLEMENTARY READING

Jesus Christ Heals by Charles Fillmore, 2nd ed., Unity House, Unity Village, Mo., 1940, Chapter 5, "The Omnipotence of Prayer," and Chapter 9, "Healing Through Praise and Thanksgiving."

Keep a True Lent by Charles Fillmore, 2nd ed., Unity House, Unity Village, Mo., 2005, pp. 151-152.

Talks on Truth by Charles Fillmore, Unity House, Unity Village, Mo., 1926,, Chapter 5, "The Development of Divine Love."

What Are You? by Imelda Shanklin, 2nd ed., Unity House, Unity Village, Mo., 2004, Chapter 9, "Nonresistance."

CHAPTER TWENTY-NINE

METAPHYSICAL BASIS FOR WHOLENESS AND HEALTH

INTRODUCTION

The intention of this chapter is to explore ideas and concepts that pertain to wholeness and health—two manifestations of the Divine Idea of Life. Our state of health and wholeness in mind and body is a reflection of our current state of consciousness, including the awareness of the Divine Idea of Life in Divine Mind. The pure Life-Energy of Divine Mind, the Divine Idea of Life, is what we draw from to experience a life of wholeness and health.

29A GROWING NATURALLY

In right relation, everyone is the inlet and the outlet of an everywhere present life, substance, and intelligence. When a person's "I" recognizes this fact and adjusts itself to the invisible expressions of the one Mind, a person's mind becomes harmonious; one's life, vigorous and perpetual; one's body, healthy. It is imperative that the individual understand this relation in order to grow naturally. It must not only be understood as an abstract proposition, but it is necessary that the person blend his or her life consciously with God life, intelligence with God intelligence, and the body with the "Lord's body." Conscious identification must prevail in the whole person before he or she can be in right relation. This involves not only a recognition of the universal intelligence, life and substance, but also their various combinations in one's consciousness. These combinations are, in the individual world, dependent for perfect expression upon recognition of and loyalty to one's origin—God-Mind. Humankind is in God-Mind as a perfect idea. God-Mind is constantly trying to express in everyone its perfect idea, the real and only human being. (Charles Fillmore, *Christian Healing*, 2nd ed., Unity House, Unity Village, Mo., 2005, p. 22)

"... there is no defeat for one who has a strong hold upon Spirit. Don't, then, let

us worry so much about making a bodily demonstration always. The body will be quickened. ... It is not so awfully important what becomes of the body; it is, what is your soul [conscious and subconscious realms of mind] doing? How strong a hold have you upon these issues of life? Don't become so much attached to the material that it will take you away from the great central idea of being, as Jesus taught in our lesson today, 'rich toward God.'" (Charles Fillmore, Unpublished Talk, *"The Nature and Use of True Riches,"* March 22, 1931)

It is true that this mortal body must be transfigured; it is but a picture or symbol of the real, the spiritual body, which is the "Lord's body." The Lord's body is the body of Spirit, the divine idea of a perfect human body. When one realizes this new body, the cells of the present body will form on new planes of consciousness, they will aggregate around new centers, and the Lord's body will appear. (Charles Fillmore, *Atom-Smashing Power of Mind*, 2nd ed., Unity House, Unity Village, Mo., 2006, p. 158)

Spiritual thoughts make a spiritual body. The body is the outer court of the soul, an exact representative in form of the ideals that are revolving in the inner realms of its domain. (Charles Fillmore, *Dynamics for Living: A Topical Compilation of Essential*

Fillmore Teachings, Unity House, Unity Village, Mo., p. 48)

Everyone is an "inlet and outlet" of Divine Life, Divine Substance and Divine Intelligence. While Fillmore's quote indicates we must blend our life, our intelligence and our body with Them, the truth is our life, intelligence and body do not have an independent existence from Them. And, as Fillmore says, we do not want to be so attached to the material or worrying so much about the body that we lose sight of what our soul (conscious and subconscious minds) is doing and take ourselves away from the central Idea of being "rich toward God," knowing Oneness.

In the Absolute we are Divine Life, Substance and Intelligence. We simply need to wake up to these Truths. As we do, we harmonize ourselves with Them and begin to express Them more and more clearly instead of infusing Them with the limiting thoughts of sense consciousness. As we realize that the Spiritual Body is made up of Spiritual Thoughts, we will give form to these Thoughts ever more clearly.

29B THE PERFECT PATTERN

There are two steps in creation—mind ideates that which it later brings forth in the outer, just as a person works out in the mind an invention before making the model. God is the all-powerful mind. God creates first in thought, and God's idea of creation is perfect, and that idea exists as a perfect model upon which all manifestation rests. The body of humankind must rest upon a divine body idea in Divine Mind, and it logically follows that the inner life substance and intelligence of all flesh is perfect. (Charles Fillmore, *Keep a True Lent*, 2nd ed., Unity House, Unity Village, Mo., 2005, p. 19)

The attainment of permanent health is based on the belief in a Divine Mind that ideated the "perfect Body Idea" as the pattern for the human physical body. This perfect pattern represents the pure potential for health and wholeness that is inherent in humankind; it is established in mind and then manifests as a physical body under the Law of Mind Action and Divine Order, or Mind-Idea-Expression. That Divine Mind ideated the perfect pattern is the fundamental basis we should always return to in our human thinking, and it is upon this pattern we must base our manifestation of the body. The physical body is the projection of humankind's idea of the perfect pattern. The quality of the projection is directly related to the level of consciousness that has been obtained in both collective and individual consciousness.

29C THE BODY

Body—The outer expression of consciousness; the precipitation of the thinking part of the human organism. God created the idea of the human body as a self-perpetuating, self-renewing organism, which we reconstruct into our personal bodies. God creates the body idea, or divine idea, and human beings, by our thinking, make it manifest. As God created us in the Divine image and likeness by the power of the word, so we, as God's image and likeness, project our bodies by the same power. (Charles Fillmore, *The Revealing Word: A Dictionary of Metaphysical Terms,* 2nd ed., Unity House, Unity Village, Mo., 2006, p. 26)

God creates first in thought, and God's idea of creation is perfect, and that idea exists as a perfect model upon which all manifestation rests. The bodies of humankind must rest upon a divine body idea in Divine Mind, and it logically follows that the inner life substance and intelligence of all flesh is perfect. (*Keep a True Lent*, p. 19)

It is helpful to know that Oneness, or Divine Mind, is not directly making or creating the physical body; it is the result of the thinking and feeling aspect of humankind. In Divine Mind there is the Divine Idea of Body, and each person utilizes It to manifest a physical body. This Divine Idea of Body is clothed in Substance based on both collective and individual consciousness. Each person is an active participant in manifesting illness or wholeness. A sick body is nothing more than the effect of limitation put on the Divine Ideas of Body and Life, which includes Wholeness and Health.

29D **MIND ACTION**

One's consciousness is formed of mind and its ideas, and these determine whether one is healthy or sick. Thus to know the mysteries of one's own being, one must study mind and its laws. (Charles Fillmore, *Jesus Christ Heals*, 2nd ed., Unity House, Unity Village, Mo., 1940, p. 31)

Every idea projects form. The physical body is the projection of a human idea; we carry the body in the mind. The body is the fruit of the tree of life, which grows in the midst of the garden of mind. If the body-idea is grounded and rooted in Divine Mind, the body will be filled with a perpetual life flow that will repair all its imperfect parts and heal all its diseases. (Christian Healing, p. 34)

So if we want to know the secrets of health and how right thinking forms the perfect body, we must go to the mind and trace step-by-step the movements that transform ideas of health into light, electrons, atoms, molecules, cells, tissues, and finally into the per-

fect physical organism. (*Jesus Christ Heals*, pp. 40-41)

The more fully our own concept of physical wholeness is aligned with Divine Mind, the more completely will our minds and bodies manifest radiant health and vitality. The Law of Mind Action and Divine Order, or Mind-Idea-Expression, is unfailing and always operating. The following series traces a probable sequence of mind into matter (the body):

Idea of Health ▸ light ▸ electrons atoms ▸ molecules ▸ cells ▸ tissues ▸ organs ▸ the perfect physical organism.

29E **LIFE**

Life is real, abiding, eternal, unchangeable. Thus, we can say that life produces health or wholeness, which is one's birthright. ... God does not compel a person to claim his or her birthright. Because each person is essentially spiritual, the potential is within each one to claim eventually the full inheritance of life, which produces health in the body. (*Foundations of Unity*, Series Two, Vol. 3, p. 39)

God is life and ... they who worship God must worship God in the life-consciousness, that is, in Spirit. When we worship God in God's way, we are vitalized all at once; there is no other way to get real, permanent life. We cannot get life from the outer personality or from anything external; we must touch the inner current.

The life source is spiritual energy. It is deeper and finer than electricity or human magnetism. It is composed of ideas, and humankind can turn on its current by making mental contact with it.

When Jesus came teaching the gospel of Spirit, people did not understand him. They did not know that universal Spirit is Principle and that we demonstrate it or fail to demonstrate it according to the character of our thinking. It has taken the [human] race 2,000 years to find that we turn on the life current by means of thoughts and words. We can have fullness of life by realizing that we live in a sea of abundant, omnipresent, eternal life and by refusing to allow any thought to come in that stops the consciousness of the universal life flow. We live and move and have our being in life, Mind life. You can think of your life as mental; every faculty will begin to buzz with new life. Your life will never wane if you keep in the consciousness of it as Mind or Spirit; it will increase and attain full expression in your body. (Jesus Christ Heals, pp. 104-105)

If we are to express the fullness of our Beingness, we must stay centered in an awareness of Divine Mind, or Oneness, as the eternal, perfect Life within us. Wholeness and health are our divine inheritance based on the eternal Truth of Life. These effects come about through the "laying hold of" and claiming of unchangeable Life, Which is always present and available in Its fullness even though we may not be demonstrating It fully. We use our thoughts, feelings and words to "turn on" this Life current.

29F SUBSTANCE AND INTELLIGENCE

Life and substance are ideas in Divine Mind. Life is the acting principle; substance is the thing acted upon. In the phenomenal world, life is the energy that propels all forms to action. Life is not itself intelligent; it requires the directive power of an entity that knows where and how to apply its force in order to get the best results. (The Revealing Word, p. 121)

The one essential fact to understand is that there can be no manifestation without intelligence as a fundamental factor or constituent part. Every form in the universe, every function, all action, all substance—all these have a thinking part that is receptive to and controllable by humankind. ... This intelligent principle in all things is the key to the metaphysician's work. (Christian Healing, p. 50)

Life is not intelligent; It needs guidance. An intelligent entity using the

Powers of Wisdom and Understanding is required to direct the Divine Idea of Life. Life is the acting Principle; what It acts on is Substance, resulting in individualized expression. This Intelligence directs the Life-Energy acting on Substance, resulting in our bodies. Our thoughts direct how the energy within our cells functions and is sustained. We must accept the responsibility for guiding the expression of the Life Principle, because positive, uplifting thoughts produce more wholeness and health. Unity co-founder Myrtle Fillmore understood this Principle and worked diligently at consciously directing thoughts of Love and Life to the cells of her body.

29G **LOVE**

We may be successful without love. We might even be healthy without love for a time. But we cannot be whole without love, and thus we cannot be happy or peaceful, or fulfilled. (Eric Butterworth, *Celebrate Yourself! and Other Inspirational Essays*, Unity House, Unity Village, Mo., 1987, p. 169)

Love, in Divine Mind, is the idea of universal unity. In expression, love is the power that joins and binds in divine harmony the universe and everything in it. (*Christian Healing*, p. 130)

Love has not will and volition, except as they are infused into it by the other faculties. (Charles Fillmore, *Talks on Truth,* Unity House, Unity Village, Mo., 1926, p. 53)

Pure love is without discriminating power. (*Talks on Truth*, p. 56)

Love is the great harmonizing and attracting Principle. It is the Power by which all the bodily functions work harmoniously together. Love is the Power that also attracts us to those ideas or qualities that help ensure the fullest expression of life, wholeness and health. Pure Love has no discriminating power, nor does it have will or volition. Therefore, like Life, Love needs intelligent direction. We must use the Power of Love with the Powers of Wisdom, Understanding and Will.

29H **WHOLENESS**

... Wholeness is the fundamental and ultimate reality of each person's being. (H. Emilie Cady, *Lessons in Truth*, Centennial Edition, Unity House, Unity Village, Mo., 2003, p. 147)

When we really live in perfect relation to principle, we shall have the power to combine ideas rightly and so manifest wholeness and perfection in mind and body. (Charles and Cora Fillmore, *The*

Twelve Powers, Unity House, Unity Village, Mo., 1999, p. 234)

When the mind is stayed on the God-thought of wholeness, we are synchronized with the flow of life. (Eric Butterworth, *In the Flow of Life,* revised paperback edition, Unity House, Unity Village, Mo., 1994, p. 23)

Wholeness is the fundamental Reality of each person. In the relative realm, it is the result of keeping thoughts and feelings centered on the pure Life of Divine Mind within consciousness. When our focus is on wholeness, we are desiring or loving wholeness. Love, then, is the Power that harmonizes all of consciousness to match wholeness. It is then that we are in conscious harmony with the rhythm and flow of omnipresent Divine Life. In order to demonstrate wholeness in mind and body, we need to understand that we are seeking to express the eternal, Divine Idea called Life. This Idea is the pure potential or pattern for wholeness that attains form through our individual consciousness. The perfect Body Idea is established in mind, then manifests in the physical world under the Law of Mind Action.

291 HEALTH

Health is the normal condition of humankind and of all creation. We find that there is an omnipresent principle of health pervading all living things. Health, real health, is from within and does not have to be manufactured in the without. Health is the very essence of Being. It is as universal and enduring as God. (*Jesus Christ Heals,* p. 24)

A state of health is a condition of wholeness, completeness, entireness ... and healing is merely the bringing forth of the natural, perfect Christ that exists within every person. (Connie Fillmore, *The Unity Guide to Healing,* Unity, Unity Village, Mo., 1982, p. 7)

Like Wholeness, Health is a Principle that underlies and pervades everything. In the Absolute, Health is an aspect of the Truth of What we are. It is not something that is imposed from without; Health expresses from within consciousness as we keep our thoughts centered on the Principle of Life. First there is the Divine Idea that is the perfect Model upon which manifestation rests. The Divine Idea is clothed in Substance according to our own level of consciousness.

SUMMARY STATEMENTS

▼ *Divine Mind ideates (creates) the <u>perfect pattern</u>, "the perfect Body Idea" that is the fundamental basis underlying the pure potential for health and wholeness inherent in humankind.*

▼ *We must <u>stay centered in an awareness of Divine Mind</u> as the eternal, perfect Life within consciousness if we are to express the fullness of our Beingness.*

▼ *The <u>body</u> is manifested from the Divine Idea of Body, by and from collective and individual consciousness.*

▼ *Life, wholeness and health manifest according to the activity of the <u>Law of Mind Action and Divine Order</u>, or Mind-Idea-Expression. As we identify with the <u>Divine Idea of Life</u> within consciousness, we experience an ever-increasing awareness of wholeness, health and vitality—first in mind, then in body.*

▼ *<u>Life</u> reveals health and wholeness.*

▼ *Our <u>thoughts</u> direct how the energy within our cells functions and is sustained. This <u>intelligence</u> directs how Life acts upon <u>Substance</u>.*

▼ *<u>Love</u> harmonizes the process of manifesting the body and all bodily activities. It also attracts those ideas and qualities that help ensure the fullest expression of Life.*

▼ *<u>Since Love</u> lacks volition and does not discriminate. It always works best with <u>Wisdom</u>, <u>Understanding</u> and <u>Will</u>.*

▼ *<u>Wholeness</u> is the fundamental Reality of each person.*

▼ *<u>The realization of Wholeness</u> is the result of keeping our thoughts centered on the Divine Idea of Life.*

▼ *<u>Health</u> is the Principle that underlies and pervades everything.*

TOPICS FOR DISCUSSION

1. *What is the metaphysical basis for health?*

2. *Describe your understanding of the "perfect body idea."*

THOUGHTS FOR REFLECTION AND MEDITATION

"Life is divine, spiritual, and its source is God, Spirit. The river of life is within people in their spiritual consciousness. They come into consciousness of the river of life through the quickening of Spirit."

(Charles Fillmore, *The Revealing Word*, p. 122)

SUPPLEMENTARY READING

Know Thyself, by Richard Lynch, Unity House, Unity Village, Mo., 1935, Chapter 10, "Our Real Body."

Myrtle Fillmore's Healing Letters by Myrtle Fillmore, revised paperback edition, Unity House, Unity Village, Mo., 2006, Chapter 5, "Drawing on the Source."

The Secret of Health by Richard Lynch, revised edition, Unity House, Unity Village, Mo., 1989, Chapter 2, "Where Health Begins."

Talks on Truth by Charles Fillmore, Unity House, Unity Village, Mo., 1926, Chapter 10, "The Lord's Body."

CHAPTER THIRTY

STUMBLNG BLOCKS AND KEYS TO DEMONSTRATING LIFE, WHOLENESS AND HEALTH

INTRODUCTION

Healing is actually a process in which the most important healing is the movement from error thinking and feeling to Truth thinking and feeling. This shift may manifest as the movement from illness to health. Since healing is a popular topic, prayer is often focused on it. People want and request healing all the time. In affirmative prayer there is no *request* for healing; there is the simple *claiming* of the Truth Principles of Life, expressing as wholeness and health. As these Truths are realized at deeper and deeper levels, the entire body-mind system manifests wholeness and health. The reader will notice that many of the excerpts in this chapter use the word *healing* as was the tradition of the time. Even today people use the word when, in Unity, the claiming of Life, wholeness and health is more accurate, as indicated in the following quote:

While healing usually means to us the curing of a particular disease or ailment, its ultimate meaning has to do with the totality of us as thinking, feeling and acting beings. The deepest sense of healing is the restoration of wholeness in our mind and heart, inner and outer selves. It goes beyond the curing of particular diseases (although includes that) to the establishment of a free flow of life and energy throughout a person's being. The evidence for the beginning of true healing is not always first in the body, but first in the depth of the mind and heart. Included in this is the sense in which a person feels "new" in himself or herself, eternally healed of whatever disease he or she may encounter, and one with the God of life. A person is in tune with an absolute sense of being "on the path" of his or her own growth and unfoldment as a spiritual being. (Foundations of Unity, Series Two, Vol. 3, p. 48)

This chapter uses the same subtopics and order as found in Chapter 28, Blocks and Keys to Demonstration.

DEMONSTRATION

When the metaphysician sits by a patient with closed eyes, he or she is not asleep, but very much awake to the reality and mental visibility of forces that enter into and make the conditions of the body. This spiritual activity is necessary to the demonstration of the law. (Charles Fillmore, *Christian Healing*, 2nd ed., Unity House, Unity Village, Mo., 2005, p. 127)

The metaphysician handles omnipresent Spirit-life and substance very much as the electrician handles electricity. Energy is locked up in all this life and substance and its release enables the metaphysician to utilize it in demonstrating health and in achieving success. (Charles Fillmore, *Jesus Christ Heals*, 2nd ed., Unity House, Unity Village, Mo., 1940, p. 42)

KEY IDEA: Demonstration can occur when Life, Wholeness and Health are realized and claimed in consciousness.

Healing is actually the process of moving from the seeming appearance of illness to the realization of Life, Wholeness and Health at all levels of Beingness. In this context, then, demonstration is when Life, Wholeness and Health are realized and claimed in consciousness, manifesting first in the mind and then in the outer realm of the body.

BLOCKS TO DEMONSTRATION AND HOW TO RESOLVE THEM

30A STUMBLING BLOCKS

The fact is, Being is always present. Mortal ignorance and lack of faith prevent our realization of this truth. The more we believe in the wisdom, power, substance, love and life of the one Mind, the greater is its activity in us and our affairs. Not only should we have faith in the All-Presence, but we should also develop our understanding to the end that we may know why the All-Presence manifests through us. (*Christian Healing*, p. 66)

When the "I will" gets so absorbed in its real of expression that it loses sight of the ideal and centers all its attention in the manifest, it is Adam listening to the serpent and hiding from Jehovah God. This breaks the connection between Spirit and manifestation, and a person loses that spiritual consciousness which is under divine law. In this state of mind the real source of supply is cut off, and there is a drawing upon the reserve forces of the organism, the tree of life. (Christian Healing, p. 34)

When a person allows the imagination to run on in a lawless way, this person brings about such discord in mind and body that the flood of error thought submerges understanding and is drowned in it. (Christian Healing, p. 100)

KEY IDEA: Stumbling blocks to demonstrating health and wholeness are always in mind. Examples are lack of Faith in the Oneness, having an outer focus, and imagining all sorts undesirable expressions in the body.

There are many stumbling blocks to manifesting health. It helps to know that all of these are in the mind, regardless of how real the outer may seem. When we lack the Faith that Divine Mind, or Beingness, is always present, we block our access to It. When we get focused on the outer, manifest realm, we lose sight of the Inner Realm and break the awareness of Spirit; when this happens, it results

in being cut off from Supply. We can also block our demonstration of wholeness and health through misuse of the Power of Imagination, which happens when we imagine and visualize all sorts of undesirable expressions in the body.

30B FEAR AND THE NEGATIVE SIDE

One also sees the law of sowing and reaping, and fears one's sins and their results. Then fear of the divine law is added to one's burdens. The way out of this maze of ignorance, sin and sickness is through understanding one's real being, and then the forgiving or the giving up of all thoughts of the reality of sin and its effects in the body. (Jesus Christ Heals, p. 61)

If the mind of a person is clogged with doubt, lethargy or fear, he or she must open the way by persistent knocking and asking. "Pray without ceasing", [1 Th. 5:17], "continuing instant in prayer". [Rom. 12:12]. Acquire in prayer a facility in asking equal to the mathematician's expertness in handling numbers and you will get responses in proportion. (Jesus Christ Heals, p. 68)

Humankind has the power to deny and dissolve all disintegrating, discordant, and disease-forming words. Knowledge of this fact is the greatest discovery of all ages. No other revelation from God to humankind is to be compared with it. You can make yourself a new creature, and you can build the world about you to your highest ideals. Do not fear, but speak to the law supreme the desires of your heart. (*Christian Healing*, pp. 69-70)

KEY IDEA: Fear, the negative side, the belief in sickness, and the use of disease-claiming words are overcome through the use of denials and affirmations and praying without ceasing.

Focusing on our fears and the negative side hampers the demonstration of Life as wholeness and health. What is focused on in consciousness, grows in consciousness. Each person has the power to dissolve these fears by focusing on the indwelling Spirit, denying giving any power to fear and negative thinking, and affirming Truth while praying without ceasing.

30C JOY/CHEERFULNESS

All healing systems recognize joy as a beneficent factor in the restoration of health to the sick. (*Jesus Christ Heals*, p. 168)

Joy is inherent in our soul but we must develop it. All of us relate joy to the things that happen in our lives rather than trying to find the source of joy within us. The joy of the Lord is a wellspring within that we can let flow out into our lives by cultivating a joyous spirit. (May Rowland, *Dare to Believe*, Unity School of Christianity, Unity Village, Mo., 1962, pp. 127-128)

The true source of joy is God, and only as we enter into the consciousness of our oneness with God can we find real joy. True joy takes hold of one's consciousness when awakening to the realization of one's divine nature and to the blessings that accompany that realization. (*Foundations of Unity*, Series Two, Vol. 3, p. 55)

That there is an intimate relation between happiness and health goes without question. When you feel good, you sing either audibly or silently. Singing promotes health because it increases the circulation and a good circulation is a sign and promoter of health. ... It follows logically then that we should cultivate those mind activities which stimulate naturally the currents of life in our body. One of these, and a very important one, is joy. ... Back of every true song is a thought of joy. It is the thought that counts in the end, because it is the thought that invites the healing Spirit. (*Jesus Christ Heals*, pp. 169-170)

KEY IDEA: Divine Mind, or Oneness, is the Source of joy that is to be cultivated into awareness; it is an Antidote to fear and promotes health and wholeness.

From human perception, joy is based on something seen or experienced in the outer realm of the senses; this is joy with an object. Divine Mind, or Oneness, is the Source of joy without the need for an object or reason; this joy's expression is natural and limitless. A conscious expression of joy and cheerfulness throughout one's entire being promotes the healing process and counteracts fear (as discussed in Chapter 28). Singing is one way to express our joy, and it sets forth mighty currents of health, restoring our awareness of Life in our bodies.

30D ATTACHMENT AND NONATTACHMENT

One must give up personal attachments before one can receive the universal. (Charles and Cora Fillmore, *The Twelve Powers,* Unity House, Unity Village, Mo., 1999, p. 126)

When we deny our attachment to matter and material conditions and affirm our unity with spiritual substance, we enter the new consciousness of real substance.
(Charles Fillmore, *Mysteries of Genesis*, Unity Classic Library edition, Unity House,
Unity Village, Mo., 1998, p. 127)

If the mind is free from attachment to money or love of it, and lovingly concentrated on the divine substance,

there is never failure in the demonstration. (Charles Fillmore, *Keep a True Lent*, 2nd ed., Unity House, Unity Village, Mo., 2005, p. 106)

KEY IDEA: Attachment to the body and outer proof inhibits demonstration by hindering awareness of the Oneness, Life and Substance. Nonattachment allows the realization of Divine Ideas, like Life and Substance.

Since attachments to the body and outer results hinder demonstration, they must be given up and replaced with an attitude of nonattachment that smoothes the path to demonstration. To become aware of Divine Ideas, especially Divine Life and Substance, deny attachments to the body and affirm Oneness. Constant looking for results or proof of demonstration indicates a consciousness stuck in the outer.

30E RESISTANCE AND NONRESISTANCE

You are capable of developing nonresistance to a degree that will render your flesh impervious to hurt. ... Thousands of persons are practicing the nonresistance that protects them from taking cold on being drenched by chilly rain. (Imelda Octavia Shanklin, *What Are You?*, 2nd ed., Unity House, Unity Village, Mo., 2004, p.144)

When you are nonresistant you do not oppose, mentally or physically. You are insured against the friction of resistance. Mental resistance excites your nerves, makes them tense, burns them out; you become irritable, apprehensive. It saps the fluids of your body and makes your flesh sensitive. Your life takes on two interests: defense of what you call your rights and defense of your body. Mental resistance challenges to warfare all the phantoms of the fictitious world. Nonresistance cancels all these, and brings you tranquility in place of perplexity. (What Are You?, p. 147)

KEY IDEA: Resistance to unwanted thoughts of sickness and disease hinder demonstration by actually increasing them in consciousness. Nonresistance eliminates an oppositional attitude.

Through the Law of Mind Action, resistance to any beliefs, thoughts or appearance of disease strengthens its hold in the mind and can lead to other unwanted physical appearances.

In demonstrating wholeness and health, nonresistance eliminates any oppositional attitude toward sickness and disease; it is based on the realization of the Divine Idea of Life.

30P UNFORGIVENESS, FORGIVENESS AND REPENTANCE

The greatest prescription for a healthy body and a full life is to forgive and forget, to cleanse our own mind that the divine plan of God may be set free to carry on its perfect work of renewal and recreation. (Sue Sikking, Beyond a Miracle, Unity School of Christianity, Unity Village, Mo., 1973, p. 45)

Repentance and forgiveness are the only means that man has of getting out of sin and its effect and coming into harmony with the law. All sin is first in the mind; the forgiveness is a change of mind or repentance. We forgive sin in ourself every time we resolve to think and act according to the divine law. The mind must change from a material to a spiritual base. Change must all be on the part of man and within him. The moment man changes his thoughts of sickness to thoughts of health the divine law rushes in and begins the healing work. (Charles Fillmore, Dynamics for Living: A Topical Compilation of Essential Fillmore Teachings, compiled by Warren Meyer, 1967, p. 143)

KEY IDEA: Unforgiveness blocks healing. Forgiveness and repentance (changing the mind) cleanse the consciousness of error thoughts and feelings related to illness and disease.

In order to experience the renewal and complete healing desired, release all unforgiving thoughts held in consciousness. Forgiveness does not require us to declare that a particular event or circumstance was not painful or did not actually occur; it releases the mental and emotional bondage currently experienced in reaction to the situation. Forgiveness, a change of mind, enables the letting go of resentment that is adversely affecting consciousness. A thorough inventory of all thoughts and feelings is necessary to enable a significant degree of consciousness cleansing. Through forgiveness and repentance, sin and error thinking are erased by replacing them with higher thoughts based on Divine Ideas—a move from mortal to spiritual thought.

KEYS TO DEMONSTRATION

30G CONSCIOUSNESS

When people awaken to the consciousness that they are in every department of their being perfect and whole, that they are hale and healthy, that moment they begin to manifest perfection. It is at first in their minds, and then that perfection begins to work in their bodies; it is the quickening of the Spirit, and every atom of their bodies starts towards Divine Perfection. (Weekly Unity, May 17, 1911, Wednesday evening Healing Meeting)

KEY IDEA: An awakened consciousness of perfection and wholeness results in manifesting perfection in mind and then in body.

The attitudes, beliefs and thoughts we focus on have a powerful impact on our demonstrating wholeness and health. An awakened consciousness of Perfection and Wholeness must be brought to bear on our health challenges. (For more on consciousness, see Chapter 2). This begins first at the level of the mind, then works its way out into the body.

30H DIVINE MIND/ONENESS

God is life. Life is a principle that is made manifest in the living. Life cannot be analyzed by the senses. It is beyond their grasp, hence it must be cognized by Spirit. (Jesus Christ Heals, p. 29)

God is life, love, Truth, substance, wisdom. Humankind is the potential I that recognizes these inherencies of Being and makes them manifest.

Wisdom, life and substance are incorporated into a person's consciousness as spirit, soul, and body; each takes form in according to his/her recognition of it. (Keep a True Lent, p. 59)

KEY IDEA: An Aspect (Divine Idea) of God, or Divine Mind, is Life. We use

Life to demonstrate wholeness and health in mind and then in body.

All demonstration of wholeness and health begins with the claiming of Life and therefore starts with Divine Mind. Intention and attention is placed on, in and from Divine Mind to realize Life and our own Divine Potential. The Divine Idea of Life is utilized to express wholeness and health. Putting Divine Mind first also aids in objectively looking at fears, resistance, or unforgiveness so that they may be overcome. (For more information on Oneness, Beingness, or Divine Mind, see Chapter 10.)

30I **DIVINE IDEAS**

Divine ideas are humankind's inheritance; they are pregnant with all possibility, because ideas are the foundation and cause of all that humankind desires. With this understanding as a foundation, we easily perceive how "all ... mine are thine." All the ideas contained in the one God Mind are at the mental command of its offspring. Get behind a thing into the mental realm where it exists as an inexhaustible idea, and you can draw upon it perpetually and never deplete the source. (Christian Healing, p. 13)

As God creates the [spiritual] universe by divine ideas, so each person may recreate his or her body by his or her gov-

erning thought. Every new and higher conception each person forms will tend to an outward, bodily expression. (Keep a True Lent, pp. 132-133)

KEY IDEA: Use inexhaustible Divine Ideas such as Life to manifest wholeness and health.

We go to the Silence to realize Divine Ideas, such as Life, which may be expressed as wholeness and health. As with all Divine Ideas, the Divine Idea of Life can never be used up or depleted; They are inexhaustible. Claim the Divine Inheritance of Life; hold to It with Faith, knowing It is already so. Wholeness and health will first be realized and expressed in mind and then in body.

30J **MEDITATION/THE SILENCE**

A daily half hour of meditation will open up the mind to a consciousness of the inner One and will reveal many things that are hidden from the natural person. (Christian Healing, p. 15)

Jesus says, "Be ye therefore shall be perfect, even as your Father which in heaven is perfect" [Mt. 5:48]. Paul says, "Your body is a temple of the Holy Spirit which is in you, which ye have from God ... therefore glorify God in your body" [1 Cor. 6:19-20]. Unity says, "God in the midst of you is mighty to quicken, to cleanse, to heal, to restore to wholeness, to prosper. Look within yourself, to the Christ Mind, for the light that will flood your soul and enable you to see yourself and your affairs in right relation to God and your fellows." (Myrtle Fillmore, *Myrtle Fillmore's Healing Letters,* revised paperback edition, Unity House, Unity Village, Mo., 2006, p. 38)

Seeing is the discerning capacity of the mind. By taking time for quiet meditation, and by confidently claiming oneness with God Mind, we keep the avenues of our mind open to the divine plan for us. There is a divine law of mind action that we may conform to, and that will always bring satisfactory results. Now, there is also a physical side to the operation of this divine law. The body and its needs must have our consideration. We must not drive the body or neglect its normal needs. (*Myrtle Fillmore's Healing Letters*, p. 38)

KEY IDEA: Meditate to experience the Silence and lay hold of the Divine Idea of Life. Divine Life quickens, cleanses and restores wholeness and health.

Through the practice of meditation and entering the Silence, the Divine Idea of Life is realized. Claim this Truth. See the body and each other in right relation bringing satisfactory results at all levels of being. (For more on the Silence, see chapter 6. For more information on meditation, see Chapter 7.)

30K **PRAYER**

This body is the result of our use of God-given faculties and powers. We have needed such a temple, and the soul [conscious and subconscious minds] *has built it. Sometimes we fail to remember that the temple is for the use of the Holy Spirit. Sometimes the belief in lack, or darkness, or time comes in to cause us to do things not good for the body temple. When there is evidence of disobedience, we should not seek to whip the body into submission and comfort by outer means or by mental treatment. We should prayerfully seek the understanding of the soul's* [conscious and subconscious minds] *need and bring ourselves into harmony with God Mind.* (*Myrtle Fillmore's Healing Letters,* p. 38)

All through the Scriptures the different attitudes of mind necessary in prayer are pointed out. We are told to be instant in prayer; to pray with the Spirit, pray in understanding. We have thought that prayer was something we could go at in any old way at any old time. But to get results, we must pray with persistence and understanding, and with faith. This practice establishes a consciousness where doubt cannot enter. (*Weekly Unity,* June 7, 1911, vital points in the Sunday school lesson for June 11)

KEY IDEA: Prayer conditions the mind so that thoughts and beliefs about illness and disease are neutralized. These thoughts and feelings are replaced by the Divine Idea of Life, which supports wholeness and health.

Persistent prayer raises the consciousness of the soul (conscious and subconscious minds). It establishes a consciousness where doubt cannot enter and where Life, Health and Wholeness are certainties. As a consciousness of Life, Health and Wholeness is established, it begins to outpicture in the manifest realm. (For more on prayer, see Chapter 8).

30L CONCENTRATION AND THE POWER OF WILL

The will plays the leading part in all systems of thought concentration. The simple statement I will to be well *gathers the forces of mind and body about the central idea of wholeness, and the will holds the center just so long as the I AM continues its affirmation. No one ever died until he or she let go his or her will to live, and thousands live on and on through the force of a determined will. (Christian Healing, p. 115)*

Conservation of thought stuff is essential to right thinking. Right thinking is using the mind to bring about right ends idealized by the thinker. All the elements necessary to the restoration of health exist in the higher dimensions of the mind. Through concentration and

conservation of thought force, one regains the consciousness of health in one's mind, and health then becomes manifest in one's body. (Jesus Christ Heals, p. 44)

KEY IDEA: Concentration through the Power of Will gathers the forces of mind and body around the central Divine Idea of Life, expressing as wholeness and health in mind and then in body.

The Power of Will is our ability to choose. A determined will plays a part in thought concentration, which is part of the process of regaining the consciousness of Health that eventually manifests in the body. Concentration on Life, Wholeness and Health brings about their realization in mind and then in body.

30M REALIZATION

The prayer for realization attains its consummation when with concentrated spiritual attention one has affirmed that God Spirit is present, that with all God's power God is bringing to pass the perfect health desired, and that all is well. When your thoughts radiate with the speed of spiritual light, they blend with creative Mind (called by Jesus "heaven"), and the thing you have asked for will be done. (Jesus Christ Heals, p. 47)

KEY IDEA: Realization of Life brings the mind and body to perfect wholeness and health.

During meditation and prayer one concentrates on Life, or perfect Health and Wholeness. This concentrated spiritual attention brings about a deep certainty, a realization of Life, Wholeness and Health, which are the Truth manifesting Itself at all levels of the soul (conscious and subconscious minds) and then the body.

30N SUBSTANCE AND SUPPLY

God is substance; but this does not mean matter, because matter is formed while God is the formless. This substance which God is lies back of all matter and all forms. It is that which is the basis of all form yet enters not into any form as finality. It cannot be seen, tasted, or touched. Yet it is the only "substantial" substance in the universe. (Jesus Christ Heals, p. 29)

Although there is almost universal skepticism with reference to the mind's ability to know consciously how relative substance is formed, there are those who have made contact with the thought processes and can apply them in transforming the cells and tissues of their own body. ...

Jesus is the outstanding pioneer in this realm where the health-producing processes of cells are released and

imbued with supermind vitality. (Jesus Christ Heals, p. 41)

... There is a technique for molding thought stuff by means of the mind, and metaphysicians follow it in their scientific thinking and in healing. The metaphysician handles omnipresent Spirit life and substance very much as the electrician handles electricity. Energy is locked up in all this life and substance and its release enables the metaphysician to utilize it in demonstrating health and in achieving success. (Jesus Christ Heals, p. 42)

KEY IDEA: Divine Mind is the unlimited Substance and Supply from which the body is manifested.

Substance is not matter; It is the ever-present, unlimited supply from which the body is formed. Substance can be used to manifest illness and sickness in the body by holding error beliefs and thoughts. Equally, Substance can be used to manifest wholeness and health by claiming Life through visualizing a whole and perfect body and using denials and affirmations.

30O THE TWELVE POWERS

Each of the 12 faculties has a center and a definite place of expression in the body. Physiology has designated these faculty locations as brain and nerve centers. Spiritual perception reveals them to be aggregations of ideas, thoughts, and words. Thoughts make cells, and thoughts of like character are drawn together in the body by the same law that draws people of kindred ideas into assemblies and communities. (*Christian Healing*, pp. 74-75)

By our thought and the mighty mind energy back of thought we can stir to action all the powers of Being and get the results of their concentrated healing currents. (*Jesus Christ Heals*, pp. 18-19)

KEY IDEA: Use all of the Twelve Powers to demonstrate the Divine Idea of Life, leading to wholeness and health.

All of the Twelve Powers are used to demonstrate wholeness and health in the body, but they work best together. (In this chapter, you will find more information in subsequent sections on some selected Powers.)

Faith—The Ability to believe in the final outcome of demonstration, despite all outer evidence to the contrary. Faith is the Power behind affirmations. Understanding and Faith are the Powers behind realization. Belief in the Divine Idea of Life resulting in wholeness and health.

Strength—The Ability to stay the course during the process of demonstration. Strength is the Power behind patience. Holding to the belief in Life, wholeness and health regardless of outer appearances.

Judgment—The Ability to evaluate, discern and be wise about what to demonstrate. Judgment is also used to evaluate what to eliminate that might be blocking the awareness and demonstration of Life, wholeness and health.

Love—The Ability to desire what to demonstrate. Love and Order are the Powers behind harmony. Desiring Life, wholeness and health. Using Love to harmonize and unify everything to match the Divine Idea of Life, wholeness and health.

Power—The Ability to master and have dominion over the process of demonstration. It is the Power behind the spoken word. Strength and Power are the Powers behind concentration. Use Power to have dominion over error thoughts and feelings. Use Power to master the Divine Idea of Life expressing as wholeness and health.

Imagination—The Ability to visualize and conceptualize what to demonstrate. Imagination is the Power behind visualization and seeing the Good. Use Imagination to visualize wholeness and health. See every little cell being whole and perfect.

Understanding—The Ability to know and understand what to demonstrate. Understanding and Faith are the Powers behind realization. Use Understanding to know the Truth of Life expressing as wholeness and health. Know, realize, Life, wholeness and health at a deep level.

Will—The Ability to decide or choose what to demonstrate as well as to make choices in the process of demonstration. Use Will to make choices that support Life expressing as wholeness and health.

Order—The Ability to demonstrate in an orderly fashion, first in mind using the process of Divine Order (Mind-Idea-Expression/mind-idea-expression). Order and Love are the Power behind harmony. Use Order to sequence and balance the processes that move Life from the infinite to the finite as wholeness and health.

Zeal—The Ability to start the process of demonstration and be passionate about what to demonstrate. Use Zeal to passionate start the process of demonstrating Life as wholeness and health as well as adding passion to the stick-with-it-ness of Strength.

Elimination—The Ability to eliminate what gets in the way of demonstration. Elimination is the Power behind denials. Use Elimination to deny and release any erroneous beliefs, thoughts and feelings that may be hindering your demonstration of Life as wholeness and health.

Life—The Ability to vitalize and enliven the process of demonstration. Use the Power of Love to demonstrate wholeness and health. Also use Life to

energize the process of demonstration of wholeness and health.

30P MORE ON THE POWERS OF FAITH AND IMAGINATION

The first move in all healing is a recognition on the part of the healer and on the part of the patient that God is present as an all-powerful mind, equal to the healing of every disease, no matter how bad it may appear. "With God all things are possible" [Mt. 19:26 KJV]. (Charles and Cora Fillmore, *Teach Us to Pray*, 2nd ed., Unity House, Unity Village, Mo., 2007, p. 177)

The secret of healing lies in the lifting up of the consciousness by faith into the realm of God perfection, thus clearing the way for God's original perfect healing to be done in the body. (Connie Fillmore, *The Unity Guide to Healing*, Unity, Unity Village, Mo., 1982, p. 47)

Now this faith that we are all cultivating and striving for is built up through continuous affirmation of its loyalty to the divine idea, the higher self. You must have faith in your spiritual capacity. (*Jesus Christ Heals*, p. 103)

Spiritual healing depends on faith, and there cannot be faith while the mind is holding thoughts directly opposed to the possibility of healing. It is therefore very necessary to dwell much on the love and power of God so that a steady, unwavering faith may be established. (Charles Fillmore, *Atom-Smashing Power of Mind*, 2nd ed., Unity House, Unity Village, Mo., 2006, p. 76)

The mind makes its forms in a way similar to that in which cooks make biscuits. First is the gathering of the materials, then the mixing, then the biscuit cutting, which gives shape to the substance. In thinking, man accumulates a mass of ideas about substance and life, and with his imagination he makes them into forms. (*Christian Healing*, p.99)

KEY IDEA: The Power of Faith affirms and activates the Divine Idea of Life that outpictures in wholeness and health. Imagination works with Faith to shape Substance according to our Faith.

Faith is the great affirming and activating Power that is linked with Imagination to shape Substance. In developing a healing consciousness and wholeness, Faith works by affirming the Omnipresence of Divine Mind and all Divine Ideas. The Divine Idea is always of a greater dimension than anything in the relative realm. In the case of a health challenge, the Divine Idea of Life is greater and more powerful than anything on the level of the existing disease and sickness. Through Faith, contact is made with the Divine Idea of Life. Imagination shapes Substance according to our Faith; this activity promotes the

process of healing that manifests itself as wholeness and health. (For more information on Faith and Imagination, see Chapters 24 and 25.)

30Q MORE ON THE POWERS OF LOVE, WISDOM AND UNDERSTANDING

When spiritual love is quickened, it becomes a healing, harmonizing force in the life of an individual. (Elizabeth Sand Turner, *Your Hope of Glory: The Gospels Metaphysically Interpreted*, Unity Classic Library edition, Unity House, Unity Village, Mo., 1994, p. 104)

Love is a healing balm. ... Every form of hate and envy and jealousy is a burning fire, a disintegrating force that disturbs the mind and tears down the body. But love will restore us when we enter the silence, affirm our oneness with love, and express it. (*Foundations of Unity*, Series Two, Vol. 3, p. 52)

There is a knowing quality in Divine Mind. God is supreme knowing. That in man which comprehends is understanding; it knows and compares in wisdom. Its comparisons are not made in the realm of form, but in the realm of ideas. (*Christian Healing*, p. 112)

It is the work of the true healer to instruct the patient, to show cause and remedy from the viewpoint of spiritual understanding. All other methods are temporary. The old states of mind will come again into action unless the causing thought is uncovered and removed. (*Christian Healing*, p. 113)

KEY IDEA: Love, Wisdom and Understanding work together to demonstrate what is desired: wholeness and health.

Love is the key to wholeness in mind and body. Love harmonizes, blesses and unifies. A loving attitude causes harmony to be the dominant factor in mind and body, and it maintains good health. Love is the Ability to desire wholeness and perfection. Therefore, cultivate an awareness of Love in every facet of life. Love must be used with Wisdom and Understanding to ensure the highest and best outcome. (See Chapters 24 and 25 on the Twelve Powers.)

30R HARMONY—THE POWERS OF LOVE AND ORDER

In health, the human body has this power of replacing worn parts and when it is in harmony it never wears out. The harmony referred to is self-adjustment to the law of Being, to the law of divine nature, to the law of God. It does not matter what you call this fundamental principle underlying all life—the important thing is to understand it, and to put yourself in harmony with it. (*Christian Healing*, p. 41)

God is Spirit, and Spirit pours its quickening life into mind and body when we turn our attention to it and make ourselves receptive by trusting Spirit to restore us to harmony and health. (*Jesus Christ Heals*, p. 17)

That mind has ideas and that ideas have expression; that all manifestation in our world is the result of the ideas that we are holding in mind and are expressing; that to bring forth or to manifest the harmony of Divine Mind, or the "kingdom of heaven," all our ideas must be one with divine ideas, and must be expressed in the divine order [Mind-Idea-Expression] *of Divine Mind.* (*Christian Healing*, p. 16)

... One must be established in the consciousness of divine love, and there must be discipline of the mental nature to preserve such a high standard. The divine law is founded in the eternal unity of all things, and "love therefore is the fulfillment of the law." ... So this law of harmony, which has its origin in love, is established in the midst of every individual. (*Christian Healing*, p. 135)

KEY IDEA: Harmony is brought about by using the Powers of Love and Order. Using Divine Law and Order (Mind-Idea-Expression), thoughts and feelings are harmonized to manifest wholeness and health.

Part of the healing process is to come into the full realization and harmony with the Divine Idea of Life. This process uses the Law of Divine Mind, which is Divine Order (Mind-Idea-Expression), to manifest wholeness and healing in mind and body. Availing oneself of this self-adjustment process is one more reason to put Divine Mind first.

30S PEACE

The reason that prayers and treatments for health are not more successful is that the mind has not been put in a receptive state by affirmations of peace. The Mind of Spirit is harmonious and peaceful, and it must have a like manner of expression in humankind's consciousness. When a body of water is choppy with fitful currents of air, it cannot reflect objects clearly. Neither can a person reflect the steady strong glow of Omnipotence when his or her mind is disturbed by anxious thoughts. (Jesus Christ Heals, pp. 176-177)

The mind of peace precedes bodily healing. Cast out enmity and anger and affirm the peace of Jesus Christ, and your healing will be swift and sure. (Jesus Christ Heals, p. 21)

KEY IDEA: The receptive state of peace assures the successful demonstration of wholeness and health.

As a healing consciousness is developed, the mind becomes receptive by creating a peaceful state through affirmations of peace. This peaceful state results in the confident expectation of a restoration of wholeness and vitality.

30T THE CREATIVE POWER OF THOUGHTS AND FEELINGS

We are vitalized all at once. There is no other way to get real, permanent life. We cannot get life from the outer manner from anything external. We must touch the inner current.

We turn on the life current by means of thoughts and words. We can have fullness of life by realizing that we live in a sea of abundant, omnipresent, eternal life, and by refusing to allow any thought to come in that stops the consciousness of the universal life flow. We live and move and have our being in Mind life. (Dynamics for Living, p. 162)

If we do not keep on thinking in accord with the prayers we have made, we do not get good results. For all thought is formative; all thought has its effect in our life. When some of our thought energy is expended in negative beliefs and feelings, and we show that we have old mental habits in the subconscious mind, we get those old negative results—even when we are praying daily and when others are praying for us. (Myrtle Fillmore's Healing Letters, pp. 18-19)

Positive declaration of the truth of one's unity with God sets up a new current of thought power, which delivers one from the old beliefs and their depression. And when the soul [conscious and subconscious minds] is lifted up and becomes positive, the body and the affairs are readily healed. (Myrtle Fillmore's Healing Letters, p. 20)

Positive thinking is a definite step toward healing. God has given us the power to think, and our thoughts can either hinder or put us on the forward path. ... You must refuse to let thoughts of inharmony and negation enter your mind. Center your thought on God; think about God and God's healing, cleansing, vitalizing life flowing in and through you. Let go anxious, fearful thoughts, for they keep you from thinking about wholeness and perfection. Remember that God created you in God's image and likeness. God's life and health fill every part of your being. Every cell is alive with energy and vitality. (Foundations of Unity, Series Two, Vol. 3, p. 49)

KEY IDEA: The power of thoughts and feelings have effects in mind, and then in the outer realm. Thoughts and feelings can either support the belief in disease and illness or support the Divine Idea of Life that leads to wholeness and health.

Thoughts and feelings can either support error or support Divine Ideas that result in effects at the level of mind as well as in the relative realm. Choose to think positively by using the Power of Dominion to master thoughts and feelings. Choose to think about beliefs, thoughts and feelings based on the Divine Idea of Life; this conscious focus leads to a deep realization of the Truth of wholeness, perfection and health. Use the power of thought to move the realization of wholeness from the level of the mind (soul) to the level of the body. Meanwhile, stay ever vigilant for any contrary thoughts or words and release them. Deny giving them any power while holding to the Truth. (For more on thought, see Chapter 20.)

30U THE WORD AND THE SPOKEN WORD

The usual conversation among people creates ill health instead of good health, because of wrong words. If the words speak of disease as a reality, disintegrating forces are set in action, and these, in the end, shatter the strongest organism, if not counteracted by constructive forces. (Christian Healing, p. 65)

Although we all get definite results in body and affairs from the words we utter, those results would be infinitely greater if we understood the power of words and had undoubting faith in their creative power. Jesus said, "The words that I have spoken unto you are spirit, and are life." (Jesus Christ Heals, p. 15)

Jesus said that every person would be justified or condemned by his or her word. He demonstrated the power of the word of faith in his mastery of natural laws and in his many marvelous healings. (Jesus Christ Heals, p. 15)

KEY IDEA: The power of words can either build up *illness* based on error consciousness or *health* based on Divine Ideas and Christ Consciousness.

Be mindful of the words you use. If there is the appearance of ill health, be sure not to speak words that continue to build up this erroneous condition. Instead, deny giving any power to those erroneous words, thoughts and feelings, then claim the Truth of Life from Christ Consciousness with affirmations of wholeness and health. (For more on the Word, see Chapter 21.)

30V DENIALS AND AFFIRMATIONS

A good healing drill is to deny the mental cause first, then the physical appearance. The mental condition should first be healed. Then the secondary state, which it has produced in the body, must be wiped out and the perfect state affirmed. (Jesus Christ Heals, p. 37)

The consistent practice of affirmations steadies the mind so that the power of God can move through us to heal even deep-rooted mental and physical ailments. (Your Hope of Glory, p. 186)

It is important, therefore, to keep in mind that healing must begin with us, with our attitudes, feelings and beliefs. If there is anything that we think, feel, or believe that keeps the life of God from expressing to its full extent through us, it must be released. In its place we will develop a full consciousness of the life of God and all that is meant by the full expression of that life in our minds, bodies and affairs. (Foundations of Unity, Series Two, Vol. 3, p. 47)

KEY IDEA: Denials cleanse consciousness of erroneous thoughts and feelings of illness and disease. Affirmations of wholeness and health build up a consciousness of Life.

The use of denials and affirmations may require patience and persistence. Deny giving power to thoughts and feelings of illness or disease, then you may deny the physical appearance. Affirmations claim the Truth of Life, Wholeness and Health. (For more on denials and affirmations, see Chapter 22.)

30W GRATITUDE, PRAISE AND BLESSING

Praising and giving thanks liberate the finer essence of soul and body when we center our attention upon Spirit. (Jesus Christ Heals, p. 138)

We increase our vitality by blessing and giving thanks in spirit. To bring about this increase efficiently we must understand the anatomy of the soul and mind centers in the body. (Charles Fillmore, Mysteries of John, 2nd ed., Unity House, Unity Village, Mo., 2008, p. 67)

Turn the power of praise upon whatever you wish to increase. Give thanks that it is now fulfilling your ideal. The faithful law, faithfully observed, will reward you. You can praise yourself from weakness to strength, from ignorance to intelligence, from poverty to affluence, from sickness to health. (Christian Healing, p. 80)

KEY IDEA: Praise, bless and express gratitude for what you want to increase. Praise, bless and be grateful for the body and the health you have.

Praise, joyous thanksgiving and blessing increase whatever they are focused on. Praise, bless and be grateful for the wholeness and health you already have; praise, bless and be grateful for your body; and praise, bless and be grateful for the Divine Idea of Life that already exists in Divine or Universal Mind. This focused activity accelerates the powerful work of Divine Life within consciousness and then in the body. Expressing gratitude in advance of demonstration reflects Faith in the unfailing God-Life.

30X THE LAW OF VISUALIZATION/SEEING THE GOOD

Be wise; pronounce nothing evil, and only good will come. Shall we call everything good? Yes. (Christian Healing, p. 93)

A person can imagine that he or she has some evil condition in body or affairs and, through the imaging law, build it up until it becomes manifest. On the other hand, he or she can use the same power to make good appear on every side. The marks of old age can be erased from the body by one's mentally seeing the body as youthful. If you want to be healthy, do not imagine so vain a thing as decrepitude. Make your body perfect by seeing perfection in it. Transient patching up with lotions and external applications is foolish; the work must be an inner transformation. "Be ye transformed by the renewing of your mind" [Rom. 12:2]. (Christian Healing, p. 105)

As you pray for health, remember that you are to see only health and perfection. You are to behold God's perfect manifestation of life and health. Instead of focusing your attention on the condition as it appears, try to keep your thoughts centered in God. Trust God and know that God's will is life, health, and strength. (*Foundations of Unity*, Series Two, Vol. 3, p. 50)

KEY IDEA: Visualize wholeness and health; see only the Good, regardless of outer appearances.

See only the perfection of Life expressing as wholeness and health, regardless of what the human senses are reporting. Do not give any attention or energy to the appearance of sickness, sin or error. Find and accept only the Good. See the body as perfect, and see the Goodness of this perfection. Visualize every little cell being well and perfect, whole and healthy. Claim the Goodness of the Principle of Life invigorating every aspect of you.

30Y PATIENCE AND TRUST

Trust God in all things, and see the result made apparent by the mental currents that you set going all about you. You may not be able to point out just how each separate word of alle-giance to the Father took effect, but as the months go by you will gradually observe the various changes that are taking place in your mind, body, and affairs. (*Jesus Christ Heals*, p. 135)

I realize that I am feeding my consciousness on divine patience. When my thoughts are in harmony with divine law, they develop my body into God's beautiful, indestructible temple. "Let us run with patience the race that is set before us, looking unto Jesus the author and perfecter of our faith." (*Keep a True Lent*, p. 182)

KEY IDEA: Patience is needed if the demonstration of wholeness and health does not come quickly.

In the process of healing—demonstrating the Principles of Life, Wholeness and Health—there must be patience and trust that a mighty work is occurring. Jesus exemplified that wholeness and health can be demonstrated immediately in the manifest realm. At other times, the demonstration seems to take time to work itself out into the manifest realm. At these times, hold to the Truth of Divine Mind as the Source of Life manifesting as wholeness and health.

SUMMARY STATEMENTS

▼ *Demonstration can occur when Life, Wholeness and Health are realized and claimed in consciousness.*

Stumbling Blocks and Keys to Demonstrating Life, Wholeness and Health

▼ _Stumbling blocks_ to demonstrating health and wholeness are always in mind (consciousness). Examples are lack of Faith in the Oneness, having an outer focus and imagining all sorts of undesirable expressions in the body.

▼ _Fear, the negative side, the belief in sickness_, and the use of disease-affirming words are overcome through the use of denials, affirmations and praying without ceasing.

▼ _Divine Mind_, or Oneness, is the Source of joy that is to be cultivated into awareness; It is an antidote for fear as well as an elixir for health and wholeness.

▼ _Attachment_ to the body and outer proof inhibits demonstration by hindering awareness of Oneness, Life and Substance. Nonattachment allows the realization of Divine Ideas like Life and Substance.

▼ _Resistance_ to unwanted thoughts and feelings of sickness and disease hinders demonstration by actually increasing them in consciousness. _Nonresistance_ eliminates an oppositional attitude.

▼ _Unforgiveness_ blocks healing. _Forgiveness and repentance_ (changing the mind) cleanse the consciousness of error thoughts and feelings related to illness and disease.

▼ An _awakened consciousness_ of Perfection and Wholeness results in manifesting perfection in mind (consciousness) and then in body.

▼ An Aspect (Divine Idea) of _God, or Divine Mind_, is Life. We use Life to demonstrate wholeness and health in mind (consciousness) and then in body.

▼ _Inexhaustible Divine Ideas_ such as Life are used to manifest wholeness and health.

▼ _Meditate to experience the Silence_ and lay hold of the Divine Idea of Life. Divine Life quickens, cleanses and restores wholeness and health.

▼ _Prayer_ conditions the consciousness so that thoughts, beliefs and feelings about illness and disease are neutralized and replaced by the Divine Idea of Life supporting wholeness and health.

▼ *Concentration,* through the Power of Will, gathers the forces of mind and body around the central Divine Idea of Life. This Idea of Life expresses as wholeness and health, first in consciousness (mind)and then in body.

▼ *Realization* of Life brings the (consciousness) and body to wholeness and health.

▼ Divine Mind is the unlimited *Substance and Supply* from which the body is formed.

▼ All of the *Twelve Powers* are used to manifest and demonstrate the Divine Idea of Life, leading to wholeness and health.

▼ The *Power of Faith* affirms and activates the Divine Idea of Life that results in wholeness and health. *Imagination* works with Faith to shape Substance according to our Faith.

▼ *Love, Wisdom and Understanding* work together to demonstrate what is desired: wholeness and health.

▼ *Harmony* is brought about by using the *Powers of Love and Order.* Using Divine Law and Order (Mind-Idea-Expression), thoughts and feelings are harmonized to manifest wholeness and health.

▼ The receptive *state of peace* assures the successful demonstration of wholeness and health.

▼ The *power of thoughts and feelings* has its effects in mind (consciousness) and then in the outer realm. Thoughts can either support the belief in disease and illness or support the Divine Idea of Life that leads to wholeness and health.

▼ The *power of words* can either build up illness based on error consciousness or health based on Divine Ideas and Christ Consciousness.

▼ *Denials* cleanse consciousness of erroneous thoughts and feelings of illness and disease. *Affirmations* build up a consciousness of Life, expressing as wholeness and health.

▼ *Praise, bless and express gratitude* for what you want to increase. Praise, bless and be grateful for the body and the health you have.

▼ _Visualize wholeness and health;_ *see only the Good, regardless of outer appearances.*

▼ _Patience_ *is needed if the demonstration of wholeness and health does not come quickly.*

TOPICS FOR DISCUSSION

1. *Why is nonresistance so important to demonstration?*

2. *Think of a time when you saw the Good despite appearances. What did you do?*

THOUGHTS FOR REFLECTION AND MEDITATION

"Your mind responds to life-giving ideas; your body responds to life-giving ideas; your whole being takes on new life as you imbue your consciousness with the idea of life—eternal life, ever-renewing life, life that flows ceaselessly from the one fountainhead, God."

(Martha Smock, *Listen Beloved*, Unity House, Unity Village, Mo., 1980, p. 21)

SUPPLEMENTARY READING

Jesus Christ Heals by Charles Fillmore, 2nd ed., Unity House, Unity Village, Mo., 1940. Chapter 3, "Realization Precedes Manifestation," and Chapter 9, "Healing Through Praise and Thanksgiving."

Listen, Beloved by Martha Smock, Unity House, Unity Village, Mo., 1980. Chapter 3, "Life-Giving Ideas."

Myrtle Fillmore's Healing Letters by Myrtle Fillmore, revised paperback edition, Unity House, Unity Village, Mo., 2006. Chapter 10, "No Incurable Disease."

The Secret of Health by Richard Lynch, Unity House, Unity Village, Mo., 1975, Chapter 8, "According to Your Faith."

CHAPTER THIRTY-ONE

METAPHYSICAL BASIS FOR PROSPERITY

INTRODUCTION

The heart-centered metaphysician knows that true prosperity is first and foremost about the mind. It is about obtaining a consciousness through and from which Substance will flow, and ultimately about unfolding more and more Christ Consciousness. Prosperity is also the abundance of every good thing our heart desires; it originates in and from the Truth of What we are (Christ or Divine Mind), the Source of all good. Prosperity is manifested in our lives through our enlightened use of Divine Ideas. When we consciously work with these Ideas and use them wisely and lovingly, bountiful blessings will flow into our lives. As our awareness of the Infinite Substance and Supply that is perpetually available to us increases, our prosperity demonstrations will also increase. Our every desire will be abundantly satisfied in the most appropriate and fulfilling ways.

This chapter explores ideas and concepts that are fundamental to the metaphysical basis of prosperity. While developing consciousness and putting the awareness of Oneness, or Divine Mind, first are very basic metaphysical ideas appropriate to this chapter, they are presented in Chapter 32 as part of the 22 Keys to Demonstration.

31A THE GOAL—TRUE PROSPERITY

... *Prosperity is not in the possession of things but in the recognition of supply and in the knowledge of free and open* *access to an inexhaustible storehouse of all that is good or desirable.* (Charles Fillmore, *Prosperity,* Unity Books, Unity Village, Mo., 1936, p. 87)

The goal should not be to make money or acquire things, but to achieve the consciousness through which the substance will flow when and as you need it. (Eric Butterworth, *Spiritual Economics: The Principles and Process of True Prosperity,* 2nd revised paperback ed., Unity Books, Unity Village, Mo, 1998, p. 27)

True prosperity is not making money or putting out goods or developing property. It is determining what our souls require in order to cause them to unfold more of God; and then how to harmonize their expression with the needs of our fellow human beings so that all are benefited and inspired to unfold and express more of their inner spiritual resources. The exchange of merchandise and money is merely incidental to this spiritual association and growth. Money success comes as a result; but there are other results that should be sought and rejoiced over even more than the financial returns. (Myrtle Fillmore, *Myrtle Fillmore's Healing Letters,* revised paperback edition, Unity House, Unity Village, Mo., 2006, pp. 54-55)

Prosperity is based on the conscious possession of the idea of God's abundance back of all things. (Charles Fillmore, *The Revealing Word: A Dictionary of Metaphysical Terms,* 2nd ed., Unity House, Unity Village, Mo., 2006, p. 158)

Considered in the broadest sense, prosperity is "spiritual well-being." This involves the whole experience of healing life, satisfying love, abiding peace and harmony, as well as a sufficiency (of every good thing). (*Spiritual Economics*, p. 10)

Prosperity is neither riches nor poverty, but a state of consciousness superior to both. The true goal of prosperity is the attainment of a level of consciousness, ultimately Christ Consciousness, not the attainment of possessions. It is about the realization and the unfoldment of more of our Divine Nature. It is entering into the awareness that Mind and Ideas of Mind, like Substance, simply *are*. These Ideas are utterly dependable and can never be used up; their natural result is outer prosperity, which is an effect and an outpicturing of one's True Prosperity—the Christ-Nature.

31B SUBSTANCE

This does not mean matter, because matter is formed, while God is the formless. The substance that God is lies back of all matter and all forms. It is that which is the basis of all form yet enters not into any form as finality. It cannot be seen, tasted or touched. Yet it is the only enduring substance in the universe." (*The Revealing Word*, p. 85)

Prosperity is not just having a lot of money. It is having a consciousness of the flow of substance. (Eric Butterworth, *In the Flow of Life*, revised paperback edition, Unity House, Unity Village, Mo., 1994, p. 49)

The spiritual substance from which comes all visible wealth is never depleted. It is right with you all the time and responds to your faith in it and your demands on it. It is not affected by our ignorant talk of hard times, though we are affected because our thoughts and words govern our demonstration. (*Prosperity*, p. 13)

Just as the earth is the universal matrix in which all vegetation develops, so this invisible Spirit substance is the universal matrix in which ideas of prosperity germinate and grow and bring forth according to our faith and trust. (Charles Fillmore, *Keep a True Lent*, 2nd ed., Unity House, Unity Village, Mo., 2005, p. 184)

The whole of God-substance is present in its entirety at every point in space at the same time. Not just some of it, but all the substance in the Universe is present at any point of human need. ... There is no place on Earth where there is an absence of substance. (*Spiritual Economics*, p. 18)

True riches and real prosperity are in the understanding that there is an omnipresent substance from which all things come and that by the action of our mind we can unify ourselves with that substance so that the manifestations that come from it will be in line with our desires and needs. (*Prosperity*, p. 167)

Substance is "Divine Energy," the Invisible Matrix from Which all possible forms of supply develop. The Divine Idea of Substance is everywhere present in Its entirety. Substance is not matter, but It makes matter possible. While Substance is the basis of matter, It does not actually enter into it any more than the idea of *table* enters into or could be found in a table. One cannot dissect matter and find Substance, much like one cannot dissect a chair and find the idea of a chair. It is our senses that report the experience of the manifestation of Substance as matter.

True prosperity is about having the consciousness of Divine Substance. It can never be depleted and responds according to our Faith and the demands we make on It. This Spiritual Substance is the Universal Matrix in which seed thoughts of prosperity germinate and grow according to our Faith and trust. While ignorant words of lack and limitation have no effect on It, they do affect the ability to demonstrate. By the action of the mind, we unify ourselves with the Divine Idea of Substance so that the manifestations we demonstrate from It are in alignment with our desires and needs.

31C **SUPPLY**

Supply—Spiritual substance. Supply often fails to flow to one whose faith is fixed in some outer source instead of in substance. Jesus understood spiritual substance and could make from it whatever he wished, whenever he wished.

Anxiety about supply can be overcome by a recognition of the omnipresence of Spirit substance and the centering of faith in it as the one source of supply. (The Revealing Word, pp. 188-189)

For many of us there is either a feast or a famine in the matter of money and we need the abiding consciousness. There is no reason why we should not have a continuous, even flow of substance both in income and outgo. If we have freely received, we must also freely give and keep substance going, confident in our understanding that our supply is unlimited and that it is always right at hand in the omnipresent Mind of God. (Prosperity, p. 20)

The law of supply is a divine law. This means that it is a law of mind and must work through mind. God will not go to the grocery and bring food to your table. But when you continue to think about God as your real supply, everything in your mind begins to awaken and to contact the divine substance, and as you mold it in your consciousness, ideas begin to come which will connect you with the visible manifestation. You first get the ideas in consciousness direct from their divine source, and then you begin to demonstrate in the outer. It is an exact law and it is scientific and unfailing. "First the blade, then the ear, then the full grain in the ear." (Prosperity, pp. 67-68)

Again, he who seeks the kingdom of substance for the sake of the loaves and fishes he may get out of it will surely be disappointed in the end. He may get the loaves and fishes, that is quite possible; but if there remains in his soul any desire to use them for selfish ends, the ultimate result will be disastrous. (Prosperity, p. 19)

The supply is always equal to the demand, but there must first be a demand before supply is of use. (Keep a True Lent, p. 50)

Our True Supply emerges from and is the Divine Idea of Spiritual Substance and other Divine Ideas. Divine Mind, or God, does not do things for us in the outer realm; so our focus must be on the *inner* means of supply rather than the *outer* means. How to get supply is one thing; how to handle supply is another—the two must balance and complement each other. If not, there is no real prosperity. Accumulating a lot of "clutter" is not true prosperity. The danger involved in the relatively easy use of getting supply through mental ways is the temptation toward selfishness or acquisitiveness; these quickly become addictions. True metaphysical thinking will enable a person to avoid this danger.

Supply can seem to stop when there is anxiety or when Faith is placed in the outer realm of form instead of in Divine Substance. These are overcome by understanding Spiritual Substance and Its Source, Divine Mind. It is also about being in a *giving consciousness* based on the faith and trust that Supply and Substance are unlimited and always at hand.

31D THE TWO-STEP APPROACH TO PROSPERITY

It is not sufficient, however, to sit down and hold thoughts of abundance without further effort. That is limiting the law to thought alone, and we want it to be fulfilled in manifestation as well. Cultivating ideas of abundance is the first step in the process. Ideas that come must be used. Be alert doing whatever comes to you to do, cheerful and competent in the doing, sure of the results, for it is the second step in the fulfilling of the law. (Prosperity, p. 92)

We should give equal emphasis to both steps in fulfillment of the law of prosperity. We begin with the formative power of thought, which is linked with the feeling nature based on Divine Ideas; then we follow through with

appropriate action. We are *thinkers/feelers* and *doers*. If we attempt to function as just one or the other, we are fulfilling only half of the law and our existence will be unsatisfactory in many ways. Part of the process is to pray by claiming Truth from our Higher Nature; and when we rise to a higher realization of that Truth, we are to follow It.

31E THE LAW OF INCREASE

There is a universal law of increase. It is not confined to bank accounts but operates on every plane of manifestation. The conscious cooperation of humankind is necessary to the fullest results in the working of this law. You must use your talent, whatever it may be, in order to increase it. Have faith in the law. Do not reason too much but forge ahead in faith and boldness. (Prosperity, p. 81)

It may seem foolish to some persons that we bless our nickels, dimes and dollars, but we know that we are setting the law of increase into operation. All substance is one and connected, whether in the visible or the invisible. The mind likes something that is already formed and tangible for a suggestion to take hold of. With this image the mind sets to work to draw like substance from the invisible realm and thus increase what we have in hand. (Charles Fillmore, Dynamics for

Living: A Topical Compilation of Essential Fillmore Teachings, Unity Books, Unity Village, Mo, 1967, p. 234)

The Hebrew Scriptures are a record of religious thinking based on belief in a "law of even exchange." The Christian Scriptures are a record of religious thinking based on the "law of increase." Jesus often tells his hearers, "You have heard that it was said ... But I say to you ..." (Mt. 5:21, 22). Such passages illustrate a rise in the level of Spiritual thinking. This rise must occur in all who seek to attain a true prosperity consciousness. The law of increase says that we must use whatever talents we have. We must bless, praise and be grateful for what we have. Whatever this prosperity may be, we use it in order to increase it.

31F THE SECONDARY LAW OF INCREASE

All this is true not only of your own affairs. The effects extend also to those with whom you come in contact. They will become more prosperous and happy. They may not in any way connect their improvement with you or your thoughts, but that does not affect the truth about it. All causes are essentially mental, and whoever comes into daily contact with a high order of thinking must take on some of it. Ideas are catching, and no one can live in an

atmosphere of true thinking, where high ideas are held, without becoming more or less inoculated with them. (*Prosperity*, pp. 39-40)

It is a fact that other persons can be the beneficiaries of our work in developing our own consciousness, including a prosperity consciousness. One way that happiness comes into our awareness is by sharing with others. As we expand our prosperity consciousness, we find great happiness by realizing that it sort of "spills over" from us and touches others. All causes start first in mind (consciousness), but "ideas are catching"—an increased consciousness radiates Truth Ideas in every direction. A change in seeming "personal consciousness" has its affect on "collective consciousness."

31G LIVING IN TWO WORLDS

Apparently we live in two worlds: an invisible world of thoughts and a visible world of things. The invisible world of thought substance is the real world, because it is the source of the world of things, and humankind stands between the two, handing out with their thoughts the unlimited substance of Spirit. When people get understanding of the right relation between the visible and the invisible into their mind and active in their thoughts, all their needs will be met. This is what Jesus meant when he said, "Seek ye first his kingdom, and his righteousness; and all these things shall be added unto you" [Mt. 6:33]. (Keep a True Lent, p. 102)

There seem to be two worlds, the Inner Invisible Realm of our Spiritual Nature and the outer visible world of the senses. Our conscious mind is pivotal, so we appear to live in both realms simultaneously. Our attention determines our state of mind at any given moment. When people get a real understanding of the right relation between these two realms, a great dimension of power is added to their consciousness and "all their needs will be met." The understanding of the right relation between these two realms determines right relations in our world: The outer visible realm is dependent upon the Inner Invisible Realm and has no independent existence, while the Inner Invisible Realm does.

When our mind is pivoted toward Oneness, we lay hold of Substance and then give shape and form to that Substance according to our own awareness (primarily by employing the Power of Imagination). As the mind pivots outward, the shape and form are determined by our thoughts and feelings. Keep in mind that our thoughts and feelings are influenced by sense consciousness and collective consciousness.

31H THE INNER APPROACH TO INCREASE

The difference between spiritual prosperity and material prosperity is that spiritual prosperity is founded on understanding of the inexhaustible, omnipresent substance of Spirit as the source of supply; the material belief is that the possession of things constitutes prosperity. (The Revealing Word, p. 158)

We must look within for the law and not without. The laws we find in the outer are the secondary laws. The infinite, creative Mind has given to every one of us a key to the workings of this unfailing inner law. (Prosperity, p. 73)

Realize, first of all, that prosperity is not wholly a matter of capital or environment but a condition brought about by certain ideas that have been allowed to rule in the consciousness. When these ideas are changed, the conditions are changed in spite of environment and all appearances, which must also change to conform to the new ideas. (Prosperity, p. 88)

If you would demonstrate true prosperity, you must turn from things and, as Jesus told his disciples, "have faith in God" [Mk. 11:22]. Do not have faith in anything less than God, in anything other than the one Mind, for when your faith is centered there, you are building for eternity. Mind and the ideas of Mind will never pass away. There will never be an end to God. There will never be an end to Truth, which God is. There will never be an end to substance, which God is. Build with the divine substance, cultivate faith in realities and "lay up for yourselves treasures in heaven." (Prosperity, p. 49)

The metaphysical, inner or Spiritual approach to prosperity need not be difficult and is not risky. It involves no competition, opportunism or any other practice that coarsens consciousness. When a person takes a metaphysical approach to prosperity, it is by working with Spiritual Substance. True prosperity has its origins in Divine Ideas, not in material things. When we understand this basic Truth, we can work creatively with these ideas to enhance our lives in many ways.

31I THE OUTER APPROACH TO INCREASE

People pile up possessions by human effort, interest and other ways of secondary increase, and grow into the thought that these are the real means of attaining prosperity.

But possessions gained in this way rest on a very insecure foundation. … Such persons are really never happy in their wealth, because there is always a lurking fear that they may lose it. They are secretly troubled with the thought of

lack, in the presence of worldly plenty. (Keep a True Lent, p. 101)

The physical or outer approach to prosperity is a difficult one; it involves competition, opportunism and other practices that may defeat the purpose of true prosperity. Also, this approach carries with it the possibility of loss that is a frightening concept to the materially-minded. Yet, the outer approach certainly does get results for some people, because it is part of the "secondary law of increase."

31J IDEA OF POSSESSION

Every thought of personal possession must be dropped out of mind before people can come into the realization of the invisible supply. They cannot possess money, houses or land selfishly, because they cannot possess the universal ideas for which these symbols stand. No person can possess any ideas as his or her own permanently. He or she may possess its material symbol for a little time on the plane of phenomena, but it is such riches that "moth nor rust consumes, and where thieves do not break in and steal" [Mt. 6:20]. (Prosperity, p. 17)

As paradoxical as it may seem, in order to be established in a state of well-being, one must turn loose, temporarily at least, in consciousness the things that represent prosperity to him or her.

(May Rowland, *Dare to Believe!*, Unity School of Christianity, Unity Village, Mo., 1961, p. 187)

Belief in exclusive possession is an error that can ruin our enjoyment of prosperity. Even those who are experts at getting supply can short-circuit their enjoyment of it by believing in exclusive ownership. One cannot truly *possess* anything because no one can possess the Universal Ideas that the possessions are based on. No one can exclusively own or possess either Substance or Supply. Possessions are symbols or effects of the originating Ideas and are subject to time and degradation, unlike Divine Ideas Themselves. One must at least temporarily release or detach from the outer symbols of prosperity and focus instead on the prospering Ideas.

31K STEWARDSHIP

You have some talent and capability that, used to the glory of God and the honor of humankind, will bring you a rich reward. There is something that you can do better than anyone else can do, and through the loving, efficient service you can render, you will fulfill a need in the world. (Myrtle Fillmore, *How to Let God Help You,* 4th ed., compiled by Warren Meyer, Unity House, Unity Village, Mo., 2006, p. 143)

As you prosper, you have the responsibility of the wise and loving use of the bounties and opportunities that come to you. (Ernest C. Wilson, *The Emerging Self,* Unity Books, Unity Village, Mo., 1970, p.127)

The one with the surplus is simply a steward of God and is merely discharging the work of one's stewardship. When one asks for divine wisdom and understanding about giving, it becomes a joy both to the giver and the recipient. (*Prosperity*, p. 153)

Webster's Ninth New Collegiate Dictionary defines stewardship as "the individual's responsibility to manage his [or her] life and property with proper regard to the rights of others." If we see ourselves as stewards of all the Good (all the Divine Ideas of Divine Mind), with exclusive ownership of nothing, we avoid trouble. Prosperity is the wage for good stewardship, and this form of prosperity can be permanent. Our bounty and unique talents are to be developed and shared generously under the direction of Divine Wisdom and Understanding. We are to be stewards of the good we have already realized in the relative realm. The truth is not in ownership, but in stewardship. To be good stewards, we must accept our good as already ours and willingly release our need to be identified with material things.

31L THE LAW OF GIVING AND RECEIVING

If you discover the wonder of giving, you will find a great blessing of inner fulfillment in your work, which will lead to better work, and, by the law of causation, to a greater experience of affluence, which may come through your job or through many different channels. The law is exact: If you give, really work in a giving consciousness, you must receive. (Spiritual Economics, p. 171)

Giving and receiving are two aspects of a prosperity law that must be exercised if we are to release the flow of abundant Good in our consciousness. Through giving and receiving, we participate in establishing balance in the manifestation of prosperity. Giving and receiving cause a flow of Substance in soul (conscious and subconscious minds) and body that manifests in every area of our lives. One aspect of the Law of Giving and Receiving is that first occurs entirely in consciousness. When we give from an open and compassionate heart, we receive the good effect in consciousness at precisely the same moment.

31M GIVING AND RECEIVING FREELY

A gift with reservations is not a gift; it is a bribe. There is no promise of increase unless we give freely, let go of the gift entirely, and recognize the universal scope of the law. Then the gift has a chance to go out and to come back multiplied. There is no telling how far the blessing may travel before it comes back, but it is a beautiful and encouraging fact that the longer it is in returning, the more hands it is passing through and the more hearts it is blessing. All these hands and hearts add something to it in substance, and it is increased all the more when it does return. (Prosperity, p. 143)

There is no reason why we should not have a continuous, even flow of substance both in income and outgo. If we have freely received, we must also freely give and keep substance going, confident in our understanding that our supply is unlimited and that it is always right at hand in the omnipresent Mind of God. (Prosperity, p. 20)

Giving freely is the only valid kind of giving. Any other kind of giving is a pretense, a loan, a gesture of self-congratulation or a bribe. Giving freely is full compliance with Divine Law, and it should be a beautiful experience. Generosity is more than a virtue—it really is a Divine Idea; it is part of Divine Love. When giving is purely an expression of love and generosity, we have willingly cooperated with a Divine Idea; there is no higher or finer action possible to humankind than this. As we give freely, we should not just stop with the pleasure of giving, but also make room for an additional experience: *receiving freely*. It completes the law, creates balance and is part of the same law that inspired us to give in the first place. Freely give; freely (and gratefully) receive.

31N THE LAW OF TITHING

Tithing—giving a tenth of one's supply to God and His work. Tithing is a tacit agreement that humankind is in partnership with God in the conduct of our finances. ... Tithing, which is based on a law that cannot fail, establishes method in giving. It brings into the consciousness a sense of divine order that is manifested in one's outer life and affairs as increased efficiency and greater prosperity. (*The Revealing Word*, p. 195)

Tithing can be a way of getting into a giving consciousness, but it is not a substitute for a giving attitude.

The great need is to give way to the divine flow, and tithing can be an excellent means of achieving the giving consciousness. (*Spiritual Economics*, pp. 189-190)

Tithing is a very special kind of giving. It is giving from the the thought of Oneness, or Divine Mind, uppermost in mind. This way of giving is why tithing is always connected with something Spiritual, usually a church or a religious organization. However, it may be given to any person, church or organization that has provided us with Spiritual nourishment. It is the thought of Divine Mind, or Oneness, in the mind (consciousness) of the giver that causes it to be a tithe. Unity co-founder Charles Fillmore suggests above that the thought of Divine Mind as our metaphorical "partner" is a good one to adopt in tithing. Others may choose the thought of Divine Mind as Source, Increase, or unfailing Substance. However we think of It, never think of It as separate. Whatever form we may choose, it is the thought of Oneness that determines the difference between tithing and other types of giving.

31O THE MONEY "IDEA"

Watch your thoughts when you are handling your money, because your money is attached through your mind to the one source of all substance and all money ... which is visible, as something directly attached to an invisible source that is giving or withholding according to your thought, you have the key to all riches and the reason for all lack. (*Keep a True Lent*, p. 102)

The wise metaphysician deals with the money idea and masters it. (Charles Fillmore, *Christian Healing*, 2nd ed.,

Unity House, Unity Village, Mo., 2005, p. 136)

Money, like everything else in existence, is connected to the invisible Source through our minds. It is the visible evidence of an invisible Idea. We must always be aware of this Truth when we use money so that we may know and experience true abundance.

31P **MONEY AS A SYMBOL**

It is not money, but the love of money, that is the root of all evil. What people need to know is that money represents a mind substance of unlimited abundance and accessibility; that this mind substance cannot safely be hoarded or selfishly used by anyone; that it is a living magnet attracting good of every kind to those who possess it; that those who train their thoughts to depend on this mind substance for supply of all kinds never lack. (Keep a True Lent, p. 106)

Money itself is not the trap one may fall into; erroneous attitudes about money are the usual traps. Focusing on money results in faith or trust in this outer form, a result which can give rise to the tendency to *worship* money rather than the Divine Source of the Mind Substance. The above statement "Money represents a mind substance of unlimited abundance and accessibility" is worth contemplating: Money is tangible; the Mind Substance it is based on is not. When this is fully understood, it can be used to change one's basic attitude about money. As we grow in understanding the Truth, money becomes a symbol of Mind Substance, Divine Source becomes the focus, and prosperity can be enjoyed to the fullest.

SUMMARY STATEMENTS

▼ *The goal of true prosperity is based on the unfoldment of our Divine Potential and realization of the Divine Idea that the abundance of Divine Mind is behind all visible form.*

▼ *Substance is Divine Energy, the invisible matrix that is the basis for all form. Substance makes all form possible.*

▼ *How to get Supply is one thing; how to handle Supply is another. The two must balance and complement each other. If not, there is no real prosperity.*

▼ *The two-step approach requires that we must take action on Divine Ideas and Guidance. First is the awareness about Divine Ideas and associated formative thought; second is taking action on these thoughts.*

▼ *The Law of Increase says we must use what prosperity we have to increase it.*

▼ *The Secondary Law of Increase says that our own prosperity consciousness can positively affect another person's prosperity consciousness.*

▼ *There seem to be two worlds: the Inner Invisible Realm of our Spiritual Nature and the outer visible world of the senses. Our conscious mind is pivotal, so we live in both realms simultaneously. Our attention determines our state of mind at any given moment.*

▼ *The inner approach to prosperity is dependent on our Inner Spiritual Realm.*

▼ *The outer approach to prosperity is dependent on the material or physical realm.*

▼ *Belief in exclusive possession is an error that can ruin our enjoyment of prosperity.*

▼ *Our bounty and unique talents are to be developed and shared generously under the direction of Divine Wisdom and Understanding.*

▼ *We are to be good stewards of the good we have already received.*

▼ *Giving and receiving are two aspects of a prosperity law that must be exercised if we are to release the flow of abundant good in our consciousness.*

▼ *Giving freely is the only valid kind of giving; it is an expression of love and generosity. Receiving freely (and gratefully) completes the law, creating balance.*

▼ *Tithing is giving with the thought of Divine Mind uppermost in our consciousness. We are encouraged to share our tithe wherever we receive our Spiritual Good.*

▼ *Money is the visible evidence of a Divine Idea.*

▼ *Money itself is not prosperity; it is a symbol that represents invisible, unlimited, ever-present Mind Substance.*

TOPICS FOR DISCUSSION

1. *What is true prosperity?*

2. *What is the metaphysical basis for prosperity?*

3. *What is your understanding of Substance?*

THOUGHTS FOR REFLECTION AND MEDITATION

"The only way to become permanently prosperous and successful is through quickening, awakening, and bringing into righteous use all the indwelling resources of Spirit. When we develop our soul and express its talents and capabilities in loving service to God and humankind, our temporal needs will be supplied in bountiful measure."

(Myrtle Fillmore's *Healing Letters*, p. 41)

SUPPLEMENTARY READING

Prosperity by Charles Fillmore, Unity Books, Unity Village, Mo., 1936. Chapter 1, "Spiritual Substance," and Chapter 2, "Spiritual Mind."

Prosperity's Ten Commandments by Georgiana Tree West, 2nd ed., Unity House, Unity Village, Mo., 1996. Chapter 1, "Thou Shalt Look to No Other Sources but God for Thy Supply."

Spiritual Economics: The Principles and Process of True Prosperity by Eric Butterworth, 2nd revised paperback ed., Unity Books, Unity Village, Mo., 1998. Chapter 1, "The Truth About Substance," and Chapter 2, "Your Fortune Begins With You."

CHAPTER THIRTY-TWO

STUMBLING BLOCKS AND KEYS TO DEMONSTRATING PROSPERITY

INTRODUCTION

In our metaphysical studies, we have explored the Divine Ideas that comprise Truth as we teach it in Unity. It is important for everyone and most especially for a heart-centered metaphysician to express Divine Attributes in a creative and fulfilling way. In this chapter, we will use the same subtopics and order that appear in Chapter 28, "Keys to Demonstration"; however, they will now be focused on demonstrating prosperity.

DEMONSTRATION

The secret of demonstration is to conceive what is true in Being and to carry out the concept in thought, word, and act. If I can conceive a truth, there must be a way by which I can make that truth apparent. If I can conceive of an inexhaustible supply existing in the omnipresent ethers, then there is a way by which I can make that supply manifest. Once your mind accepts this as an axiomatic truth, it has arrived at the place where the question of processes begins to be considered. (Charles Fillmore, *Prosperity,* Unity House, Unity Village, Mo., 1936, p. 37)

KEY IDEA: The demonstration of prosperity is from a consciousness that perceives and knows the Truth of an inexhaustible Supply.

This is the key to the demonstration of prosperity: a consciousness that perceives and knows the Truth of an inexhaustible Supply. This level of perceiving and knowing is termed "realization," a deep inner knowing that you know something is true regardless of outer appearances. Realization must be backed by our thoughts, words and actions to demonstrate prosperity.

BLOCKS TO DEMONSTRATION AND WAYS TO RESOLVE THEM

32A STUMBLING BLOCKS

If you are not a success, some adverse state of consciousness is ruling in you. Do not drop into self-justification, but let go of the evil[1] and it will pass away. It has no power but that which you are giving to it, and when you withdraw your power, the evil will disappear. The divine Law always brings success. You were born to succeed. Power, authority, and dominion were given to humankind in the very beginning. Nothing can oppose you if you believe in the omnipresence of good and praise and worship it. All people should be successful, healthy and happy. Why are we not all in that state of mind? Because of the belief in the reality of evil. Remember that no matter how large the evil may seem, good is the one and only reality, and good will become dominant in all your life's experiences if you behold it as the Supreme and only Power in existence. (From Charles Fillmore's Sunday morning talk at Unity Auditorium, April 30, 1911, published in *Weekly Unity,* May 4, 1911)

We are to cease depending on outer, material avenues for prosperity, because when we look to the outer, we look away from the one resource that is within us. (Myrtle Fillmore, *Myrtle Fillmore's Healing Letters,* revised paperback edition, Unity House, Unity Village, Mo., 2006, p. 49)

In what do you have faith? In outer things? If so, you are building shadows without substance, shadows that cease as soon as your supporting thought is withdrawn from them, forms that will pass away and leave you nothing. If you would demonstrate true prosperity, you must turn from things and, as Jesus told His disciples, "have faith in God." Do not have faith in anything less than God, in anything other than the one Mind, for when your faith is centered there, you are building for eternity. Mind and the ideas of Mind will never pass away. There will never be an end to God. There will never be an end to Truth, which God is. There will never be an end to substance, which God is. Build with the divine substance, cultivate faith in realities and "lay up for yourselves treasures in heaven." (*Prosperity*, p. 49)

When we put our faith in the power of material riches, we wean our trust from God and establish it in this transitory substance of rust and corruption. This point is not clearly understood by those who are hypnotized by the money idea. When the metaphysician affirms God to be his opulent supply and support and declares that he has money in abundance, the assumption is that he loves money and depends upon it in the same way that the devotees of Mammon do. The difference is that one trusts in the law of God, while the other trusts in the power of Mammon. (*Charles Fillmore, Christian Healing, 2nd ed., Unity House, Unity Village, Mo., 2005, p. 36*)

Many who have found the law of true thinking and its effect wonder why supply does not come to them after months and years of holding thoughts of bounty. It is because they have not developed love. They have formed the right image in mind, but the magnet [Love] that draws the substance from the storehouse of Being has not been set into action." (Charles Fillmore, *Talks on Truth,* Unity House, Unity Village, Mo., 1926, p. 55)

If you let yourself think of any person or any outer condition as hindering your increase, this becomes a hindrance to you, for you have applied the law of increase to it. Fear of it may cause you to become timid and bury your talent, which defeats the law. Keep your eyes on the abundant inner reality and do not let the outer appearance cause you to falter. (*Prosperity*, p. 81)

KEY IDEA: Beliefs, thoughts and feelings held in mind can block or hinder increase. Examples include an adverse condition in consciousness, a belief that a person or outer condition can hinder you, or a belief in the outer realm and things such as money.

These blockages may also be due to the underdeveloped or misused Power of Love.

There are many stumbling blocks to the demonstration of prosperity. In demonstrating any desire one must remember that everything begins in mind, whether it be *lack* consciousness or *prosperity* consciousness. The best place to start is clearly identifying the stumbling blocks that occur in consciousness. These may include:

• Clinging to some adverse state of consciousness such as an old belief or thought.

• Thinking that a person or outer condition hinders our increase.

• Focusing on the outer realm including things like money.

• Misusing the Power of Love that may also be underdeveloped.

In order to grow in consciousness, let go of any adverse states of consciousness—give no power to evil (error) and they will disappear. Turn the Power of Faith that was once used to believe and trust in the outer to believe and trust in Divine Mind and Ideas.

32B FEAR AND THE NEGATIVE SIDE

Money saved as "an opportunity fund" brings an increase of good, but money hoarded from fear as a motive or with any miserly thought in mind cannot possibly bring any blessing. Those who hold the thought of accumulation so dominant in the world today are inviting trouble and even disaster, because right along with this thought goes a strong affirmation of the fear of loss of riches. Their actions bespeak fear, and the loss they dread is certain to be manifested sooner or later. (Prosperity, pp. 165-166)

You can send forth this vibratory energy of Spirit and break down the inertia caused by thoughts of fear and lack, carve out ways, open new avenues to the demonstration of your good. (Prosperity, p. 48)

There are various methods of erasing fear from the mind and preventing its congestions in the body. One of the most direct and effective shatterers of fear is laughter. Laugh your fears away. See how ridiculous they are when traced to their source. Nearly all persons have some pet fear, and they give up to it without trying to find its source. (Charles Fillmore, *Jesus Christ Heals,* 2nd ed., Unity House, Unity Village, Mo., 1940, p. 168)

The Mind of Spirit is harmonious and peaceful, and it must have a like manner of expression in man's consciousness. When a body of water is choppy with fitful currents of air it cannot reflect objects clearly. Neither can man reflect the steady strong glow of

Omnipotence when his mind is disturbed by anxious thoughts, fearful thoughts or angry thoughts. (Jesus Christ Heals, p. 176)

KEY IDEA: In order to demonstrate Good (prosperity), avoid and eliminate the fear of lack and a negative attitude toward money by focusing the mind on Spirit, laughter and song, as well as on using denials and affirmations.

The Law of Mind Action is always operating in the life of every person. Belief in lack, fear of loss, or anticipation of insufficiency—all these things go to make up what Jesus termed a "have-not" consciousness. Jesus in his parable of the talents (Mt. 25:14-30) said that "from those who have nothing, even what they have will be taken away" (Mt. 25:29). Jesus is essentially saying that a have-not consciousness would manifest itself not simply as a have-not experience but as a have-*less* experience. In other words, when the focus is on lack, an abundance of lack appears. Jesus also said, "For to all those who have, more will be given, and they will have an abundance" (Mt. 25:29). Jesus is saying that the "have" consciousness would not simply manifest as a have experience but as an "even more" experience. When the focus is on prosperity, an abundance of prosperity appears. Therefore, be conscientious about how the power of consciousness is used. Fear of loss produces limitation in our lives, whereas faith in Divine Mind produces bountiful blessings. <u>Release and transcend all fears so as to stay centered in an attitude of positive expectation.</u> Release can be accomplished by focusing the mind on Spirit, laughter and song, as well as on using denials and affirmations.

32C **JOY/CHEERFULNESS**

The free, open mind thus stayed on God is certain to bring forth joy, real satisfaction in living, and true prosperity. (*Prosperity*, p. 142)

As we find cheerfulness conducive to health, we also find it paving the way for prosperity. (Charles and Cora Fillmore, *Teach Us to Pray*, 2nd ed., Unity House, Unity Village, Mo., 2007, pp. 105-106)

When one asks for divine wisdom and understanding about giving, it becomes a joy both to the giver and the recipient. (*Prosperity*, p. 153)

KEY IDEA: <u>There is a direct relationship between our prosperity and being joyful when we give.</u>

We want to cultivate joy and cheerfulness to support our prosperity. Being a cheerful giver aligns us with Divine Law and True Prosperity. Joy is a result of keeping our mind on and living from a consciousness of Divine Mind. When we give, there is a direct relationship between our prosperity and being joyful.

32D **ATTACHMENT AND NONATTACHMENT**

KEY IDEA: Attachment to the outer realm and outer results hinders demonstration; an attitude of nonattachment smoothes the path to demonstration.

While no Unity quotations could be found related specifically to prosperity, attachment and nonattachment, the general concept still applies: Attachments to the outer realm and outer results (money and things) hinder demonstration. This is because attachments to the outer realm and results pulls ones focus from Divine Mind, or the Oneness, the starting point of all demonstration. Therefore attachments must be given up and replaced by an attitude of nonattachment, which smoothes the path to demonstration. Deny attachments to matter and material conditions and <u>affirm Oneness to become aware of Divine Ideas, especially Divine Substance, to manifest prosperity.</u>

32E RESISTANCE AND NONRESISTANCE

When you are nonresistant toward your good, your good runs to meet you. … This declaration or any declaration of similar spirit must be wholly sincere, or confusion and disappointment will follow its use. Sincerely avowed, what is worthwhile responds; what is not worthwhile fades from consciousness. (Imelda Octavia Shanklin, *What Are You?*, 2nd ed., Unity House, Unity Village, Mo., 2004, p. 154)

Living in the consciousness that your interests and the interests of the universe are identical, adjustment precedes every act. Nonresistance preserves and prospers you. (*What Are You?*, pp. 148-149)

KEY IDEA: Resistance against thoughts of lack hinders demonstration by increasing them in consciousness. Nonresistance creates a consciousness where we attract ourselves to what is worthwhile, and what is not worthwhile fades away.

Through the Law of Mind Action, resistance against thoughts of lack hinders demonstration by increasing them in consciousness. Having an attitude of nonresistance sets up a consciousness where we attract ourselves to what is worthwhile, and what is not worthwhile dissipates. Living in a nonresistant consciousness will prosper us. Not only must there be non-resistance toward the Good, there must also be nonresistance toward fear and lack.

32F UNFORGIVENESS, FORGIVENESS AND REPENTANCE

If you have in your mind any thought that someone has wronged you, you cannot let in the cleansing power of Spirit and the richness of spiritual substance until you have cast out the thought of the wrong, [and] have forgiven it fully. You may be wondering why you have failed to get spiritual illumination or to find the consciousness of spiritual substance. Perhaps the reason is here: a lack of room for the true thoughts because other thoughts fill your mind. If you are not receiving the spiritual understanding you feel you should have, you should search your mind carefully for unforgiving thoughts. "Thoughts are things" and occupy space in the mind realm. They have substance and form and may easily be taken as permanent by one not endowed with spiritual discernment [The Power of Discernment]. They bring forth fruit according to the seed planted in the mind, but they are not enduring unless founded in Spirit. (*Prosperity*, pp. 117-118)

Fill your mind with thoughts of divine love, justice, peace and forgiveness.

This will pay your debts of love, which are the only debts you really owe. Then see how quickly and easily and naturally all your outer debts will be paid and all inharmonies of mind, body and affairs smoothed out at the same time. (Prosperity, p. 123)

KEY IDEA: <u>Unforgiveness keeps us from the cleansing power of Spirit and Spiritual Substance</u>. Forgiveness leading to repentance exchange the unforgiving thought that someone has wronged you for empowering thoughts of love, justice and peace.

Any unforgiveness held in mind may prevent new ideas that will lead to greater prosperity. Unforgiveness keeps us from the cleansing power of Spirit and Spiritual Substance. Unforgiving thoughts must be rooted out, forgiven and *repented* (replaced with an empowering thought), allowing the "cleansing power of Spirit and the richness of spiritual substance" to establish a firm foundation for our prosperity. Forgiveness is about changing ones mind about a person or event. While repentance is more a more global change of mind and state of consciousness. It occurs when we let go of unforgiving thoughts and replace them with empowering thoughts like love, justice and peace.

KEYS TO DEMONSTRATION

32G CONSCIOUSNESS

As we continue to grow in the consciousness of God as omnipresent life and substance, we no longer have to put our trust in accumulations of money or other goods. We are sure that each day's need will be met, and we do not deprive ourselves of today's enjoyment and peace in order to provide for some future and wholly imaginary need. In this consciousness our life becomes divinely ordered, and there is a balance in supply and in finances as in everything else. We do not deprive ourselves of what we need today; neither do we waste our substance in foolish ways nor deplete it uselessly. (Prosperity, pp. 171-172)

We have access to the realm of rich ideas; we enrich our consciousness by incorporating these rich ideas into it. A rich consciousness always demonstrates prosperity. (Myrtle Fillmore's Healing Letters, p. 49)

KEY IDEA: Growth in prosperity consciousness depends increasingly on Spirit. Emphasize the Powers of Faith, Wisdom and Understanding to balance needs, wants and wastefulness.

Expanding prosperity consciousness depends on Divine Mind. Focus on Divine Mind as the omnipresence of Substance in order to grow in prosperity consciousness. Have Faith that today's needs will be met. A balanced prosperity consciousness utilizes Divine Wisdom and Understanding that help to determine the proper balance of needs, wants and discern wastefulness.

32H DIVINE MIND—ONENESS

We must depend wholly on the inner kingdom of supply and the indwelling Christ, for this inner way is the only way to receive permanently. (Myrtle Fillmore's Healing Letters, p. 49)

"The kingdom of God is in the midst of you" (Lk. 17:21). Jesus said, "Seek first his kingdom and his righteousness, and all these things shall be yours as well" (Mt. 6:33). This means that we are to find the wealth of capabilities and spiritual resources within us and bring them into expression. When we develop the power to accomplish things and the qualities that we need in order to accomplish them, our success is assured. (Myrtle Fillmore's Healing Letters, p. 49)

The only way to become permanently prosperous and successful is through the quickening, awakening and bringing into righteous use all of the indwelling resources of Spirit. When we develop our soul [conscious and subconscious minds] and express its talents and capabilities in loving service to God and humankind, all of our

temporal needs will be supplied in bountiful measure. (Myrtle Fillmore's Healing Letters, p. 49)

KEY IDEA: Divine Mind and Its Resources (Divine Ideas) are the starting point of all true prosperity. Enliven, awaken and bring into righteous use all the indwelling Resources of Spirit and use Them in loving service.

All Spiritual approaches to prosperity begin with realizing Divine Mind, the one Power and Presence. Cease looking to the outer, material means of prosperity. Seek first the Inner Kingdom of God, depend wholly on It, and faithfully know that all needs are met through the infinite Supply of Divine Ideas. Faithfully enliven, awaken and bring into righteous use all the indwelling Resources of Spirit. Develop the soul, the conscious and subconscious mind, and express its talents and capabilities through loving service.

32I DIVINE IDEAS

Divine Mind has ideas of substance as unlimited and everywhere present, equally available to all. Since humankind's work is to express substance ideas in material form, we must find a way to connect ideas of substance with ideas of material expression, to adjust the ideas of humankind's mind with the ideas of Divine Mind. This is accomplished by faith through prayer. (Prosperity, p. 31)

That part of the Lord's Prayer which reads "Give us this day our daily bread" [Mt. 6:11] is more correctly translated, "Give us today the substance of tomorrow's bread." By prayer we accumulate in our mind ideas of God as the substance of our supply and support. There is no lack of this substance in infinite Mind. Regardless of how much God gives, there is always an abundance left. God does not give us material things, but Mind substance—not money but ideas—ideas that set spiritual forces in motion so that things begin to come to us by the application of the law. (Prosperity, p. 31)

Prosperity is basically an attitude of thought and feeling, only secondarily a matter of money. For ideas are coins of the mind realm. (Ernest C. Wilson, *Like a Miracle*, Unity House, Unity Village, Mo., 1971, p. 144)

KEY IDEA: Divine Ideas are the only true wealth, for they are the Primary Causes for all that is good in life.

Strictly speaking, God does not give us anything. God is Divine Mind consisting of Divine Ideas. Divine ideas are always fully available and cannot be depleted or annihilated. The mind causes the energies of Divine Ideas to project into the realm of form (manifestation). We must adjust humankind's ideas with Divine Ideas in Divine Mind through prayer and Faith. Supply is our *experience* of prosperity, but the Divine Ideas behind Supply *are* prosperity.

32J MEDITATION/THE SILENCE

Go into the silence daily at a stated time and concentrate on the substance of Spirit prepared for you from the foundation of the world. This opens up a current of thought that will bring prosperity into your affairs. A good thought to hold in this meditation is this: The invisible substance is plastic to my abundant thought, and I am rich in mind and in manifestation. (Prosperity, p. 41)

In true meditation one becomes joined with the Giver, contact is made with the Source of all good, and such faith, harmony and peace are established in mind that through it the body and affairs are opened to receive. (Frances W. Foulks, *Effectual Prayer*, 3rd ed., Unity House, Unity Village, Mo., 2000, p. 78)

When we are endeavoring to listen, to understand, and to follow our divine guidance from the spiritual center of our own soul, we find that every wind that blows (whether it appears at first to be good or ill) does fill us with the spirit of plenty—because the winds are evidence of God's Ideas and Substance, and plenty is the one reality. So we may rejoice in our prosperity and use it day by day, in full assurance that it will never fail. (Myrtle Fillmore, *How to Let God Help You,* 4th ed., compiled by Warren Meyer, Unity House, Unity Village, Mo., 2006, p. 145)

KEY IDEA: Investing time in the Silence by meditating puts Divine Mind first and ensures a state of receptivity to the prospering Ideas of Spirit.

Daily meditation is the primary way to put Oneness, or Divine Mind, first. It is imperative for Spiritual growth and helpful in creating a prosperity consciousness. Investing our time, intention and attention in meditation ensures a state of receptivity to the prospering Ideas of Spirit. (For more on meditation, see Chapter 7). In meditation, hold this thought from Charles Fillmore: *"The invisible substance is plastic to my abundant thought, and I am rich in mind and manifestation."*

32K PRAYER

Divine Mind has ideas of substance as unlimited and everywhere present, equally available to all. Since our work is to express substance ideas in material form, we must find a way to connect ideas of substance with ideas of material expression, to adjust the ideas of our minds with the ideas of Divine Mind. This is accomplished by faith through prayer. *(Prosperity,* p. 31)

By prayer we accumulate in our mind ideas of God as the substance of our supply and support. There is no lack of this substance in infinite Mind. (*Prosperity,* p. 31)

Pray, but let your prayer be affirmative, for that is the prayer of faith. A begging prayer filled with "ifs" is a prayer of doubt. Keep praying until affirmations become a habit of mind. The race thought of lack must be penetrated and so charged with the truth of God's omnipresent abundance that all consciousness of lack and poverty disappears from the face of the earth. (*Prosperity,* p. 85)

KEY IDEA: The purpose of affirmative prayer is to express Substance Ideas into material form by connecting Substance Ideas with ideas of material expression.

Affirmative prayer rooted in Faith adjusts the human mind with the Ideas of Divine Mind. God, or Divine Mind, is the realm of unlimited Mind Substance, or Divine Ideas. Pray knowing and claiming that Divine Mind is the Source of Divine Ideas and Substance. The habit of affirmative prayers of abundance and ever-present Substance disempowers or erases all thoughts of lack and poverty. We should not utilize prayers that beg, for they are prayers of doubt. (For more on prayer, see Chapters 8 and 9.)

32L **CONCENTRATION**

Daily concentration of mind on Spirit and its attributes will reveal that the elemental forces that make all material things are here in the ether awaiting our recognition and appropriation. It is not necessary to know all the details of the scientific law in order to demonstrate prosperity. (*Prosperity*, p. 41)

By thinking about all things as now present, you focus the thoughts in the now and this concentration brings large results. (From Charles Fillmore's Sunday morning talk at Unity Auditorium, October 3, 1910, published in *Weekly Unity,* October 10, 1927, "Retrospection and Introspection")

KEY IDEA: Concentrate on Divine Ideas that relate to abundance and prosperity in order to have good results.

Concentrate the mind on and from the awareness of Spirit, or Divine Mind, to get into contact with the Attributes of Spirit and the elemental forces that make material things possible. Our concentration on Divine Mind and Its Divine Ideas having to do with abun-

dance and prosperity brings good results. Again, affirm this thought from Charles Fillmore: *The invisible substance is plastic to my abundant thought, and I am rich in mind and manifestation.* (For more on concentration, see Chapter 8.)

32M **REALIZATION**

The other person's realization of substance will not guarantee your supply. You must become conscious of it for yourself. Identify yourself with substance until you make it yours; it will change your finances, destroy your fears, stop your worries, and you will soon begin to rejoice in the ever-present bounty of God. (*Prosperity*, p. 24)

When your mind comes around again to the subject of prosperity, realize most strongly that your prosperity comes from God. It came with you from God, from your contact with God Mind in your silence, and your prosperity is right with you wherever you are. Supply may seem to come through outer channels, but your real success depends on your inner hold on the prosperity realization. (*Prosperity*, pp. 54-55)

Nothing will so broaden your mind and your world as the realization that all is yours. When you realize the boundlessness of your spiritual inheritance, nothing shall be lacking in all your world. See with the bountiful eye; for "he that hath a bountiful eye shall be blessed" [Prov. 22:9]. This passage states an exact law, the law of increase. (Prosperity, p. 186)

The anxious thought must be eliminated and the perfect abandon of the child of nature assumed, and when to this attitude you add the realization of unlimited resources, you have fulfilled the divine law of prosperity. (Prosperity, p. 91)

KEY IDEA: Realization of the Truth of our unlimited Resources, combined with the elimination of any anxious thoughts of lack and limitation, fulfills the law of prosperity.

Realization of prosperity establishes the Truth at a core level of being. We must be patient and wait in silent meditation for the realization that Oneness, or Divine Mind, is the Source of unlimited abundance, no matter the outer channels from which it seems to flow. Realization of the Truth of unlimited Resources, combined with the elimination of any anxious thoughts of lack and limitation, fulfills the law of prosperity. (For more on realization, see Chapter 7.)

32N SUBSTANCE AND SUPPLY

The mind in us, that reasons and looks to the physical side of things, has also the ability to look within. It is the door through which divine ideas must come. ... It is the divine plan that all expression or demonstration shall come through this gateway of man's mind. But above all these are the ideas that exist in the primal state of Being, and this is the truth of which we must become conscious. We must become aware of the source of our substance. Then we can diminish or increase the appearance of our supply or our finances, for their appearance depends entirely on our understanding and handling of the ideas of substance. (Prosperity, p. 32)

Spiritual substance is the source of all material wealth and cannot suffer loss or destruction by human thought. It is always with us, ready to be used and to make the consciousness potent and fertile. ...

Just as the earth is the universal matrix in which all vegetation develops, so this invisible Spirit substance is the universal matrix in which ideas of prosperity germinate and grow and bring forth according to our faith and trust. ...

To gain control of Spirit substance I grasp it with my mind; that is, lay hold of the idea back of it. Right thinking is necessary in using my mind constructively to bring about right results. (Charles Fillmore, Keep a True Lent, 2nd ed., Unity House, Unity Village, Mo., 2005, p. 184)

KEY IDEA: Substance and Supply are Divine Ideas; They are also the Universal Matrix in which Divine Ideas of prosperity germinate and grow. Each person can control and use Substance constructively, depending entirely on the level of understanding and proper handling of the Ideas of Substance.

Divine Mind is the Source of Substance and Supply, which are essentially synonymous. These Divine Ideas in the primal state of Beingness are also the "universal matrix in which ideas of prosperity germinate and grow." Divine Ideas that make up Substance and Supply must pass through the doorway of the mind of humanity in order to manifest. Each person must gain control of Substance by grasping It, realizing It, with the mind. Therefore, right thinking and understanding are important in handling Substance so that we may constructively bring about righteous results.

320 THE TWELVE POWERS/FACULTIES/ABILITIES

You want to learn how to demonstrate prosperity in your home by the righteous exercise of powers and faculties that God has given you. Realize in the very beginning that you do have these powers and faculties. You are in possession of everything necessary for the demonstration of prosperity and can undertake it with the utmost confidence and faith. (Prosperity, p. 108)

So in the demonstration of spiritual powers as they are expressed through humankind, we must be willing to follow the directions of someone [Jesus] who has proved his understanding of the law by his demonstrations. (Prosperity, p. 37)

When a person releases the powers of his soul, he or she does marvels in the sight of the material-minded, but has not departed from the law. (Prosperity, p. 19)

Release your rich thoughts, set free your innate powers, and take from the rich substance of the Father what you will. (Prosperity, p. 74)

KEY IDEA: The awakening and conscious use of the Twelve Powers is important in demonstrating prosperity.

First, we must realize that the Powers/Faculties/Abilities are always present and available. Most people are using the Powers unconsciously, giving rise to undesired results. So begin to consciously set the Twelve Powers free and reap from the rich Substance of Divine Ideas that is ever present and cannot be diminished or depleted in any way.

Faith—Believes, intuits and perceives Divine Ideas, Laws and Principles of prosperity.

Strength—Endures, persists and perseveres with the Divine Ideas, Laws and Principles of prosperity.

Judgment/Wisdom/Discernment—Evaluates, discerns, appraises and knows how to use Divine Ideas, Laws and Principles of prosperity.

Love—Harmonizes, unifies, attracts oneself to Divine Ideas, Laws and Principles of prosperity as well as to whatever will bring about prosperity in the outer realm.

Power/Dominion—Masters, dominates and controls thoughts and feelings of lack and limitation as well as thoughts and feelings of abundance.

Imagination—Images, conceptualizes and shapes Substance to express the Divine Ideas, Laws and Principles of prosperity.

Understanding—Knows and perceives the Divine Ideas, Laws and Principles of prosperity.

Will—Chooses based on the Divine Ideas, Laws and Principles of prosperity.

Order—Organizes, balances, sequences and adjusts one's affairs to demonstrate the Divine Ideas, Laws and Principles of prosperity.

Zeal—Enthusiastically and passionately acts and motivates based on the Divine Ideas, Laws and Principles of prosperity.

Elimination/Renunciation—Releases, removes, denounces, denies and lets go of beliefs, thoughts and feelings of lack and limitation.

Life—Energizes, vitalizes and enlivens the process of demonstrating from the Divine Ideas, Laws and Principles of prosperity.

32P **FAITH AND IMAGINATION**

In this lesson we are considering the subject of faith especially as it applies to the demonstration of prosperity. People, being like God, must also base their creations on faith as the only foundation. Here then is our starting point in building a prosperity consciousness and making our world as we would have it. We all have faith, for it is innate in every person. Our question is how may we put it to work in our affairs. (Prosperity, p. 42)

The imagination builds things out of the one substance. If you will associate faith with it in its creative work, the things you make will be just as real as those that God makes. Whatever you make in mind and really put faith in will become substantial. Then you must be constantly on your guard as to what you believe, in order that you may bring what is for your good into manifestation. (*Prosperity*, p. 49)

KEY IDEA: Faith in Divine Ideas, Laws and Principles in Divine Mind, linked with the Power of Imagination, assures abundance.

Having Faith in God is having Faith in the Divine Ideas, Principles and Laws that make up Divine Mind. Faith linked with Imagination is an essential factor in the metaphysical approach to prosperity; It is the great affirmative Power of the mind linked with the Ability to shape Substance. This affirmative attitude is constantly saying "yes" to Divine Ideas while Imagination uses them to build from the one Substance. With such an attitude, a person must be truly prosperous; such a person will experience prosperity of the highest order even if he or she does not care much for material wealth.

32Q LOVE, WISDOM, UNDERSTANDING AND ZEAL

Nothing will so quickly enrich your mind and free it from every thought of lack as the realization of divine love. Divine love will quickly and perfectly free you from the burden of debt and heal you of your physical infirmities, often caused by depression, worry and financial fear. Love will bring your own to you, adjust all misunderstand-

ings, and make your life and affairs healthy, happy, harmonious and free, as they should be. Love indeed is the "fulfillment of the law." (*Prosperity*, pp. 123-124)

The supply and support that love and zeal will set in motion are not as yet largely used by humankind, but those who have tested their providing power are loud in their praise. (*Prosperity*, p. 9)

The things formed are the result of efforts to combine wisdom and love, and their character indicates the success or the failure of the undertaking. (Charles Fillmore, *Dynamics for Living: A Topical Compilation of Essential Fillmore Teachings,* Unity House, Unity Village, Mo, p. 181)

When wisdom and love are unified in the individual consciousness, humankind is a master of ideas and brings forth under the original creative law. (Charles Fillmore, *Mysteries of Genesis,* 2nd ed., Unity House, Unity Village, Mo., 1998, p. 27)

Through your thoughts you deal with the wonderful spiritual substance, and it takes form in your consciousness according to your thought about it. That is why we must hold the thought of divine wisdom and understanding: so that we may use these creative mind powers righteously. We use them all the time either consciously or unconsciously and we should use them to our advantage and blessing. (Prosperity, p. 52)

The mind of humankind is like the net catching every kind of idea, and it is humankind's privilege and duty under the divine law to separate those that are good from those which are not good. In this process the currents of unselfish, spiritual love flowing through the soul act as great eliminators, freeing the consciousness of thoughts of hate, lack and poverty, and giving the substance of Spirit free access into the consciousness and affairs.

... When this divine current of love and spiritual understanding begins its work, we must make this separation. We put the sheep, the good and obedient and profitable thoughts, on the right, and we put the goats, the stubborn, selfish, useless thoughts, on the left. Each must handle his own thoughts and overcome them by aligning them with the harmony and order of the divine thought. There is an infinite, omnipresent wisdom within us that will deal with these thoughts and guide us in making the discrimination between the right and the wrong when we trust ourselves fully to its intelligence. We can establish a connection between the conscious mind and the superconscious mind within us by meditation, by silence, and by speaking the word. (Prosperity, p. 173)

KEY IDEA: The Power of Love is used to desire prosperity and abundance; It works best when combined with Wisdom, Understanding and Zeal, resulting in righteous use.

Attaining prosperity results from more than the right use of a particular method; it also results from the unconditional expression of our Faculty of Love. If a demonstration of prosperity is lacking or failing in spite of all efforts, examine the Faculty of Love. Love needs to be part of all motivation (Zeal), including the desire for prosperity. Love is the Spiritual Power that offers blessings to others and attracts a person to the blessings desired.

If the focus in life is on lack, then that is what seems to be desired (loved); and since what is focused on increases, the result is an abundance of lack. And because the Power of Love used alone is indiscriminate, it is vital that Love be used with Wisdom and Understanding. Love combined with Zeal (motivation), Wisdom and Understanding motivates their righteous use to advantage and blessing.

32R HARMONY

The law [divine law of equilibrium] is based on love and justice, and it equitably and harmoniously adjusts all the affairs of people. It goes even further, for it restores a harmony and balance in both mind and body that results in happiness and health as well as prosperity. (Prosperity, p. 149)

Wisdom, justice, judgment are grouped under one head in spiritual consciousness. (Charles and Cora Fillmore, *The Twelve Powers, Unity House, Unity Village, Mo., 1999, p. 46*)

The law of supply is a divine law. ... It is a law of mind and must work through mind. God will not go to the grocery and bring food to your table. But when you continue to think about God as your real supply, everything in your mind begins to awaken and to contact the divine substance, and as you mold it in your consciousness, ideas begin to come which will connect you with the visible manifestation. You first get the ideas in consciousness direct from their divine source, and then you begin to demonstrate in the outer. ...

When you work in harmony with this universal law every needed thing is abundantly supplied. Your part is simply to fulfill the law; that is, to keep your mind filled with mind substance, to store up spiritual substance until the mind is filled with it and it cannot help but manifest in your affairs in obedience to the law "Whosoever hath, to him shall be given." *(Prosperity, p. 68)*

KEY IDEA: To enjoy a full measure of joy and experience harmony in life, employ the Powers of Love and Wisdom that harmonize with Divine Law, Ideas and Principles.

Harmony has its basis in Love, and Love works hand in hand with justice (the Power of Wisdom/Judgment). "When justice and love meet at the heart center, there are balance, poise and righteousness" (*The Revealing Word*, p. 114). Harmony can be seen in two ways: First, there must be harmony with Divine Law (The Law of Supply and the Power of Order, Mind-Idea-Expression) in order to enjoy its full measure of Good. Second, when we are in harmony with Divine Law, we experience harmony in our lives, resulting in happiness, health and prosperity.

32S **PEACE**

... If we would have peace and harmony in our environment, we must establish it within ourselves. We must faithfully and persistently deny the appearance of that which seems to be inharmonious and silently and faithfully affirm the omnipresent peace, love and harmony that we want to see manifested. That which we hold in consciousness will be made manifest for us, therefore we should not hold the thought of anything that we do not want to see appear. (Charles Fillmore,

Atom-Smashing Power of Mind, 2nd ed., Unity House, Unity Village, Mo., 2006, p. 72)

The Mind of Spirit is harmonious and peaceful. It must have a like manner of expression in humankind's consciousness. If we are not anchored to supreme and immovable reality, we shall be exposed to the storms of mortal thought and shipwrecked on the rocks of materiality. The mind may be compared to the sea, which is calm or stormy according to the wind that moves it. Thought utilizes the substance of the mind and forms that which a person ideates. A restful state of mind is greatly to be desired because of its constructive character. (Dynamics for Living, p. 159)

KEY IDEA: A peaceful mind greatly aids the demonstration of prosperity.

The mind anchored in the awareness of Spirit is peaceful. A peaceful mind utilizes Substance for harmonious and constructive results and greatly aids the demonstration of prosperity.

32T THE CREATIVE POWER OF THOUGHT AND FEELINGS

We hear a great deal about the creative power of thought. Correctly speaking it is mind that is creative and thought is its action. Thought is the use we make of mind with its vast creative power ...

we should practice using the creative power of mind to construct only the images of the good we desire to see made manifest in our lives. (Georgiana Tree West, Prosperity's Ten Commandments, 2nd ed., Unity House, Unity Village, Mo., 1996, pp. 26-27)

The spiritual substance from which comes all visible wealth is never depleted. It is right with you all the time and responds to your faith in it and your demands on it. It is not affected by our ignorant talk of hard times, though we are affected because our thoughts and words govern our demonstration. The unfailing resource is always ready to give. It has no choice in the matter; it must give, for that is its nature. (Prosperity, p. 13)

Everything that appears in the universe had its origin in mind. Mind evolves ideas, and ideas express themselves through thoughts and words. Understanding that ideas have a permanent existence and that they evolve thoughts and words, we see how futile is any attempted reform that does not take them into consideration. (Prosperity, p. 26)

Thoughts are seeds that, when dropped or planted in the subconscious mind, germinate, grow and bring forth their fruit in due season. The more clearly we understand this truth, the greater will be our ability to plant the seeds that bring forth desirable fruits. After sowing, the plants must be tended. After using the law, we must hold to its fulfillment. This is our part, but God gives the increase. You just work in divine order [mind, idea and expression] *and not expect the harvest before the soil has been prepared or the seed sown. You have now the fruits of previous sowings. Change your thought seeds and reap what you desire. Some bring forth very quickly, others more slowly, but all in divine order* [mind, idea and expression]. (Charles Fillmore, *Jesus Christ Heals,* 2nd ed., Unity House, Unity Village, Mo., 1940, p. 112)

KEY IDEA: Thoughts, feelings and words govern the demonstration of prosperity.

Everything in the physical universe originates in mind. Mind is creative and its action is thought. Mind evolves Ideas which have a permanent existence. Ideas evolve and express thoughts and words. Thoughts give form to what a person ideates utilizing the Substance of Mind/mind. Thoughts, feelings and words of Truth derived from Divine Ideas are seeds and must go through a process before becoming a harvested crop. Thoughts propelled by feelings are implanted in the subconscious mind and omnipresent Substance, becoming the seeds of manifestation. It is during this time that impatience is most dangerous. Remember, the more patience is exercised during this processing time, the less time it takes for demonstration. There is the possibility that if impatience is totally overcome, demonstrations could become "instantaneous." (For more on thought, see Chapter 20.) While feelings are not mentioned in the excerpts above, there is ample support for the idea that thoughts boosted by feelings are very powerful. (See section 32Y on Patience.)

32U THE WORD AND THE SPOKEN WORD

I know that any seed words that are planted in omnipresent Spirit substance will germinate and grow and bring forth fruit "after their kind." Just as the farmer selects the best seed for planting, so I must choose the words that will bring forth the rich harvest of plenty. (Keep a True Lent, p. 184)

Spiritual thoughts are infinite in their potentiality, each one being measured by the life, intelligence, and substance with which it is expressed. The thought is brought into expression and activity by the word. Every word is a thought in activity, and when spoken it goes out as a vibratory force that is registered in the all-providing substance. (Prosperity, p. 36)

The spiritual substance from which comes all visible wealth is never depleted. It is right with you all the time and responds to your faith in it and your demands on it. It is not affected by our ignorant talk of hard times, though we are affected because our thoughts and words govern our demonstration. The unfailing resource is always ready to give. It has no choice in the matter; it must give, for that is its nature. Pour your living words of faith into the omnipresent substance, and you will be prospered though all the banks in the world close their doors. Turn the great energy of your thinking toward "plenty" ideas, and you will have plenty regardless of what people about you are saying or doing. (Prosperity, p. 13)

When we know that certain potent ideas exist in the invisible mind expressions, named by science both "ether" and "space," and that we have been provided with the mind to lay hold of them, it is easy to put the law into action through thought and word and deed. (Prosperity, pp. 12-13)

KEY IDEA: Pour living words empowered by Faith into omnipresent Substance and the subconscious mind will manifest prosperity and abundance.

Divine Ideas inspire thoughts, and thoughts infused with feeling are brought into expression through the activity of words. We use words to plant seeds in the subconscious mind; we also use the omnipresent Substance to manifest our prosperity and abundance. (For more on the word and the power of the spoken word, see Chapter 21).

32V DENIALS AND AFFIRMATIONS

Eliminate all negative thoughts that come into your mind. Yet do not spend all your time in denials but give much of it to the clear realization of the everywhere present and waiting substance and life. (Prosperity, p. 98)

Charge your mind with statements that express plenty. No particular affirmation will raise anyone from poverty to affluence, yet all affirmations that carry ideas of abundance will lead one into the consciousness that fulfills the law. Deny that lack has any place or reality in your thought or your affairs and affirm plenty as the only appearance. (Prosperity, p. 41)

Old thoughts must be denied and the mind cleansed in preparation before the affirmative Christ consciousness can come in. Our minds and even our bodies are loaded with error thoughts. Every cell is clothed with thought: every cell has a mind of its own. By the use of denial we break through the outer crust, the material thought that has enveloped the cells, and get down into the substance and the life within them. Then we make contact with that substance and life which our denials have exposed, and by it express the positive, constructive side of the law. When we consistently deny the limitations of the material, we begin to reveal the spiritual law that waits within ourselves to be fulfilled. When this law is revealed to our consciousness, we begin to use it to demonstrate all things that are good. (Prosperity, p. 175)

KEY IDEA: Use denials to clear and release any error thoughts of fear or lack. Use affirmations to build up the Truth of abundance and prosperity.

We use denials to disempower and clear away any negative thoughts, including erroneous thinking related to our prosperity as well as old thoughts that oppose the manifestation of prosperity. We use affirmations to build consciousness of the Principles, Ideas and Laws that are the Truth of our prosperity. (For more on denials and affirmations, see Chapter 22.)

Sample denials:

◆ *I dissolve in my own mind and the minds of all others any thought that my own can be withheld from me. (Prosperity, p. 185)*

◆ *I give no power to fear of poverty. I give not power to thoughts of obligation to others.*

◆ *I give no power to any thoughts of lack or poverty; they have no Influence.*

Sample affirmations:

◆ *Jesus Christ is now here, raising me to his consciousness of the omnipresent, all-providing Divine Substance, and my prosperity is assured. (Prosperity, p. 25)*

◆ *I have unbounded Faith in the all-present Spiritual Substance increasing and multiplying at my word. (Prosperity, p. 25)*

◆ *I am prosperous.*

32W GRATITUDE, PRAISE AND BLESSING

You should expect prosperity when you keep the prosperity law. Therefore, be thankful for every blessing that you gain and as deeply grateful for every demonstration as for an unexpected treasure dropped into your lap. This will keep your heart fresh; for true thanksgiving may be likened to rain falling upon ready soil, refreshing it and increasing its productiveness. (Prosperity, p. 105)

This insight of the grateful heart is a dynamic key to personal prosperity. (Eric Butterworth, Spiritual Economics: The Principles and Process of True Prosperity, 2nd revised paperback ed., Unity House, Unity Village, Mo, 1998, p. 89)

As you feel grateful you become attractive, not only in your beauty and radiance, but in your relationships with people. More importantly you release a vital energy that draws to you opportunities, employment, and secure flow of substance. (Spiritual Economics, p. 97)

Praise what you have, be it ever so little, and insist that it is constantly growing larger. (Prosperity, p. 41)

Blessing the substance increases its flow. If your money supply is low or your purse seems empty, take it in your hands and bless it. See it filled with the living substance ready to become manifest. When you dress, bless your garments and realize that you are being constantly clothed with God's substance. Do not center your thought on yourself, your interests, your gains or losses, but realize the universal nature of substance. The more conscious you become of the presence of the living substance, the more it will manifest itself for you and the richer will be the common good of all. (Prosperity, p. 24)

KEY IDEA: Invest time and energy in blessing, praising and expressing gratitude for all that you have. The more conscious of the presence of universal Substance you become through blessing, praising and gratitude, the more

It increases for you and the common good of all.

Be grateful for every demonstration of abundant Good as well as for any unexpected treasure. Bless the money, food, clothes and whatever else you have. Do not center thoughts on yourself, your gains or losses; simply realize the universal Nature of Substance. In other words, make blessing, praising and gratitude a perpetual attitude of mind. Becoming more conscious of the presence of universal Substance increases It for you and the common good of all.

32X **THE LAW OF VISUALIZATION/SEEING THE GOOD**

We are not talking about seeing things (cars, houses, jobs, jewels, etc.), but rather seeing from a consciousness of ever-present substance, which will become the magnetic force that draws the things to you but without any of them ever becoming the object of your life. (Spiritual Economics, p. 54)

If I can conceive of an inexhaustible supply existing in the omnipresent ethers, then there is a way by which I can make that supply manifest. Once your mind accepts this as an axiomatic truth, it has arrived at the place where the question of processes begins to be considered. (Prosperity, p. 37)

KEY IDEA: Using the Power of Imagination, visualize and conceptualize what you desire. See only the Good, the reality of ever-present Substance and Divine Ideas, without regard to outer appearances.

Calmly and consistently visualize, conceptualize and focus on the reality of abundant Substance; this creative Activity through the Power of Imagination is an all-important key to demonstrating true and lasting Prosperity. No matter what the outer appearance seems to be, attention is not to be focused on it because anxiety *and* lack will result; it may even result in manifesting more of the outer appearance. Attention is to be focused on the inner knowing that there is an all-sufficiency of Good, Divine Ideas, and ever-present Substance, resulting in demonstrating what is desired without attachment.

32Y PATIENCE AND TRUST

Patience is a state of mind that beholds the world from the harmony of the Christ Mind, a freedom from personal thinking. It is an attitude of mind characterized by poise, calmness and a quiet restful trust, especially in the face of trying conditions. It has its foundation in love. (Keep a True Lent, p. 181)

We have discovered that there is within us a life force that can be quickened

into greater activity by thinking. Everyone has at some time demonstrated that he or she could overcome the negative condition of weakness by holding the thought of strength. Sometimes the strength follows the thought immediately, sometimes the thought must be persistently held for days or weeks. In demonstrating the law of ever-present abundance, we should and do expect the same results. If the demonstration seems slow in coming, patience and persistence will win. That may be because the poverty consciousness has a tenacious hold and takes effort to be got rid of. (Prosperity, pp. 71-72)

You will become more prosperous and successful so gradually, simply and naturally that you will not realize that it derives from a divine source and in answer to your prayers. We must realize all the while however that whatever we put as seed into the subconscious soil will eventually bring forth after its kind and we must exercise the greatest caution so that we do not think or talk about insufficiency or allow others to talk to us about it. As we sow in mind, so shall we reap in manifestation. (Prosperity, p. 67)

KEY IDEA: Patience and trust ease whatever waiting period there may be for the demonstration of prosperity.

Do not feel inadequate if the demonstration of prosperity comes slowly. No one is inadequate who trusts Oneness, or Divine Mind, and affirms the Truth. Success will come just as surely as day follows night; however, it may come in a gradual and sensible way. Patience, trust and inner gratitude will ease whatever waiting period there may be. So be at peace with the process through patience and trust; have Faith.

SUMMARY STATEMENTS

▼ *The <u>demonstration</u> of prosperity is a consciousness that perceives and knows the Truth of an inexhaustible Supply.*

▼ *Beliefs, thoughts and feelings held in mind can <u>block or hinder increase</u>. Examples include an adverse condition in consciousness, a belief that a person or outer condition can hinder you, a belief in the outer realm and things such as money, or an underdeveloped or misused Power of Love.*

▼ *In order to demonstrate Good (prosperity, Divine Ideas), avoid and eliminate the <u>fear of lack and a negative attitude</u> toward money by focusing the mind on Spirit, laughter and song, as well as on using denials and affirmations.*

▼ *There is a direct relationship between our prosperity and our being <u>joyful</u> when we give.*

▼ *<u>Attachment</u> to the outer realm (money and things) and outer results hinders demonstration.*

▼ *An attitude of <u>nonattachment</u> smoothes the path to demonstration.*

▼ *<u>Resistance</u> to thoughts of lack hinders demonstration by increasing them in consciousness.*

▼ *<u>Nonresistance</u> creates a consciousness where we attract ourselves to what is worthwhile, and what is not worthwhile fades away.*

▼ *<u>Unforgiveness</u> keeps us from the cleansing power of Spirit and Spiritual Substance.*

▼ _Forgiveness and repentance_ is the exchange of unforgiving thoughts that someone has wronged you for the empowering thoughts of love, justice and peace.

▼ Growth in _prosperity consciousness_ depends more and more on Spirit. Emphasize the Powers of Faith, Wisdom and Understanding so as to balance needs, wants and eliminate wastefulness.

▼ _Divine Mind_ and Its Resources (Divine Ideas) are the starting point of all true prosperity. Enliven, awaken and bring into righteous use all the indwelling Resources of Spirit and use Them in loving service.

▼ _Divine Ideas_ are the only true wealth, for they are the Primary Causes for all that is good in life.

▼ Investing time in the _Silence by meditating_ puts Divine Mind first and ensures a state of receptivity to the prospering Ideas of Spirit.

▼ The purpose of _affirmative prayer_ is to express Substance Ideas in material form by connecting Substance Ideas with ideas of material expression.

▼ _Concentrate_ on Divine Ideas that relate to abundance and prosperity in order to have good results.

▼ _Realization_ of the Truth of unlimited Resources that are already ours, combined with the elimination of any anxious thoughts of lack and limitation, fulfills the law of prosperity.

▼ _Substance and Supply_ are Divine Ideas as well as the Universal Matrix in which Divine Ideas of prosperity germinate and grow.

▼ Each person can control and use _Substance_ constructively, depending entirely on the level of understanding and the proper handling of the Ideas of Substance.

▼ The awakening and conscious use of _the Twelve Powers_ are important to demonstrating prosperity.

▼ _Faith_ in Divine Ideas, Laws and Principles in Divine Mind, linked with the Power of _Imagination_ (ability to shape and mold the one Substance), assures abundance.

▼ _Love_ is used to desire prosperity and abundance; it works best when combined with _Wisdom, Understanding and Zeal,_ resulting in righteous use.

▼ Through Love and Wisdom, we _harmonize_ with Divine Law, Ideas and Principles to enjoy a full measure of joy and experience harmony in life.

▼ A _peaceful_ mind greatly aids the demonstration of prosperity.

▼ _Thoughts, feelings and words_ govern the demonstration of prosperity.

▼ Pour _living words_ of Faith into omnipresent Substance and the subconscious mind brings prosperity and abundance into manifestation.

▼ Use _denials_ to clear and release any negative or error thoughts of fear or lack.

▼ Use _affirmations_ to build up the Truth of abundance and prosperity.

▼ Invest time and energy in _blessing, praising and expressing gratitude_ for all that you have.

▼ Become more conscious of the presence of universal Substance through _blessing, praising and gratitude so that_ It increases for you and the common good of all.

▼ Using the _Power of Imagination, visualize and conceptualize_ what you desire. See only the Good, the reality of ever-present Substance and Divine Ideas, without regard to outer appearances.

▼ _Patience_ and trust (the Power of Faith) ease whatever waiting period there may be for the demonstration of prosperity to appear.

TOPICS FOR DISCUSSION

1. Why is nonresistance so important to demonstrating true prosperity?

2. Think of a time when you saw the Good despite appearances. What did you do?

3. How are concentration and realization related in the process of manifesting more and more of your Good?

THOUGHTS FOR REFLECTION AND MEDITATION

"Just in proportion as a person yields willingly and obediently to the transforming process, does he or she demonstrate Truth.

All that pertains to self must be put away as fast as it is revealed, and that which is of the universal, the Christ, must take its place."

(Charles Fillmore, *Atom-Smashing Power of Mind*, 2nd ed., Unity House, Unity Village, Mo., 2006, pp. 73-74)

SUPPLEMENTARY READING

Dynamics for Living: A Topical Compilation of Essential Fillmore Teachings by Charles Fillmore, Unity House, Unity Village, Mo, 1967, pp. 109-122, "Truth Demonstrates Itself."

Jesus Christ Heals by Charles Fillmore, 2nd ed., Unity House, Unity Village, Mo., 1940, Chapter 5, "The Omnipotence of Prayer," and Chapter 9, "Healing Through Praise and Thanksgiving."

Keep a True Lent by Charles Fillmore, 2nd ed., Unity House, Unity Village, Mo., 2005, pp. 151-152, "Love."

Talks on Truth by Charles Fillmore, Unity House, Unity Village, Mo., 1926, Chapter 5, "The Development of Divine Love."

What Are You? by Imelda Octavia Shanklin, 2nd ed., Unity House, Unity Village, Mo., 2004, Chapter 9, "Nonresistance."

CHAPTER THIRTY-THREE

CREATING A METAPHYSICAL DEMONSTRATION PLAN

INTRODUCTION

The overall purpose of this chapter is to present a coherent process and plan by which you can apply the various principles, beliefs, ideas and techniques presented in this book. While this material will be comprehensive, it is not intended to include every practical idea presented in the book.

Our primary work is always in consciousness, because life is consciousness. Use this chapter as a tool and starting point to help you apply these magnificent Principles, beliefs and ideas to everyday life so that you can change your consciousness to meet a challenge, create something new in your life or eliminate something you do not want. Remember, underlying every "do not want" is a "want." If there is something you do not want, first pause and reflect on what you do want in its place.

33A **KEYS TO DEMONSTRATION**

Demonstrate—to demonstrate Truth is to effect a change of consciousness. This includes the elimination of error [through denials] *and the establishment of Truth* [trough affirmations]*.* (Charles Fillmore, *The Revealing Word: A Dictionary of Metaphysical Terms,* 2nd ed., Unity House, Unity Village, Mo., 2006, p. 52)

Demonstration—the proving of a Truth principle in one's body or affairs. The manifestation of an ideal when its accomplishment has been brought about by one's conformity in thought, word, and act to the creative Principle of God. (*The Revealing Word*, p. 52)

With respect to what you want to demonstrate, where are you with the following ideas from Chapter 28, "Keys to Demonstration"?

BLOCKS TO DEMONSTRATION

- Stumbling blocks—some examples are: 1) thought barriers, the result of your heredity, your education and your own thinking; 2) lack of Faith in the Oneness; 3) having an outer focus and imagining all sorts undesirable expressions in the body; 4) adverse conditions in consciousness; 5) believing that a person or outer condition can hinder you; or 6) a belief in the outer realm and things such as money.

RESOLVING THE BLOCKS AND SUPPORTING DEMONSTRATION/ MANIFESTATION

- Fear and the negative side— resolved by focusing on Spirit, laughter and song.
- Joy/cheerfulness—supports whatever you want to demonstrate or manifest including but not limited to prosperity, health and wholeness.
- Attachment—resolved through nonattachment.
- Resistance—resolved through non-resistance.

- Unforgiveness—resolved through forgiveness and repentance.

KEYS TO DEMONSTRATION

- Consciousness
- Divine Mind First—Oneness
- Divine Ideas
- Meditation/The Silence
- Prayer
- Concentration
- Realization
- Substance and Supply
- The Twelve Powers
- Faith and Imagination
- Love, Wisdom and Understanding
- Harmony—the Powers of Love and Order
- Peace
- The Creative Power of Thoughts and Feelings
- The Word and the Spoken Word
- Denials and Affirmations
- Gratitude, Praise and Blessings
- Law of Visualization/Seeing the Good
- Patience

33B OVERVIEW OF SPIRITUAL PRINCIPLES AND TOOLS

The following chart is a place to start in creating a metaphysical treatment plan. This chart is not inclusive of all the ideas and concepts presented in the book.

PRINCIPLE OR CONCEPT	CHAPTER	IMPORTANCE / "TOOL"
Absolute Realm and the Relative Realm	Chapter 1	■ Knowing that there is an utterly dependable Absolute Realm from which we deal with the ever-changing relative realm. ■ Knowing that everything in the relative realm is based on some Divine Idea(s) in the Absolute. The relative realm does not have an independent existence.
Life Is Consciousness	Chapter 2	■ What type of consciousness are you using? (Section 2E) ■ What level of consciousness are you operating from? (Section 2F) ■ What level do you live in (victim, victor, vessel or Verity)? Are you self-aware when you visit another level? Example: Do you live most of the time in "vessel consciousness" with occasional visits to "victim consciousness"?
Self-Knowledge	Chapter 3	■ Use your power of self-awareness to observe yourself in the situation, then answer the questions in Section C of this chapter.
Spiritual Evolution	Chapter 4	■ Are you experiencing chemicalization, resistance, nonresistance, crucifixion, resurrection and/or regeneration?
Divine Purpose, Divine Will	Chapter 5	■ When you know that there is no predetermined plan or specific action, you realize your power. ■ You give form and shape to the amorphous "Will," which is simply that each person express more and more good and intend to be the best Christ you can be!
Power of Meditation and the Silence	Chapter 6 Chapter 7	■ Meditate—Go to the Silence and let your Christ Nature reveal Divine Ideas. ■ Do you have a regular meditation time so that you are regularly investing time in the Silence?

PRINCIPLE OR CONCEPT	CHAPTER	IMPORTANCE / "TOOL"
Power of Prayer	Chapter 8 Chapter 9	■ Create a prayer about the situation that claims and affirms the Truth and sees the Good. To paraphrase Eric Butterworth from *The Universe Is Calling*, "See rightly rather than set things right." ■ Contemplative prayer—use Bible quotes or affirmations to reflect on what you want to manifest in your consciousness and in your life.
Four Functions of Consciousness	Chapter 19	■ Are your sensing, feeling, thinking and intuiting functions balanced? ■ What do you sense, feel, think and intuit about the situation or about what you want to manifest?
Kingdom of Heaven	Chapter 20	■ Are you aware that you move Divine Ideas from the invisible to the visible through thoughts and the power of your word? ■ Are you aware that you are the assembly and disassembly point for thoughts and feelings related to Divine Ideas? ■ Are you aware that you take the invisible Ideas, thoughts and feelings and give them form and shape in time and space?
Thought—Law of Mind Action	Chapter 20	■ The thoughts we hold in mind are what we experience. If we do not like what we are experiencing, we can change our thoughts. ■ What thoughts, feelings and beliefs are you holding? Error thoughts and feelings can inhibit and block manifestation. ■ You have Dominion over your thoughts and feelings. In fact, thoughts and feelings are the only things you have absolute dominion over. ■ All cause is in mind. ■ What new cause do you want to put into motion now? ■ What Divine Idea or thoughts about a Divine Idea do you want to express or manifest?

PRINCIPLE OR CONCEPT	CHAPTER	IMPORTANCE / "TOOL"
Power of the Spoken Word	Chapter 21	■ Watch your language. What are you telling yourself and claiming with your current language? ■ The power of your word starts with the intention behind the word. ■ What have you been claiming and affirming with your thoughts, feelings and words? ■ Do they support your error thinking and feeling? ■ Do they rehearse some hurt or harm over and over again?
Denials and Affirmations	Chapter 22	■ Write denials and affirmations. ■ Speak denials gently. ■ Denials cleanse consciousness of error thinking and feeling. ■ Speak affirmationsm with Power and Dominion. ■ Affirmations claim the Truth, beginning with the realization of Truth. ■ Realization comes as a result of investing time in the Silence as well as concentration and contemplation.
Creation	Chapter 23	■ What experience of your life are you creating moment to moment? ■ To some extent you are creating the outer events of your life. Are you aware of the ones you are creating? Do you like what you arc creating?
Twelve Powers/Christ Nature	Chapter 24 Chapter 25	■ Which of the Twelve Powers would you like to apply in your situation? ■ Which of the Twelve Powers do you need to quicken or strengthen? ■ How would you use all of the Twelve Powers working together to demonstrate a change in consciousness and in your outer world?
The Creative Process	Chapter 27	■ Can you utilize the seven-step creative process in this situation? ■ Light, Faith, Imagination, Understanding and Will, Judgment, Wisdom and Love, Sabbath. How?

PRINCIPLE OR CONCEPT	CHAPTER	IMPORTANCE / "TOOL"
Review chapters 28— Demonstration in General Review Chapter 30— Demonstrating Wholeness and Health Review Chapter 32— Demonstrating Prosperity	Chapter 28	■ The keys to demonstration are reviewed in section A of this chapter.
Metaphysical Basis for Healing	Chapter 29	■ Review this chapter if you want to demonstrate wholeness and health.
Metaphysical Basis for Prosperity	Chapter 31	■ Review this chapter if you want to demonstrate prosperity.

33C METAPHYSICAL IMPLEMENTATION PROCESS AND PLAN

Use the following questions to create a plan to change your consciousness so that you can handle any situation or create "more good" in your life. Please keep in mind that not all the questions and points may be applicable to your situation. In his book *The Universe Is Calling*, Eric Butterworth said, "It is not about making things right but seeing things rightly." In every situation, we put our Christ Nature first, expecting illumination and understanding. Change must be in consciousness first; if not, sins (errors) will surely arise. Change in the outer world of the senses may then follow. The most important change we can make is from the limitations of sense and personal consciousness to unlimited Christ Consciousness. We must come to the realization that while we have bodies, we are so much more than our bodies. In fact, our True Nature is not our physical form. We are not matter, nor are we simply the conscious and subconscious minds; we are Spirit, Christ, Oneness, Beingness, Divine Mind.

This is an exercise in self-awareness and self-knowledge. Just as a global positioning system (GPS) must first know where it is to direct us to our destination, so, too, we must be self-aware so that we may proceed in a productive and efficient way to raise consciousness as well as to demonstrate and manifest.

1. What is the situation, problem, challenge or need? (Describe.)

2. What do I hold in my mind that contributes to the situation, problem, challenge or need?

  • How does this "serve" me? (What benefit do I think I am getting from this?)

  • How is this person mirroring an aspect of myself?

  • Am I resisting, and if so, how? Why?

  • What am I feeling? (Chapter 18)

  • What am I thinking? (Chapter 18)

  • What am I sensing? (Chapter 18)

  • What am I intuiting? (Chapter 18)

  • What are my old mental messages or beliefs about this?

  • Can I detect any other error thinking?

3. What do I know about Oneness, my Christ Nature, or Principle that can apply here? (Chapter 10)

4. What Divine Ideas, Principles and Laws can I apply to this situation and how?

5. What tools will help me with this situation? (Be specific.)

  • How am I going to apply them?

  • When?

  • How often?

  • Where?

  • Am I committed to doing this?

6. Write a prayer of gratitude for the demonstration you are about to manifest, first in consciousness and then in form.

Chapter 19:

[1]Lord—The activity of the spiritual I AM as the ruling consciousness. The Lord God of the Scriptures is Christ, the Spiritual Man; our divine consciousness; the creative power within us. (*The Revealing Word*, p. 124)

Chapter 32:

[1]Evil—That which is not of God; unreality; error thought; a product of the fallen human consciousness; negation. ...

There is but one presence and one power, God omnipotent. But man has the privilege and freedom of using this power as he will. When he misuses it he brings about inharmonious conditions. These are called evil. (*The Revealing Word*, p. 64)